The Cambridge Companion to John Cage

John Cage (1912–1992) was without doubt one of the most important and influential figures in twentieth-century music. Pupil of Schoenberg, Henry Cowell, Marcel Duchamp, and Daisetz Teitaro Suzuki among others, he spent much of his career in pursuit of an unusual goal: "giving up control so that sounds can be sounds," as he put it.

This book celebrates the richness and diversity of Cage's achievements – the development of the prepared piano and of the percussion orchestra, the adoption of chance and of indeterminacy, the employment of electronic resources and of graphic notation, and the questioning of the most fundamental tenets of western art music. Besides composing around 300 works, he was also a prolific performer, writer, poet, and visual artist. Written by a team of experts, this Companion discusses Cage's background, his work, and its performance and reception, providing in sum a fully rounded portrait of a fascinating figure.

Cambridge Companions to Music

Composers

The Cambridge Companion to Bach
Edited by John Butt

The Cambridge Companion to Bartók
Edited by Amanda Bayley

The Cambridge Companion to Beethoven
Edited by Glenn Stanley

The Cambridge Companion to Berg
Edited by Anthony Pople

The Cambridge Companion to Berlioz
Edited by Peter Bloom

The Cambridge Companion to Brahms
Edited by Michael Musgrave

The Cambridge Companion to Benjamin Britten
Edited by Mervyn Cooke

The Cambridge Companion to John Cage
Edited by David Nicholls

The Cambridge Companion to Chopin
Edited by Jim Samson

The Cambridge Companion to Debussy
Edited by Simon Trezise

The Cambridge Companion to Handel
Edited by Donald Burrows

The Cambridge Companion to Ravel
Edited by Deborah Mawer

The Cambridge Companion to Schubert
Edited by Christopher Gibbs

Instruments

The Cambridge Companion to Brass Instruments
Edited by Trevor Herbert and John Wallace

The Cambridge Companion to the Cello
Edited by Robin Stowell

The Cambridge Companion to the Clarinet
Edited by Colin Lawson

The Cambridge Companion to the Organ
Edited by Nicholas Thistlethwaite and Geoffrey Webber

The Cambridge Companion to the Piano
Edited by David Rowland

The Cambridge Companion to the Recorder
Edited by John Mansfield Thomson

The Cambridge Companion to the Saxophone
Edited by Richard Ingham

The Cambridge Companion to Singing
Edited by John Potter

The Cambridge Companion to the Violin
Edited by Robin Stowell

Topics

The Cambridge Companion to Pop and Rock
Edited by Simon Frith, Will Straw and John Street

The Cambridge Companion to

JOHN CAGE

....

EDITED BY
David Nicholls

CAMBRIDGE
UNIVERSITY PRESS

PUBLISHED BY THE PRESS SYNDICATE OF THE UNIVERSITY OF CAMBRIDGE
The Pitt Building, Trumpington Street, Cambridge, United Kingdom

CAMBRIDGE UNIVERSITY PRESS
The Edinburgh Building, Cambridge CB2 2RU, UK
40 West 20th Street, New York, NY 10011-4211, USA
477 Williamstown Road, Port Melbourne, VIC 3207, Australia
Ruiz de Alarcón 13, 28014 Madrid, Spain
Dock House, The Waterfront, Cape Town 8001, South Africa

http://www.cambridge.org

First published 2002

Printed in the United Kingdom at the University Press, Cambridge

Typeface Minion 10.75/14 pt   *System* LATEX 2$_\varepsilon$ [TB]

A catalogue record for this book is available from the British Library

Library of Congress Cataloguing in Publication data

The Cambridge companion to John Cage / edited by David Nicholls.
    p.   cm. – (Cambridge companions to music)
Includes bibliographical references (p.) and index.
ISBN 0 521 78348 8 (hb.) – ISBN 0 521 78968 0 (pb.)
1. Cage, John – Criticism and interpretation.   I. Nicholls, David, 1955 – II. Series.
ML410.C24 C36 2002
780′.92–dc21
[B]   2001052401

ISBN 0 521 78348 8 hardback
ISBN 0 521 78968 0 paperback

Contents

Illustrations

Contributors

David W. Bernstein is Professor of Music at Mills College and head of the music department. His publications and lectures are on Arnold Schoenberg's tonal theories; the history of music theory; John Cage; and Fluxus. He organized a conference/festival entitled "Here Comes Everybody: The Music, Poetry, and Art of John Cage" which took place at Mills College in November 1995. He coedited (with Christopher Hatch) and contributed to a book of essays stemming from this event entitled *Writings through John Cage's Music, Poetry, and Art.*

William Brooks presently holds faculty positions at the Universities of Illinois and York (England). He has written extensively on various aspects of American music from eighteenth-century music theatre to experimental music of the present. A composer as well as a scholar, he likes to think that each domain informs the other. Future projects include an episodic overview of American music for the University of Illinois Press and an extended work for spatially distributed forces on the poetry of Emily Dickinson.

Kathan Brown is the founder and director of Crown Point Press, an etching workshop that will celebrate its fortieth anniversary in 2002. The Press invites artists to travel to San Francisco to produce etchings in its studio. Brown's memoir, *ink, paper, metal, wood: Painters and Sculptors at Crown Point Press*, was published in 1996, and the following year the National Gallery of Art, Washington, D.C. and the Fine Arts Museums of San Francisco showed the Press's work and published a catalog. Brown lives and works in San Francisco.

Kyle Gann, a composer, has been new-music critic for the *Village Voice* since 1986 and Assistant Professor of Music at Bard College since 1997. His books include *The Music of Conlon Nancarrow* (Cambridge University Press), *American Music in the 20th Century*, and *It's Only As Good As It Sounds: Village Voice Articles on American Music after Minimalism*. Gann studied composition with Ben Johnston, Morton Feldman, and Peter Gena. His major works include a one-man microtonal opera *Custer and Sitting Bull*, a ten-movement suite *The Planets*, and *Transcendental Sonnets* for chorus and orchestra. CDs of his music are available on the Lovely Music, New Tone, and Monroe Street labels.

John Holzaepfel received his Ph.D. in historical musicology from the City University of New York, where he wrote his dissertation 'David Tudor and the Performance of American Experimental Music, 1950–1959'. He is currently preparing a biography of David Tudor.

Leta E. Miller, Professor of Music at the University of California, Santa Cruz, is co-author, with Fredric Lieberman, of *Lou Harrison: Composing a World* and editor of *Lou Harrison: Selected Keyboard and Chamber Music, 1937–1994* (MUSA, vol. 8). She has written articles on Harrison, Cage, and Henry Cowell; those on Cage appear in *Perspectives on American Music, 1900–1950, John Cage: Music,*

Philosophy, and Intention, 1933–50, and *Musical Quarterly.* Miller is also an active flutist who has been featured on over a dozen compact disc recordings.

David Nicholls is Professor of Music at the University of Southampton. Author of *American Experimental Music, 1890–1940* (Cambridge University Press) and numerous articles on topics in American music, he has also acted as contributing editor for the reissue of Henry Cowell's *New Musical Resources* (Cambridge University Press), *The Whole World of Music: A Henry Cowell Symposium,* and *The Cambridge History of American Music* (Cambridge University Press). He is editor of the journal *American Music,* and is currently preparing a monograph on Cage for Illinois's *American Composers* series.

David W. Patterson is an Assistant Professor of Musicology at the University of Illinois at Urbana-Champaign. His 1996 dissertation on John Cage's aesthetic evolution during the 1940s and 1950s received the Sonneck Society Dissertation Prize, and his work since then continues to focus on the work and thought of Cage and the New York School, appearing in *American Music, Perspectives of New Music, repercussions,* and other journals. Patterson is the contributing editor of *John Cage: Music, Philosophy, and Intention, 1933–1950.*

Christopher Shultis is Regents Professor of Music at the University of New Mexico. In 1993–94 he was a Fulbright guest professor in American Studies at the Institut für Anglistik, RWTH Aachen and in 1999–2000 at the Anglistisches Seminar, Universität Heidelberg. Shultis has written a book on John Cage – *Silencing the Sounded Self: John Cage and the American Experimental Tradition* – as well as several articles. His "Cage in Retrospect: A Review Essay" (*Journal of Musicology,* 1995) won an ASCAP Deems Taylor Award. Shultis is presently an associate editor for *Perspectives of New Music.*

Alastair Williams, Senior Lecturer in Music at Keele University, is author of *New Music and the Claims of Modernity* and *Constructing Musicology.* He has also published articles in *Cambridge Opera Journal, Music Analysis,* and *Perspectives of New Music.*

Preface

John Cage (1912–92) was without doubt one of the most important and influential figures in twentieth-century culture; yet he was also one of the least understood. Pupil of, among others, Arnold Schoenberg, Henry Cowell, Marcel Duchamp and Daisetz Teitaro Suzuki, he spent much of his career in pursuit of an unusual goal: "giving up control so that sounds can be sounds," as he put it on page 72 of *Silence*, his first and best-known collection of writings. Among his many notable accomplishments were the development of the prepared piano and of the percussion orchestra, the adoption of chance and of indeterminacy, the employment of electronic resources and of graphic notation, and the questioning of the most fundamental tenets of western art music. As well as composing around 300 works, he was also active as a performer, writer, poet, and visual artist.

The present volume is neither a biography of Cage nor an analytical study of his music. Rather, it is a multi-faceted celebration of the richness and diversity of a remarkable creative artist and his art. Compiled by a team of experts drawn from the new generation of Cage scholars, it builds on earlier research while providing new facts, insights, and interpretations. Part I – *Aesthetic contexts* – considers and contrasts the three principal sources of Cage's developing cultural background: America, Europe, and Asia. Part II – *Sounds, words, images* – contains the majority of the detailed discussion of his artistic legacy in music, writing, and visual art. However, some of this discussion (notably of key works from the late 1940s through late 1950s) is of necessity also contained in the chapters constituting Part III – *Interaction and influence* – which otherwise examines various aspects of Cage's artistic practice, and attempts to contextualize him in relation to both his peers and his successors. If, in this arrangement, there are overlaps between the fourteen chapters, or differences of opinion among the ten authors, then all the better: for John Cage was both much loved and much maligned, and his work both hugely influential and totally ignored. His aesthetic stance poses multiple questions, and demands multiple answers: indeed, it thrives on plurality – of sources, influences, methodologies, interpretations, and outcomes. And so, hopefully, does this *Cambridge Companion to John Cage*.

A few general thanks are in order: my former colleagues at Keele University and my present colleagues at the University of Southampton have provided academic support and intellectual stimulation in equal measure. Further afield, I have enjoyed enormously working on this project with my co-authors (though the number of them sharing my forename has at times proved confusing).

My wife, Tamar, and our children, Ben and Daisy, have (as ever) been tolerant way beyond the call of duty during the gestation period of this volume.

Finally, at Cambridge University Press, Penny Souster has waited very patiently for the delivery of a book that owes its existence entirely to her vision.

David Nicholls
University of Southampton

Acknowledgements

The front cover photograph, of John Cage *c.* 1970, was taken by James Klosty, and is provided courtesy of the John Cage Trust.

An expanded and fully illustrated version of Chapter 7 is published in Kathan Brown, *John Cage Visual Art: To Sober and Quiet the Mind*, San Francisco: Crown Point Press, 2000.

Extracts from the following music examples are © Henmar Press Inc., New York, and are reproduced by permission of Peters Edition Limited, London: examples 2.1; 4.1, 4.2, 4.9, 4.10; 6.1; 9.1, 9.2, 9.3, 9.4; 10.1; 11.1, 11.5.

The music examples in Chapter 14 are reproduced by courtesy of the individual composers, except those by William Duckworth which are used by permission of Monroe Street Music.

The following sketch materials are reproduced by permission of The Getty Research Library, 980039 and the John Cage Trust: Examples 10.2, 10.3, 10.4, 10.5, 10.6, 10.7; 11.9.

The following sketch materials are reproduced by permission of the New York Public Library and the John Cage Trust: Examples 11.4, 11.6, 11.7.

The images reproduced in Chapter 7 are reproduced courtesy of Crown Point Press (Figures 7.1, 7.3, 7.5, 7.6); Achenbach Foundation for Graphic Arts, The Fine Arts Museums of San Francisco (Figure 7.2); Margarete Roeder Gallery, New York City (Figure 7.4).

Chronology

1912 September 5: born in Los Angeles.

1928 Graduates from Los Angeles High School: enters Pomona College.

1930 Drops out of Pomona College. Travels in Europe (to 1931). Begins to compose.

1934 Studies in New York City, with Adolph Weiss and Henry Cowell.

1935 Marries Xenia Andreevna Kashevaroff.

1935–36 Studies with Arnold Schoenberg.

1938 Meets Lou Harrison (in San Francisco) and Merce Cunningham (in Seattle).

1938–40 Teaches at the Cornish School of Music in Seattle; *c.* 1940 writes "The Future of Music: Credo."

1939 *First Construction (in Metal)*

1940 Devises prepared piano.

1941–42 Teaches at the Chicago School of Design.

1942 Moves to New York City. Meets Marcel Duchamp.

1944 Begins personal and artistic partnership with Merce Cunningham.

1945 Separates from Xenia Andreevna Kashevaroff, whom he subsequently divorces. Commences study of Asian philosophy, later including classes with Daisetz Teitaro Suzuki.

1946–48 *Sonatas and Interludes*

1948 During summer, teaches at Black Mountain College. Meets R. Buckminster Fuller and Robert Rauschenberg.

1949 Receives awards from Guggenheim Foundation, and American Academy and National Institute of Arts and Letters. Travels to Paris, where he meets Pierre Boulez. Becomes involved in the Artists' Club in New York.

1950 Meets Morton Feldman, Christian Wolff, and David Tudor, later known collectively as the "New York School" of composers. Earle Brown joins the group in 1952. Starts to employ chance operations based on the *I Ching*.

1951 *Music of Changes*

1952 During summer, teaches again at Black Mountain College: *Black Mountain Piece*. *4′33″*

1954 Meets Jasper Johns. Moves to Stony Point, Rockland County, New York State. With Tudor, tours Europe; meets Karlheinz Stockhausen.

1956–60 Teaches regular classes at the New School for Social Research in New York City.

1958 May 15: Twenty-Five-Year Retrospective Concert at Town Hall, New York City. Scores exhibited at the Stable Gallery.

With Tudor, tours Europe; meets Luciano Berio. Wins Italian quiz show *Lacia o Raddoppia*, answering questions on mushrooms.

1960–61 Fellow at Center for Advanced Studies at Wesleyan University.

1961 *Silence* published; signs exclusive contract with Henmar Press, Inc.

1962 Co-founds New York Mycological Society.

With Tudor, tours Japan.

1963 *Variations IV*

1964 With Cunningham Dance Company, undertakes world tour.

1967 Composer-in-residence at University of Cincinnati.

Introduced to the work of Henry David Thoreau.

1967–69 *HPSCHD*

1968 Elected to the American Academy and Institute of Arts and Letters.

1968–69 Associate at the Center for Advanced Study at the University of Illinois.

1969 Artist-in-residence, University of California at Davis.

First work in visual art.

1970 Fellow at Center for Advanced Studies at Wesleyan University.

1972 Moves back to New York City.

1978 First printmaking sessions at Crown Point Press in San Francisco.

Elected to Fellowship of the American Academy of Arts and Sciences.

1980 Regents Lecturer at the University of California at San Diego.

For the remainder of his life, is increasingly affected by health problems.

1982 70th birthday celebrations include Wall-to-Wall Cage and Friends in New York City, plus events throughout Europe and America.

1986 Awarded the honorary degree of Doctor of All the Arts by California Institute of the Arts.

1987–91 *Europeras 1–5*

1988 Charles Eliot Norton Professor of Poetry at Harvard University.

1992 August 12: dies in New York City.

PART I

Aesthetic contexts

1 Cage and America

DAVID NICHOLLS

Prelude

Given that he was born, bred, and educated in the United States, the supposition that John Cage's aesthetic outlook was nurtured and majorly influenced by his home nation might seem obvious to the point of redundancy. However, not every American has achieved the same degree of national and international fame and infamy, as has Cage; nor has any other American artist – with the possible exception of Andy Warhol – had such a huge impact on the global development of culture, whether "high" or "pop." Thus the fact that Cage was arguably unique among Americans – let alone among American musicians – suggests that his particular relationship with America may have been somewhat out of the ordinary.

Each of us, by the time of our maturity, will have defined what might be termed an individual aesthetic locus. Put simply, this is a set of choices – relating to lifestyle, garb, décor, deportment, belief, culture, and so on – with which we (hopefully) feel comfortable; it is also, de facto, the image of ourselves we project to others. Many complex factors will have engaged and entwined during our formative years, in order that such an aesthetic locus may form: some will be genetic, others environmental; some inevitable, others unpredictable. For artists (in the broadest sense of that word) the process is knottier still, for the aesthetic locus is projected not only materially (through clothing, food, or furniture), but also transcendentally (through the artistic objects created by, but existing apart from, the artist).

In March 1943, a percussion ensemble founded and conducted by Cage was the subject of a spread in *Life* magazine. The article had been prompted by a concert, at New York's prestigious Museum of Modern Art a month earlier, in which "an orchestra of earnest, dressed-up musicians sat on the stage and began to hit things with sticks and hands . . . The audience, which was very high-brow, listened intently without seeming to be disturbed at the noisy results." The concert had been sponsored by the League of Composers, and included works by Lou Harrison (*Counterdance in the Spring* and *Canticle*), Henry Cowell (*Ostinato Pianissimo*), Jose Ardévol (*Preludio a 11*) and Amadeo Roldán (*Ritmicas V & VI*). Pride of place was reserved for Cage himself, who was represented by three works: *First Construction (in Metal)* (1939), *Imaginary Landscape No. 3* (1942), and the recently completed *Amores* (1943). The composer-conductor was described by

Life as "a patient, humorous, 30-year-old Californian...the most active percussion musician in the U.S., [who] believes that when people today get to understand and like his music...they will find new beauty in everyday modern life..." Among the photographs in the spread is one captioned "Pieces of shaped bronze sound like anvils...Player is Xenia Cage, the conductor's wife, who took up percussion after marriage." Among the other performers was Merce Cunningham.[1]

There were, of course, a number of important periods after 1943 when American influences of various kinds affected Cage: witness, for instance, the impact of the Abstract Expressionist painters in the early 1950s, or of the work of Henry David Thoreau, from the early 1970s onwards. Details of such influences will emerge elsewhere in this volume. But by 1943 Cage's *fundamental* aesthetic locus, which so intrigued *Life*, had largely formed; what followed in the remaining half century of his life, while contributing to his developing persona, was also to a considerable degree a result of choices predicated on the needs of that persona. The principal purpose of the present chapter, then, is to examine via a series of topical headings the complex factors that had engaged and entwined during Cage's formative years, leading him to the momentous MOMA concert in 1943.[2]

Family

"Their marriage was a good one between bad people"[3]

When John Milton Cage Jr. was born in Los Angeles on September 5, 1912, his ancestors had already resided in America for the best part of two centuries. As he noted in 1976, "My family's roots are completely American. There was a John Cage who helped Washington in the surveying of Virginia" (Kostelanetz 1988, p. 1). Many later family members lived mainly west of the Appalachians; and several (on the male side) were active as preachers. Thus Cage's experience of growing up in the United States was already thrice removed from that of two close contemporaries – Aaron Copland (1900–1990) and George Gershwin (1898–1937) – for he was neither East Coast in location, Jewish in ethnicity and religion, nor first-generation American by birth. Accordingly, he was entirely free from any perceived necessity (whether personal or societal) to assimilate or conform.[4] In this, he was very much his parents' (only) child: both John Milton Cage Sr. (1886–1964) and Lucretia ("Crete") Harvey (1885–1969) were somewhat unconventional, the former an idealistic inventor (for instance of a submarine that gave off bubbles), the latter a sometime journalist for the *Los Angeles Times*. Anecdotes concerning Crete (and to a rather lesser extent John Sr.) adorn the pages of *Silence* and

A Year from Monday, notably in the texts "Indeterminacy" and "How to Pass, Kick, Fall, and Run" (Cage 1961, pp. 260–273; 1967, pp. 133–140). Some sense of the Cages' marital equilibrium may be gleaned from an aphoristic aside on page 72 of *A Year from Monday*: "I was arguing with Mother. I turned to Dad. He spoke. 'Son John, your mother is always right, even when she's wrong.' "

If independence of thought and mind is a particularly (or even peculiarly) American character trait, then there was certainly a good deal of it in the family gene pool for Cage to inherit. As mentioned above, a high percentage of his forebears were ministers, and of these several were notable for a certain doggedness in the pursuit of unpromising quarry. Before the Civil War his great grandfather, Adolphus Cage, preached to both blacks and whites in Tennessee, before moving on to Colorado. Cage's grandfather, Gustavus Adolphus Williamson Cage, followed Adolphus into the Methodist Episcopalian Church: amongst other exploits, Gustavus traveled to Utah to decry Mormonism, and to Wyoming to work as a missionary. His grandson described him as "a man of extraordinary puritanical righteousness [who] would get very angry with people who didn't agree with him. As a child my father used to run away from home whenever he got the chance" (Kostelanetz 1988, p. 1). John Cage Jr. may not have inherited his grandfather's temper, but the latter's religious zeal found early expression: as a child, John Jr. was "very much impressed by the notion of turning the other cheek" (quoted in Revill 1992, p. 31); in his teenage years, he wished – like Gustavus – to become a Methodist Episcopalian minister; and slightly later, at age sixteen, he provoked family furor when he announced his intention of joining the Liberal Catholic Church as an acolyte. A striking degree of self-belief also characterizes both Gustavus and (as will become apparent elsewhere in this volume) John Jr. Indeed, this was true of John Cage Sr., too, for he was so convinced of the merits of his gasoline-powered submarine that he set "the world's record for staying underwater . . . by making an experimental trip on Friday the thirteenth, with a crew of thirteen, staying under water for thirteen hours" (Kostelanetz 1988, p. 1).

A further American family trait was a pioneer tendency to seek out pastures new: in the late eighteenth century William Cage moved his family from Virginia to the (then) frontier territory of Tennessee, while the westward relocation of William's grandson, Adolphus, is discussed above. Later, the financial instability associated with John Sr.'s inventions led to frequent changes of home, state, and even country: before John Jr. was twelve, he had already lived in California (six or more locations in greater Los Angeles), Michigan (Ann Arbor and Detroit), and Ontario, Canada. One can only speculate on the effect so many moves (and the financial necessities underlying them) may have had on the marriage between John

Sr. and Crete, though some of John Jr.'s anecdotes are indicative and Revill (1992, p. 22) reports that "Every so often [Crete] would leave the house, saying she was never coming back, and each time John senior would console his frightened son, assuring him that before long she would return." What *is* known is that Crete "never enjoyed having a good time" (Cage 1967, p. 69), and had been married twice before her espousal to John Sr., though she could never remember the name of her first husband (Cage 1972, p. 102). John Sr., meanwhile, was once overheard saying to Crete, "Get ready: we're going to New Zealand Saturday." His son got ready, reading "everything I could find in the school library about New Zealand. Saturday came. Nothing happened. The project was not even mentioned . . . " (Cage 1961, p. 6). The effects of such volatility on John Jr. were predictable, and are discussed below.

Three other family members deserve mention: Cage's maternal grandmother, who (like several other of Crete's relatives) lived in the family home during Cage's childhood, also possessed a powerful religious zeal (Hines 1994, pp. 67, 72). As Cage attempted one day to tiptoe across the living room to retrieve a manuscript, she woke from a deep sleep to address him sharply: "John, are you ready for the second coming of the Lord?" (Cage 1967, p. 20). Crete's sister Marge "had a beautiful contralto voice [which] Cage loved to hear . . . at church every Sunday", while another sister, Phoebe, was among John Jr.'s piano teachers: "She was devoted to late nineteenth-century music and expected her charge to feel the same way" (Revill 1992, p. 24). This perhaps in part explains Cage's early obsession with the music of Edvard Grieg: "I . . . imagined devoting my life to the performance of his works alone, for they did not seem to me to be too difficult, and I loved them" (Tomkins 1976, p. 77). While not wishing to over-emphasize the marterteral influences of Marge and Phoebe, it is perhaps significant that Cage's first published vocal work – the Five Songs of 1938 – is for contralto, and that he later became devoted to the music of another *fin-de-siècle* miniaturist, Erik Satie. Music was clearly an important part of Cage's family life, for Crete – at the time of her meeting John Sr. – had been the pianist in Gustavus's church. Indeed, it was apparently Crete who took John Jr., aged five, to his first symphony concert, where "he stood in the aisle utterly absorbed" (Revill 1992, p. 23). However, it was only after great persistence that he was allowed music lessons, and in later life was barely tolerated as a musician: on hearing her son's Quartet for any percussion (1935) Crete stated "I enjoyed it, but where are you going to put it?" Many years on, she could still remark, disparagingly, "I've listened to your record several times. After hearing all those stories about your childhood, I keep asking myself, 'Where was it that I failed?'" (Cage 1961, pp. 264, 273).[5]

Place

"When I was growing up in California there were two things that everyone assumed were good for you ... sunshine and orange juice." (Cage 1961, p. 88)

As has already been noted, Cage spent much of his childhood in transit. He was an only child, and one effect of so many relocations both within and without greater Los Angeles must have been the necessity of self-reliance. During his first decade, Cage would have had little opportunity to develop lasting friendships, and it is noteworthy that of the many anecdotes he related concerning his childhood, few contain mention of any other children.[6] Rather, we read of an isolated boy – perhaps trying to avoid the tensions of his home – who "sought adventure, exploring the canyons and marshes of [Los Angeles's] inland countryside, spying one day on a gypsy encampment" (Revill 1992, p. 23). Elsewhere, Cage writes of a period when the family was residing in Ocean Park:

> I was *sent out* every morning to the beach where I spent the day building rolly-coasters in the sand, complicated downhill tracks with tunnels and inclines upon which I rolled a small hard rubber ball. Every day toward noon I fainted because the sun was too much for me ... It took me much longer, about thirty-five years in fact, to learn that orange juice was not good for me either.   (Cage 1961, p. 88; emphasis mine)

Other children do momentarily flit through the Cagean world – albeit anonymously – in 1924 or 1925, when Cage was twelve and a tenderfoot Boy Scout. He persuaded a Los Angeles radio station, KNX, to broadcast a weekly Scout programme: Cage was "the master of ceremonies" (Kostelanetz & Cage 1989, p. 273) and the content of the hour-long show (which ran for around two years) was provided by "Individual Scouts [who] all gave their services willingly. There were boy sopranos; trumpet, trombone, and piano soloists; and Scouts who spoke on their experiences building fires and tying knots" (Cage 1967, p. 132). There was also a "ten-minute inspirational talk from a member of the clergy" and "When there was no one else to perform I played piano solos ... " (Kostelanetz & Cage 1989, p. 273).

Cage's enforced solitude had a downside, of course: whatever elementary school he attended in his childhood, the precociously talented boy achieved "A" grades; unfortunately, he was also often the victim of bullying. "I was what is called a sissy, so that I was continually under attack from other children. They would lie in ambush [outside school] and would laugh at me every time I answered a question in school" (Revill 1992, p. 22). In this general context, one can begin to understand why Cage's anecdotes concerning childhood cluster around his own (out-of-school) experiences, family reminiscences, and topics of pleasure or success (such as music lessons or the radio show) rather than the more obvious classroom or "gang" activities. Although the bullying and other such unpleasantnesses had halted by the time Cage was a teenage pupil at Los Angeles High School (1923–28), he appears nowhere to recall, with fondness (or otherwise), any teacher other than those he visited for piano.

Until the summer of 1930, when he dropped out of Pomona College, Cage remained in Los Angeles. The remainder of the period until 1943, though, saw him experience as a young adult a wide range of new, and often very different, environments. Foremost among these was Paris. Having left Pomona, persuaded his parents that "a trip to Europe would be more useful than two more years of college," hitch-hiked to Galveston, and boarded a trans-Atlantic steamer, he arrived in a city that "enchanted but rather overwhelmed the seventeen-year-old Cage" (Tomkins 1976, p. 78). It is difficult to pinpoint precisely the source of Cage's tendency towards obsessiveness – though one can speculate that both Gustavus and John Sr. may have set the mold – but by 1930 it was already well developed. Cage's desire to devote his life to the performance of Grieg's piano works was noted earlier. In the 1950s and 1960s he amassed an impressive library of mycological texts, later donated to the University of California at Santa Cruz; and from the 1970s onwards, the mushroom books were replaced by plants, of which there were eventually several hundred. Cage's obsession while in Paris was Gothic architecture, especially "the flamboyant style of the fifteenth century. In this style my interest was attracted by balustrades. These I studied for six weeks in the Bibliothèque Mazarin, getting to the library when the doors were opened and not leaving until they were closed" (Cage 1961, p. 261). While in Paris, Cage also discovered the music of Bach, Stravinsky, and Scriabin; with supreme irony, he probably left the city before the June 6, 1931, concert given there by the Pan American Association of Composers, which included pieces by Charles Ives, Carl Ruggles, and two of Cage's future teachers, Adolph Weiss and Henry Cowell. The further importance of this visit to Europe is discussed in Chapter 2.

In late 1931, Cage returned to America. He spent the next two or so years in California, where – among other things – he wrote music, painted pictures, gave lectures to housewives in Santa Monica, carried out research assignments for his father, fell in love with Xenia Andreevna Kashevaroff (whom he eventually married in June 1935) and, in Carmel, had his first encounters with mushrooms. As discussed below, in "Education," Cage also began to receive formal tuition in composition during this period; ultimately, this led him in 1934 to New York, where he stayed for approximately eight months, studying with Weiss.[7] In her book *Making Music Modern*,

Carol J. Oja describes in vivid detail the city's extraordinary musical life during the 1920s and early 1930s, and the possibilities that existed for young composers: "New York City placed [them] at an auspicious cultural crossroads. There they could stand, with all their belongings in one suitcase, free to roam in whatever direction their imaginations might lead" (Oja 2000, p. 6). Although by 1934 the Depression had cut deeply into most aspects of American life, there were still concerts of contemporary music in New York, as well as Cowell's various activities at the New School for Social Research, and in connection with his New Music Edition. Thus it is rather odd to find Cage failing completely in later years to mention the inevitable impact on him that the city must have had. Indeed, his recollections are almost suspiciously down-beat: in *Silence* (p. 268) he writes about his experiences working at the Brooklyn YWCA; elsewhere, he talks of acting as Cowell's New School assistant, and of "play[ing] bridge every evening with Mr. and Mrs. Weiss and Henry Cowell – or sometimes with the Weisses and Wallingford Riegger" (Kostelanetz 1988, p. 7).

It may be that in this, as in other aspects of his autobiography, Cage was less than direct when discussing the most formative influences on his aesthetic locus. The sources for his stunning manifesto, "The Future of Music: Credo" (Cage *c.* 1938–40) were casually revealed in an obscure list, made in 1960–61, of the ten books that had most influenced his thought (Nicholls 1990, p. 190). And it was only in 1959, in his "History of Experimental Music in the United States" (Cage 1961, pp. 67–75), that Cage first mentioned a number of American composers with whose work he would first have come into contact at this time: these include Edgard Varèse, Charles Ives, Carl Ruggles, William Russell, Leo Ornstein, Dane Rudhyar, Henry Brant, Ruth Crawford, and Harry Partch.[8] The key to unlocking this little puzzle – as with so much else in American music in the earlier twentieth century – is Henry Cowell, whom Cage describes in his article as

> for many years the open sesame for new music in America. Most selflessly he published the New Music Edition and encouraged the young to discover new directions. From him, as from an efficient information booth, you could always get not only the address and telephone number of anyone working in a lively way in music, but you could also get an unbiased introduction from him as to what that anyone was doing.
>
> (Cage 1961, p. 71)

Cage had met Cowell in 1933, and it was at Cowell's suggestion that he moved temporarily to New York. As far as can be determined, Cowell was based in Manhattan from September through December 1934 inclusive; also resident in, or visitors to, the city during Cage's sojourn were Varèse, Ives, Ruggles, Russell, Brant, Crawford, and Partch. (Ornstein was by this time living in Philadelphia, but he had been an important influence on Cowell's use of tone clusters. Rudhyar, meanwhile, had lived since 1920 in California. Cage may have met him there, or Rudhyar may have made an unverifiable visit to New York during this period.) While there is documentary evidence for Cage actually meeting only Partch at this time – "I was with him [in NYC] when he received his first grant" (Cage 1981a) – Cowell's *New Music* activities create further, much stronger, links with the remainder of the group. During 1934–35, *New Music Quarterly* published works by Rudhyar (*Granites*) and Ives (Eighteen [*recte* Nineteen] Songs), while the associated Orchestra Series issued Varèse's *Ionisation*, Rudhyar's Sinfonietta, Ruggles's *Sun-Treader*, and the second movement of Ives's Fourth Symphony. During the same period, the newly founded *New Music Quarterly Recordings* released Weiss's Three Songs, the slow movement of Crawford's String Quartet, Ives's *Barn Dance* (from *Washington's Birthday*), *In the Night*, and *General William Booth Enters Into Heaven*, and Ruggles's *Lilacs* and *Toys*. Given that Cage had been associated with Cowell in California prior to his move to New York, and was Cowell's assistant at the New School for some of the time he spent in Manhattan, it would be very odd indeed if he had not become acquainted with these works during this short but crucial formative period. What is certain is that in Cage's 1959 essay, the works or techniques named or alluded to include Varèse's *Ionisation*, Russell's percussion pieces (the *Fugue for Eight Percussion Instruments* had appeared in *New Music*'s Orchestra Series in 1933, and the *Three Dance Movements* would follow in 1936), "the clusters of Leo Ornstein, the resonances of Dane Rudhyar . . . the sliding tones of Ruth Crawford [which could refer to either the String Quartet or the Three Songs, which Cowell had published in 1933] and . . . the microtones and novel instruments of Harry Partch" (Cage 1961, pp. 71–73). What is equally certain is that 1935 saw the emergence of those features that would by 1943 make Cage's music worthy of attention in *Life* (see Chapter 4).

Cage's locations during the remaining years through 1943 were similarly significant. During 1935–38 he was again in Los Angeles, though this time as a married man: at first he studied with Schoenberg; later he met and putatively collaborated with the experimental film maker Oscar Fischinger, before finally taking up a variety of temporary positions at U.C.L.A. Among the long-term benefits of this period was Fischinger's suggestion that there is a "spirit . . . inside each of the objects of this world[;] . . . all we need to do to liberate that spirit is to brush past the object, and to draw forth its sound" (Cage 1981, pp. 72–73); more mundanely, in connection with an aquatic ballet at U.C.L.A., came the invention of the water gong (Revill 1992, p. 55). Both influences were part of the mix that led Cage to form his first percussion orchestra. In 1938, through Lou Harrison, Cage taught first at

Mills College, near San Francisco, and then at the Cornish School in Seattle. The musical importance of his time at the latter institution is discussed in Chapter 9, but while based in the Pacific Northwest Cage also met a number of dancer-choreographers – including Merce Cunningham, later to become his partner in both life and art – as well as the painters Morris Graves and Mark Tobey. The latter, Cage has said, "had a great effect on my way of seeing, which is to say my involvement with painting, or my involvement with life even" (Kostelanetz 1988, p. 174). Graves presumably impressed Cage as much by his eccentric and devil-may-care behavior, as by his painting. Among several memorable stories is that in "Indeterminacy," which describes Graves breaking up a party chez John and Xenia: "about 3:00 A.M. an Irish tenor was singing loudly in our living room. Morris . . . entered . . . without knocking, wearing an old-fashioned nightshirt and carrying an elaborately made wooden birdcage, the bottom of which had been removed. Making straight for the tenor, Graves placed the birdcage over his head, said nothing, and left the room" (Cage 1961, p. 272). After Seattle, the Cages returned in 1940 to San Francisco, before moving to Chicago (1941) where John Jr. was able to experiment further with proto-electronic sounds. Finally, in 1942 and at the invitation of Max Ernst and Peggy Guggenheim, came a second (and more permanent) move to New York, where Cage met a succession of artistic luminaries: among the more important of these, *vis-à-vis* Cage's later activities, were Marcel Duchamp, and Virgil Thomson (Revill 1992, pp. 78–82).

Time

"Standing in line, Max Jacob said, gives one the opportunity to practice patience."
(Cage 1961, p. 268)

The first thirty years of Cage's life were, in historical and social terms, probably the most unpredictable and erratic of the twentieth century. The period is framed by the two world wars: in between came boom, bust, and reconstruction. Unsurprisingly, Cage was to varying degrees affected by all of these events. Although John Jr. was only six years old at the conclusion of World War I, the worldwide militarization that had foreshadowed and accompanied it impacted considerably on the Cage family fortunes. For instance, John Sr.'s bubble-blowing submarine – demonstrated in 1912 and patented in 1915 – was, despite its imaginative design, of no possible use to the U.S. Navy. The resulting bankruptcy prompted the family's move to Michigan, where John Sr. worked on various related projects with a professor at the University of Michigan (Revill 1992, pp. 20–22).

The general upturn in the economy during the 1920s is reflected in greater domestic stability: based from 1921 onwards in and around Los Angeles, the principal reason underlying successive Cage family moves was an improving financial situation. Indeed, the parallel expansion of both Los Angeles and the U.S. economy during the 1920s is remarkable. In rural areas, there was little of cheer: for most of the decade, "farmers were in distress, and the [Republican] government did little of value to help them out" (Morison, Commager, & Leuchtenburg 1977, p. 580). But in urban areas, the picture was quite different: "In the Coolidge years [1923–28] the nation reaped the benefits from the application of electricity to manufacturing and the adoption of the scientific management theories of Frederick Winslow Taylor" (Morison, Commager, & Leuchtenburg 1977, p. 583). Between 1914 and 1929, the percentage of factory machinery operated by electricity rose from 30 per cent to 70 per cent; and an electrochemical revolution "dramatically altered factory procedures and improved output in industries like petroleum and steel" (Morison, Commager, & Leuchtenburg 1977, p. 583). Worker productivity rose, taxes were lowered, and the real income of those in employment increased by approximately a third. Significantly, a population that in 1890 had been 65 per cent rural was by 1930 56 per cent urban (Morison, Commager, & Leuchtenburg 1977, p. 566). In Los Angeles, the changes were even more marked, mainly as a result of the construction of the first Los Angeles aqueduct in 1913 – which ensured a bountiful supply of fresh water – and the opening of the Panama Canal the following year – which led to the dynamic growth of the city's port. In addition, the climate was benevolent and land was cheap. Between 1910 and 1940, then, the population of Los Angeles County more than quintupled to 2.78 million; as a proportion of the total population of California, this represents a rise from 21 per cent to 40 per cent.

Among the consequences of these large-scale changes in society were dramatic increases in the ownership of goods, and in the availability of mass entertainment. The number of automobiles in America rose from 9 million in 1920 to 26 million a decade later. In the home, "Labor-saving appliances liberated millions of [newly enfranchised] women from the stove and the wash-tub, and knowledge of birth control from the demands of large families" (Morison, Commager, & Leuchtenburg 1977, p. 567). While Cage's singleton status may have been attributable to parental relief at his normalcy (Crete's two previous pregnancies had resulted in two boys, the first stillborn, and the second so deformed that he died within a fortnight) it could also reflect changing gender dynamics: Revill (1992, p. 22) reports that John Sr., who worked at home, was "kept busy running errands" for the clearly assertive Crete.

The motion-picture industry, with which Los Angeles became inextricably linked during Cage's formative years, grew enormously in the period between the wars: "Stars of the silent screen supplanted luminaries of the 'legitimate' stage . . . Sound, introduced in 1927, greatly expanded film potentialities . . . [and] by 1937 the motion-picture business was eleventh in assets among the industries of the nation[:] . . . some 75 million persons visited the movies each week" (Morison, Commager, & Leuchtenburg 1977, p. 567). Even more popular than film was radio. "The first broadcasting station opened at Pittsburgh in 1920; within a decade there were almost 13 million radios in American homes, and by 1940 there were close to 900 broadcasting stations and 52 million receiving sets" (Morison, Commager, & Leuchtenburg 1977, p. 566). For Cage – whether as tenderfoot Scout broadcaster, potential collaborator with Oscar Fischinger, or borrower of electrical equipment from the CBS studios in Chicago and New York – such developments were clearly crucial to the shaping of his aesthetic locus. And, notwithstanding his rural retreat to Stony Point in the 1950s and 1960s, Cage was fundamentally a child of the city and of technology.

Equally influential on Cage's character was the dramatic downturn in the economy after the Wall Street crash of October 1929: in less than a month "stocks suffered an average decline of 40 per cent" (Morison, Commager, & Leuchtenburg 1977, p. 594) and the effects of the resulting Great Depression only truly receded in 1941, with the onset of America's involvement in World War II. Although Cage was to some extent immured from the early effects of the recession – he was at college in California, then traveling in Europe – by the time of his return home in 1931 things had clearly changed. His parents, as a result of new financial difficulties, moved to a Los Angeles apartment; Cage himself took a job as gardener at a Santa Monica auto court, "working in return for an apartment and a large room over the garage" (Revill 1992, p. 39). Showing remarkable initiative and self-motivation, he raised funds by organizing a series of lectures on modern art and music, which were delivered to Santa Monica housewives. A little later – "I had no job. No one could get work" (Kostelanetz 1988, p. 7) – he carried out library research for (among others) his father; he also helped in his mother's nonprofit arts and crafts shop – through which he met Xenia – and as a dishwasher at the Blue Bird Tea Room in Carmel.

In New York, Cage would have been exposed to the full horrors of the Great Depression, and it is perhaps this that explains the tone of one of the few stories concerning his first visit there:

> I had very little money. To eat and pay my rent and so forth, I was washing walls at a Brooklyn YWCA . . . [Every day] I would get on the subway, at the last possible moment, to go to Brooklyn . . . The way I knew it was the last

> possible moment was because I saw the same people every morning, in the
> same car. Because *they* all went there at the last possible moment; they
> didn't like their jobs any more than I liked mine.   (Kostelanetz 1988, p. 7)

On his return to the West Coast, the situation was no better. After marrying
Xenia, the couple lived for a while with Cage's parents, before moving in
with bookbinder Hazel Dreis and her apprentices. Cage learnt some design
skills, continued with library research projects (this time for lawyers), and
organized the household residents as a percussion orchestra. But "Everyone
was as poor as a church mouse" (Revill 1992, p. 52), and as a consequence Schoenberg taught Cage without charge (Hicks 1990, p. 128), while
the orchestra's battery included kitchen utensils, bookbinding equipment,
and objects salvaged from scrap yards. In this context, the instrumentation of such works as the *First Construction (in Metal)* (1939) and *Living
Room Music* (1940) becomes attributable as much to poverty as to sonic
imaginativeness.

    Although, following his meeting with Lou Harrison in 1938, Cage was
for a while in fairly regular employment, by the time the MOMA concert approached his circumstances were again dire: "there was no possible
employment. We were penniless, absolutely penniless . . . we had a place
to live, but no money for food, I mean literally" (Kostelanetz 1988,
pp. 11–12). Cage never *per se* mentions "standing in line" – in a soup queue,
or to receive welfare handouts – but the 1930s clearly taught him considerable patience, as well as self-reliance. Unafraid of taking on menial tasks –
such as washing walls or dishes, or working in hospitals and community
centers for the WPA – it is impossible to conceive of Cage becoming a hobo,
as did Harry Partch. More importantly, he "used to have a feeling . . . that I
had, so to speak, a guardian angel" (Revill 1992, p. 31): thus, at the worst
point of his fortunes, in 1942, rather than succumbing to depression he
displayed "a characteristic buoyancy in the face of an insuperable problem"
(Revill 1992, p. 81). Indeed, he felt "relieved because I found that I had
not even a cent – nothing" (Kostelanetz 1988, p. 12) and, with complete
pragmatism, "simply took the attitude that people should give me money"
(Revill 1992, p. 81). As a result of having written to friends, approximately
fifty dollars was received; shortly thereafter, he was again able to undertake research for his father (which, by virtue of its military nature, excused
Cage from being drafted), and also accumulated a number of dance commissions, "at the rate of five dollars per minute of music" (Revill 1992, p. 81). And
there was one further, immensely pragmatic, lesson learnt during the 1930s,
albeit unintentionally, from Adolph Weiss: "he had written a large
amount of music and almost none of it was played. He was somewhat
embittered because of this . . . I determined then and there . . . that I won't

write something unless it is going to be performed" (Kostelanetz 1988, p. 101).

Education

"I didn't study music with just anybody; I studied with Schoenberg. I didn't study Zen with just anybody; I studied with Suzuki. I've always gone, insofar as I could, to the president of the company."   (DUCKWORTH 1989, p. 27)

It could be argued that much of what has been discussed previously contributed significantly to Cage's general education. But it is important to distinguish between the time he spent in relatively formal tuition, and that spent in autodidactic activities: both were equally important in shaping his aesthetic locus. Cage's unfortunate years at elementary school were discussed earlier; at Los Angeles High School he appears to have been a model student, eventually graduating with the highest scholastic average in the school's history. He had been contributing editor of a student-run French-language monthly, had won prizes for oratory (Cage's speech "Other People Think" is reproduced in Kostelanetz 1971, pp. 45–49, and makes fascinating reading given his later political views), and was class valedictorian. This success continued, initially, at exclusive Pomona College, but he rebelled against the rigid textbook-based system, revising for exams by reading materials chosen randomly, and answering assignments in a prose style akin to that of Gertrude Stein (whose work he had recently discovered, and whose non-syntactic texts he set in the Three Songs of 1933, and the second movement of *Living Room Music*). Pomona did, however, contribute to Cage's education after he had dropped out. One of his former professors there, José Pijoan, met him in Paris and, on hearing of his activities at the Bibliothèque Mazarin, gave him "a swift kick in the pants" (Cage 1961, p. 261) and arranged for him to work with the architect Ernö Goldfinger.

A new phase in Cage's education began on his return to California. Perhaps as a result of his solitary childhood, he was a gifted researcher: consequently, his teaching of Santa Monica housewives was predicated in the notion that "I will learn each week something about the subject that I will then lecture on" (Cage 1961, p. 273). When the time came to talk on Arnold Schoenberg, in whose work Cage had become increasingly interested, he attempted to engage Richard Buhlig, a Los Angeles resident who had given the American première of Schoenberg's opus 11 piano pieces. Buhlig refused, but offered to look at Cage's compositions; subsequently, he recommended that Cage contact Henry Cowell. What, in specific terms, Cage learnt from Cowell is difficult to ascertain: Cowell maintained that Cage "studied dissonant counterpoint and composition with me for a season in California" (see Chapter 4) and in New York "continued intensive explorations of his own into rhythmic form and percussion music, and the musical systems of other peoples, particularly in the Orient, in my classes at the New School" (quoted in Kostelanetz 1971, pp. 94–95). Cage has only concurred that he "studied with Henry Cowell at the New School and became his assistant for a while" (Kostelanetz 1988, p. 7).

Cowell recommended that Cage should study with Schoenberg, and it was to this end that he moved first to New York, to undertake preparatory studies with Weiss (Hicks 1990, p. 126). In later years Cage strongly emphasized the importance of his Schoenbergian tutelage (as, for instance, in the statement quoted above) and often related stories emanating from his lessons with him. For instance, five of the anecdotes in "Indeterminacy" (Cage 1961, pp. 260–273) are concerned with Schoenberg, most famously that in which Cage determines to devote his life to beating his head against the "wall" of harmonic incomprehension (Cage 1961, p. 261). On other occasions, Cage proudly repeated Schoenberg's supposed opinion that he was "Not a composer, but an inventor. Of genius."[9] Yet in reality, Cage's aesthetic locus was probably influenced to a far greater extent by Cowell than by Schoenberg. From the latter, ultimately, he learnt compositional discipline, and of the fundamental necessity of structure (in whatever form). But from Cowell – author of the seminal text *New Musical Resources*, and (in Cage's earlier-quoted words) "the open sesame for new music in America" – he inherited a spirit of musical adventurousness, as well as important practical examples of how such adventurousness might manifest itself. In the context of the 1943 MOMA concert – and beyond – these include the use of newly invented or adapted instruments (percussion; prepared piano), the use of durational structures (such as "square-root form"), and more generally the iconoclastic idea, expressed in "The Future of Music: Credo," that "Any sound is acceptable to the composer of percussion music; he explores the academically forbidden 'non-musical' field of sound insofar as is manually possible" (Cage 1961, p. 5).

Postlude

Towards the end of his 1993 book *Creating Minds*, Howard Gardner – having earlier examined the lives of Freud, Einstein, Picasso, Stravinsky, Eliot, Graham, and Gandhi – paints "A Portrait of the Exemplary Creator," this being a generalized description of the common themes that emerge in the lives of many (if not most) outstanding creators. Gardner is

> well aware of the limitations of this hypothetical portrait . . . [for] when it comes to offering generalizations about creativity, one must assess how essential each generalization is. In all probability, no single one of the factors . . . highlighted is critical for a creative life; but it may be that one needs at least a certain proportion of them, if the chances for a creative breakthrough are to be heightened.   (Gardner 1993, pp. 362–363)

The Exemplary Creator is nicknamed "E.C." and is made female; however, it is interesting (and instructive) in the following précis of Gardner's idealized portrait to substitute "J.C." for "E.C." and "he" for "she."

> E.C. is raised "somewhat removed from the actual centers of power and influence in her society" in a family "neither wealthy nor in dire financial straits." The home atmosphere "is more correct than it is warm" and "moral, if not . . . religious . . . E.C. develops a strict conscience [and] often passes through a period of religiosity . . . " The family "is not highly educated, but [values] learning and achievement." When, relatively early on, E.C.'s "area of strength emerged . . . the family encouraged these interests" though with some ambivalence concerning "a career that falls outside of the established professions." By the time of adolescence, E.C. has "outgrown her home environment" and before long "ventures toward the city that is seen as a center of vital activities for her domain." There, she finds "a set of peers who share the same interests"; the results include "organizing institutions, issuing manifestos, and stimulating one another to new heights."   (Gardner 1993, pp. 360–362)

And so on: the similarities continue through the remainder of the portrait.

It is highly unlikely that J.C. was in Gardner's mind when he described E.C. (though J.C. is mentioned, in another context, on p. 402); and there are some small but significant differences between them. Yet the degree to which Gardner's "hypothetical portrait" maps onto the early (and, indeed, later) life of John Cage is both remarkable and striking. Of particular note is the issue of location, for Cage's home state was at *two* levels "somewhat removed from the actual centers of power and influence" of early twentieth-century society (Gardner 1993, p. 360). California was the best part of 3,000 miles from America's East Coast, where could be found the country's capitals both political and – more importantly – cultural. Thus, in the period under review, Cage was twice drawn, in 1934 and 1942, to New York City, which he saw as "a center of vital activities for [his] domain" (Gardner 1993, p. 361). Indeed, he ultimately made Manhattan his home. However, America itself was *also* "somewhat removed" from that traditional "[center] of power and influence," Europe; and thus Cage – like such contemporaries as Aaron

Copland, Roy Harris, and Virgil Thomson, together with the Pan American Association of Composers – was inevitably drawn to Paris, an even more vital center of "activities for [his] domain." In this context, the importance of America to the development of Cage's aesthetic locus takes on a different, more subtly shaded, meaning.

Creating Minds also suggests a final connection between Cage's American upbringing and his artistic achievements. Gardner argues very convincingly for there being "significant links between the world of the young school child and the world of the accomplished master" (Gardner 1993, p. 401), with these links "abound[ing] in the artistic realm." Like four of Gardner's seven subjects, Cage was – as a child – "already fascinated with the domains of [his] artistry": witness him playing on a newly purchased baby grand "while the movers were carrying it into the house" (Tomkins 1976, pp. 76–77). As adults, Gardner's subjects continued "to examine the productions of young children and of populations that seemed . . . primitive and childlike, and . . . often sought to capture such aspects in their own work." Although this does not resonate particularly strongly with Cage, he was at various times fascinated by – for instance – Native American sand painting, the music of Erik Satie, and the toy piano (for which he wrote a suite in 1948). But "perhaps most fundamentally, the modern masters centered their own work around the elements that are salient for the young child" (Gardner 1993, p. 401). For Cage, in 1943 and beyond, this manifested itself in multifarious ways, most of which center on a childlike need to question basic syntax. These include:

- A fascination with raw sound, as is revealed in the opening paragraph of "The Future of Music: Credo": "Wherever we are, what we hear is mostly noise. When we ignore it, it disturbs us. When we listen to it, we find it fascinating. The sound of a truck at fifty miles per hour. Static between the stations. Rain." (Cage 1961, p. 3)
- A predilection for adapted or newly created instruments, such as the junk percussion of the 1930s, the natural instruments – conch shells and amplified plant materials – of the 1970s, and (most famously) the prepared piano.
- The use of simple durations (rather than complex harmonies) as the basis for his "square-root form" compositional method before circa 1950, and thereafter of chance-derived methods including the *I Ching*, a variety of templates, and the identification and highlighting of imperfections in the manuscript paper.

As is discussed elsewhere in this volume, similar observations might be made regarding Cage's writings and his visual art; it is also noteworthy that he was attracted at an early stage to the writings of Gertrude Stein, e. e. cummings, and James Joyce, and the visual art of Mark Tobey, Marcel Duchamp, and – to a lesser extent – Morris Graves, all of whom in their work similarly question basic syntax.

Gardner concludes the penultimate section of *Creating Minds* by noting that, "it may well be part of the birthright of the most creative individuals that they retain a privileged access to sensations and points of their earlier development, including the years of early childhood. As Baudelaire once remarked, genius is the ability to recapture one's childhood at will" (Gardner 1993, p. 402). For John Milton Cage Jr., certainly, the experience of growing up in America in the first third of the twentieth century had a profound and permanent impact on the development of his aesthetic locus, and of the remarkable work that subsequently emanated from it.

2 Cage and Europe

CHRISTOPHER SHULTIS

John Cage was an American original. His inventiveness, which he claimed as originating from his father, has an "American-ness" that has a long history, dating back to the very beginnings of European migration to the "new world." Historian Brooke Hindle asks, "how could the custodians of an empty continent, far distant from the economic power centers of Europe and from its busy workshops and rising factories, move on to take leadership in one line after another of mechanization and innovation?" (Hindle 1981, p. 3). While that question requires an entire book for Hindle to answer, by the time Cage was writing music, the notion that the United States was an important source of newness, innovation and invention was well established. Cage's sense of invention – whether it be the discovery of new sounds through percussion or the creation of the prepared piano in the 1930s and 1940s, or the more (in)famous explorations into chance and indeterminacy in the 1940s and 1950s – is the stuff of legend and, as well, the very things most strikingly *not* European in Cage's work.

Other so-called American originals intentionally grounded their work in a way that differentiated it from Europe. Authors that later became especially influential to Cage, Ralph Waldo Emerson and particularly Henry David Thoreau, saw themselves as writing a way out of European influence. Emerson wrote, "It is for want of self-culture that the superstition of Travelling, whose idols are Italy, England, Egypt, retains its fascination for all educated Americans" and "why need we copy the Doric or the Gothic model? Beauty, convenience, grandeur of thought and quaint expression are as near to us as to any..." (Emerson 1982, pp. 197, 198). Following in the footsteps of Emerson and Thoreau, Charles Ives, another composer who claimed his father as an important influence, also sought to distinguish his music from what was being written in Europe. His choice of materials often included quotations of music he had heard growing up including hymns, folk tunes and popular musics native to his New England experience. Henry Cowell, an important early influence on John Cage, called Charles Ives "the father of American Music" (Cowell & Cowell 1983, p. 4) a parentage that now only makes sense when qualified as belonging to the "experimental tradition," a tradition to which Cage eventually attached himself and which now is considered a movement where his position, along with Ives, is central.

And yet, Cage, unlike these aforementioned predecessors, had no such aversion to European influence. In fact, just the opposite, he actively courted it. A comparison with an equally iconic American artistic figure, Jackson Pollock (born in January 1912 and thus an almost exact contemporary of Cage), shows just how different Cage's beginnings were. And that difference is closely tied to the degree of European influence on their work.

Both Cage and Pollock were in the Los Angeles area in the mid-1920s. In 1928, when Cage graduated as valedictorian of his class at the age of sixteen, Pollock was failing miserably as a student and would be expelled the following year. When Cage began attending Pomona College in 1929, Pollock was in Ojai, California where he spent a week listening to talks given about and by Krishnamurti, a young man from India discovered by Theosophists and called by them "the new messiah" (Naifeh 1989, p. 128). By 1930, Pollock was in New York studying with Thomas Hart Benton who was involved with what he called a "country-wide revival of Americanism" (Naifeh 1989, p. 160). That same year, Cage had dropped out of Pomona College, hitchhiked to Galveston, Texas, and took his first trip to Europe. Cage would stay there a little less than two years. But the direct influence of Europe would last for almost three decades.

Cage was only eighteen when he went to Europe for the first time. He wanted to be a writer. With his early interest in Gertrude Stein, as well as his knowledge of French, it is no surprise that he ended up in Paris. What is surprising is that, upon arrival, he began studying architecture and music. According to Cage, "I went to the Bibliothèque Mazarin. And I studied flamboyant Gothic architecture for a solid month" (Retallack 1996, p. 83). He also took pilgrimages to the cathedrals themselves, Notre Dame, Chartres and Beauvais (Hines 1994, p. 79). This story is well known, as is his being discovered by a teacher from Pomona College, José Pijoan. Pijoan found Cage a job with architect Ernö Goldfinger, drawing "Ionic and Doric and Corinthian columns," a far cry obviously from what Emerson would have recommended to a young American writer! (Retallack 1996, p. 84).

Cage eventually stopped working for Goldfinger and began studying music. He had studied piano as a child, most notably with his aunt Phoebe James and later with the composer Fannie Charles Dillon. According to Cage, "my first experience with music was through neighborhood piano teachers, and particularly my Aunt Phoebe. She said of the work of Bach and Beethoven that it couldn't possibly interest me, she herself being devoted to the music of the nineteenth century. She introduced me to Moszkowski and what you might call the piano music the whole world loves to play. In that volume, it seemed to me that the works of Grieg were more interesting than the others" (Cage 1962a, p. 45).[1] On the recommendation of La Baronne d'Estournelles de Constant, who found his playing "very bad but somehow musical," Cage studied piano with M. Lazare-Lévy, who taught at the Paris Conservatoire (Cage 1948a, p. 29). Cage was assigned a Beethoven sonata and sent off to listen to concerts, particularly ones that programmed the music of Bach. According to Cage, "I took only two lessons. I could see' that his teaching would lead to technical accomplishment, but I wasn't really interested in that" (Tomkins 1976, p. 79). He did, however, continue to attend concerts, most notably a concert of modern piano music given by John Kirkpatrick "that included Scriabin and Stravinsky and this led me to – I was given to sight reading – to buy a book called *Das neue Klavierbuch* that had short easy pieces by all the modern composers, including Schoenberg and Satie"[2] (Retallack 1996, p. 84). Modern music would eventually become Cage's passion. He would "devote his life to it" in response to Schoenberg, something Cage refused to do following a similar remark made by the architect Goldfinger: "I overheard him say that to become an architect you must devote your life to architecture, and I immediately – I didn't interrupt him immediately – but the next time I talked to him I said, I have to give up architecture because I am interested in so many other things . . . And so I did" (Retallack 1996, p. 84). Cage spent the rest of his time traveling around Europe visiting, among other places, Germany and Spain, Capri and Mallorca. In the last of these, he wrote his first pieces of music.

Cage's "German period"

Architecture continued, however, to have an influence on Cage, in the sense of how it connects with the visual arts. The Bauhaus, one of the most important art movements of that time, or of the twentieth century as a whole for that matter, made a deep and lasting impression on him. It was, according to Frans van Rossum, one of the most important European influences on Cage's early creative life.[3] But the Bauhaus was not just an art movement; it was an art school founded in Weimar by architect Walter Gropius in 1919. By the time Cage arrived in Paris, in the spring of 1930, the Bauhaus had moved to Dessau and the school's director by that fall was the architect Ludwig Mies van der Rohe. Gropius and László Moholy-Nagy had left for Berlin by then but others, including Josef Albers, remained. And many people came there to visit: "By the end of the twenties, the Dessau Bauhaus belonged among the attractions of Europe. According to the records kept by its administration, the institution had 100–250 visitors, among them Americans, each week" (Kentgens-Craig 1999, p. 83). One of those visitors was John Cage.

According to van Rossum, Cage and Don Sample, an artist he met in Paris, visited the Bauhaus in Dessau during this first European visit. Sample, twelve years Cage's senior, was Cage's companion during most of his European travels; according to Cage, "it was through him that I became aware of [the journal] *transition* and of art and literature" (Hines 1994, p. 81). When they returned to the United States in 1931, Cage and Sample brought with them a collection of books and magazines about the Bauhaus and Bauhaus aesthetics. Again according to van Rossum, Harry Hay, a friend from Los Angeles High School, sang early songs of Cage that were staged by Hay, Cage and Sample in the Bauhaus style, including the costumes.[4] And Harry Hay said that "Back home, they checked the Bauhaus catalogue Sample had brought back from Europe for commentary on furniture and design detail" (Timmons 1990, p. 58). In the spring of 1930, just after he arrived in Paris, it is possible that Cage saw an exhibition of the Société des Artistes Décorateurs Français. If not, in all likelihood, Don Sample, for whom the Bauhaus was very important, did see the exhibition. The German section was designed by Bauhaus artists: Walter Gropius, László Moholy-Nagy, Herbert Bayer and Marcel Breuer (Giersch 1999, p. 607). And since the Paris exhibition featured "interior décor, lamps and furniture," it is likely the catalog Hay describes was from this event (Giersch 1999, p. 607).

When Cage returned to the United States he was only nineteen. But the former valedictorian of Los Angeles High School, who had originally intended to become a Methodist minister, was now completely under the influence of modernism in music, literature and the visual arts. Although Cage's years at Pomona College had begun that transformation in literature, and Cage's initiation to modern music began soon after his arrival in Paris, it was the Bauhaus that made the most powerful aesthetic impact on Cage's later work. In 1927, Ludwig Mies van der Rohe wrote: "Is form really an aim? Is it not instead a product of the design process? Is it not the process which is essential?" (Kentgens-Craig 1999, p. 162). Thirty years later Cage would deliver a series of three lectures to a predominantly German-speaking audience on that very subject. As we will see, "Composition as Process," given in Darmstadt in 1958, brought an end to the European influence on Cage being described in this chapter. And there is remarkable irony to the fact that important aspects of what was upsetting to Cage's audience, and what separated him from the mainstream of the post-war European musical avant-garde, were ideas that he had first discovered many years before in Germany.

Back in Los Angeles, Cage continued to pursue his newly cultivated European interests. These, and the contacts involved in pursuing them, were predominantly German. Among other places, he and Don Sample lived for "probably a little less than a year" at the guest house of the King's Road residence of architect Rudolph Schindler (Hines 1994, p. 84). As would be the case for several years to come, the Bauhaus connection was ever-present. Galka Scheyer, whom Cage met through his connection with the

King's Road circle of artists and intellectuals in the Los Angeles area, was a Bauhaus devotee and made regular visits there in the 1920s. She was the person who represented the "Blue Four" (Alexey von Jawlensky and Bauhaus teachers Paul Klee, Wassily Kandinsky, and Lyonel Feininger) in the United States. Through Scheyer, who "turned her house into a gallery" (Kentgens-Craig 1999, p. 68), Cage had the opportunity to get to know these artists' works better: "she was straight from the Bauhaus. She brought with her all the work she could . . . of Klee and Kandinsky and Feininger . . . and she would loan those beautiful things to me . . . and . . . when I would bring a Klee back to her, for instance, after having had it for several months, she would say, 'oh you could have kept it'" (Retallack 1996, p. 88). Scheyer also introduced Cage to Walter Arensberg (at whose home he first saw the work of Marcel Duchamp, later to become an increasingly important influence), and the architect Richard Neutra, who was a guest faculty member at the Bauhaus in 1930 (Kentgens-Craig 1999, p. 94).

Another Bauhaus visitor who had a lasting influence on Cage was Henry Cowell. Cowell had collaborated with Imre Weisshaus of Budapest for a concert given at the Dessau Bauhaus, "Contemporary Music and its Developmental Potentials," on December 1, 1931 (Kentgens-Craig 1999, p. 84). Cage met Cowell through Richard Buhlig, his teacher at the time. Although Cage's Sonata for Clarinet was ultimately not published by Cowell's *New Music Quarterly* (*Amores* from 1943 holds that distinction), it did receive enough notice by Cowell to merit his further involvement with Cage and his youthful career as a composer. According to Michael Hicks, "That year, 1933, Cowell deemed Schoenberg the greatest living composer, and Cage not only told Cowell that he wished to study with the master, who would be immigrating to the United States that fall, he also asked Cowell to help him get a scholarship to do that. Cage writes in a 1934 letter that Cowell was 'rather vague' in reply but urged him to approach Adolph Weiss in New York" (Hicks 1990, p. 126). Cage did study composition with Weiss (who was Schoenberg's only student living in the United States at the time) in New York for several months. He left Carmel with Don Sample that spring and stayed until December, after which he returned to California with Cowell.[5] His plans from the beginning were to study with Schoenberg and, since the latter had moved to Los Angeles while Cage was in New York, it made sense for him to return.[6]

Cage's studies with Buhlig, Weiss and Schoenberg gave him a thorough grounding in then-current German "modernist" compositional methods. According to Weiss, Cage was already "very proficient" in counterpoint, something he must have worked on through his association with Buhlig (George 1971, p. 46). Weiss himself continued to work with Cage on counterpoint and also added the study of harmony: "He was lucky to have come to me, for I gave him a free hand in his creative work. Of course in the A B C's of harmony and counterpoint the traditional rules were observed and exceptions to rules were noted and tolerated by later historical evidence" (George 1971, pp. 50–51). Because Schoenberg wouldn't look at his compositions, Cage continued to show them to Weiss while he was taking classes with Schoenberg: "when, later, I sent them to him [Weiss] by mail, he returned them with long letters and his verbal notations (in pencil) on my manuscripts" (George 1971, p. 48).

Cage's studies with Schoenberg included classes in, once again, counterpoint and harmony, as well as courses in analysis and composition. There is evidence of Cage's taking courses, both privately and at U.S.C. and U.C.L.A., beginning in 1935 (after mid-semester holiday recess) through the fall semester 1936. This was significant contact between a professor and student and it was definitely the longest period of formal study Cage had with anyone in music. According to Robert Stevenson, "His January 1932 alumni record at Los Angeles High concludes thus: 'Cage studied art in Europe for past year exploring fields such as abstraction, Germanic, & expression'" (Stevenson 1982, p. 8). Upon his return, as the above has shown, Cage's study of the "Germanic" concentrated on music. And it was, by Cage's own admission, one of the great influences of his compositional life.[7]

Cage's "French period"

Cage's German connections continued to be important in the 1930s and 1940s. He met László Moholy-Nagy at Mills College in 1940, a contact that would influence his being offered a position in Chicago in 1941.[8] Cage had been greatly influenced by a well-received book Moholy-Nagy had written in 1935, *The New Vision* (Retallack 1996, p. 87), that "described the idea and pedagogic concept of the Bauhaus" (Kentgens-Craig 1999, p. 142) and Cage used his contact with Galka Scheyer to bring exhibitions of the works of the "Blue Four" to Seattle while he was there (Retallack 1996, p. 88). Thomas Hines states that in 1934, while in New York, Cage through Virgil Thomson met Phillip Johnson (Hines 1994, p. 92). The previous year, Mies van der Rohe had sent Johnson a letter (dated February 22, 1933) authorizing him "to act officially as the Bauhaus's American representative" (Kentgens-Craig 1999, p. 95); and it was Johnson who was also instrumental in bringing Anni and Josef Albers to Black Mountain College, NC, in November, 1933. The Albers' arrival predated Cage's meeting with Johnson, and it is thus possible that their relationship was a catalyst for Cage's own initial interest in Black Mountain. According to Martin Duberman, "by the late thirties, John Cage, then at the Cornish School in Seattle, had heard of Black Mountain as 'an advanced place,' [quoting Cage] and wrote to ask if they had an opening for him" (Duberman 1993, p. 277).

But by the time Cage finally came to Black Mountain College in 1948, his interests had shifted from Germany to France. The Bauhaus connection was still there: Lincoln Kirstein, who curated a Bauhaus show in New York (1930), had in 1947 commissioned Cage and Cunningham to create the ballet that became *The Seasons* (1947).[9] However, instead of being the Schoenberg follower of the 1930s, something the faculty would have likely supported, Cage came instead as a promoter of French composer Erik Satie. Regarding Cage's "Defense of Satie," the infamous lecture that attacked Beethoven, Mary Emma Harris writes, "it was a declaration of war on the assumed supremacy of the Germanic tradition that dominated American musical life, including the music program at Black Mountain" (Harris 1987, p. 154).

How did this change come about? The reasons for Cage's shift in interests were likely of two kinds: social and political, personal and professional. As early as 1934, Americans had increasingly negative feelings toward Germany, with friends of Cage like Galka Scheyer making comments such as those found in a letter written to Paul Klee: "I would appreciate if, in the future, you quote your prices in Swiss francs. It is easier to discuss Swiss prices with people here than German ones because Germany is on the black list" (Kentgens-Craig 1999, p. 176). Cage, in turn, could not have been unaware of the changing political situation that had brought so many writers, composers and artists – including his teacher, Arnold Schoenberg – to the United States. However, while this may explain to some extent the turn away from obvious German influences, it does not explain the redirection of Cage's interests to France. This belongs predominantly to Cage's reacquaintance with Virgil Thomson, when he and his wife Xenia moved to New York in 1942.

As with everything concerning the interrelation between Cage's private and professional life, there is some confusion regarding Cage's first meeting with Thomson. According to Phillip Johnson, Cage met Thomson (perhaps through Cowell) in New York in 1934 (Hines 1994, p. 92). Thomson was himself a Francophile and had spent a considerable amount of time in France, studying with Nadia Boulanger, and socializing with many of the artists living in Paris between the wars. By the time Cage moved to New York in 1942, Thomson had spent two years as the chief music critic for the *New York Herald Tribune*. His was a position of enormous power, especially for someone who, as an active composer, was himself a "player" in the very musical scene he was charged to cover. That influence would eventually assist Cage in receiving a Guggenheim and an award from the National Institute of Arts and Letters which, in turn, would send him to Europe for a second time[10] (Tommasini 1997, p. 441). Important as these professional contacts and influence were for Cage's career, the most significant connections concerning the French influence consisted in Thomson's introducing Cage to the music of Erik Satie, and recommending that he contact Pierre Boulez when he traveled to Paris in 1949.

As has been shown, Cage was familiar with some of Satie's music as early as 1930. But he became devoted to it through Thomson, who had been a champion of Satie since his Harvard days in the early 1920s (Tommasini 1997, p. 82). According to Tommasini, Thomson introduced Cage and his friend and fellow composer Lou Harrison "to Satie's *Socrate*, singing and playing the work at the piano, an experience which moved Harrison, but profoundly changed Cage. Like Thomson, Cage grew to revere Satie" (Tommasini 1997, p. 368).

However, the question of influence had changed for Cage in the 1940s. No longer was he the impressionable student, but instead an increasingly self-sufficient artist. He would have known, for example, that his compositions for percussion and prepared piano, although clearly influenced by the experimental school of composition he had become acquainted with through Cowell, were themselves original contributions to that same tradition. And Thomson himself had, in an early review of Cage's work, transferred the question of pedigree (Cage's studies with Schoenberg) from one of teacher's influence to one of student's improvement:

> Mr. Cage has carried Schoenberg's harmonic maneuvers to their logical conclusion. He has produced atonal music not by causing the twelve tones of the chromatic scale to contradict one another consistently, but by eliminating, to start with, all sounds of precise pitch ... By thus getting rid, at the beginning, of the constricting element in atonal writing – which is the necessity of taking care to avoid making classical harmony with a standardized palette of instrumental sounds and pitches that exists primarily for the purpose of producing such harmony – Mr. Cage has been free to develop the rhythmic element of composition, which is the weakest element in the Schoenbergian style, to a point of sophistication unmatched in the technique of any other living composer.
>
> (Thomson 1945, p. 72)

This review helped Cage's career greatly; but it also points to the new-found maturity of Cage's work beginning in the late 1930s and early 1940s. Cage's influences were beginning to concern ways in which he matched sympathies on the outside with already formed ideas of his own. In a certain sense, Cage himself said as much in his remark concerning Ives: "we become aware, I believe, of the past by what we do. What we do throws a light on the past" (Cage 1964, p. 37). However, more to the point is the idea that Cage's influences were increasingly related to his own now self-determined sense of place in the world of art. Marjorie Perloff mentions this in light of Cage's interest in the work of Marcel Duchamp, whom Cage also met in the mid-1940s, another French artist whose influence on Cage was deeper than that of Boulez and at least as deep as that of Satie.[11] According to Perloff, Cage was drawn to Duchamp because of his "subversion of causality and psychological depth, coupled with his predilection for chance operations and his larger refusal to distinguish between 'life' and 'art' ... " (Perloff 1994, p. 101). These interests, however, were not original influences. In other words, it is not because Duchamp worked in these areas that Cage, in turn, began doing so as well. Duchamp instead became, "a duchamp unto my self" (Cage 1979, p. 53), where the intersection between Duchamp and Cage's own ideas becomes how Cage used Duchamp's work within his own already somewhat determined (although changing) sensibility.[12]

It is in this sense that Cage was influenced by Satie. Cage thought he saw and heard similarities to his own work in Satie's scores. According to Tomkins, "Cage thought he could detect in Satie's then little-known symphonic drama, *Socrate*, a type of rhythmic structure similar to his own, a structure which, he firmly believed, had enabled Satie to break with the harmonic structure of Beethoven" (Tomkins 1976, p. 102). In the mid- to late 1940s, Cage was still composing with variations of his "square root form," a method he had used regularly since the *First Construction (in Metal)* of 1939. Cage's use of this form saw compositional structure as something that could be independent of what was placed within it. Years later Cage would say the following about form concerning his *Sonatas and Interludes* (1946–48), a piece that corresponds to both Cage's study of Satie and to this moment in Cage's career: "In contrast to a structure based on the frequency aspect of sound, tonality, that is, this rhythmic structure was as hospitable to non-musical sounds, noises, as it was to those of the conventional scales and instruments. For nothing about the structure was determined by the materials which were to occur in it; it was conceived, in fact, so that it could be as well expressed by the absence of these materials as by their presence" (Cage 1958a, pp. 19–20).

What Cage saw in Satie was a view of form that did not follow "conventional scales" or harmonies, particularly in the sense of following common rules of harmonic progression or melodic phrasing. These can, of course, also be found in the music of Debussy, a composer who also greatly admired Satie. Paul Griffiths uses *Prélude à 'l'après-midi d'un faune'* (1892–94) to address this point: "One of the principal characteristics of modern music, in the not strictly chronological sense, is its lack of dependence on the system of major and minor keys which had provided motivation and coherence for most western art music since the seventeenth century. In this respect, Debussy's *Prélude* undoubtedly heralds the modern era" (Griffiths 1978, p. 7). That Satie had earlier performed a similar task, writing music that did not use tonality in a "functional" way, was likely obvious to Debussy himself, who had met Satie in 1891. Debussy would certainly have been familiar with the three *Gymnopédies* (1888), two of which he may have assisted in getting published in 1895 (Gowers 1986, pp. 130, 132).

However, anyone familiar with both composers can immediately hear differences in how such digressions from so-called common practice were used. While Debussy's music seeks to move beyond the harmonic world of late nineteenth-century German music, it still has its own tonal logic and can be followed as such without in itself seeming somehow to be a "transgression." Satie, on the other hand, intentionally plays with musical conventions in a way that clearly wishes to reorient the listener's normative sense of melodic contour and harmonic progression. A good example of the latter is found in the well-known first of the *Gymnopédies*, where the harmonic shifts between D major and d minor have no traditional grounding. They instead function musically like the story Cage tells of the man standing on a hill, a story told at the end of "Composition as Process," the lecture mentioned earlier. Three men go to the top of the hill to ask the man why he stands there:

> "What reasons do you have for my standing here?" he asked. "We have
> three," they answered. "First, you are standing up here because it's cooler
> here and you are enjoying the breeze. Second, since the hill is elevated
> above the rest of the land, you are up here in order to see something in the
> distance. Third, you have lost your friend and that is why you are standing
> here alone on this hill. We have walked this way; we never meant to climb
> this hill; now we want an answer: Which one of us is right?" The man
> answered, "I just stand."   (Cage, 1958a, pp. 33–34)

Those harmonic shifts in Satie seemingly exist for the same reason: they just happen.

The comparison between Debussy and Satie is important because it mirrors the respective influence of these composers on Boulez and Cage. Cage, on Virgil Thomson's recommendation, visited Boulez when he traveled to Europe in 1949. They became friends and shared an intense correspondence that lasted for the next five years. Cage spent a considerable amount of time in Paris studying Satie's work. Of Satie, Cage wrote, "It's not a question of Satie's relevance. He's indispensable" (Cage 1958e, p. 82). In contrast and by comparison, Boulez wrote the following in an encyclopedia entry on Debussy:

> much has been said of [Satie's] influence on Debussy (the use of streams of
> parallel ninth chords and superimposed fourths); it is even said that Satie's
> *Sarabandes* and *Gymnopédies* showed him the way for the harmonic
> innovations which he was to bring to such a pitch of refinement. While

this influence did occasionally make itself felt, it remains the case that it is really to Debussy alone that we owe the discovery of a new harmonic vocabulary: Satie by comparison never got beyond the level of a collector of rare objects; he completely failed to integrate his "discoveries" into a coherent vocabulary.   (Boulez 1958, pp. 265–66)

Boulez could likely have said the same of Cage.

Much of what Cage heard in Satie spoke to his own interest in formal properties, with which he found affinities in the latter's music. From the 1940s, his sense of Satie as a precursor lasted for the rest of his life. Boulez chose Debussy as a precursor for similar reasons that inform his own need for coherence, where "harmonic innovations" result in a "new harmonic vocabulary." In his introduction to the published correspondence between Boulez and Cage, Jean-Jacques Nattiez writes that "in aesthetic terms, the two men's encounter could not have been anything other than a misunderstanding" (Nattiez 1993, p. 15). Possibly: but I think it more likely that Cage and Boulez simply enjoyed each other's company when they met and, in the late 1940s, became friends and colleagues with whom they could share their work. As the correspondence shows, it is only their shared sense of purpose that Boulez speaks of, when he writes in "Eventuellement . . . " about Cage's use of "non-tempered sound spaces" and "the idea of sound complexes" (as found, for example, in Cage's *String Quartet in Four Parts*, which was being written at the time the two composers first met). Boulez closes with the following:

> I would again draw attention to his [Cage's] way of conceiving rhythmic structure as something dependent on real time, expressed through numerical relationships in which the personal element plays no part. Moreover, a given number of units of measure yield an equal number of units of development. We thereby arrive at an *a priori* numerical structure which Cage calls "prismatic" but which I prefer to call "crystallized." More recently, he has been working on setting up structural relations between the different components of sound, and for this he uses tables which organize each component into parallel but autonomous distributions. The tendency of these experiments by John Cage is too close to my own for me to fail to mention them.   (Boulez 1952a, pp. 134, 135)

The results of their shared experiments were Boulez's *Structures 1A* and Cage's *Music of Changes*. Tellingly, neither composer chose to continue in the direction required by the individual methods used to write these pieces.

The "French influence" on Cage rests more directly on how the pieces of this period sound. I agree with Kostelanetz's opinion that Cage's *Sonatas and Interludes* "echo the piano music of Erik Satie" (Kostelanetz 1989, p. 57). There is, I think, a direct correlation between the tonal world of Satie (and

Virgil Thomson for that matter) and the music Cage wrote under its influence. And there is no doubt that the sound world of *Music of Changes* is a direct result of Cage having heard and studied Boulez's Piano Sonata No. 2 (1948).

"End of the influence": Germany in the 1950s

Cage made his third trip to Europe in 1954, a concert tour with David Tudor featuring music that was grounded in Cage's new area of interest: indeterminacy. His fourth trip included an appearance at Darmstadt in 1958. And, while Cage would go on influencing Europe until the day he died, the influence of Europe on Cage, at least in the sense of how it has been presented here, would, after these two visits, come to an end.

In 1954, Cage and Tudor performed in several European cities, and appeared, infamously, at the Donaueschinger Musiktage where they performed a shortened version of *34′ 46. 776″ for two pianists*.[13] This was, according to sources at Donaueschingen, Cage and Tudor's "first European appearance" now regarded as "a star-studded hour in Donaueschingen's history, comparable with the guest appearance of Schoenberg and Webern thirty years earlier" (Häusler 1996, p. 90). The reason why the piece (which had been commissioned by the festival) was shortened is due to Heinrich Strobel himself, longtime director of Southwest German Radio in Baden-Baden, and in charge of programming in Donaueschingen from 1950 until his death. Strobel, "fearing the worst," according to the previously cited notes, "had persuaded the composer to reduce the work . . . to around a third of its length." Wolfgang Steinecke, who, as director of the summer courses, would later invite Cage to Darmstadt, reviewed the concert calling it "childish sensationalism" (Häusler 1996, pp. 90, 91).

The pieces Cage and Tudor played are from a series of compositions that James Pritchett has called "The Ten Thousand Things" (Pritchett 1993, p. 96). These particular pieces were for the prepared piano, an instrument that had brought Cage a significant amount of fame. This would have been the first opportunity for most of the "Neue Musik" audience to hear this invention played by the composer and his famous accomplice. However, if they were expecting something along the lines of his *Sonatas and Interludes*, what they got was something else altogether. The scores of these pieces show pitch and placement in time according to seconds. The title, in fact, shows to what level of specificity time is measured, at least compositionally. As Example 2.1 shows, there is also a table above the notation, "three narrow bands with markings corresponding to the notes below them." According

Example 2.1 John Cage, *31'57.9864" for a pianist* (1954), page 1

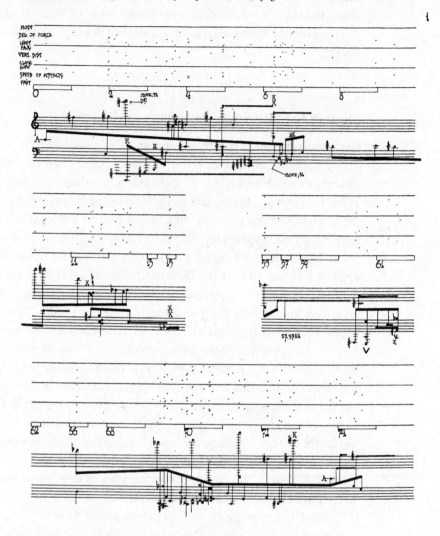

to Pritchett, "these bands denote force of attack, distance of attack from the keyboard, and speed of attack, the three physical factors that Cage thought determined dynamics" (Pritchett 1993, p. 100).

There is much that is determined in these compositions. And yet, following Cage's at-that-time current interests, and a development that would become increasingly important to him during the course of the 1950s, indeterminacy plays an important role as well. A few quotations from the score instructions demonstrate this: "Any amount of this music may be played or not . . . " "Where impossibilities are notated (of any kind), the pianist is free to use his own discretion"; and finally, "the notation may be read in any focus (as many or as few of its aspects as desired being acted upon)." The performance was so controversial that, as a result, Cage didn't appear at Donaueschingen for almost twenty years. His return in 1972 was for the presentation of a film for television co-composed with Hans G. Helms and entitled *Birdcage.*

Reading through Cage's contemporaneous writings, as collected in *Silence,* it becomes clear that he begins to have critical things to say about Europe correspondent to this tour, the negative responses to the performances he received, and the cooling off of his relationship with Boulez. On the other hand, it is important to mention that these European visits and contacts, along with his lessons with Schoenberg, were essential to his early successes as a composer. Cage would himself have been quite sensitive to the importance of European reception to his work in regard to continuing the upward trajectory of his career, as the following correspondence suggests. Getting the address from Everett Helm, an American who was an important figure in the post-war German new music scene, Cage wrote his first letter to Wolfgang Steinecke, then director of the Darmstadt summer courses, on March 30, 1954. In that letter Cage stated: "My hopes and intentions with regards to this coming trip are not only connected with the performance of new American music but I am also anxious to become acquainted with new works by European composers."[14]

Cage's fourth European trip was in 1958. He was scheduled to appear at Darmstadt where David Tudor would perform a program of "Neue Klaviermusik in den USA und Europa." The program (which was not performed) was supposed to have included *Music of Changes* by Cage, Boulez's Third Piano Sonata, and Stockhausen's *Klavierstück XI* (IMD, 1958). He was also scheduled to perform at the Brussels Worlds Fair (the recording *Indeterminacy* documents the work prepared for that appearance). At the last minute Boulez, who was supposed to teach the summer composition courses with Bruno Maderna, cancelled. According to Wilhelm Schlüter, longtime librarian at the Internationales Musikinstitut Darmstadt, a discussion ensued between Wolfgang Steinecke, then director of the courses, and both Bruno Maderna and Luigi Nono. It was Maderna's suggestion to invite Cage and Steinecke did so. Steinecke's invitation is dated August 8, and Cage's telegram in response, a simple "yes. subject composition as process" was written on August 15 (IMD, 1958). In little more than two weeks, the courses would begin.[15]

The 1958 Darmstadt summer courses (Ferienkurse für Neue Musik) began on September 2. On September 3, Cage, once again assisted by Tudor, presented the evening concert. This would have been the second concert of the courses, the first "Eröffnungskonzert" consisting of chamber music by Alban Berg. Cage and Tudor's concert, contrary to prior publicity, continued – as it had at Donaueschingen – to promote the work of Cage and other members of the New York School: Morton Feldman, Earle Brown, and Christian Wolff.

Indeterminacy was, as mentioned, a fundamental compositional concern for Cage at the time. His *Concert for Piano and Orchestra* (1957–58), one of his most famous large-scale indeterminate pieces, had received its première at the twenty-five-year retrospective concert that Emile de Antonio, Jasper Johns, and Robert Rauschenberg organized on May 15, 1958 in Town Hall, New York City. Stockhausen, having heard a performance of the *Concert* in Cologne, would lecture on the piece at Darmstadt the following summer, in 1959. "Indeterminacy" was also the title of the talk Cage gave in Brussels early in October 1958; and it was this talk that Stockhausen requested from Cage for publication in *die Reihe* (No. 5, 1959, pp. 116–121).

One of the compositions performed at the September 3 concert was *Variations* (1958). No piece up until that time had taken indeterminacy as far as did *Variations*. And it should be remembered that it was indeterminacy, not chance, that really caused the split between Cage and his European contemporaries. *Variations I*, as it subsequently became titled, was written in January 1958 and dedicated to David Tudor on the occasion of his birthday. This was Cage's first use of transparencies, a method that produced some of his most indeterminate compositions. According to Pritchett, this piece has its origin in notations appearing in the *Solo for Piano* (*Concert for Piano and Orchestra*) which uses many types of notation and compositional methods (Pritchett 1993, p. 135).

The transparencies consist of lines and dots that are then superimposed. According to the score instructions, "The 5 lines are: lowest frequency, simplest overtone structure, greatest amplitude, least duration, and earliest occurrence within a decided upon time. Perpendiculars from points to lines give distances to be measured or simply observed." In other words, the distances between lines and points would determine, one assumes according to a performer's own criteria, issues of frequency, overtones, amplitude, duration, and when sounds would begin. Cage's final instructions are certainly among the most indeterminate he had ever written: "Any number of performers; any kind and number of instruments."

It is important to emphasize the discrepancy between what Europe expected from Cage and what it got. In Donaueschingen, what was expected was prepared piano music similar to that Cage had written in the 1940s, culminating in his masterpiece *Sonatas and Interludes*. And, as Cage himself tells us in his first Darmstadt lecture, Steinecke had asked him to "discuss in particular my *Music of Changes*," another of Cage's pianistic masterpieces (Cage 1958a, p. 18). *Music of Changes* was a monumentally difficult work written using extensive chance operations. Highly regarded by the European avant-garde, at least by reputation, it was seen as a part of the compositional ideology they had been in the process of rebuilding after the war. A short excerpt from a letter by Pierre Boulez, written in December 1951 in response to a letter from Cage describing the composition of *Music of Changes*, confirms this view: "Everything you say about the tables of sounds, durations, amplitudes, used in your *Music of Changes* is, as you will see, along exactly the same lines as I am working at the moment." It is the following sentence that betrays Boulez's future criticism: "The only thing, forgive me, which I am not happy with, is the method of absolute chance (*by tossing the coins*). On the contrary, I believe that chance must be extremely controlled . . ." (Nattiez 1993, p. 112). Important to note, even in the criticism, is that it is not chance in itself that is being criticized, but the *method* of how it is used. It is also important to note that it was at this same time (excerpts are actually included in the letter) that Boulez wrote his infamous "Schoenberg is Dead" essay where he throws down the following gauntlet: "all non-serial composers are *useless* . . ." (Boulez 1952b, p. 214). While Boulez did not include that remark in the letter, Cage would certainly have read it later.

At Darmstadt, Cage chose to throw his own gauntlet, in part a response to Boulez in particular, but mostly to the European new music scene in general. His relations with Boulez had soured long before 1958, so attacking Boulez at Darmstadt would only be Cage's side of a conflict already begun in public by Boulez's published criticisms of Cage (of which "Alea" [Boulez 1957, pp. 26–38] is the most representative). The third European visit likely contributed to Cage's ire, projecting his personal feelings toward Boulez onto a European scene that valorized Boulez and those other serial composers who didn't merit Boulez's label of being "useless." Cage's gauntlet was not, however, the concert at which he and Tudor performed *Variations*: as we have seen, his music had already received a similar response (mostly negative) four years earlier at Donaueschingen. Instead, it was the lectures he gave – ironically only because Boulez couldn't make it – entitled "Composition as Process," that caused the furore.

John Cage was not only a great composer: he was also a great writer; and the three lectures he gave at Darmstadt include some of his very best writing. The first lecture, entitled "Changes," is a history of what Cage saw as the developments that had occurred in his work beginning with his percussion pieces and ending with those espousing indeterminacy. It was delivered on Saturday, September 6. This first lecture includes a discussion of *Music of Changes*, which was supposed to be the subject of his talk in its entirety, and was actually written within the time length of the work so that Tudor could play the corresponding part of the piece whenever there were pauses in Cage's text.

"Indeterminacy," where the first lecture's subject matter left off, is where the second lecture begins and remains. Cage called it "intentionally pontifical" (Cage 1958a, p. 35). Delivered on Monday, September 8, Cage gave examples of European music that he regarded as being indeterminate, ranging from Bach's *The Art of Fugue* to Karlheinz Stockhausen's then recently composed *Klavierstück XI*. However, he used these two examples for entirely different purposes. Bach was cited in order to give credibility and historical context to indeterminacy in music. Stockhausen was cited in order to criticize European appropriation of Cage's work, through what Boulez called "aleatory," a completely different subject from either Cage's use of chance or indeterminacy, though history books even today often regard the terms interchangeably. Here is what Cage wrote about Stockhausen's work:

> The indeterminate aspects of the composition of the *Klavierstück XI* do not remove the work in its performance from the body of European musical conventions. And yet the purpose of indeterminacy would seem to be to bring about an unforeseen situation. In the case of *Klavierstück XI*, the use of indeterminacy is in this sense unnecessary since it is ineffective. The work might as well have been written in all of its aspects determinately. It would lose, in this case, its single unconventional aspect: that of being printed on an unusually large sheet of paper which, together with an attachment that may be snapped on at several points enabling one to stretch it out flat and place it on the music rack of a piano, is put in a cardboard tube suitable for safekeeping or distribution through the mails.
>
> (Cage 1958a, p.36)

This would have been seen as (and still is) strong criticism for a composer like Stockhausen, whose quest for innovation and newness was perhaps rivaled only by that of Cage himself.

The third lecture was on "Communication" (a title that one suspects was devised especially for its inclusion as the third Darmstadt lecture). It was first delivered at Rutgers University and also, since it is mentioned in the text, somewhere in Illinois, probably the University of Illinois. The lecture is nothing but questions, clearly from the outset an attack by Cage concerning the need for "answers" and the "controlling composer" behind such results, that Cage saw as typifying the work of his European colleagues and critics. Cage instead asked questions, an approach he used consistently for the rest of his compositional life.

Later in the lecture, Cage is obviously speaking about Boulez when he says, "If one of us says that all twelve tones should be in a row and another says they shouldn't, which one of us is right?" (Cage 1958a, p. 48). And he is obviously reacting to his experience with European audiences, especially

German audiences, when he writes "Why is it so difficult for so many people to listen? Why do they start talking when there is something to hear? Do they have ears not on the sides of their heads but situated inside their mouths so that when they hear something their first impulse is to start talking? The situation should be made more normal, don't you think? Why don't they keep their mouths shut and their ears open? Are they stupid? And, if so, why don't they try to hide their stupidity? Were bad manners acquired when knowledge of music was acquired? Does being musical make one automatically stupid and unable to listen?" (Cage 1958a, pp. 48–49). Harsh words to be sure. But note how Cage is able to deflect the harshness linguistically by shifting to the third-person "they" when the criticism is leveled. "Are *they* stupid?" is softened somewhat by such deflection especially in a context where the personal "you" is also deployed, "The situation should be made more normal, don't *you* think?" This enables one to apply an "if the shoe fits wear it" approach that keeps the criticism intact without necessarily being personally insulting to the audience.

Hans G. Helms, Heinz-Klaus Metzger, and Wolf Rosenberg were asked by Wolfgang Steinecke to write German translations of Cage's three lectures.[16] They were passed out prior to each of the talks and those who couldn't understand Cage's English were thus able to read along in German. Thirty-eight years later, Metzger remarked, "das scheint mir retrospektiv so ungeheuerlich, dass mir schwindlig wird – der Mittler zwischen dem Denken Cages und der deutschen Sprachkultur" (Metzger 1996, p. 250). In English, his remarks read as follows: "As I look back, it now seems so immense that it makes me dizzy – my being the medium between the thought of Cage and German-speaking culture."[17]

The translation is very good. Here's a particularly difficult passage: "Do they have ears not on the sides of their heads but situated inside their mouths so that when they hear something their first impulse is to start talking?" This is translated as: "Sitzen bei ihnen die Ohren, anstatt rechts und links vom Kopf, veilleicht zwischen den Zähnen, sodaß ihr erste Impuls es ist, wenn sie etwas hören, zu reden?"[18] The translation appropriately leaves "their" as "ihnen" and "ihr" and "sie," all third-person German equivalents. At the place where Cage switches from the impersonal "they" to "you," "The situation should be made more normal, don't you think?" the translation reads: "Meinen Sie nicht, daß man zu einer anständigeren Aufführung gelangen sollte?" Here the translation goes "beyond the call of duty" to get a German equivalent to "normal situation." "Gelangen" means to "achieve the end" of an "anständigeren Aufführung" which is a "decent performance." The translators very clearly distinguish between "man" for the impersonal "one," not required in the original but needed to render it in German, and the formal "Sie" for the you found in "don't you think."

This makes a later error in translation much more obvious and, as will be seen, intentional. The next line of Cage's lecture in English is: "Why don't they keep their mouths shut and their ears open?" The translation is: "Warum schließen Sie nicht den Mund und machen auf die Ohren?" This accurately translates the English in every sense except one. "They" is translated into "Sie," the formal German equivalent of a personalized "you." In the typescript, it was originally rendered correctly and then the capital S was typed over the small one. Adding then further insult to the injury, Cage's next line "Are *they* stupid?" becomes "Sind Sie beschränkt?" A direct retranslation back from the German would read "Are *you* stupid?" (literally "narrow minded"). And then continuing to translate the translation, one gets, "And if so, why do you not at least try to hide *your* stupidity." Harsh words, made harsher.

Interestingly enough, this translation was recently published in a Musik-Konzepte Sonderband: *Darmstadt-Dokumente I* in January 1999; and while corrections are made throughout, for example, changing "machen auf die Ohren" to "machen die Ohren auf" (Cage 1958d, p. 168), the mistake addressed above was left uncorrected, without annotation or further comment. Why?

That question is best answered by Hans G. Helms, one of the three translators of the lectures. According to him, turning "they" into "Sie" was "the result of an extended discussion between the translators and John. We suggested to him several possible versions of the sentences in question, explaining to John what each of those versions implied and how the audience might react to each of them. It was John's decision to adopt the most direct and most accusatory version: 'Sie' instead of 'sie' because – as he argued – he wanted to address each individual sitting in front of him. In other words: it was an intentional change in addressing the audience which he preferred."[19] In an undated letter to Stockhausen listing the time as "7:00 AM!" Cage himself describes his satisfaction with the translations: "Please write a note or speak to Steinecke about Metzger, Helms + Rosenberg. We worked 'till 7:00. Let Steinecke know that Metzger has worked beautifully. On the translations about 40 hours extra work by all 3 together have been spent" (Stockhausen 2001, p. 205).

No other event in Darmstadt's history ever generated more controversy than Cage's 1958 lectures. In the Musik-Konzepte issue, Cage's appearance is the only one that merits a separate section on the press reaction entitled "Kritik und Kontroversen zu Cage und Darmstadt 1958." Articles included titles like "Catch as Cage Can" (Metzger 1999, p. 175). The Darmstadt library has a significant number of articles from the press including "Die Neue Musik hat ihren frechen Clown" where the critic writes, "Cage had the soul and visage of a tragic clown, he reminded one compellingly of Buster

Keaton" (*Der Mittag*, Düsseldorf, September 11, 1958). Mauricio Kagel, on the other hand, wrote (in an article that was published in Buenos Aires) that "In the history of modern music, a new era has begun" (Metzger 1999, p. 180). And Nam June Paik, not yet the Fluxus artist but instead a student of Wolfgang Fortner in Freiburg, wrote an even more positive article for a newspaper in his native country, Korea (Metzger 1999, p. 181). His meeting with Cage changed Paik's profession as well as his future, as it did for many who were at the Darmstadt summer courses in 1958.

The reaction to Cage's Darmstadt appearance was so strong that Cage didn't return until 1990, just two years before his death. We know from Cage's own words that he took it personally. Here is what he read when he returned in 1990: "This is an introduction for those who do not know me, who do not know what I do and what I think, that is to say, how I live. I write it because I have not been here for thirty-two years and those of you who are listening may not have read my books" (Cage 1990a, p. 7). When reading the German translation, one cannot help but wonder if the Darmstadt audience also "took it personally." Had those "third-person" criticisms translated intentionally into direct personal attacks somehow contributed to an already tenuous relationship – Cage's participation in the European new music scene – being sent over the edge as a result? One thing is certain: Boulez's criticism of Cage placed an "either/or" around the possibilities of music using or not using serial methods. Cage then did the same thing with indeterminacy. Neither extreme lasted long for either composer. Only the "either/or" stayed in place. Until the very end, Cage and Boulez maintained their distance and ever since, certain followers have "chosen sides."

After the Darmstadt courses, Wolfgang Steinecke asked Cage to write an article for the *Darmstädter Beitrage*. In response, Cage wrote "History of Experimental Music in the United States." It is Cage's "declaration of independence" from European influence, placing himself in a tradition of American experimentalism, which is where he belonged from the very beginning. Cage contrasts his European influences with those experimental influences that were happening at the same time in the 1930s and 1940s. This time, however, he downplays the European side, privileging Varèse and noise over the Schoenberg/Stravinsky questions of dissonance/consonance, and then proclaiming his mentor Henry Cowell as predecessor to both Varèse and noise as well as the "European indeterminacy" of his former colleagues Boulez and Stockhausen (Cage 1959, p. 71).

Although Cage later in this essay writes that the "world is one world now," this idea is grounded in the statement that precedes it: "It will not be easy, however, for Europe to give up being Europe" (Cage 1959, p. 75). Cage's attack on history and tradition was, I believe, a direct result of his negative European experiences in the 1950s. Cage tells the following story: "Once in Amsterdam, a Dutch musician said to me, 'It must be very difficult for you in America to write music, for you are so far away from the centers of tradition.' I had to say, 'It must be very difficult for you in Europe to write music, for you are so close to the centers of tradition'" (Cage 1959, p. 73). When Jackson Pollock watched his painter friends going off to Europe, he is reported to have commented cynically, "I have a feeling they'll be back." For John Cage, although he traveled the world time and time again for the rest of his life, in a sense, after 1958, he *did* come back. In "History of Experimental Music in the United States," he placed himself within the American Experimental Tradition. And he never really left again.

3 Cage and Asia: history and sources

DAVID W. PATTERSON

"What I do, I do not wish blamed on Zen ... "   (Cage 1958–59b, p. 79)

John Cage and Asian music

In determining the legitimate impact of Asian culture on John Cage's development, a clear distinction must be made between those influences that are purely musical and those that are philosophical in nature. As to the former, there is little if anything in Cage's music that suggests any kind of compelling interest in the musics of Asia, and even less that might constitute direct stylistic borrowing. Certainly in his early years, Cage had ample opportunity to be exposed to Asian music, whether in California, in New York while studying with Cowell (1934), or through longstanding friendships with others whose interest in this music was pronounced, such as Lou Harrison or sculptor Richard Lippold. Furthermore, during the 1940s it was popular among critics and sophisticated listeners to equate Cage's percussion ensemble works with the gamelan or interpret the prepared piano's delicate timbres as evidence of musical orientalism. Indeed at one point, Cage himself commented that his square-root method of rhythmic organization was in part "a structural idea not distant in concept from Hindu tala (except that tala has no beginning or ending, and is based on pulsation rather than phraseology) ... " (Cage 1951, p. 63). However, such comparisons, whether drawn by critics or Cage himself, are actually quite superficial, and no significant structural or procedural affinities between Cage's oeuvre and the music of Asia have been demonstrated to date.

The occasional "Asian" element in Cage's compositions was often little more than programmatic, as in the *Seven Haiku* (1951–52) or *Ryoanji* (1983). An earlier and subtler example might be the *Sonatas and Interludes* for prepared piano (1946–48), which, as Cage explained,

> were written when I ... first became seriously aware of Oriental
> philosophy. After reading the work of Ananda K. Coomaraswamy, I
> decided to attempt the expression in music of the "permanent emotions"
> of Indian tradition: the heroic, the erotic, the wondrous, the mirthful,
> sorrow, fear, anger, the odious, and their common tendency toward
> tranquility. These pieces were the first product of that effort ...
> (Cage 1958b, p. 129)

These nine permanent emotions were also the programmatic basis for *Sixteen Dances* (1950–51). In the case of either composition, though, the genuine relation of the *rasas* to the music is a murky issue; it is impossible, for example, to cross-match any one sonata with a discrete emotion (if in fact, Cage's account is meant to be taken that literally at all). And while each of the *Sixteen Dances* identifies explicitly its connection to a single *rasa*, the nature of Cage's chance compositional procedures during this stylistic transition period all but precludes the possibility of extra-musical "depiction"; instead, the *rasas* are concretely manifested only in the programmatic schemata of Cunningham's choreography.

In addition to the "permanent emotions," the notion of the seasons can also be read as an Asian-derived programmatic theme in Cage's works during the 1940s. His first orchestral score, *The Seasons* (1947) (which was also Cunningham's first ballet), was offered to audiences as "an attempt to express the traditional Indian view of the seasons as quiescence (winter), creation (spring), preservation (summer), and destruction (fall)" (Cage 1962, p. 11). Yet like the dubious musical relationship between the *rasas* and *Sixteen Dances*, any genuine affinity between the Indian concept of the seasons and the music that Cage composed for the ballet is stylistically intangible. Shortly after *The Seasons*, Cage related each of the movements of the *String Quartet in Four Parts* (1949–50) to a particular season as well. However, in this case, his explicit program utterly westernizes the concept, summarizing the work's theme as:

> that of the seasons, but the first two movements are also concerned with place. Thus in the first movement the subject is Summer in France while that of the second is Fall in America. The third and fourth are also concerned with musical subjects, Winter being expressed as a canon, Spring as a quodlibet.
>
> (Cage 1962, p. 51)

Ultimately, Cage must be categorized as an emphatically "western" composer, particularly when compared to contemporaries such as Lou Harrison, Colin McPhee, Henry Cowell, or even Harry Partch. He never systematically explored pre-existent, non-western tuning systems, for example, and his overall attempts to integrate authentically "Asian" instruments into his compositions were typically confined to the small handful of instruments specified among the vast battery of devices found in the early percussion works and to a few of the later "number" pieces, such as One^9 (1991), Two^3 (1991), and Two^4 (1991), each of which calls for a *sho*. Even in a work such as *Haikai* (1986), written for gamelan ensemble, Cage deliberately disassociated the work from the musical style and performance practices standard to this ensemble, incorporating classically Cagean passages of silence into the musical texture and calling for the pot gongs to be turned upside down and played from their bottom edges. As he explained, "I wanted to make some use of the gamelan that, as far as I knew, hadn't been made. I think that if I'm good for anything, that's what I'm good for: finding some way of doing things other than the traditional way" (Cage 1988, p. 20).

John Cage and Asian philosophy

While claims of any causal relation between Asian music and Cage's compositions are highly contentious, both his interest in and appropriation of terms and concepts from Asian philosophy and aesthetics, on the other hand, are indisputable, and such borrowings came to constitute a cornerstone of his rhetoric. Yet in appropriating terms and concepts from his sources, his borrowings were not so much faithful transcriptions of ideas as they were carefully constructed intellectual subversions. This is not to lend an insidious tone to Cage's attitude toward his materials but more objectively refers to a particular type of appropriation whereby the basic elements and unifying structure of an idea are maintained, though the intended effect is first undercut and then reversed (i.e., subverted) by a motivation contrary to the idea's original purpose. Of course, the notion of "subversion" could well apply to an even larger portion of Cage's activity during the 1940s, particularly in regard to the prepared piano, whose extraneous objects decisively thwarted the aesthetic function of the premier instrument of the nineteenth century. In fact, one could say that Cage transformed his rhetorical sources much as he did the standard piano through his use of preparations – taking delight in the historical weight these sources derived from their traditions, yet then alienating them utterly from their original contexts, manipulating their internal arguments to sound to his taste and for his purposes.

The specific dating of Cage's earliest exposure to Asian texts is problematic, as is the identification of the texts themselves. Both Cage and Harrison have recalled the instance in the 1930s in which Harrison first showed the *I Ching* to Cage in San Francisco, although developmentally, Cage was hardly at the point where it was of much interest (Cage 1986, p. 177). Cage also made frequent reference to his attendance at a lecture entitled "Zen Buddhism and Dada" given by Nancy Wilson Ross at the Cornish School in Seattle, though this, too, seems an isolated instance of no obvious consequence (Cage 1958–59b, pp. 78–79). Throughout the late 1930s, Cage's own musical rhetoric was consistently western in its expression, and even during the war years, his prose bore little overt sign of Asian influence. In 1944, for example, his mentality reflects that of the still-to-be-converted westerner when he states, "Personality is a flimsy thing on which to build an art. (This does not mean that it should not enter into an art, for, indeed, that is what is meant by the word *style*.)" (Cage 1944, p. 90.)

In August of 1942, Cage met dancer Jean Erdman, who along with Merce Cunningham, co-choreographed and premièred Cage's *Credo in US* (1942) during the Martha Graham Company's summer tenure at the Bennington School of the Dance. Upon relocating permanently to New York City just a few weeks later, Cage and his wife, Xenia, received an offer of lodging from Erdman and her husband, the mythologist Joseph Campbell, and for several months thereafter, Erdman, Campbell, Cage and Xenia fit snugly into a four-room apartment on Greenwich Village's Waverly Place. This environment, and more specifically, the exchanges between Cage and Campbell that occurred therein, provides a point of departure for the study of Cage's encounters with concepts derived from Asian texts. The relationship between the two men was, of course, hardly one of teacher–student. On the other hand, it is difficult to dismiss as mere coincidence the parallels between Campbell's intellectual interests and those topics that would soon come to fascinate Cage. From these sources, as well as from selected texts by medieval Christian mystics, Cage shaped his first genuine "collection" of appropriations. Among his writings from this decade, the influence of these sources on his own rhetoric is especially evident in "The East in the West" (Cage 1946), the "Vassar Lecture," also known as "A Composer's Confessions" (Cage 1948a), "Defense of Satie" (Cage 1948b) and "Forerunners of Modern Music" (Cage 1949).

South Asian sources – Ananda Coomaraswamy

The war years, then, became a seminal period in which Cage first actively enhanced his own knowledge of Asian philosophy and aesthetics, and while seldom articulated in Cage scholarship to date, his initial frame of reference was not East Asian but South Asian. Cage's studies may well have begun with his reading of Ananda Coomaraswamy's 1934 publication entitled *The Transformation of Nature in Art* (Coomaraswamy 1934), a set of essays that derives a general theory of art from the examination of not only Indian and Chinese treatises, but through the writings of the fourteenth-century German mystic, Meister Eckhart, as well. Cage discovered Coomaraswamy directly through Campbell, who had worked with Indologist Heinrich Zimmer at Columbia University and was himself steeped in Indian artistic and aesthetic studies during the early 1940s, overseeing the completion of several of Zimmer's unfinished volumes.

Cage's first extant reference to Coomaraswamy appears in the 1946 article entitled "The East in the West," in which he remarks, "There is, I believe, a similarity also between Western medieval music and Oriental. In other fields than music, Dr. Ananda K. Coomaraswamy has discussed such a relation" (Cage 1946, p. 24). However modest the citation, "The East in the West" signals the new role of Asia in Cage's creative thought and anticipates what would become his extensive use of Asian concepts and terms in his own aesthetic rhetoric. Over the years, his references to Coomaraswamy were both frequent and redundant of one another, citing the importance of *The Transformation of Nature in Art* to his aesthetic development. When asked for additional information on the subject, he typically contributed a reference to a single concept contained within this text: "Art is the imitation of Nature in her manner of operation."[1]

In fact, many of Cage's aesthetic statements from this period could well be derived from or at least heavily influenced by the aesthetic set forth by Coomaraswamy. Yet Cage was seldom direct in acknowledging Coomaraswamy's work, making it difficult at times to distinguish conclusively those coincidental instances of aesthetic parallelism from genuine appropriations. For example, Coomaraswamy invokes the term "impersonality" to refer to the proper manner in which one is to execute tasks artistically. In this context, self-expression, equated with "aesthetic exhibitionism," or "the substitution of the player for the play," is interpreted as an artistic vice, and Coomaraswamy continually warns of its degenerate nature. At the very least, the appearance of the artist's person in any work is intrusive; at worst, it is a glaring indication of defective workmanship. In several instances throughout his writings, Coomaraswamy explains the necessity of artistic impersonality through the example of Indian dramatic art and dance:

> As to the Indian drama, the theme is exhibited by means of gestures, speech, costume, and natural adaptation of the actor for the part; and of these four, the first three are highly conventional in any case, while with regard to the fourth not only is the appearance of the actor formally modified by make-up or even a mask, but Indian treatises constantly emphasize that the actor should not be carried away by the emotions he represents, but should rather be the ever-conscious master of the puppet show performed by his own body on stage. The exhibition of his own emotions would not be art.　　　　　(Coomaraswamy 1934, p. 14)

Cage concurred wholeheartedly with Coomaraswamy on this point, though in his own particular expression of the idea, he framed his position as the antithesis to nineteenth-century European attitudes. In the 1952 "Juilliard Lecture," he compares these two opposing attitudes, reinforcing

his own position with references to the autonomy of sound, a central facet
to his own aesthetic:

> The most that can be accomplished by no matter what musical idea is to
> show how intelligent the composer was who had it ... the most that can be
> accomplished by the musical expression of feeling is to show how
> emotional the composer was who had it. If anyone wants to get a feeling of
> how emotional a composer proved himself to be, he has to confuse himself
> to the same final extent that the composer did and imagine that sounds are
> not sounds at all but are Beethoven and that men are not men but are
> sounds. Any child will tell us: this is simply not the case. To realize this,
> one has to put a stop to studying music. That is to say, one has to stop all
> the thinking that separates music from living.   (Cage 1952a, p. 97)

Likewise, the needless duality between art and life is a prominent theme
in the work of either Coomaraswamy or Cage. To Coomaraswamy, every
action executed is linked inherently to an aesthetic process, whether an
act of religion, philosophy, cooking, planting, teaching, sculpting, etc., and
therefore must be considered "artistic." In Coomaraswamy's view, "the artist
is not a special kind of man, but every man is a special kind of artist,"
and one's particular "art" is simply determined by individual nature, as he
noted:

> Indian literature provides us with numerous lists of the eighteen or more
> professional arts (*silpa*) and the sixty-four avocational arts (*kala*); and
> these embrace every kind of skilled activity, from music, painting, and
> weaving to horsemanship, cookery, and the practice of magic, without
> distinction of rank, all being equally of angelic origin.
>   (Coomaraswamy 1934, p. 9)

Further, he contended, the modern (i.e., post-Renaissance) western definition of art had alienated mankind from the experience of life as art. "All
alike have lost," he lamented, "in that art being now a luxury, no longer
the normal type of activity, all men are compelled to live in squalor and
disorder and have become so inured to this that they are unaware of it"
(Coomaraswamy 1934, p. 65).

Cage's adoption of Coomaraswamy's attitudes toward art as life and of
all persons as "artists" is nothing short of categorical, and the reader already somewhat familiar with Cage can acknowledge readily the status of
these concepts as mainstays in his aesthetic for the rest of his life; "Art's
obscured the difference between art and life. Now let life obscure the difference between life and art" (Cage 1965a, p. 19). In his earliest expres-
sions of this idea, the very language he chooses is clearly derived from
Coomaraswamy; in a 1950 rebuttal of criticisms leveled against Satie, his
rhetorical plagiarism is flagrant:

Art is a way of life. It is for all the world like taking a bus, picking flowers, making love, sweeping the floor, getting bitten by a monkey, reading a book, etc., ad infinitum . . . Art when it is art as Satie lived it and made it is not separate from life (nor is dishwashing when it is done in this spirit).

> (Cage 1950a, p. 93; Cage's italics)

Armed with the essential themes and terms of Coomaraswamy's aesthetic – the challenge to limited western conceptions of "art," the technique of juxtaposing examples of works of "art" with works of life (and the ultimate equation of the two), etc. – Cage often modified these materials to make specific claims for contemporary music as to its function and value not only *in* life but *as* life. His contentions are made clear in the 1958 essay, "Composition as Process," in which he takes aim at the very same western conception of "art" to which Coomaraswamy objects so strenuously:

When we separate music from life what we get is art (a compendium of masterpieces). With contemporary music, when it is actually contemporary, we have no time to make that separation (which protects us from living), and so contemporary music is not so much art as it is life and any one making it no sooner finishes one of it than he begins making another just as people keep on washing dishes, brushing their teeth, getting sleepy, and so on. Very frequently no one knows that contemporary music is or could be art. He simply thinks it is irritating. Irritating one way or another, that is to say keeping us from ossifying. For any one of us contemporary music is or could be a way of living.

> (Cage 1958a, pp. 44–45)

Despite such affinities, however, it is imperative to acknowledge outright that Cage and Coomaraswamy are hardly kindred spirits, aesthetically speaking. In fact, from certain standpoints, it is hard to imagine two philosophic attitudes less sympathetic with one another, yet these divergences illuminate the nature of Cage's appropriative subversions. To Coomaraswamy, for instance, art was an act of communication, and communication mandated a language that all spoke and understood – tradition. "Originality" was a foolish egoism; consequently, he openly loathed modern art, admonishing, "New songs, yes; but never new kinds of music, for these may destroy our whole civilization. It is the irrational impulses that yearn for innovation" (Coomaraswamy 1971, p. 176).

Several of Cage's remarks strongly suggest that he was well aware of the limits of his aesthetic alliance with Coomaraswamy, and though he never named him explicitly as an intellectual detractor, many of his statements from this period seem to respond directly to Coomaraswamy's objections to contemporary art. In contrast to Coomaraswamy's insistence upon adherence to tradition for instance, Cage contended that it was pointless for contemporary artists to hold fast to the western tradition, since the tradition itself was both dysfunctional and in an advanced state of deterioration:

> we are still at the point where most musicians are clinging to the complicated torn-up competitive remnants of tradition, and, furthermore, a tradition that was always a tradition of breaking with tradition, and furthermore, a tradition that in its ideas of counterpoint and harmony was out of step not only with its own but with all other traditions.
>
> (Cage *c.* 1951–52, p. 144)

Ultimately, therefore, the manner in which Cage incorporated Coomaraswamy into his own aesthetic became typical of the way in which he approached later sources as well, appreciating their philosophic or aesthetic tenets on a highly selective basis, then recontextualizing, reconfiguring and in some cases transgressing the intentions and ideals of their original authors.

South Asian sources – *The Gospel of Sri Ramakrishna*

In April 1948, Cage told a Vassar audience of his recent completion of "eighteen months of studying oriental and medieval Christian philosophy and mysticism" (Cage 1948a, p. 41). This study, however, revolved not so much around the work of Coomaraswamy as it did *The Gospel of Sri Ramakrishna* (Gupta 1942), a volume recording the life and lessons of an Indian mystic of the late nineteenth and early twentieth centuries. This text came to Cage in 1946, shortly after the twenty-five-year-old Geeta Sarabhai arrived in New York from India. Sarabhai had just finished eight years of study of Hindustani singing, drumming and music theory. Concerned over the ever-increasing threat that western music posed to the propagation of traditional Indian music, she made the trip intending to study this music in order better to comprehend and confront this creeping cultural invasion. One of the first friendships she established in New York was with the artist Isamu Noguchi, who, upon hearing of her plans, led her to Cage's door:

> John very readily offered to teach me what he had learnt from Schoenberg. When I inquired from him what I would have to pay for the lessons . . . he replied that if I taught him Indian music there would be no question of payment. I was overjoyed. (Sarabhai Mayor, 1993)

Contrary to the original agreement, Sarabhai did not teach Cage as much about Indian music as she did the general philosophy surrounding this art, and for the next five months, the two met three or four times a week, their meetings often followed by dinner and general conversation about Indian and western cultures. Their aesthetic perspectives easily complemented each other. Cage had already repudiated the idea of music as self-expression, just as Sarabhai had learned from her own teacher in India that music was "not the activity of the (conscious) mind but is given to one or comes to one in those spaces in time when one is willing to remain open to receive it" (Sarabhai Mayor, 1993). She and Cage also concurred that the real purpose of music was "to integrate and center one's personality or being, to bring it to a state of repose or tranquillity and that communication, as understood in the west, is not its true and prime function" (Sarabhai Mayor, 1993). Based on his exchanges with Sarabhai, Cage repeatedly quoted "the traditional reason for making a piece of music in India: 'to season and sober the mind thus making it susceptible to divine influences,'"[2] a statement that, in at least one instance, he allied with the concept of art as life:

> We learned from Oriental thought that those divine influences are, in fact,
> the environment in which we are. A sober and quiet mind is one in
> which the ego does not obstruct the fluency of the things that come in
> through the senses and up through our dreams. Our business in living is to
> become fluent with the life we are living, and art can help this.
>
> (Cage 1966a, p. 77)

Before returning to India in the latter part of December, Sarabhai gave Cage a copy of *The Gospel of Sri Ramakrishna*. Cage's study of this text constitutes the second phase of his South Asian studies, and his own recollections of spending the next year reading this material (Cage 1961, p. 127) are verified by the reminiscences of friends and colleagues who recount his voracious consumption, some describing chance meetings with Cage on the street in ensuing months, the book securely tucked under his arm (Harrison 1993, Lippold 1993).

Because of the Indian philosophical origins it shares with *The Transformation of Nature in Art*, *The Gospel of Sri Ramakrishna* includes many conceptual parallels with Coomaraswamy's writings, and therefore could be considered at least an auxiliary source in Cage's aesthetic development. Unlike *The Transformation of Nature in Art*, however, *The Gospel of Sri Ramakrishna* is not a volume on aesthetics; consequently, its relation to Cage's artistic thought is relatively tangential. Still, this publication was essential to him, providing inspiration as well as general relief from the tensions surrounding his more personal transitions of the mid-1940s, including his separation and ultimate divorce from Xenia. Cage's own acknowledgments of the text are not aesthetic but consistently personal in nature, describing it as "a gift from India, which took the place of psychoanalysis."[3] Not surprisingly, then, many of Cage's appropriations from Sri Ramakrishna are more generically spiritual than aesthetic in their thrust, as his references from this source often demonstrate:

Ramakrishna spent an afternoon explaining that everything is God. Afterward, one of his disciples entered the evening traffic in a euphoric state and barely escaped being crushed to death by an elephant. He ran back to his teacher and asked, "Why do you say everything's God when just now I was nearly killed by an elephant?" Ramakrishna said, "Tell me what happened." When the disciple got to the point where he heard the voice of the elephant's driver warning him several times to get out of the way, Ramakrishna interrupted, "That voice was God's voice."

(Cage 1967, p. 111)[4]

East Asian borrowings: sources and issues

Artistically and aesthetically, Cage's most striking transformations occurred in the early 1950s. Compositionally, three works in particular stand as points of arrival. *Music of Changes* (1951), *4'33"* (1952) and the multi-media *Black Mountain Piece* (1952). The explanatory prose that accompanied this new compositional agenda also took an equally noteworthy turn in these years, and although Cage never entirely abandoned his metaphors from South Asia and medieval Europe, they were all but eclipsed in the 1950s by the sudden influx of terms, concepts and metaphors drawn from distinctly East Asian sources, and in particular, from Taoism, Buddhism and, in specific instances, Zen. As the conceptual and philosophic cousins to the thought of Coomaraswamy and Sri Ramakrishna, these traditions supplied Cage with a new terminology that was both sympathetic to his previous South Asian studies and pregnant with the potential to illuminate his new agenda of compositional indeterminacy. His appropriations of terms and concepts from these sources were far more explicit than those from previous sources, and he applied them vigorously to his own aesthetic statements. The "Lecture on Nothing" (Cage *c.* 1949–50), "Lecture on Something" (Cage *c.* 1951–52) and the "Juilliard Lecture" (Cage 1952a) are the earliest products of this new rhetoric. East Asian philosophy continued to play a predominant role in Cage's aesthetic language throughout the 1950s – whether in brief statements such as "Manifesto" (Cage 1952c) or "Robert Rauschenberg" (Cage 1953), larger essays such as "Experimental Music: Doctrine" (Cage 1955) and "Composition as Process" (Cage 1958a), or spoken performance works such as "45' for a Speaker" (Cage 1954) and "Indeterminacy" (Cage 1958–59a).

It is entirely reasonable to assume that Cage's aesthetic appetite for Buddhism and Taoism was at least being whetted during the 1940s concurrently with his readings of Coomaraswamy and Sri Ramakrishna. But if East Asian philosophy was, in fact, seeping into Cage's psyche during the 1940s, his subsequent rhetorical appropriations did not seep into his prose during this same period as much as they simply appeared in 1950, as demonstrated by the rhetorical lurch between "Forerunners of Modern Music" (Cage 1949) and "Lecture on Nothing" (Cage *c.* 1949–50). "Forerunners," for example, is Cage's last essay of the 1940s and still bears the clear imprint of his studies of South Asian philosophy and Christian mysticism. It opens with a description of music as an art involving the reconciliation of dualities, another notion specifically associated with Cage's aesthetic of the 1940s and the philosophies of Coomaraswamy and Sri Ramakrishna: "Music is edifying for from time to time it sets the soul in operation. The soul is the gatherer-together of the disparate elements (Meister Eckhart), and its work fills one with peace and love"[5] (Cage 1949, p. 62).

Written only a few months after "Forerunners," the "Lecture on Nothing" is rooted in a startlingly new and well-developed rhetoric, opening with the seemingly paradoxical remark, "I am here and there is nothing to say." Ultimately, the use of paradox became central to Cage's rhetorical strategy of this period, reappearing, for instance, as the opening gambit in the "Juilliard Lecture":

> In the course of a lecture last winter on Zen Buddhism, Dr. Suzuki said: "Before studying Zen, men are men and mountains are mountains. While studying Zen things become confused: one doesn't know exactly what is what and which is which. After studying Zen, men are men and mountains are mountains." After the lecture the question was asked: "Dr. Suzuki, what is the difference between men are men and mountains are mountains before studying Zen and men are men and mountains are mountains after studying Zen?" Suzuki answered: "Just the same, only somewhat as though you had your feet a little off the ground."[6]   (Cage 1952a, pp. 95–96)

Cage's network of East Asian rhetorical appropriations is elaborate, and the conceptual richness of the traditions from which he borrowed makes these appropriations some of the most provocative to be found in his prose. Their individual instances can be both overt and subtle; the use of the paradox, for instance, is itself indicative of Cage's new mimicry of Buddhistic (and in particular, Zen) methods of instruction. At times, it is necessary to distinguish more specifically those East Asian appropriations that affected Cage's approach to music conceptually (i.e., aesthetically) from those that affected his technical approach to composition; the *I Ching* was the essential primary mechanism by which Cage generated his compositions from 1951 onward, and yet its texts and terms were never a particularly noticeable part of his aesthetic vocabulary. In any event, just as in the case of his appropriations from South Asian aesthetics and philosophy, Cage's rhetorical borrowings from East Asia do not constitute the wholesale adoption of an agenda but are actually quite specific and idiosyncratic, limited to a fairly extensive yet relatively definable set of terms.

With a few exceptions, documentation of Cage's earliest East Asian source readings is elusive, and the most essential source of information – Cage's library itself – was sold off book by book in the economically lean 1950s (Brown 1992). His rhetorical borrowings provide a clue only on occasion, for in many cases, these are so basic as to defy association with any single textual source, as in the case of the reference below, in which Cage melds the biography of the Buddha with his own:[7]

> But no ivory tower exists, for there is no possibility of keeping the Prince forever within the Palace Walls. He will, willy nilly, one day get out and seeing that there are sickness and death (tittering and talking) become the Buddha. Besides at my house, you hear the boat sounds, the traffic sounds, the neighbors quarreling, the children playing and screaming in the hall, and on top of it all the pedals of the piano squeak. There is no getting away from life.   (Cage c. 1951–52, p. 135)

In other instances, however, Cage actually identifies his textual model, explicitly citing works from the respective canons of Buddhism and Taoism (such as Huang Po's *Doctrine of Universal Mind* (Huang Po 1947) and the writings of Kwang-tse in general) as well as contemporary publications by western authors, such as *Haiku* (Blyth 1950–52) and *Zen in English Literature* (Blyth 1942).

The works of Reginald Horace Blyth, for example, are similar to those of Coomaraswamy in their frequent use of diverse cultural cross-references, reinforcing observations on East Asian poetry and philosophy with examples from western literary sources spanning the late Renaissance to the nineteenth-century transcendentalists. Cage's first published acknowledgement of Blyth – or, for that matter, of any of his East Asian source readings – appears in a 1950 apologia of Satie; the parenthetical reference to Beethoven is Cage's own:

> If we glance at R. H. Blyth's book on *Haiku* (the Japanese poetic structure of five, seven, and five syllables), we read (p. 272): "Haiku thus makes the greatest demand upon our internal poverty. Shakespeare (cf. Beethoven) pours out his universal soul, and we are abased before his omniscience and overflowing power. Haiku require of us that our soul should find its own infinity within the limits of some finite thing."   (Cage 1950b, p. 90)

Cage also cited Blyth's *Zen in English Literature and Oriental Classics* on a handful of occasions,[8] and in at least one subtler instance, implied this work through his choice of literary examples:

> No matter how rigorously controlled or conventional the structure, method, and materials of a composition are, that composition will come to life if the form is not controlled but free and original. One may cite as examples the sonnets of Shakespeare and the *haikus* of Basho.
>   (Cage 1958a, p. 35)

1950 marks not only the new East Asian rhetoric of the "Lecture on Nothing" and Cage's first overt citation of Blyth, but also his first extant reference to Daisetz Teitaro Suzuki, a Japanese scholar of East Asian philosophy.[9] In the latter part of this same year, Suzuki himself (by then eighty years old) arrived in New York, and within a few years, reaction to his English publications and public and university lectures transformed Buddhism, and in particular the relatively esoteric school of *Ch'an*, or in Japanese, *Zen*, into a full-blown New York fad. As one observer noted:

> Ultra-modern painting, music, dance, and poetry are acclaimed as expressions of Zen. Zen is invoked to substantiate the validity of the latest theories in psychology, psychotherapy, philosophy, semantics, mysticism, free-thinking, and what-have-you. It is the magic password at smart cocktail parties and bohemian get-togethers alike.[10]

In terms of Cage's development, the figure of Suzuki poses some historical difficulties. In his own recollections of the 1940s, Cage often cited Suzuki's lectures at Columbia University as one of the early catalysts of his East Asian studies. Yet his historical memory was characteristically sketchy; at times he recalled attending Suzuki's lectures for two years (Cage & Anderson 1992, p. 54); at others, he claimed it was three.[11] His dating of these lectures was also variable, ranging from 1945–1947[12] to 1949–51 (Cage & Anderson 1992, p. 53). But even a cursory investigation into Suzuki's lectures proves that these could not possibly have been events that spurred Cage's East Asian studies, since Suzuki did not even arrive in New York until the late summer of 1950; moreover, he only first lectured publicly at Columbia in March 1951 and was not employed by Columbia until spring 1952, when he taught his first course. Although this redating corrects a popular misconception, its also creates an historic vacuum, for unfortunately, this spurious citation to Suzuki's lectures has been the predominant (and often only) historical reference to Cage's early East Asian studies, and no new information on this period has yet surfaced that might fill the void. There are also no extant records at Columbia University that can confirm Cage's actual attendance at Suzuki's lectures, although accounts from fellow auditors verify his presence at least in the spring and fall of 1952.[13] Further, there are very few materials that elaborate on Suzuki's lectures themselves, and oddly, there are almost no official university records that document Suzuki's stay at Columbia. Consequently, there seems to be almost "nothing to say" about these essential events related to Cage's studies of East Asian philosophy. Still, the published reminiscences of former students and colleagues at least provide scattered glimpses into Suzuki's pedagogy, recounting how he emphasized "the fact that Zen thought is, in opposition to the Western rational way of thinking, an irrational, non-rational way of thinking" (Shimomura 1986, p. 66) or "took the Hua-yen or Kegon doctrines of the *Avatamsaka Sutra* as the starting point of his Columbia seminars" (Fields 1992, p. 197).

Even after investigating the chronological details of Suzuki's Columbia lectures, his particular role in Cage's aesthetic development is a frustratingly speculative issue. Surprisingly, Cage did not cite any of Suzuki's English publications in his own prose of the 1950s, leaving a considerable body of literature open for consideration. Moreover, Cage's published remarks on Suzuki are primarily anecdotal, seldom indicating the impact that Suzuki's actual writings or lectures may have had, as illustrated by the related references below:

> There was an international conference of philosophers in Hawaii on the subject of Reality. For three days Daisetz Teitaro Suzuki said nothing. Finally the chairman turned to him and asked, "Dr. Suzuki, would you say this table around which we are sitting is real?" Suzuki raised his head and said Yes. The chairman asked in what sense Suzuki thought the table was real. Suzuki said, "In every sense." (Cage 1967, p. 35)

> In order to fulfill all our commitments, we need more ears and eyes than we had originally. Besides, the old ones are wearing out. In what sense am I losing my ear for music? In every sense. (Cage 1961a, p. 112)[14]

On more than one occasion, Cage himself elevated Suzuki to a position of considerable prominence:

> I think I am actually an elitist. I didn't study music with just anybody; I studied with Schoenberg. I didn't study Zen with just anybody; I studied with Suzuki. I've always gone, insofar as I could, to the president of the company. (Duckworth 1989, p. 27)

Still, the pairing of Suzuki with Schoenberg seems an obvious overstatement, and at times Cage countered his own testimonials with reminiscences of the anonymous, passive – and sometimes, he confessed, napping (Cage 1958–59a, p. 262) – audience of as many as three hundred in attendance at Suzuki's lectures, or ascribed only a symbolic significance to his Columbia studies:

> Suzuki was not very talkative. He would frequently say nothing that you could put your finger on. Now and then he would. When I say now and then I mean one Friday or another, but on any given day, nothing that you could remember would remain. (Cage & Anderson 1992, p. 54)

In the long run, therefore, it is tremendously difficult to gauge the proper weight that Suzuki is to be afforded in Cage's aesthetic development.

Unlike Coomaraswamy or Sri Ramakrishna, who were sources of inspiration peculiar to Cage, Suzuki was a figurehead to a fair number of creative artists of the 1950s. Yet it bears note that Suzuki was not always pleased with the ramifications of his success, and like Coomaraswamy, he could well be classified an unwilling adoptee of the western avant-garde. By the late 1950s, in fact, he deemed it necessary to distance his work publicly from its artistic reverberations in the United States in the brief article, "Zen in the Modern World":

> Zen is at present evoking unexpected echoes in various fields of Western culture: music, painting, literature, semantics, religious philosophy, and psychoanalysis. But as it is in many cases grossly misrepresented or misinterpreted, I undertake here to explain most briefly, as far as language permits, what Zen aims at and what significance it has in the modern world, hoping that Zen will be saved from being too absurdly caricatured.
> (Suzuki 1958, p. 452)

While Suzuki's critique focuses exclusively on the appropriation of Zen by the "Beat" authors, one can nonetheless infer a great deal about his attitude toward Cage's artistic applications of East Asian philosophic concepts as well:

> I can say this about the "Beat Generation": they have probably not yet tapped the headspring of creativity. They are struggling, rather superficially, against "democracy," bourgeois conformity, economic respectability, conventional middle-class consciousness, and other cognate virtues and vices of mediocrity. Because they are still "rootless," as Simone Weil would condemn them, they find themselves floundering in the mud in their own search for "the only way through into truth (which) is by way of one's own annihilation; through dwelling a long time in a state of extreme and total humiliation." They have not yet quite passed through their experiences of humiliation and affliction and, I may add, revelation.[15]
> (Suzuki 1958, p. 453)

Unlike the highly speculative relationship between Cage's aesthetic and Suzuki's work, Cage's borrowings from the slim ninth-century Chinese Zen text, *Doctrine of Universal Mind,* attributed to Huang Po, are far more evident and are occasionally reinforced by historical information, such as accounts of Cage's late-night reading of this text at North Carolina's Black Mountain College in the summer of 1952. Among Cage's writings, the brief "Manifesto" (Cage 1952c) is one of his most obvious adaptations of Huang Po, lifting the rhetorical motif of "accomplishing nothing" directly from this source:

> It is by not allowing wrong thinking to take place that you will realize Bodhi [Truth; Enlightenment]; and, at the moment of realization, you will be but realizing the Buddha who has always existed in your own mind. Kalpas [aeons] of striving will prove to have been so much wasted effort, just as, when the warrior found the pearl, he merely discovered what had been on his forehead all the time, and just as his finding of it was not

dependent on his efforts to find it elsewhere. Therefore the Buddha said: "I obtained nothing from complete, unexcelled Enlightenment."

(Huang Po 1947, p. 25)

Written in response to a request for a manifesto on music, 1952: instantaneous and unpredictable, nothing is accomplished by writing a piece of music, nothing is accomplished by hearing a piece of music, nothing is accomplished by playing a piece of music. Our ears are now in excellent condition. (Cage 1952c, p. xii)[16]

In the essay "Experimental Music: Doctrine" (Cage 1955), Cage not only borrowed individual rhetorical figures from Huang Po but openly copied the text's formal substructures, parodying its master–student question-and-answer (or in Zen terminology, *mondo*) sections. At an even deeper level, other passages from this mock *mondo* include recastings of actual passages from Huang Po's original:

> Question: When I spoke to your Reverence, just now, in what way was I mistaken?
> Answer: You are the one who does not understand what is said to him. What is all this about being mistaken? (Huang Po 1947, p. 41)

> Question: But, seriously, if this is what music is, I could write it as well as you.
> Answer: Have I said anything that would lead you to think I thought you were stupid? (Cage 1955, p. 17)

Less frequently credited than Buddhist sources, the texts of Taoism contributed to Cage's aesthetic vocabulary of the 1950s as well. Cage's borrowings from Kwang-tse, for example, were often quite overt, making direct reference to several parables.[17] One such parable depicts Chaos, a Taoist concept roughly analogous to what Coomaraswamy might call a primordial Ultimate Reality:

> The Four Mists of Chaos, the North, the East, the West, and the South, went to visit Chaos himself. He treated them all very kindly and when they were thinking of leaving, they consulted among themselves how they might repay his hospitality. Since they had noticed that he had no holes in his body, as they each had (eyes, nose, mouth, ears, etc.), they decided each day to provide him with an opening. At the end of seven days, Kwang-tse tells us, Chaos died. (Cage 1965b, p. 137)[18]

Cage referred to this particular story in subsequent essays and lectures in apparent appreciation of both its interpretation of Chaos as a dynamic, natural entity as well as its contention that purposeful (i.e., intentional) action is deleterious to this greater essential state. The story also provided Cage with a motivic reference, as is seen in one of the best-known passages from his writings, where it is combined with the idea of "purposelessness" (itself an appropriation from Huang Po):

> And what is the purpose of writing music? One is, of course, not dealing with purposes but dealing with sounds. Or the answer must take the form of a paradox: a purposeful purposelessness or a purposeless play. This play, however, is an affirmation of life – *not an attempt to bring order out of chaos nor to suggest improvements in creation,* but simply a way of waking up to the very life we're living, which is so excellent once one gets one's mind and one's desires out of its way and lets it act of its own accord.
>
> (Cage 1957, p. 12; italics mine)

In addition to Kwang-tse, Cage was no doubt familiar with the *Tao Te Ching,* although its importance as a distinct source of rhetorical appropriations is relatively peripheral. In explaining the purpose of *Imaginary Landscape No. 4* (1952), for example, Cage states:

> When I wrote the *Imaginary Landscape* for twelve radios, it was not for the purpose of shock or as a joke but rather to increase the unpredictability already inherent in the situation through the tossing of coins. Chance, to be precise, is a leap, provides a leap out of reach of one's own grasp of oneself. Once done, forgotten.   (Cage 1954, pp. 162–163)

Following its more obviously provocative allusions to chance operations and the *I Ching,* the concluding sentence of this passage may be passed over too quickly as a mere cadential figure. However, it may also be considered a motivic reference that draws upon a prominent concept in Taoist literature, as the *Tao Te Ching* explicitly illustrates:

> . . . Therefore the sage goes about doing nothing, teaching no-talking.
> The ten thousand things rise and fall without cease,
> Creating, yet not possessing,
> Working, yet not taking credit.
> *Work is done, then forgotten.*
> Therefore it lasts forever.
>
> (Lao-Tse 1972, second section; italics mine)[19]

Conclusions

In his writings, Cage never abandoned any of his previous sources entirely; instead his pool of sources increased additively, and an undergrowth of the rhetorical borrowings that had been prominent in earlier periods is often detectable beneath the layers of his more recent appropriations. In the 1960s, he propelled many of the notions originally expressed through

South or East Asian terminology through an entirely different set of terms. As usual, his sources were based outside the field of music – and, for that matter, outside of the arts altogether. These post-1960 appropriations also signaled a noteworthy turn in Cage's aesthetic motivations, for while the sources from which he derived his metaphors during the 1940s and 1950s ultimately centered upon "God" (in its most abstract sense) in some aspects, the sources from which he co-opted his metaphors from the 1960s until his death – namely, the social philosophy of Marshall McLuhan, the writings of Henry David Thoreau and anarchist theory in general – are unified in their focus on Man. During the 1960s, for instance, it was not the Buddha's enlightenment that served as a metaphor for musical works deliberately designed without a single, central focus, but the futurist lingo of McLuhan: "Nowadays everything happens at once and our souls are conveniently electronic (omniattentive)" (Cage 1966b, p. 167). Yet while this shift in emphasis marks a fundamental change of attitude, it does not so much disrupt the continuity of his aesthetic thought as much as it simply represents its next stage. Moreover, based upon the ideological affinities that Zen and Taoism share with anarchic political theory, one could comfortably suggest that East Asian philosophy was a logical precursor to Cage's subsequent interest in social theorists.

The depth to which Cage may have ever personally accepted the principles of any Asian philosophic tradition is, for the purposes of this essay, a matter of disinterest. He regularly attended Suzuki's Columbia University lectures in the 1950s; he read a fair amount of South Asian aesthetics and East Asian philosophy. He did not affiliate himself officially with any Buddhist temples or other organizations; nor did he sit *zazen* (the traditional seated form of Zen meditation), contending that just about anything else could serve as a perfectly acceptable substitute: "Distractions? Interruptions? Welcome them. They give you the chance to know whether you're disciplined. That way you needn't bother about sitting cross-legged in the lotus position" (Cage 1965a, p. 11). Similarly, in surveying his use of excerpts from Asian sources during the 1940s and 1950s, it becomes apparent that Cage's aesthetic was never any more consistently Hindu or Taoist than he himself ever was, that his works composed through chance operations are no more authentically "Buddhist" than his percussion works are "Balinese." Indeed, from the 1960s onwards, Cage's personal intersections with Asia and Asian composers were more frequent – he visited Japan on several occasions, meeting with Suzuki in the early 1960s; he was and continues to be venerated in Japanese New Music circles. However, these later biographical details seem more surface than substance. In truth, and as the preceding pages have attempted to document, the most elemental facet of

Cage's contact with Asian culture is the way in which he studied, absorbed, and sifted through a variety of texts during the 1940s and 1950s, extracting with single-minded discrimination only those malleable ideas that could be used metaphorically to illuminate the artistic themes that were always the focus of his writings or reshaped to reinforce the tenets of his own modernist agenda.

PART II

Sounds, words, images

4 Music I: to the late 1940s

DAVID W. BERNSTEIN

John Cage's earliest exposures to music were rather limited, being, for the most part, confined to late nineteenth-century repertoire. Cage began studying the piano at the age of eight, later taking lessons with his Aunt Phoebe James and then with Fannie Charles Dillon, a composer interested in the musical potential of birdsong (Cage 1948a, pp. 27–28). While in Paris in 1930, a concert of works by Stravinsky and Scriabin by pianist John Kirkpatrick inspired Cage's interest in modern music. He enthusiastically explored this new repertoire on the piano and composed several works derived from mathematical calculations, which he later described as having "no sensual appeal and no expressive power" (Cage 1948a, p. 29).

On returning to Los Angeles in the fall of 1931, Cage continued composing, this time through improvisation at the piano. In his Three Songs (1933) with texts by Gertrude Stein, the music closely follows the text. The first song, "Twenty Years After," consists almost entirely of two motives (D–E–G–A–A and G♯–F♯–D♯) repeated with almost the same rhythms in both the piano and the voice part. These repetitions mirror Stein's poetic style; they are, as the composer later explained, "transcriptions from a repetitive language to repetitive music" (Cage 1989, p. 238). They also prefigure Cage's later predilection for repeated pitch/rhythmic motives in both his twelve-tone and his percussion music. Their texture is sparse. For example, the second song, "Is it as it was," contains only the voice melody accompanied by a single line in the piano. Their harmony is a curious combination of triadic figures and dissonant part writing. Cage's Three Songs have a certain charm, but they clearly represent the efforts of a novice composer.

Twelve-tone music

Richard Buhlig, an American pianist known for his performances of Schoenberg's *Drei Klavierstücke*, Op. 11, was Cage's first composition teacher. Cage met Buhlig in 1932 (Hines 1994, p. 91). Buhlig advised him to stop composing through improvisation and Cage began to develop compositional techniques based on Schoenberg's twelve-tone system. The second movement of the Sonata for Clarinet (1933) employs Schoenberg's method in a limited manner.[1] It opens with the row's prime form (mm. 1–5: D♭, D, B,

Example 4.1 John Cage, Sonata for Clarinet (1933), i, measures 1–2, 20–21, 4–5, 23–24

C, Bb, Ab, G, Gb, F, A, E, Eb), the last note of which begins its transposed inversion (mm. 5–9: Eb, D, F, E, Gb, Ab, A, Bb, B, G, [Db], [C])[2] and retrograde
beginning on its second note (mm. 10–12: E, A, F, Gb, G, Ab, Bb, C, B, D, Db).
Fragments of each of the row forms appear in measures 12 through 19. The
movement concludes with the retrograde inversion (mm. 20–24: C, Db, G,
B, Bb, A, Ab, Gb, E, F, D, Eb) and ends on a low E, thus repeating the pitches
from the initial overlap of prime and inversion in measure 5 in reverse order.

Cage noted that the last movement of his Sonata is a retrograde (although
not rhythmically) of the first (Cage 1962, p. 6). Similar palindromic structures also appear on a smaller scale; the outer movements have a quasi-serial
structure based upon retrogrades of melodic and rhythmic segments. For
example, in the first movement, measures 1 and 2 reappear in measures 20
and 21 in retrograde with the same rhythm. Measures 4 and 5 return in 23
and 24; this time the two phrases are retrogrades in both pitch and rhythm.
(See Example 4.1)

In the next group of works – the Sonata for Two Voices (1933), *Solo with
Obbligato Accompaniment for Two Voices in Canon and Six Short Inventions
on the Subject of the Solo* (1934), and *Composition for Three Voices* (1934) –
Cage began to explore his own, more idiosyncratic version of Schoenberg's
twelve-tone system. The underlying principle of this new technique was to
avoid pitch repetitions within a given twenty-five tone (two-octave) range.
Accordingly, in this much freer approach to serial counterpoint, each voice
is obliged to state all of the twenty-five notes before a pitch is repeated. For
example, in the first five measures of the Sonata for Two Voices, the top voice
contains the twenty-five tones of the two-octave span from c^1 to c^3 without
a repeated pitch; the lower voice consists of the twenty-five tones from C to
c^2, again without a repetition.

Cage's Sonata for Two Voices contains the sort of palindromic passages present in his Sonata for Clarinet. In the first movement, measures 1
through 11 in the lower voice reappear in measures 13 through 23 as a pitch
and a rhythmic retrograde in the upper voice (Nicholls 1990, p. 178). A similar relationship occurs between movements: the first five measures of the

top voice in the last movement are a pitch and a rhythmic retrograde of the lower voice of measures 19 to 23 in the first movement. The first and last movements lack the degree of motivic integration present in the Sonata for Clarinet, undoubtedly the result of the composer's self-imposed obligation to use collections of twenty-five tones without repetitions. However, the middle movement, labeled *fugato*, contains passages in imitative counterpoint based on a subject and its rhythmically altered inversion (Nicholls 1990, p. 178).

Henry Cowell had a profound impact upon Cage's early development as a composer. It is through Cowell that Cage most likely encountered "dissonant counterpoint," a technique discussed by Cowell and his teacher Charles Seeger (Cowell 1930, pp. 35–42 and Seeger 1930). In dissonant counterpoint dissonance, rather than consonance, is the norm; consonance is resolved by dissonance. This approach applies also to melody and rhythm. "Dissonant melody" consists of rapidly differentiated rhythmic values and/or meters, with dissonant intervals more common than consonant intervals. Consonances in dissonant melody are most often resolved by dissonant leaps. Rhythmic dissonance exists between the parts through unaligned syncopations and cross-rhythms such as three against two and four against three.

The opening six measures of Cage's *Solo with Obbligato Accompaniment of Two Voices in Canon*, a composition to which Cage later added his *Six Short Inventions on the Subject of the Solo*, provides an excellent example of dissonant counterpoint (see Example 4.2).[3] Melodic consonances rarely appear and are most often followed by dissonant "resolutions"; the

Example 4.2 John Cage, *Solo with Obbligato Accompaniment of Two Voices in Canon* (1934), measures 1–6 counterpoint is also "dissonated." The infrequent occurrences of vertical consonance are, for the most part, properly resolved. For example, the minor sixth (a^1–f^2) between voices two and three in measure 4 is resolved by a tritone (b^1–f^2); the perfect fifth between voices one and three in measure 6 (c^1–g^2) resolves to a minor seventh (b–a^1).

Both Cage's *Solo* and its companion work, the *Six Short Inventions*, also show an increased interest in conventional contrapuntal techniques. The upper two parts in canon at the unison accompany the subject in Cage's *Solo*. In measures 94 through 105 the subject appears in augmentation (although not exact). Several of the inventions contain imitative counterpoint, such as the quasi-fugal sixth invention. But perhaps the most distinguishing feature of this and other works written during this period is their rhythm. Their quickly changing rhythmic patterns and syncopations create a "dissonated" rhythmic style with an abstract, almost mechanical quality similar to that found in works by Cage's ultramodernist colleagues.

Cowell, who was among Schoenberg's most loyal supporters in America, recommended that Cage study composition with the Viennese master, but also suggested that he prepare by taking lessons with Adolph Weiss in New York. Weiss, a former Schoenberg student, was an acknowledged expert on his music and theories. Cage studied with Weiss in 1934 (Hicks 1990, p. 126) and also attended Cowell's classes in contemporary and world music at the New School for Social Research. Cage returned to Los Angeles in December 1934 and began studying with Schoenberg the following month (Hicks 1990, p. 127). He continued to develop his own approach to twelve-tone composition. Unlike Schoenberg, Cage avoided presenting his rows in their entirety, as themes. He constructed motivic segments based upon the row's intervallic structure and formed connections between these motives by referring to the final note of each segment and its position within the row. The row for Cage's Two Pieces for Piano (1935) appears in Example 4.3; Example 4.4 contains several of the motives derived from the row. Motive a consists of interval classes 1 and 5; the same succession occurs between the fifth, fourth, and third notes in the row. Motive b contains interval classes 6 and 1; the same interval classes appear between the row's last, first, and second notes. Motive d follows motive a in measures 2 and 3 in the right hand. The first note of motive d, G♭, follows the last note of motive

Example 4.3 John Cage, Two Pieces for Piano (1935), twelve-tone row

Example 4.4 John Cage, Two Pieces for Piano (1935), pitch/rhythmic motives

a, Ab. Ab and Gb are linear adjacencies in Cage's row. Motive c follows motive d in the same measures in the left hand. They are similarly joined by linear adjacencies from the row – in this instance, Eb and Db. The row is thus the source for the work's motivic materials and the basis for their interconnection.

In Two Pieces for Piano each motive has its own specific rhythm, which remains unchanged. The work's two movements consist of repetitions of the motives at different levels of transposition. For example, in the first movement motive a appears in measures 2 and 24 in the right hand and measures 8, 9, 16, and 34 in the left. Motive b occurs in measures 4, 6, 22, 23, and 26 in the right hand; motive c appears in measure 8 in the right hand, measures 3, 11, 14, and 33 in the left.

The repetitions in Cage's Two Pieces, particularly in the second movement, look forward to *Metamorphosis* (1938), a composition that uses the same twelve-tone method. The first movement of *Metamorphosis* opens with a five-note motive that remains unchanged, except for octave displacements and transpositions, for twenty-five measures. This material is accompanied by repetitions of a three-note motive beginning in measure 17. Much of the work's five movements consists of literal or quasi-literal repetitions such as those at the beginning of the first movement. During his classes with Schoenberg, Cage learned that variation was an important means for creating continuity.[4] But since, according to Schoenberg, repetition and variation are equivalent, Cage did not see a need for variation:

> In all of my pieces coming between 1935 and 1940, I had Schoenberg's
> lessons in mind; since he had taught me that a variation was in fact a
> repetition, I hardly saw the usefulness of variation, and I accumulated
> repetitions. All of my early works for percussion, and also my compositions
> for piano, contain systematically repeated groups of sounds or durations.
>
> (Cage 1981, p. 37)

Later in his career, Cage criticized the incessant repetitions in *Metamorphosis*. But this criticism aside, the accumulation of repetitions allowed

Example 4.5 John Cage, Five Songs for Contralto (1938), i, melodic motives

Cage to compose *Metamorphosis* according to sections of predetermined time lengths, a method which he refined in his later works (Nicholls 1990, pp. 192–217).

Although Cage's Five Songs for Contralto (1938) use the same twelve-tone system as *Metamorphosis*, the two works sound markedly dissimilar. While there are passages in *Metamorphosis* that resemble (albeit superficially) Schoenberg's serial music, the Five Songs look more toward the musical style of Erik Satie or perhaps Virgil Thomson. This is a result of their diatonic and whole-tone motivic materials, repetitions, and occasional tonal references. Their syllabic settings of five poems by e. e. cummings employ a limited repertoire of motives derived from the same twelve-tone row. The first song, "little four paws" contains four motives (see Example 4.5). In the piano introduction motive a is repeated twice in the left hand; motives b and c follow in the right hand. The voice begins with motive d, followed by its transposition and motives b and c. The melodic materials in the song are predominantly stepwise, perhaps mimicking the quiet steps of the poem's feline protagonist. Despite the simplicity of these materials, the song has a rich harmonic palette constructed through motivic superimpositions, such as the stacking of four different transpositions of motive b in the piano at measure 6, followed by five simultaneous forms of motive a.

The second song, "little Christmas tree" is contrapuntally and rhythmically more complex than the first, but it also employs a limited repertoire of motives. The texture of the third song "in Just–" looks back to the first. Its voice part uses only three pitches (the third occurring only at the very end), anticipating a similar austerity in such later vocal works as *The Wonderful Widow of Eighteen Springs* (1942) and *Experiences No. 2* (1948). The diatonic scalar motive in "Hist whist," the fourth song, acerbically accompanied by chromatically related open fifths and other dissonant combinations, and dissonant transpositions of the motive, both simultaneous (m. 9) and in imitation (mm. 12–13), make this work sound very much like Satie. The cycle concludes with "Tumbling hair" a brief, almost aphoristic nine-measure setting, which ends with a sparse duet between the piano and voice emphasizing the chromatic motive from its opening measure.

The form of the first song is carefully laid out into seven sections, each twenty-four eighth notes in length. Cage follows a similar procedure in "in Just–," but here, although the piano and voice each contain the same pattern of five, fourteen, eighteen, and twenty-three eighth notes, the patterns are out of phase. In addition, in a manner recalling the palindromic passages from Cage's earlier works, the second statement of the pattern (mm. 27ff.) in the piano appears in retrograde.

Cage's interest in formal structure built from rhythmic units in *Metamorphosis* and his Five Songs marks an important stage in the development of his compositional style. His *Imaginary Landscape No. 1* (1939) was also composed according to a preconceived phrase structure: four sections each containing three five-measure phrases separated by a refrain which gradually increases in length from one to four measures.

We should note here that several of Cage's contemporaries shared similar concerns. For example, Cowell's String Quartet No. 1 (1916) and *United Quartet* (1936), Crawford's *Diaphonic Suite No. 1* (1931), and Seeger's song *The Letter* (1931) show an interest in musical form based upon repeated units of time. Perhaps the most extended discussion of this approach to form occurs in Seeger's "Tradition and Experiment in (the New) Music," a treatise including investigations into relationships between prose and music. His "verse-form" divides a work into fixed numbers of beats within a phrase, of phrases within sections, and of sections within the complete work. He lists several numerical successions, such as 5–5–5–2–3–2–3–2–3 and 4–3–2–3–2–4, which could determine the lengths of each of these levels (Seeger 1994, p. 196).

Percussion music and the "all-sound music of the future"

By the late 1930s, Cage's attentions had shifted noticeably and were increasingly focused on percussion music and specifically on the musical potential of noise – a preoccupation that would last his entire career. He equated the arbitrary distinction between noise and "musical" sounds in the same light as the historical distinction between consonance and dissonance (Cage c. 1938–40, p. 4). His attraction to what he termed the "all-sound music of the future" was in keeping with musical developments taking place during the 1930s. Edgard Varèse and Amadeo Roldán had written percussion works at the beginning of the decade; there were also contributions to this new genre by Henry Cowell, Johanna Beyer, William Russell, and several others. Another source for Cage's new interest was his interaction with filmmaker Oscar Fischinger, who piqued his curiosity not only in the musical potential of percussion instruments, but also in the virtually unlimited possibilities of found objects.[5]

Cage composed his first percussion works, the Quartet (1935) and the Trio (1936), shortly after meeting Fischinger (Cage 1948a, p. 31). The

Example 4.6 John Cage, Quartet (1935), iii, rhythmic motives

Quartet is scored for unspecified percussion instruments; its four movements utilize a series of rhythmic motives, repeated without variation much in the same manner as in Cage's twelve-tone music. The third movement, subtitled "Axial Asymmetry," uses four motives (see Example 4.6). Cage explained that the motives in his Quartet were deployed in a systematic manner, which he would later use in his *First Construction (in Metal)* (1939): the motives were arranged around a circle from which they were selected by proceeding either backward or forward (Cage 1989, p. 239). The simplicity of the Quartet's motivic materials and the manner of their deployment make the work sound overly mechanistic. It is surely only a tentative step into a new world of percussion music, although an imaginative selection of instrumentation can yield a successful performance. The Trio is perhaps a more sophisticated work; it is rhythmically more complex than the Quartet and also shows the beginnings of Cage's rapidly growing knowledge of percussion instruments. He thought enough of its last movement ("Waltz") to later include it as the third part of *Amores* (1943), a mature work for prepared piano and percussion.

Cage learned from Schoenberg that musical structure results from the division of a work into parts. However, he did not agree that harmony should define the parts of a composition. In a polemical essay denouncing the music of Beethoven, he explained that structure should not depend on tonal or thematic articulation, but on a rhythmic structure consisting of precompositionally determined temporal divisions. He criticized Beethoven for developing formal procedures based upon harmony. For Cage, time is the most fundamental musical category; it exists prior to both pitch and harmony and can contain musical sound as well as noise and silence (Cage 1948b, p. 81).

Cage traced his views concerning rhythmic structure to Satie and Webern. He also recognized that composers in the Middle Ages worked with rhythmic structure and that certain non-western musics had similar attributes. As we have seen, Cage's contemporaries had contributed to the development of rhythmic structure. We should also note that Cage's interest in this area was further influenced by his work with modern dancers, for whom he often composed music for previously completed works whose form was determined by numbers of counts. In a manner strikingly similar to Seeger's "verse form," he devised an approach to rhythmic structure that entailed a close coordination between large- and small-scale structural units: the same proportion determines both the phrase structure of sections (microstructure) and the grouping of these sections into larger units (macrostructure).

The *First Construction (in Metal)* (1939), perhaps the first significant work of Cage's early period, employs this new method using the proportion $4:3:2:3:4$.[6] Accordingly, the microstructure consists of sixteen measures segmented into phrases of four, three, two, three, and four measures in length; the macrostructure consists of sections of four, three, two, three, and four sixteen-measure units. Cage termed this sort of rhythmic structure "square-root form," since the overall plan consists of a given number of measures repeated the same number of times (in this case 16×16).

Cage called the first unit of the macrostructure, four sixteen-measure units (1, 1, 1, 1), an "exposition" and the remaining three, two, three, and four sixteen-measure units a "development." The work concludes with a nine-measure "coda." As in his earlier works, he began with a collection of motives; the *First Construction* uses the sixteen motives given in Example 4.7.[7] Cage employed the same method purportedly used in the Quartet in deploying the motives. As illustrated by Example 4.7, he divided the motives into four groups of four each arranged around a circle. He selected motives by moving forward and backward around a given circle. Repeated motives were allowed, but moves across a circle were not.[8] Table 4.1 shows the results of this system in the exposition. For example, in the last two phrases of the first sixteen-measure section, the sixth percussionist moves around the first circle, playing motives 3, 3, 1, 3, 3, 1, 3, 2, 2, and 4. Precisely adhering to Cage's precompositional rules, there are moves in both directions to contiguous motives along the circle and repeated motives, but no moves across the circle. Similarly, the third percussionist plays motives 4, 1, 4, 2, 3, 3, and 4. This follows Cage's system except for the final motive 4 (marked by an asterisk) preceded by motive 3 from across the first circle. Cage was willing to deviate from his plan for musical reasons. By breaking the rules, the third and sixth percussionists play motive 4 in unison, thus articulating the end of the first sixteen-measure section. Another noteworthy departure from the rules occurs in the first two measures, where the second percussionist plays motives 1, 7, 9, and 5 (see Example 4.8). However, if motive 1 is segmented into groups of four and three eighth notes, the durational values in eighths of these motives are 4, 3, 2, 3, 4 (as indicated by the brackets in Example 4.8). Cage's opening "theme" thus foreshadows the rhythmic proportion governing the entire movement.

Although, for the most part, Cage adheres to his system, there are other instances in the exposition where he breaks the rules; these are also marked by asterisks in Table 4.1. For example, the fourth percussionist plays motives 7 and 8 in the third and fourth phrases of the second section.

Example 4.7 John Cage, *First Construction (in Metal)* (1939), rhythmic motives

Example 4.8 John Cage, *First Construction (in Metal)* (1939), second percussion part, measures 1–2

Table 4.1 John Cage, *First Construction (in Metal)* (1939), disposition of rhythmic motives in the exposition

Section I	4	3	2	3	4	Section II (A)	4	3	2	3	4
Player 1	th. sh.		o. b.		o. b.	Player 1		th. sh.	th. sh.		1, 1, 1, 1, o. b.
Player 2	1, 7, 9, 5, 4, 1	1, 1, 1		1, 7, 9, 5, 4	1, 1, 1, 1,	Player 2		3, 2, 2, 2		3, 3, 5, 5, 5, 5	8bc, 8ca
Player 3		4, 4		4, 1, 4	2, 3, 3, 4*	Player 3		4, 3, 3, 3		5, 5, 3, 3, 5, 7, 7	6, 7, 6, 6, 7, 6, 6, 7, 6, 6, 7, 6
Player 4	th. sh.		b. d.		b. d.	Player 4	5, 7, 5, 7, 5, 7, 5, 7, 5, 7, 7		7, 7, 7, 7, 7, 7, 7, 7,	8acb*	5, 7, 5, 7, 5, 7, 5, 7, 5, 7, 7
Player 5	th. sh.		t. c.		t. c.	Player 5	5, 8a, 6, 7, 6, 8b, 5		8cb	7 (x 12)*	t. c.
Player 6	th. sh.	th. sh.		3, 3, 1, 3, 3, 1	3, 2, 2, 4	Player 6		2, 2, 2, 3		2, 4, 1	3., 3, 5, 5, 5, 7, 7, 7, 7, 7, 7
Section III (B)	4	3	2	3	4	Section IV (C)	4	3	2	3	4
Player 1	o. b.		th. sh.	th. sh.	th. sh.	Player 1	10, 11, 13, 11, 10, 11, 10, 11	13, 13, 13	16a, 16a, 14, 14, 14, 14	16b, 14, 14, 14, 14, 14, 16b, 14
Player 2	5, 5, 3, 2, 4, 1	3, 3, 3, 3, 3	st. p.			Player 2		st. p.	st. p.	st. p.	st. p.
Player 3			6, 7, 6, 6, 7, 6	6, 6, 6, 6, 6, 6, 6, 6		Player 3	13 (x 11)	13 (x 5), 16b	16b, 16b	s. b., th sh s. b.	14 (x16)
Player 4	6, 7, 6, 7, 6, 7, 6, 7, 7, 7, 6, 7, 6	8b, 6, 6, 6, 6		th. sh.	th. sh.	Player 4	th. sh.	th. sh.		10, 10, 10, 10, 9*, 9, 9. 9, t. g.	
Player 5	t. c.	7, 6, 6, 7, 6, 6, 6, 7, 9	12bc		th. sh.	Player 5	th. sh.		c. c.	c. c.	c. c., 14, 14, 14, 14, 16c
Player 6		w. g.	w. g.	w. g.	w. g.	Player 6	w. g.		th. sh.		t. t., g., t. t.

Sustained Sounds
th. sh. = thunder sheet   s. b. = sleigh bells
w. g. = water gong   o. b. = orchestral bells
t. t. = tam tam   b. d. = brake drums
g. = gong   st. p. = string piano
c. c. = Chinese cymbals   t. c. = turkish cymbal

However, one may interpret this "jump" across the second circle as a "voice-exchange" with the fifth percussion part which contains two segments of motive 8 (8cb) followed by twelve iterations of motive 7. The rhythmic motives in the *First Construction* are often accompanied by sustained sounds, such as the thundersheet rumblings in the opening or the brake drum half notes in measures 8 and 9. These accompaniments are included in Table 4.1. Although they do not appear to correspond to the motives in Example 4.7, there are some cases in which their total duration matches that of the motives.

Cage moved through each of his four circles during the four sixteen-measure sections in his exposition. For example, motives from the second circle appear in the second section; motives from the third and fourth circles enter in sections three and four. In the development the motives circulate at a slower rate. Following the remaining units of the macrostructure (3 : 2 : 3 : 4), the next three sixteen-measure units (rehearsal letters D, E, and F) contain motives from the first circle followed by two sixteen-measure units (rehearsal letters G and H) with motives from the second circle, three sixteen-measure units (rehearsal letters I, J, and K) containing motives from the third circle, and four sixteen-measure units (rehearsal letters L, M, N, and O) with motives from the fourth circle. As in the exposition there are some overlaps, and some of the longer motives are segmented. In the nine-measure coda the first percussionist plays motive 16, the last motive from the fourth circle.

Cage abandoned the mechanistic procedures used in the *First Construction* in his *Second Construction* (1940). By this time he had developed considerable skill as both a performer and a composer of percussion music. His ensemble – which included Cage, his wife Xenia, Doris Denison, and Margaret Jansen – had begun to tour the country, performing works by Cage, Russell, Harrison, Cowell, Roldán, and others. The *Second Construction* is much more fluid and unified than the earlier work. Much of its motivic material appears on the score's first page. The rhythmic structure consists of 16×16 measures with a proportion of 4 : 3 : 4 : 5. The macrostructure does not entirely follow this proportion. The microstructure also breaks down after the first sixteen-measure statement of a rhythmic fugue (based on the opening motivic material), which begins at rehearsal number 10. Over the course of the four sixteen-measure units in this section, the initial fugal entrances get closer and closer; separated by four measures in the first unit, three measures in the second, two in the third, and one in the fourth. The microstructure re-emerges in the final two sixteen-measure units.

Apart from the absence of the brake drums in the *Second Construction*, the instrumentation resembles that of the *First Construction*. Both works have a part for string piano, but it is noteworthy that in the *Second Construction* this part calls for a screw and a strip of cardboard inserted between several strings, anticipating the development of Cage's prepared piano techniques (as noted in Nicholls 1990, p. 211). The instrumentation in the *Third Construction* (1941) is more elaborate: there are parts for a variety of percussion instruments (including teponaxtle, claves, lion's roar, cricket callers, and quijadas) and several "found" objects (a conch shell and graduated tin cans). The proportion governing the microstructure is 2 : 8 : 2 : 4 : 5 : 3, but this proportion is cyclically permutated in each of the four parts, a situation which results in a non-alignment of the phrases and a breakdown of the rhythmic structure on this level (Pritchett 1993, pp. 19–20). The macrostructure does not appear to follow the same proportion.

Cage noted his attempt to construct "rhythmic cadences" in the *Third Construction* (Cage 1962, p. 8). This probably refers to techniques developed by Cowell and discussed in his *New Musical Resources* (Cowell 1930, pp. 49–66). Cowell had explored relationships between rhythm, meter, and harmony, and claimed that the same proportions that yield harmonic consonance and dissonance produce rhythmic and metric "consonance" and "dissonance." A major triad, for example, expressed by the proportion 6 : 5 : 4, can translate into a rhythmic "major triad" consisting of a cross-rhythm of 6, against 5, against 4. Cage did not apply this system with the same rigor as had Cowell in, for example, his *Quartet Romantic* (1917). It does appear, however, that he chose to articulate the close of many of the twenty-four-measure units in the *Third Construction* with "consonant" rhythmic relationships, thus creating "rhythmic cadences." For example, the eighth twenty-four-measure unit closes with a rhythmic unison (one measure before rehearsal letter H), and the tenth unit closes with a 3 : 1 relationship (one measure before rehearsal letter J).

Cage saw percussion music as a transition to the "all sound music of the future," predicting that through the use of electronic instruments, composers would have access to entire fields of sound and time (Cage *c.* 1938–40, p. 5). In the early 1940s he sought funding to establish a Center of Experimental Music where composers could collaborate with sound engineers (Cage 1948a, p. 37). Although these efforts were largely unsuccessful, he did have an opportunity to work with the sound-effects apparatus at a Chicago radio station. During this time he composed the *Imaginary Landscapes Nos. 2 and 3. Imaginary Landscape No. 2* (1942) is a percussion quintet scored for a selection of the instruments used in the *Third Construction*. It also has parts for an electronic buzzer and a radio aerial coil connected to a phonograph pick-up amplified through a loudspeaker. The coil, struck by a performer's fingernail and stroked with a handkerchief, produces startling effects. The work's rhythmic structure is 3 : 4 : 2 : 3 : 5. The opening section (three seventeen-measure units) begins with an almost frightening polyrhythmically dense clamor. This is followed by the second section of the macrostructure (four seventeen-measure units: rehearsal letters C through F), consisting of a solo for graduated tin cans. The third section (two seventeen-measure units: rehearsal letters G and H) begins with a motive from the preceding section played in unison. Material from the opening section returns in the fourth section (three seventeen-measure units: rehearsal letters I through K). Cage abandoned the macrostructure in the final section (rehearsal letter L), which is only forty-eight measures long, rather than the expected eighty-five (5×17). Similarly, except for the final seventeen-measure unit, the microstructure does not adhere to the proportion governing the earlier part of the work, although the phrase lengths are two, three, four, and five measures long.

Despite being much more concise than *Imaginary Landscape No. 2*, *Imaginary Landscape No. 3* (1942) has a larger repertoire of electronic sounds. In addition to a buzzer and an amplified radio aerial coil, it has parts for an audio frequency oscillator, variable-speed turntables (such as those used in *Imaginary Landscape No. 1*) which play frequency records and a recording of a generator whine, and an amplified marimbula. The rhythmic structure – 3 : 2 : 4 : 3 – is followed consistently. The use of percussion instruments and electronic resources creates an interesting combination of non-western and "futuristic" sounds.

Credo in Us (1942) also uses electronic sounds in addition to a percussion ensemble. It has parts for electronic buzzer and a radio or phonograph;[9] if the latter is used Cage suggests records of classical music by such composers as Dvořák, Beethoven, Sibelius, or Shostakovich. Cage composed the work to fit the phraseology of a dance choreographed by Merce Cunningham and Jean Erdman. The work, with a title that is a quasi-Joycean play on words, is a satirical depiction of contemporary American mores (Vaughan 1997, p. 27). Its stylistic heterogeneity is striking; *Credo in Us* is an original, almost postmodern mix of sounds from a Cowell string piano (as in the opening), "Stravinskyan" polytonal harmonies (for example, in the section entitled "Second Progression," mm. 57ff.), diatonic folksong-like melody ("First Progression," mm. 143ff.), blues and ragtime ("Third Progression," mm. 1ff.), excerpts from records of classical music, and random fragments from radio broadcasts. (Both the element of chance and the radio anticipate Cage's later works, especially his *Imaginary Landscape No. 4* of 1951.)

Cage's remaining percussion works from this early period include *Living Room Music* (1940), a quartet for unspecified "living room" objects – i.e., "furniture, books, paper, windows, walls, and doors" (Cage 1962, p. 7); *Forever and Sunsmell* (1942) a work for singer and two percussionists written

Example 4.9 John Cage, *She is Asleep* (1943), measures 53–57

for a dance choreographed by Jean Erdman; *Double Music* (1941); and *She Is Asleep* (1943). Cage composed *Double Music* with Lou Harrison (see Chapter 9). In a manner anticipating his later collaborations with Merce Cunningham, each worked independently on two of the work's four percussion parts, deciding in advance only upon the length, tempo, and meter. In *She Is Asleep*, a composition for four tom-toms paired with a duet for voice and prepared piano with the same title, Cage experimented with a new technique which involved controlling the number of attacks within units of the microstructure (Cage 1962, p. 9). The rhythmic structure, 4 : 7 : 2 : 5 : 4 : 7 : 3 : 5, applies only at the micro-level. In some instances, the number of attacks in each part differentiates the phrases. For instance, each part in the five-measure phrase (mm. 53–57) appearing in Example 4.9 contains fifteen attacks (including the grace notes in the third part). Similarly the third percussionist plays twenty notes in a four-measure phrase beginning with measure 40. The second percussionist also plays twenty notes in the four-measure phrase starting at measure 58. It does not seem that Cage used this technique consistently in *She Is Asleep*, though he apparently employed the same method in the second movement of *Amores* (1943), a trio for nine tom-toms and pod rattle (Pritchett 1993, p. 22).

Works for prepared piano – "A feather in the hat of indeterminacy"

During the 1940s, Cage's attentions turned increasingly to composing for prepared piano, most likely due to the logistical difficulties of running his percussion ensemble. Although, as we have seen, the prepared piano made its first appearance in the *Second Construction*, Cage attributed its origins to *Bacchanale* (1940), a work written several months later. As Cage recounted, in 1940, while he was working at the Cornish School, Syvilla Fort asked him to compose music for a new dance work.[10] The Repertory Playhouse, the space in which the performance was to take place, did not have ample room for Cage's percussion ensemble; the wings were too small and there was no pit. So Cage decided to write for the piano and began to consider composing a piece based on an "African" twelve-tone row, since an African accompaniment seemed appropriate for Fort's dance. But he quickly became dissatisfied with the limited range of sounds available on the piano. Cage was familiar with Cowell's "string piano" pieces which employed such techniques as reaching into the piano and plucking the strings and running fingers and fingernails along their length. In *Bacchanale*, he extended this idea by placing a small bolt between the second and third strings for one note, a screw with nuts between the second and third strings and a strip of fibrous weather stripping between the first and second for another, and fibrous weather stripping between the first and second strings for ten other notes. The resultant collection of twelve preparations, which Cage termed a "gamut," made the piano sound as if it were a small percussion ensemble.

Bacchanale drew its musical structure from Fort's dance. Like many of Cage's works for prepared piano from the early 1940s, it contains many repetitions, such as the driving sixteenth-note rhythms in the opening. Its sections and phrases are differentiated by changes in timbre and by moving from one rhythmic pattern to another.[11] Cage's gamut consists predominately of weather stripping; the muted sounds it produces are reminiscent of the muted string-piano sounds used in earlier works such as *Imaginary Landscape No. 1*. Despite its relatively simple gamut, *Bacchanale* is a successful work. Particularly striking is its non-western sound, a result of the preparations and the arrangement and selection of notes from the largely chromatic gamut into patterns resembling non-western scale fragments.

After *Bacchanale*, Cage continued to explore the virtually unlimited possibilities for creating new sounds with the prepared piano. He inserted different sizes and types of screws and bolts as well as other materials such as bamboo, plastic, rubber, cloth, and wood between the strings at specific distances from the damper. He used screws or bolts with washers or nuts to create a rattle, buzz, or jangle. In cases where a given piano hammer hits three strings, he inserted different objects between the first and second and the second and third strings. This method allows for a change from a prepared note to a "normal" note or from one preparation to another by depressing the soft pedal (as in, for example, mm. 74ff. of *Bacchanale*). Cage's piano preparations can produce a change of pitch and timbre for a single note; they might also yield an interval or a larger "aggregate" of altered pitches and timbres.

Many of Cage's works for prepared piano were composed to accompany modern dance (see Chapter 9). *Totem Ancestor* (1942), for example, was written for a solo by Merce Cunningham. Rhythmically less complex than *Bacchanale*, it consists of a series of timbrally differentiated modules ranging from four to fifteen measures in length, each containing a repeated rhythmic pattern. *Totem Ancestor* is among a series of works – *Tossed as it is Untroubled* (1943), *Root of an Unfocus* (1944), *Spontaneous Earth* (1944), and *The Unavailable Memory of* (1944) – also choreographed and performed by Cunningham. *Tossed as it is Untroubled* (another Joycean paraphrase) and *The Unavailable Memory of* are even sparser than *Totem Ancestor*; each is primarily scored as a single melodic line. The gamuts for this group of works are limited. For example, *Root of an Unfocus* – a rhythmically simple minimalistic work – employs an eight-note gamut with screws and bolts. Cunningham's dance was "concerned with fear" (Vaughan 1997, p. 29). The music aptly evokes this mood with its incessant repetitions, particularly with the violent shudders produced by two notes prepared with long bolts touching the sounding board (see, for example, mm. 46ff.).

Cage also composed several large-scale prepared piano works for the dance. *In the Name of the Holocaust* (1942) and *Primitive* (1942) have similar gamuts; they both combine modal passages (centered around D) with chromatic and percussive effects. *In the Name of the Holocaust* utilizes a variety of Cowell's string-piano techniques including plucking muted and open strings and clusters for the flat of the hand and forearm. *Daughters of The Lonesome Isle* (1945) has a thirty-nine-note gamut enhanced by the often simultaneous use of the sustain and soft pedals, while *Mysterious Adventure* (1945) similarly employs a large gamut consisting of twenty-seven notes. Composer Elliott Carter has described its beautiful palette of sounds as "a maze of shivery strange and delicate noises" (Vaughan 1997, p. 36).

Cage also composed concert music for the prepared piano; the pieces in this category are perhaps his most accomplished works from this period. The first and last movements of *Amores* are scored for prepared piano, the earliest pieces for this instrument not written for modern dance. The first movement serves as an introduction. Despite its length of only fourteen measures, it contains a variety of expressive effects produced by ornate rhythmic gestures and an eighteen-note gamut. The last movement is longer and adheres to a rhythmic structure of 3 : 3 : 2 : 2. Although there are repeated phrases and ostinati as in Cage's dance works for prepared piano, these are often shorter and more varied.

In general, Cage's concert works for the prepared piano contain more contrasting materials and a far broader range of expression than his dance works. For example, each of the six movements in *The Perilous Night* creates its own atmosphere and expressive world through timbral contrast, shifts in dynamics, and rhythmic variety. Nine of the ten ten-measure units in the first movement contain an empty seventh measure. During the 1940s silence played an increasingly important role in Cage's music, a tendency that culminated in *4′33″* (1952), Cage's famous "silent" piece. Several of the movements also anticipate other works. The 6 × 6-measure second movement is a miniature perpetuum mobile, much in the same manner as Sonata V from Cage's *Sonatas and Interludes* (1946–48). The fourth movement, 7 × 7 measures long, consists of an eighth-note ostinato in the right hand accompanied by a shifting pattern of long notes in the left hand. Similar to the second movement, it also anticipates the style of the "Gemini" sonatas (nos. XIV and XV, named after a sculpture by Richard Lippold) from the later work. The liquidation of rhythmic activity culminating in the final section of the last movement consists of static repeated long notes, resembling similar passages in *Four Walls* (1944), a work for piano without preparations.

The extroverted virtuosity of two works written for the duo pianists Arthur Gold and Robert Fizdale, *A Book of Music* (1944) and *Three Dances* (1945), contrasts sharply with the intimate mood of *The Perilous Night*. The two pianos combine to form impressive percussive effects. The music often has a machine-like quality (as in the third movement of *Three Dances*) similar to Conlon Nancarrow's works for player piano. In composing *A Book of Music*, Cage recalls that he was influenced by Mozart's predilection for writing scalar passages and arpeggios in his piano works (Cage 1948a, p. 40). This is certainly evident in the score, but only visually. Cage's gamut sounds more like a large orchestra of non-western percussion instruments. In earlier works, Cage did not make adjustments to his rhythmic structures to account for tempo changes. As a result, the actual length of time for two units of the same number of measures might vary. In *A Book of Music* and *Three Dances*, he modified both the number of measures and the rhythmic structure when the tempo changed. For example, in *Three Dances* the first movement is 30 × 30 measures long with a rhythmic structure of 2 : 5 : 2 : 2 : 6 : 2 : 2 : 7 : 2. The tempo is 88 pulses per minute. The tempo increases in the second movement to 114 and Cage adjusts its form to 39 × 39 measures with a rhythmic structure of 3 : 6 : 3 : 3 : 7 : 3 : 3 : 8 : 3.[12]

Most critics agree that *Sonatas and Interludes* (1946–48) is the finest composition of Cage's early period. A large-scale concert work, it consists of four groups of four Sonatas and four Interludes; the first Interlude follows the first group; the second and third Interludes follow the second group; the fourth Interlude follows the third group. Most of the Sonatas are in binary form (aabb) except for Sonatas IX–XI which are in various permutations of ternary form (abbcc, aabbc, and aabcc, respectively). The first two Interludes are through-composed, while the third and fourth Interludes are in four parts (aabbccdd). The gamut includes forty-five preparations. It provides a diverse spectrum of sonic possibilities, the result of eight years of experience composing for prepared piano and more than a decade of explorations for "new sounds."

Sonatas and Interludes incorporates many of the styles developed in Cage's earlier prepared piano music. For example, the motoric rhythm and ostinati of Sonata V recall such works as *Totem Ancestor* and, as noted above, the second movement of *The Perilous Night*. The sparse single-line texture in the first Interlude looks back to *Tossed as it is Untroubled* and *The Unavailable Memory of*, while the "clanging" repetitions in the left hand in the opening of Sonata III resemble similar passages in *Root of an Unfocus*.

The rapid scale patterns and arabesque-like rhythmic gestures in movements such as the second and third Interludes resulted from improvisation at the piano. These, in combination with the repetitive patterns and simpler gestures mentioned above and extensive repertoire of sounds, allowed Cage to create a broad range of expressive effects. We should note, however, that with the *Sonatas and Interludes* Cage's views on self-expression had changed. During the 1940s he had suffered through a period of emotional distress resulting from the end of his marriage, a reorientation of his sexuality, and a realization that he was unable to communicate his emotional experiences through music. He began to question the notion that music is a means by which a composer expresses his or her emotions. Cage's emphasis had begun to shift from the composer to the listener, a change that would later lead him to chance operations and an almost complete withdrawal of self-expression from the creative process.

As discussed in Chapter 3, Cage became increasingly interested in mysticism and Asian philosophy. He learned that music should have a spiritual and ethical effect; its purpose was to "sober the mind, thus rendering it susceptible to divine influence" (Cage 1954, p. 158). In the *Sonatas and Interludes* he sought to depict in music the eight permanent emotions as described in Indian aesthetic theory: the odious, anger, mirth, fear, sorrow, the erotic, the heroic, and wonder. All of these eight emotions have a tendency toward tranquility. As Pritchett observes, it is possible that each movement in the *Sonatas and Interludes* expresses a single emotion, but this ultimately remains a matter of subjective interpretation. It does seem certain, however, that the whole cycle leads to the tranquility of Sonatas XIII–XVI (Pritchett 1993, p. 30).

Interconnections between the movements enhance the cycle's formal unity. For example, the bb^2 (mm. 61–63) and d^3 (mm. 67–70) in Sonata IV subtly foreshadow the prominence of these notes in Sonatas XIV and XV. The repeated g^2-bb^2 in the left hand of measures 7 through 9 of Sonata VII recur in Sonata VIII (the bb^2 returns enharmonically respelled as $a\sharp^2$ in the left hand mm. 2–3 and as bb^2 in m. 4; the g^2 returns in the right hand, mm. 2, 3, 5, 6, 8ff.). The second Interlude concludes with a dramatic ostinato section. The repeated a♭^{2} and g^2 in the right hand anticipates a similar pattern in Sonatas XIV and XV. Ten measures before the end of the second Interlude, the left hand plays g^2, b♭^{2}, and d^3, a succession that both looks back to Sonatas VII and VIII and anticipates the b♭^{2}–d^3 dyad in Sonatas XIV and XV.

Cage used rhythmic structures containing fractions for the first time in *Sonatas and Interludes*. Sonata I, for example, consists of seven seven-measure units, arranged according to the proportion $1^1/_4 : {}^3/_4 : 1^1/_4 : {}^3/_4 : 1^1/_2 : 1^1/_2$. An examination of this movement (see Example 4.10) illustrates the virtuosity with which Cage handled matters of rhythmic detail. The

Example 4.10 John Cage, *Sonatas and Interludes* (1946–48), Sonata I

— = PEDAL

---- = UNA CORDA

microstructure of the first seven-measure unit clearly follows the above proportion. However, the following $^7_4$ and $^6_4$ measures do not parse into units of $1\frac{1}{4}$ and $\frac{3}{4}$ (durations respectively of five and three quarter notes in length). The microstructure begins to re-emerge in the concluding measures of the "a" section (mm. 10–12) and appears unambiguously at the beginning of the "b" section (mm. 25ff.). Cage was quite willing to deviate from his preconceived rhythmic plan, or in his own words "play with and against the clarity of the rhythmic structure" for expressive purposes (Cage 1944, pp. 91–92). In this case, while the microstructure becomes obscured, the macrostructure is clear. Since each seven-measure unit consists of twenty-eight quarter notes, the $^7_4$ measure comprises a quarter of a unit. Thus, the opening eight measures articulate the first $1\frac{1}{4}$ unit of the macrostructure. Similarly, the remaining two $^6_4$ and two $^9_8$ measures in the "a" section are twenty-one quarter notes long and represent the following $\frac{3}{4}$ unit of the macrostructure $(^{21}/_{28} = \frac{3}{4})$. The repetition of the "a" section supplies the third and fourth units of the macrostructure. Cage deftly handled the problem of the two remaining $1\frac{1}{2}$ seven-measure units by ending the "b" section with a complete statement of the rhythmic structure, but in half the time. After a full seven-measure unit (mm. 25–31), the last seven measures follow the proportion, but are only fourteen quarter notes long, comprising a half unit. The "b" section thus contains a $1\frac{1}{2}$ seven-measure unit which, when repeated, finishes the macrostructure. These manipulations allowed Cage to adjust his rhythmic plan to the limitations of binary form. Similar rhythmic manipulations occur elsewhere in the work (see, for example, the closing sections of Sonatas II and III). The *Sonatas and Interludes* are among Cage's most sophisticated applications of his rhythmic techniques.

Cage was fond of telling the following story concerning his studies with Schoenberg:

> After two years it became clear to both of us that I had no feeling for harmony. For Schoenberg harmony was not just coloristic: it was structural. It was the means one used to distinguish one part of a composition from another. Therefore he said I'd never be able to write music. "Why not?" "You'll come to a wall and never be able to get through." "Then I'll spend my life knocking my head against that wall."
>
> (Cage 1989, p. 238)

But there is a subtle interplay between degrees of harmonic tension and relaxation in the *Sonatas and Interludes* which contradicts this assertion. Cage often plays with our sense of tonal "closure."[13] For example, Sonata IV builds a centricity around A. The "a" section emphasizes the pitch b^1, which tentatively resolves on a^1 in measure 21. The "b" section begins with a "tonal" contrast, but the a^1 returns seven measures before the end, followed by the b^1, which hastens the repetition of the "b" section.[14] There exists a centricity around B in Sonata VI, but this "resolves" to e minor at the end of the movement. A centricity around B also occurs in Sonata X, a movement striking for its mixture of "pianistic" and prepared sounds. It concludes (mm. 29–36) with a single melodic line in the right hand which gravitates toward b^2, followed by a b^2–$f\sharp^3$ open fifth in the right hand accompanied by a line in the left hand which includes a descent from d^1 to B. Sonata XII also has a B centricity, but a tendency toward D emerges in the "b" section and the movement concludes with a D major triad. The entire cycle ends with Sonata XVI's understated, yet unambiguous G major.

These "tonal" references stem from a harmonic palette that incorporates both microtonal as well as complex "noise" elements. The result is a harmonic language with unprecedented richness. Many elements of this language remain unfixed. No two pianos are exactly alike and thus the results of the preparations vary from piano to piano. Cage quickly discovered this situation; it troubled him at first, but later he was pleased by this lack of control. He preferred the unique qualities and characteristics of each realization of his scores, rather than the reproduction or what he termed the "possession" of sound (Cage 1973, p. 119). Cage observed that his music for prepared piano and particularly the *Sonatas and Interludes* paved the way for his move toward indeterminacy and chance operations. *Sonatas and Interludes* was not only the culmination of a period within which Cage began to explore the "entire field of sound" (Cage *c.* 1938–40, p. 4): a "feather in the hat of indeterminacy" (Duckworth 1995, p. 12), it also brought to his attention compositional issues which would engage him for the rest of his musical career.

5 Words and writings

DAVID W. PATTERSON

Throughout his career, John Cage was an active author, his first musical essays dating from around 1937, and few American composer-authors can rival him in terms of the sheer quantity of musical prose that he generated (Copland and Sessions come to mind as potential peers). Even fewer equal him in formulating an explicit, thoroughly detailed aesthetic, and those who are content with the simplistic image of Cage as the all-permissive composer who espoused a goal to "let sounds be themselves" need to recall that he ultimately wrote several hundred pages' worth of essays and lectures qualifying exactly what he meant by that statement. His first twenty years' worth of writings became available to the general public only in the early 1960s, concurrent with or even before the publication of most of his compositions. Historically, therefore, these prose works were not read by Cage enthusiasts as tangential afterthoughts but served as the initial springboard by which many were first introduced to the composer, sometimes long before the actual opportunity to hear one of his compositions ever arose. In fact, in the context of Cage's total creative output, these writings are not to be regarded as mere peripheral supplements to his music, art or poetry, but as the central means to the comprehension of such works. It would be impossible to accurately summarize the aesthetic parameters of Cage's writings in the brief space of this chapter. However, and instead, the following essay provides an introduction to the central sources of Cage's texts, groups these texts according to chronology, content and style, and then describes some of the most common means by which Cage manipulated rhetoric culled from a plurality of sources in order to prepare and forearm the serious reader who wishes to explore further Cage's prose, poetry, or less formal statements, such as interviews.

The early texts

The bulk of Cage's prose has been handed down in piecemeal fashion through a series of compilation volumes. The first of these publications, *Silence* (Cage 1961), set the standard for subsequent collections of his writings, consisting of a hodgepodge of aesthetic manifestos (such as "The Future of Music: Credo" [Cage *c.* 1938–40] or "Goal: New Music,

New Dance" [Cage 1939a]), lecture-performances (e.g., "45′ for a Speaker" [Cage 1954] or "Lecture on Nothing" [Cage *c.* 1949–50]), critiques of other composers (e.g., "Edgard Varèse" [Cage 1958f] or "Erik Satie" [Cage 1958e]), autobiographical statements (e.g., "Composition as Process" [Cage 1958a]) and descriptions of recent works (e.g., "To Describe the Process of Composition Used in *Music of Changes* and *Imaginary Landscape No. 4*" [Cage 1952b]). Because these writings span a twenty-year period, they also summarize Cage's approaches to the abstract notions of "Structure" and "Form," elements often delineated through a given text's layout, whether it be the use of square-root form in the lectures of the early 1950s, the fundamental clock-time divisions in "45′ for a Speaker" (Cage 1954) or the more whimsical one-minute rule that applies to the stories of varying lengths found in "Indeterminacy" (Cage 1958–59a). Throughout, the collection is also seasoned with shorter, undated anecdotes and epigrams that often serve as supportive material, reinforcing or elaborating on themes found in the more substantial writings.

While considered a "classic" text in Cage studies, *Silence* also documents the ways in which such collections have skewed conceptions of Cage both biographically and aesthetically. Since the late 1980s, for example, *Silence* and other related collections by Cage have undergone reassessment with a more conscious awareness that they are not so much objective presentations of material to be taken as the Cage "gospel," as it were, as they are the purposeful construction of a persona, and recent scholars have been engaged in making complex distinctions between fact and fiction, romance and reality. More subtly, but of even greater consequence, owing to the deliberately non-chronological ordering of the contents of *Silence* – an ordering that Cage himself determined in this case – the inattentive reader can easily confuse Cage's writings of one period with those of another, a casual intermingling of diverse texts that can lead to mistaking as static an aesthetic that was actually quite dynamic in its historical evolution. In actuality, when taken chronologically, Cage's writings can be grouped into periods based upon their particular philosophic slants that are articulated through discrete collections of appropriated rhetoric from an idiosyncratic variety of sources. David Nicholls, for instance, has already pointed out the ways in which Cage's earliest aesthetic manifesto, "The Future of Music: Credo" draws upon materials from Carlos Chavez's *Toward a New Music* as well as Luigi Russolo's *The Art of Noise*, including its use of particular terms and the mimicry of the latter's typographical layout (Nicholls 1990, pp. 190–191). Moreover, the fact that this text is conjoined with Cage's percussion ensemble compositions connects it even more meaningfully with these same precursors, as well as to the works and thought of Henry Cowell.

The prose of the 1940s and 1950s constitutes a sizable, bipartite period in Cage's writings. On the one hand, this period is unified overall through the obvious and profound influence of Asian thought upon Cage's developing aesthetic (see Chapter 3). More specifically, the writings from the first half of this period, from roughly 1942 to 1949, document how, after moving to New York in the late summer of 1942, Cage's artistic and personal needs led him to the study of Indian aesthetics and philosophy, primarily as expressed through the writings of Ananda Coomaraswamy and the late nineteenth-century text *The Gospel of Sri Ramakrishna* (Gupta, 1942). While earlier essays of that decade demonstrate the general impact of these sources, "Forerunners of Modern Music" (Cage 1949), which appears in *Silence*, is the essay that features these new rhetorical sources most prominently. The texts of this period would be concurrent with the bulk of the prepared piano compositions, as well as the ballet *The Seasons* and the *String Quartet in Four Parts*, the last of these considered one of the "transitional" works just preceding the adoption of chance techniques. In the early 1950s, Cage's sources of rhetoric became East Asian, as he drew from Buddhist, Taoist, and other texts on a highly selective basis. The impact of these new sources explodes onto the page beginning as soon as the "Lecture on Nothing" (Cage *c.* 1949–50), which followed "Forerunners of Modern Music" by a mere matter of months. In their very layouts, the essays of the early 1950s in particular represent a radical stylistic departure from that of earlier writings, a departure that mirrored Cage's simultaneous adoption of chance operations as the basis of his compositional technique, as manifested in works such as *4′33″*, *Music of Changes*, and the "Ten Thousand Things" collection as described by James Pritchett (Pritchett 1993).

In addition to the materials found in *Silence*, researchers have recently contributed to our knowledge of Cage's aesthetic during the crucial turning point in the late 1940s and early 1950s through the publication of *The Boulez-Cage Correspondence* (Nattiez 1993). This collection consists of approximately fifty documents, all but two dating from 1949 to 1954, the period preceding Cage's estrangement from Boulez over the issue of chance operations as a compositional system. At times chatty and at others quite theoretical, these letters offer multi-level insights into the lives and works of both figures. Most immediately, they are valuable for the extensive descriptions of the compositional techniques involved in particular works. Equally valuable, though, are the citations to friends and colleagues, descriptions of performances and critiques of other compositions that one may find scattered throughout these pages. Taken as a whole, these letters form a vibrant though incomplete account of the post-war experimental milieu in both New York and Paris.

The 1960s texts

As discussed in Chapter 3, the 1960s mark the point at which Cage's aesthetic steered away from religious and spiritual metaphors and instead adopted a language that made frequent reference to more humanistic social philosophers, such as Marshall McLuhan and Buckminster Fuller. On several occasions, Cage himself attempted to describe the continuities and divergences between his aesthetic of the 1950s and that of the 1960s:

> I believe, as [McLuhan] says, that we do not live in the day of the invention of the wheel (which extended one's ability to get from one place to another), but we live as the effect of electronic inventions by means of which our central nervous systems have become exteriorized. This means, for me, that where, formerly, by disciplines of yoga, zazen, meditation, the arts, and other fully engaging activities, one could make life durable by changing his mind, now that change of mind is socialized and is taking place inevitably and can be sped up comprehensively by thinking and designing as does Buckminster Fuller. The world we live in is now a global mind. (Cage 1967a, p. 170)

In the Foreword to the succeeding prose compilation, *A Year From Monday* (Cage 1967), Cage also indicates that while his ideas "certainly started in the field of music," he was no longer limited in applying them to that specific art form. This collection, which focuses on writings from roughly 1963 to 1967 (with exceptions such as the 1952 "Juilliard Lecture"), demonstrates the ways in which Cage extended these originally musical concepts during the 1960s into the realm of poetry and creative writing in general. The underpinnings of this volume are the three entries entitled "Diary: How to Improve the World (You Will Only Make Matters Worse)," works that Cage described as "mosaics" that are marked by their construction through chance operations as well as by their experiments with type faces and marginations. Several statements on other composers and artists, such as Charles Ives, Marcel Duchamp, Jasper Johns, Joan Miró, and Nam June Paik, also highlight this collection. In total, the collection covers a plethora of approaches to the issue of text, as traditional, syntactic essays and epigrams are mixed with the non-syntactic or telegraphic (as in certain passages of the "Juilliard Lecture" or the "Diary" series), while the second of the "Two Statements on Ives" (Cage 1964) infuses the text with a unique graphic notation.

The third collection of Cage's writings, entitled simply *M* (Cage 1972), highlights writings from the late 1960s and early 1970s and consists primarily of additional entries to the "Diary" series. This volume also features ample mesostics, which were emerging at the time as Cage's preferred poetic form. With the 1970s, anarchic philosophy and the specific example of Henry David Thoreau also made their way into Cage's aesthetic; the work "Mureau" also appears here, "a mix of letters, syllables, words, phrases and sentences," as Cage describes it, that manipulated various statements by Thoreau through chance operations. The pages of *M* are also dotted with brief exercises in typographical art. But perhaps one of the most illuminating contributions to the collection is the brief Foreword, in which Cage contextualizes his work both in the larger creative milieu of the era (making reference to the work of Norman O. Brown, Jackson MacLow and Clarke Coolidge), and in the span of his own development. It is particularly fascinating to read Cage's efforts toward reconciliation with the decade's ever-growing artistic movement demanding social "relevance," an ideology that would have been espoused by younger composers such as Frederic Rzewski and Christian Wolff. In Cage's case, part of his strategy involved adopting Mao Tse-Tung as a source of inspiration: "Throughout his thinking, I admired Mao's clear-headedness," Cage explained, ultimately reflecting, "What can I as a composer do to bring about the revolution?" (Cage 1972, pp. xii, xv) Fortunately, Mao was one of Cage's shorter-lived fascinations, and as with many other composers of the period, he was quickly discarded as the unpleasant details of the Cultural Revolution were made public.

Other passages in Cage's prose during this period illustrate the ways in which he might elide, modify, or reinterpret elements from his various sources to serve his specific artistic needs. In 1960, for example, eastern allusions to "dementation" and "purposelessness" become reinforcing images for a political, rather than purely philosophical, position:

> The complex of existence exceeds mentation's compass. Emptiness of purpose does not imply contempt for society, rather assumes that each person whether he knows it or not is noble, is able to experience gifts with generosity, that society is best anarchic.   (Cage 1960, p. 135)

The notion of "gifts" such as that seen above is a prime example of the malleable nature of Cage's appropriations. The term appears in several instances in Cage's social rhetoric of the 1960s, but its origin is entirely East Asian, constituting his solitary appropriation from the "Ten Ox-Herding Pictures," a series of ten illustrations that depict the successive stages of Zen enlightenment. As he explained:

> There are two versions of the ox-herding pictures. One concludes with the image of nothingness, the other with the image of a fat man, smiling, returning to the village bearing gifts. Nowadays we have only the second version. They call it neo-Dada.   (Cage *c.* 1962–66, p. 71)

Cage did not begin drawing upon the motif of the "gift bearer" until the 1960s when his interest in social philosophy was well under way, and it is telling that he insisted upon the more pragmatic conclusion to this set of illustrations than that which ends only with a spiritual ecstasy of the Great Void. His aesthetic of the 1950s, ensconced in heady philosophic rhetoric, may well have been perpetuated in principle throughout the rest of his life; however as the 1960s unfolded, his socially conscious rhetoric indicates that he himself was attempting to return to the village bearing gifts, giving a human purpose to his artistic purposelessness. This attitude is clearly reflected in his remarks on the compositions of the period, for the ramifications of his works were now expressly societal. In these later years, Cage no longer stressed music as the means by which "to sober and quiet the mind and thus make it susceptible to divine influences" (Cage 1954, p. 158), but more often advanced his later works as models of non-militaristic, non-hierarchical social structures. Paradoxically, he balked all the while at any suggestion that these works – and his new aesthetic tack – might be interpreted as "political," maintaining that his new social agenda conflicted in no way with the notion of "sounds as sounds themselves."

Cage's new socially motivated aesthetic was also accompanied by the infusion of a new type of appropriation in some of his musical works. Previously, he had used excerpts from pre-existent music in his works only sporadically, as in *Credo in Us* (1942); yet he did not overcome his basic distaste for musical quotation as a compositional device until he was nearly sixty, considering its evocative powers illusory or at least antithetical to his own priorities. "Clearly all the Americana aspects of Ives are in the way of sound coming into its own," he once critiqued, "since sounds by their nature are no more American than they are Egyptian" (Cage 1959, p. 71). The multi-media work *HPSCHD* (1969), however, marks the point at which Cage openly admitted musical quotation to his technical arsenal, and works based upon quotation constitute a noteworthy portion of his output during his last twenty years, culminating in the *Europera* series (1985–92), which is nothing if not a succession of audio-visual pageants based upon musical quotation and other "found" objects.

The late texts, 1970–92

The last two decades of Cage's work with texts both continue ideas established during the 1960s yet extend their utility into other arenas as well. *Empty Words* (Cage 1980), consisting of texts written between 1973 and 1978, is one of Cage's most abstract collections, culminating in the formidable performance work, "Empty Words," which reduces an already abstract source text to single syllables, nonsense words and individual letters. When performed, this text is revealed to be an essentially "musical" work.

Mesostics are also quite prominent, including the "Sixty-One Mesostics Re and Not Re Norman O. Brown" (Cage 1977). In general, the volume reaffirms that in these later years, Cage no longer identified himself simply as a musician or composer, but as a creative artist who might apply a system of construction (chance operations) to any of a variety of fields. "For many years I've noticed that music – as an activity separated from the rest of life – doesn't enter my mind," he explained. "Strictly musical questions are no longer serious questions" (Cage 1974, p. 177). Likewise, as Cage describes in the Foreword to *X* (Cage 1983), the last collection of writings that he supervised, "I have more and more written my texts in the same way I write my music," and the texts included in this volume represent an attempt "to find a way of writing which comes from ideas, is not about them, but which produces them." Consequently, the contents of *X*, comprising material written from 1979 to 1982, are not so much the kinds of direct aesthetic pronouncements found in the earliest collections as they are more abstract artistic works in themselves that operate within that underlying aesthetic. Excepting a sizable "Diary" entry and a few minor works, the bulk of this collection consists of mesostics – on the names "James Joyce," "Erik Satie," "Marcel Duchamp," "Ben Weber" and others; one especially unusual item is the atypically formatted mesostic on "Ezra Pound." The formidable 1981 mesostic-lecture "Composition in Retrospect" is also included in these pages.

The final large publication of Cage's work to be issued in his own lifetime consists of the massive set of mesostics that he delivered in the spring of 1989 as Harvard University's Charles Eliot Norton Lectures series. Dauntingly entitled *MethodStructureIntentionDisciplineNotationIndeterminacyInterpenetrationImitationDevotionCircumstancesVariableStructureNonunderstanding ContingencyInconsistencyPerformance [I–VI]* (Cage 1990), these predominantly non-syntactic epics were created from roughly five hundred passages that were extracted from various newspapers as well as from the writings of Joyce, Thoreau, Wittgenstein, McLuhan, Fuller and others, subsequently fed through chance operations and structured as mesostics based on each of the words in the title. In their cumulative effect, these mesostics are at once representative of some of Cage's last efforts in poetry, music and aesthetic prose, making this collection the "monumental" work of Cage's late years.

Additional anthologies

In addition to those compilation volumes assembled by Cage himself, those coordinated by editor Richard Kostelanetz also comprise a significant portion of Cage's published prose. *John Cage: An Anthology* (Kostelanetz 1991), initially published as (Kostelanetz 1971) and later re-released with additional material, was the first of these, featuring both previously unpublished or reprinted essays and lectures by Cage as well as brief essays and popular reviews about Cage written over the years by Virgil Thomson, Henry Cowell and Kostelanetz himself, among others. The Cage writings included span more than forty years, ranging from his prize-winning high school oration on U.S.–Latin American relations to explanations of the concept of the "musicircus" in the late 1960s. In between, the newspaper reviews that Cage wrote during the 1940s, essays from the 1950s on Satie, Morris Graves and Robert Rauschenberg, and his then most recent writing on topics as diverse as Marshall McLuhan and the New York Mycological Society serve to fill in many of the gaps in Cage's own collections.

John Cage: Writer (Kostelanetz 1993) is a more recent and invaluable collection of primary materials, consisting exclusively of Cage's writings, some previously unpublished. Presumably, it will also be the last large collection of Cage's prose. The first hundred pages of this volume fill in the gaps left by its predecessors, featuring isolated works scattered anywhere between the late 1930s through the 1960s. The remainder of the book, however, is unique as an assemblage of Cage's writings from the last twenty years of his life and includes not only essays, articles and lectures from this period, but also various examples of the mesostic. Cage's typically paragraph-length descriptions of his compositions since 1933 also appear in this volume, while the 1989 essay, "An Autobiographical Statement," constitutes the skeletal framework for what is now regarded as "Cagelore." Of course, while the documents in *John Cage: An Anthology* and *John Cage: Writer* are chronologically arranged, in both instances, each individual document is set in isolation from the others, and their mere chronology does not produce a continuous narrative of Cage's life (and surely this was not intended in the first place). In the long run, then, the most accurate sense of Cage's development is best achieved through the arduous though rewarding exercise of leap-frogging from one compilation to the other, studying the essays in the sequence in which they were originally written.

Interview collections

Beyond the compilations of Cage's "official" prose output, other sources record his more informal statements. Many published pages on Cage take the form of smaller interview transcriptions found in all manner of journals and magazines, and a few large-scale publications on Cage are based exclusively on such transcriptions. In the mid-1980s, Kostelanetz assembled and edited what was to be a Cage interview-history; the result, *Conversing with Cage* (Kostelanetz 1988), is not a single independent interview it-self, but rather a melange of extracts from various interviews conducted by Kostelanetz and others over a number of years. Prior to its release, Kostelanetz published an excerpt from this work, referring to it – somewhat problematically – as an "Ur-Conversation" (Cage & Kostelanetz 1987). As the individual questions are essentially stripped of their context and the result is a synthetic cut-and-paste assemblage, *Conversing with Cage* is an entertaining book that unfortunately cannot be used for more serious re-search purposes. In contrast, the interviews with Daniel Charles, entitled *For the Birds* (Cage 1981), are more legitimate as a unified "interview," having been conducted, transcribed and compiled by a single researcher.

Like the compilations of Cage's prose, these interviews pose their own set of difficulties. Cage's willingness to be interviewed was well known, and in-deed, this generosity was an invaluable kindness in many ways. At the same time, the limitations of these interviews are readily apparent. Typically, they lack any explicit critical commentary or independent factual verification whatsoever; Cage offers his recollections to the interviewer, who then sim-ply and dutifully transmits these remarks to the reader. Further, in studying these interviews, one often comes across the same answers to questions repeated time and again; near-verbatim rehashings are not uncommon. The lines between these interviews and Cage's own published prose may also overlap; it is often a relatively simple task to cross-reference interview excerpts with passages from *Silence* or *A Year From Monday*, for example. On the surface, this redundancy can be dulling at times; it can also be discon-certing, however, as in those instances in which the composer offers nearly identical answers to noticeably different questions. (These instances should not be confused with those pedagogical "question-and-answer" sessions in which Cage demonstrated his aleatoric techniques by preparing a series of answers – usually through chance operations – that he used as responses to given questions, regardless of the context of the questions themselves.)

The chronological proximity of the majority of Cage's extant interviews also creates historical difficulties, especially complicating accurate percep-tions of his earlier years. While he spoke about all periods of his life in his interviews, one must remember when reading these documents that the interviewee was most often the sixty-, seventy- or nearly eighty-year-old composer whose reminiscences in some cases had decades to mellow or be recast more directly. One especially clear example of this kind of anecdotal overhauling involves one of Cage's best-known autobiographical vignettes, describing a conversation with Schoenberg during the 1930s:

> when Schoenberg asked me whether I would devote my life to music,
> I said, "Of course." After I had been studying with him for two years,
> Schoenberg said, "In order to write music, you must have a feeling for

harmony." I explained to him that I had no feeling for harmony. He then said that I would always encounter an obstacle, that it would be as though I came to a wall through which I could not pass. I said, "In that case I will devote my life to beating my head against that wall."

(Cage 1958–59a, p. 261)

While Cage's Sisyphian self-depiction is widely accepted, few are aware that this is also a later manifestation of the story, considerably changed from previous versions. The same event, as recounted twelve years earlier by a Cage then only thirty-three, is by no means a fable on the cosmic merit of resignation to a hopeless and lifelong task, but instead is almost Boulezian in its aggressive dismissal of Schoenberg. As one New York newspaper reported:

> For two years, Cage told us, he had studied composition with Arnold Schoenberg, the German composer who writes atonal music for a 12-tone scale, and who is generally regarded in musical circles as a pretty radical fellow. Schoenberg wasn't radical enough for Cage, though. Cage finally quit because his instructor insisted he must have a sense of harmony to be a composer. "To me," Cage says indignantly, "that was like my grandmother saying I should be born again. It may have been true and it may not have been, but it didn't have anything to do with what I was doing."

(Anon. 1946)

The Cage of this latter quotation is a Cage few know today, a younger, brassier Cage now buried under the gentility of older age that typifies the interviews of his later years. This is not meant to suggest that he actively and intentionally construed his own history to his own specifications and for his own purposes at the expense of truth. One gets the strong impression, though, that over the years Cage may have settled into a basic "routine," i.e., a series of stories, responses and "facts," which became a stock part of any standard question-and-answer session or biographical sketch.

A recent addition to the Cage interview collection genre is Joan Retallack's *Musicage: Cage Muses on Words Art Music* (Retallack 1996), which is a refreshing departure from the standard Cage interview. As a researcher, Retallack proved to be especially skilled at pressing a point, often goading Cage beyond superficialities into an atypical specificity and depth in his comments, and as the title suggests, she intelligently approaches Cage in the broader context of his accomplishments in various arts, rather than delimiting him to the field of music. A sample mesostic, over a dozen black-and-white illustrations of Cage's artworks, and pages from selected manuscripts or worksheets for musical compositions, reinforce the documentation provided by Cage's comments. Accompanied by Retallack's own lengthy opening essay and a thorough index, this three-part interview was conducted during the last two years of Cage's life, making it an invaluable "final" statement, complementing the essay material of *John Cage: Writer* and the mesostic poetry of the 1989 Norton Lectures.

Confronting Cage's words

As is true of his compositions, the comprehension of Cage's words, whether in prose, poem, or interview, is an "insider's art," and the greatest challenge to this comprehension resides in translating or decoding the plethora of rhetorical borrowings that appear therein. In essence, these borrowings comprise the "found objects" in Cage's prose, and they are aesthetically provocative in their ability to trigger an abundance of conceptual associations. Because of the intentional lingering connections that these rhetorical borrowings maintain with their textual sources, they have reasonably invited comparisons against their original functions and/or contexts. Ultimately, Cage's idiosyncratic perspectives, and the ways in which his use of these borrowings diverges from their original context, are far more interesting and informative than is his adherence to the original spirit or meaning of these appropriations.

In later years, Cage's rhetorical techniques assumed their most complicated forms, clustering appropriations from divergent sources, as seen in the collage-like "Diary" series. Other essays from the period illustrate just as clearly the overwhelming effect that this technique could achieve, melding quotation from one source with specialized terminology from another or bracketing allusion within allusion, the result all but leaving reader comprehension in its wake:

> Self-discipline. That is to say: self-alteration, particularly with regard to ego likes and dislikes, ego memory and resultant fixed habit ("Leave thy father and mother and follow Me." Disciple. Yoga: yoking, or, rather, making nonexistent the ego. Cf. the ten ox-herding pictures of Zen Buddhism. Once caught, the ox [the ego] is no longer visible. What happens? The ox-herder, fat, smiling [Cf. Konrad Lorenz, conclusion of *On Aggression, re* laughter, humor], returns to the village bearing gifts). The ego can act as a barrier to daily experience (the senses) by cultivating its judgment-making faculty and as a barrier to nocturnal experience by paying no attention to the poetic warnings given by dreams. Disciplined (by means, traditionally, of myth, religion – e.g., meditation, sitting crosslegged, philosophical exercises – e.g., koan, Wittgenstein, arts, crafts – when these are not self-expressive, ego-flattering activities, the sciences – e.g., Thoreau: "I am sorrel; I am ice" whatever to which one gives oneself away), the ego is no longer a barrier. (Cage 1968, p. 178)

Fortunately, Cage's borrowings were not always so densely compressed, and through a survey of the many far simpler instances of rhetorical appropriation in his earlier texts, different modes of assimilation begin to emerge that aid the reader in understanding Cage's method. The *direct reference*, for example, is the most obvious of Cage's borrowings. Usually assuming the form of an unaltered textual excerpt or anecdote, the direct reference, for all intents and purposes, is the simple lifting of a "primary" source:

> Some centuries later in a Japanese monastery, there was a monk who was always taking baths. A younger monk came up to him and said, "Why, if there is no dust, are you always taking baths?" The older monk replied, "Just a dip. No why." (Cage 1958–59a, p. 273)

> Xenia told me once that when she was a child in Alaska, she and her friends had a club and there was only one rule: no silliness. (Cage 1958–59a, p. 271)

The *reinterpretive reference* is an epigrammatic parody of a direct reference or other primary source, maintaining its narrative integrity yet redirecting its purpose through new imagery. In some cases, corresponding *direct* and *reinterpretive* references appear within the pages of the same book. The reply of the bathing monk above, for example, which appears at the very end of *Silence*, is counterbalanced by its *reinterpretive reference* that appears toward the book's first few pages:

> Question: Then what is the purpose of this "experimental" music?
> Answer: No purposes. Sounds. (Cage 1955, p. 17)

In the *fused reference*, materials from two or more unrelated sources are dovetailed into one another, often within the span of a single sentence. In an atypical example, Cage identifies his sources explicitly:

> When life is lived, there is nothing in it but the present, the "now-moment" (I quote Meister Eckhart); it is thus impossible to speak of being ahead of one's time or of historical development. When life is lived, each one is "the most honored of all creatures" (I quote the Buddha), living in "the best of all possible worlds" (I quote Voltaire), and when this is done there is "no silliness" (I quote my former wife, Xenia Cage). (Cage 1950a, p. 93)

While the above is used to comic effect, Cage's fused references most often unite aesthetic themes or images from divergent fields. Again, the pages of *Silence* conveniently supply examples of both a *direct reference* – in this case, the story of Hui-neng, the Sixth Patriarch of Zen – and its transformation as part of a *fused reference* that, in this case, serves to reinforce Cage's own aesthetic principles:

> In the poetry contest in China by which the Sixth Patriarch of Zen Buddhism was chosen, there were two poems. One said: "The mind is like a mirror. It collects dust. The problem is to remove the dust." The other and winning poem was actually a reply to the first. It said, "Where is the mirror and where is the dust?" (Cage 1958–59a, p. 272)

> Only one monk in the monastery the oldest one wrote a poem but he stayed up all night and day deliberating on it. The other monks didn't try because they were certain the oldest one would win. When his poem finally came out, it said: Continuity takes place of its own accord and things do go on at the same time. All of this is correct and true: there is no concern necessary for, say, intonation, counterpoint, scales, going to and coming from; and, then, when? (Cage 1954, p. 176)

While far simpler in structure than the fused reference above, the *motivic reference* can be the most difficult of Cage's rhetorical devices to identify. At best, it may be signified by a catchphrase, but it may also consist of two or three words bearing no obvious jargon that might indicate it as derivative. The original source of the terminological reference within Cage's 1965 remarks on Wolff's *Duo II for Pianists*, for example, is revealed in one of his writings from the succeeding year:

> Have you ever noticed how you read a newspaper? Jumping around, leaving articles unread, or only partially read, turning here and there. Not at all the way one reads Bach in public, but precisely the way one reads in public *Duo II for Pianists* by Christian Wolff. (Cage 1965b, pp. 136–137)

> McLuhan insists on the newspaper front-page as the present existence type. Reading, we no longer read systematically (concluding each column, or even turning the page to conclude an article): we jump.
> (Cage 1967, p. 26)

The *generic reference* differs from all previously outlined types in its lack of an identifiable authorial origin; dubbing a reference *generic* often acknowledges little more than a conceptual "flavoring," an elusive quality which, nonetheless, should not be overlooked. Such references are characteristic of many of the Buddhistic passages in Cage's prose. The terminology of his 1953 statement on Robert Rauschenberg's "white" paintings, for instance, may seem commonplace at first, yet its similarities to passages found in some of the most commonly read Buddhist literature – while falling short of providing a verifiable textual connection – are rich with innuendo:

To whom
   No subject
   No image
   No taste
   No object
   No beauty
   No message
   No talent
   No technique (no why)
   No idea
   No intention
   No art
   No feeling
   No black
   No white (no *and*)
     (Cage 1953, p. 111)

Avalokita, The Holy Lord and Bodhisattva, was moving in the deep course of the Wisdom which has gone beyond. He looked down from on high, He beheld but five heaps, and he saw that in their own-being they were empty. "Here, O Sariputra, form is emptiness and the very emptiness is form; emptiness does not differ from form, form does not differ from emptiness; whatever is form, that is emptiness, whatever is emptiness, that is form, the same is true of feelings, perceptions, impulses and consciousness . . . in emptiness there is no form, nor feeling, nor perception, nor impulse, nor consciousness; No eye, ear, nose, tongue, body, mind; No forms, sounds, smells, tastes, touchables or objects of mind; No sight-organ element, and so forth, until we come to: No mind-consciousness element; There is no ignorance, no extinction of ignorance, and so forth, until we come to: There is no decay and death, no extinction of decay and death. There is no suffering, no origination, no stopping, no path. There is no cognition, no attainment and no non-attainment."   (Conze 1958)

Conclusion

Cage scholarship, still itself quite new, has only begun to address its subject on biographical, analytic and aesthetic grounds, and even the best work at present still constitutes a preliminary foray into extremely elaborate subject matter. To date, of the various facets of his work, Cage's contributions to both the visual arts and prose/poetry have been studied less than his music, although some excellent efforts have begun to emerge. The categories of appropriative techniques described above are only some of the most common means by which Cage's prose might be constructed on the local level. Larger issues, such as the specific content or interpretations of the extended essays, the historic context in which Cage wrote, and the critical assessment of his later works as "poetry" are only a few of the broader concerns regarding this output that in themselves would take hundreds of pages to assess. Indeed, the study of Cage's writings is particularly intimidating, for in sum, these documents trace a profound and almost restless aesthetic course over more than half a century, during which the author combed myriad source materials for supportive documentation, cross-bred the techniques employed in his musical works with the agenda of his prose, experimented with style and structure and advanced new genres. It is easier, perhaps – and certainly more common – to enjoy these writings solely for their many moments of wit. But this naïve attitude proves to be a disservice to author and reader alike, for Cage's texts – essays, epigrams, mesostics, stories, lectures, and interviews – are nothing less than the keys into his world. Further, it is an historical fact that through his words Cage became a focal point for the creative arts in general, beginning with his ascent to avant-garde guru-hood in the early 1960s, due in large part to the publication of *Silence* and *A Year From Monday*. The longevity of these words is also testament to their artistic poignancy; when read today, Cage's essays and manifestos carry a pepper no less potent than they did decades ago, and they continue to influence countless others in the arts, regardless of their specific status (or non-status) as "musicians." Ultimately, then, as in the case of his musical works, Cage's prose and poetic writings deserve and should command our most ardent scholarly and artistic attention.

6 Towards infinity: Cage in the 1950s and 1960s

DAVID NICHOLLS

The 1950s and 1960s were, arguably, the most important decades of Cage's creative life. During that period, he moved in his work from determinacy to indeterminacy, from conventional notation to graphic and texted notation, from standard instrumental resources to technology and "the entire field of sound" (Cage *c.* 1938–40, p. 4), from music to theatre, and – in terms of performance space – from the concert hall to the world at large. He also started to engage in a serious way with words and images, and – domestically – moved from the noise and bustle of New York City to the peace and tranquility of Stony Point, in New York State. Finally, willingly or otherwise, he exchanged relative anonymity for relative notoriety, and – for the first time in his artistic life – found himself having to respond to commissions. As he put it in 1971, "Roughly I would say 1952, or perhaps 1954, [was] the turning point. Before that time, I had to make the effort to get [my work] performed. Now other people make the effort and I have to respond by travelling" (Kostelanetz 1988, p. 101). Unsurprisingly therefore, given the importance of this period, many of Cage's multifarious activities of the 1950s and 1960s are subjected to detailed analysis elsewhere in this volume; consequently, the present chapter attempts not to provide a closely argued critique of particular innovations or developments, but rather to create a contextual overview within which can be placed the various facets of Cage's work discussed elsewhere.[1]

The multi-faceted broadening of Cage's artistic vision during these two decades may well have been due in part to a contemporaneous widening of his artistic contacts. Until the late 1940s he had been associated with a close-knit but relatively small group of friends and acquaintances, among the most consistent of whom were Lou Harrison, Xenia Cage, Merce Cunningham, and – to a lesser extent – Henry Cowell and Virgil Thomson. Although all were very supportive, none except Harrison and especially Cunningham provided him with sufficient intellectual stimulation to push his work forward with the same vigor that had been evident in the 1930s. Indeed, one might argue that for much of the 1940s Cage appeared contented with the pleasures of the prepared piano and/or scores for dance accompaniment. True, much of this rather focused activity arose from financial necessity (as was noted in Chapter 1) with Cage writing dance scores "at the rate of five dollars per minute of music" (Revill 1992, p. 81) in order to make

[100]

ends meet. But there is also a sense of him needing time to refine his musical language (with its structural basis in square-root form, its timbral universe defined principally by the prepared piano, and its aesthetic horizons slowly expanding to include the results of his introduction to Asian philosophy), before he was ready to take the next great leap forward in his artistic development.

In the late 1940s and early 1950s, however, a serendipitous synchronicity of circumstances provided the necessary springboard for such an advance. First, the receipt of grants from the National Institute of Arts and Letters and the Guggenheim Foundation (both awarded in recognition of his work with, and for, the prepared piano) allowed Cage to spend a prolonged period in Paris. Second, while in Paris Cage became intimately acquainted with the music of two quintessentially different French composers, Erik Satie and (via an introduction from Virgil Thomson) Pierre Boulez. Both influenced his development considerably, the former musically and aesthetically, the latter arguably more concretely by providing an entrée to the emerging European avant-garde scene. Third, as a result of their work together in Paris, Cage and Cunningham decided that the latter should form his own dance company, for which Cage became musical director. And fourth, shortly after returning to New York, Cage met Morton Feldman.

The New York School(s)

On January 17, 1950, only days before meeting Feldman, Cage had conveyed to Boulez some sense of his frustration at the artistic vacuum in which he was trapped: "The great trouble with our life here is the absence of an intellectual life. No one has an idea. And should one by accident get one, no one would have time to consider it" (Nattiez 1993, p. 50). Yet, only a few months afterwards, Cage had through Feldman become reacquainted with David Tudor, and had coincidentally met Christian Wolff. The earlier artistic vacuum was replaced by an invigorating new atmosphere, in which "Things were really popping all the time. Ideas just flew back and forth between us, and in a sense we gave each other permission for the new music we were discovering" (Tomkins 1976, p. 108).

Although the end results of these new contacts were primarily musical, much of the stimulus towards them actually came from the visual arts, most notably the work of the "New York School" of painters. Cage had already since the late 1940s been a member of the Artists Club, "the primary arbiter of what would be called abstract expressionism" (Jones 1993, p. 638) and spoke to the club on three occasions: two of the resulting talks were the "Lecture on Nothing" (Cage *c.* 1949–50) and the "Lecture on Something"

(Cage *c.* 1951–52). Another (similarly disaffected) member of the club was Robert Rauschenberg, whose all-white and all-black canvasses prompted Cage in 1952 to bring to fruition, as *4'33"*, the "Silent Prayer" he had first envisioned in 1948.[2] Cage and Feldman, meanwhile, found a common interest in visual art: "there was an incredible amount of talk about painting. John and I would drop in at the Cedar Bar at six in the afternoon and talk until it closed" (Zimmermann 1985, p. 37).

As detailed primarily in Chapter 11, by the time of his meeting Feldman, Cage – in works such as the *String Quartet in Four Parts* (1949–50), *Sixteen Dances* (1950–51), and Concerto for Prepared Piano and Orchestra (1950–51) – had already moved a considerable way towards "getting rid of [the] glue . . . so that [the] sounds would be themselves" (Cage 1959, p. 71), by freeing his music from the imposition of personal taste. The gift, from Christian Wolff, of a copy of the *I Ching* – recently published in English translation by Wolff's father – propelled Cage further along that route: "I saw immediately that the [*I Ching*'s sixty-four-hexagram] chart was better than the Magic Square [used previously]" (Kostelanetz 1988, p. 64); "right then and there I sketched out the whole procedure for my *Music of Changes* . . . I ran over to show the plan to Morty Feldman, who had taken a studio in the same building, and I can still remember him saying, 'You've hit it!'" (Tomkins 1976, p. 109).

Yet it was actually Feldman, rather than Cage, who took the most dramatic and decisive step away from what he considered to be the "photographically still" music and notation of the past (see Zimmermann 1985, p. 38). Some time in late December 1950 – before Cage had even started work on the *Music of Changes* – "Feldman left the room one evening, in the midst of a long conversation, and returned later with a composition on graph paper" (Tomkins 1976, p. 108). The work in question was *Projection 1* for solo cello, in which duration and timbre are specified, but precise pitch is not. Rather, relative pitch (high, medium, and low) is indicated by vertically aligned "fields." Similar graphs – including those for chamber music combinations such as the flute, trumpet, violin, cello, and piano of *Projection 2* (January 5, 1951), and the full orchestra of *Intersection 1* (February 1951) – followed in quick succession. With the arrival of Earle Brown – who, much to Feldman's chagrin, during 1952 joined what later came to be known as the "New York School" of *composers* – these graphic tendencies were pushed to their extreme. The score of Brown's *December 1952* consists of a single sheet of card, approximately A3 in size, on which are drawn a variety of lines and rectangles of different thicknesses and lengths. The sheet may be read from any of its four axes, may be played by one or more instruments and/or sound-producing media, and its performance may continue for any length of time; the score must therefore be "set in motion" by the performer(s), whose role it is to "bring about a . . . 'mobility' of sound-objects in time" (Brown, quoted in Ewen 1983, p. 96).

Cage's response to such stimuli, though not immediate, was decisive. Initially, he continued to compose using a combination of durational structures and charts of materials: the results are found in works such as *Imaginary Landscape No. 4* for twelve radios (1951) and *For MC and DT* for piano (1952); subsequently, he adopted Feldman-like graphs in *Imaginary Landscape No. 5* for any forty-two phonograph records, and *Music for Carillon No. 1* (both 1952). Around this time, though, he seems to have realized the profound implications of employing chance-determined compositional procedures: durational structuring, which had been the keystone of his compositional technique since 1939, was no longer necessary; and conventional notational practices could be completely side-stepped. Thus Cage also created during the *annus mirabilis* of 1952, the "point-drawing system" of the *Music for Piano* series – which consisted solely in "observing and marking minute imperfection in the manuscript paper" (Pritchett 1993, p. 94) – and the huge (55″ × 34″) quasi-pictorial score of *Water Music* (see Example 6.1). In the former work, pitch and timbre are rendered precisely, but rhythm and velocity are uncontrolled (except by the decisions of the performer, and the sustaining power of the instrument being played); in the latter piece, music and theatre collide as the player – interpreting a score which is suspended in front of the audience – performs not only on a (partly prepared) piano, but also with whistles, playing cards, a radio, and water.

The connections between the two "New York Schools" are worth emphasizing at this point, however briefly. Apart from the many interpersonal relations that existed among the schools' members – Cage was very close to Rauschenberg and Jasper Johns, Feldman to Philip Guston, and Brown to Jackson Pollock and Alexander Calder – there are clear parallels between their working practices. Feldman, for instance, "used to work by putting his manuscripts on the wall so that he could step back and look at them the way an artist looks at a picture" (Patterson 1994, p. 72), while Brown actively pursued both "the dynamic and 'free' look of the work . . . of Pollock" and Calder's "idea . . . of making 'two or more objects find actual relation in space'" (Ewen 1983, p. 96).[3] Cage, meanwhile, made frequent reference to the "New York School" painters in particular, and to other visual artists (and their techniques) in general. For instance, he shared with Pollock an interest in Navaho sand painting, as is evinced by the title of his 1949 Artists Club talk – "Indian Sand Painting or The Picture that is Valid for One Day" – and a contemporaneous article in *the Tiger's Eye* (Cage 1949); as has already been noted, the final committing to paper of *4′33″* was fired by the example of Rauschenberg, concerning whom he later wrote at least two celebratory texts; and he also likened the manner of composition employed in

Example 6.1 John Cage, *Water Music* (1952)

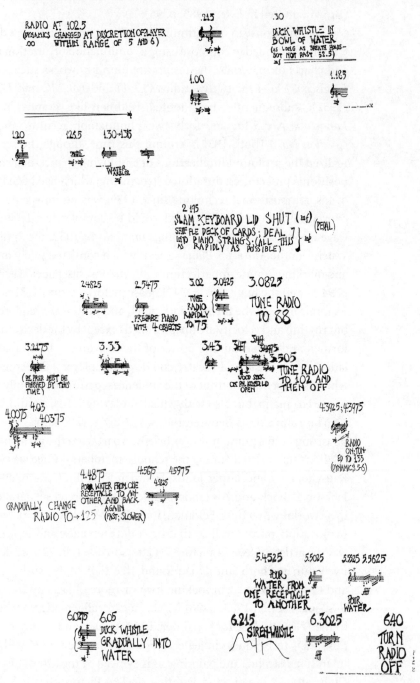

the extended *Music for Piano* series (1952–56) to working with water colors (as opposed to the oils of *Williams Mix*) (Cage 1981, p. 44). But there is also a further connection: Cage's scores had always been miracles of calligraphic beauty, but with the exhibiting, in 1958 at the Stable Gallery, of individual pages from the *Concert for Piano and Orchestra* (1957–58) as works of art in their own right, Cage made a significant step towards the creation of the prints and other visual media discussed in Chapter 7.

Stony Point

The "New York School" of composers – as a physical entity – was in fact short-lived: "the appearance of Earle Brown on the scene infuriated . . . Feldman" to the point where "the closeness that I had had with Morty and David and Christian was disrupted" (Kostelanetz 1988, p. 14). Subsequently, a discussion concerning Boulez – who was criticized by Feldman but supported by Brown – led to a major blow-up. During 1952, Feldman left the "Bozza Mansion" on Monroe Street, where both he and Cage lived, for Washington Square; Christian Wolff had already started his studies at Harvard; and in the following year, Cage was evicted from Bozza Mansion prior to its demolition. His eventual destination, along with David Tudor and several other colleagues, was an artistic community founded by ex-Black Mountain College student Paul Williams – dedicatee of *Williams Mix* (1952) – at Stony Point in Rockland County, New York State.

Cage moved to Stony Point in August 1954 and remained there until the late 1960s; the effects on both his lifestyle and his work were large scale and unexpected. As noted in Chapter 1, Cage was fundamentally a child of the city – whether Los Angeles, Chicago, or New York – which heretofore had provided him with both a multiplicity of artistic stimuli and a surprising degree of privacy and quietude. Suddenly, however, "I found myself living in small quarters with four other people, and I was not used to such a lack of privacy, so I took to walking in the woods . . . in Stony Point, I discovered that I was starved for nature" (Kostelanetz 1988, pp. 15–16). To paraphrase the fourth-century poet Lu Yun, Cage's cottage became a universe,[4] as the "accidental sounds" highlighted two years earlier by *4′33″* became the *musique d'ameublement* of his new home: Ninette Lyon wrote of "the only melodies in [the] sparsely furnished two-room cabin [being] the creaking of a big white hammock, [and] the muffled sound of bare feet on cocoa matting" (quoted in Kostelanetz 1971, p. 153), while Cage himself noted in 1974 that "the sounds of the environment constitute a music which is more interesting than the music which they would hear if they went into a concert hall" (quoted in Kostelanetz 1988, p. 65). Less (or perhaps more) serious was his view twenty years previously, not long after the move to Stony Point:

> I have spent many pleasant hours in the woods conducting performances
> of my silent piece, transcriptions, that is, for an audience of myself, since
> they were much longer than the popular length which I have had

published. At one performance, I passed the first movement by attempting the identification of a mushroom . . . The second movement was extremely dramatic, beginning with the sounds of a buck and a doe leaping up to within ten feet of my rocky podium.[5]

No wonder, then, that in 1967 Cage should have become so drawn to the work of Henry David Thoreau (see Chapter 8), nor that it became a corner-stone of his aesthetic once he returned to the city.

Among the original attractions of moving to Stony Point was Paul Williams's intention that it would serve as a base for Cage's long-wished-for center for experimental music. In the event, nothing came of this; but one significant facet of Cage's work over the next decade was its increasing inter-action with electronic media. Thus, following on from *Imaginary Landscape No. 4* and *Water Music*, he wrote a series of works involving radios: these include *Speech 1955*, *Radio Music* (1956), and *Music Walk* (1958). Comple-menting these are two television pieces – *Water Walk* and *Sounds of Venice* (both 1959) – several tape works, such as *Fontana Mix* (1958), *Music for "The Marrying Maiden"* (1960), and *Rozart Mix* (1965), and a sequence of compositions involving amplification and/or assorted audio-visual devices, most notably *Cartridge Music* (1960), *0'00"* (1962), various of the *Variations* series, *Reunion* (1968), and *HPSCHD* (1967–69). Many of these projects were brought to fruition in locations other than Stony Point – *Fontana Mix*, for instance, was created (at the invitation of Luciano Berio) at the Studio di Fonologia in Milan, and *HPSCHD* at the University of Illinois – but there is a sense in which the particular ambience of Cage's country home may have encouraged him in "reaching out" from Stony Point, both literally and metaphorically, in this case via electricity.

Indeed, there are parallels to this "reaching out" in other contempora-neous areas of Cage's activity. The bustle of New York City had provided him with relatively few opportunities to work elsewhere; yet removed to the isolation of Stony Point, invitations began to flood in, whether to festi-vals in Europe (see Chapter 2) or residencies in American universities and colleges. Similarly, 1961 saw both the publication of Cage's first (and most influential) collection of writings, *Silence* (Cage 1961), and his signing of an exclusive publishing contract with the Henmar Press, part of the C. F. Peters Corporation. Finally, Cage's work began to influence younger composers, including the Fluxus group, and Nam June Paik.[6]

Apart from the electronic pieces mentioned above, two further series of works were largely conceived and executed during this period. The first was the never-completed group collectively titled "The Ten Thousand Things" (see Pritchett 1993, pp. 95–109). Each is for a solo instrument, and has a title defining a precise duration – examples include *26' 1.1499" for a string player* (1953–55), the pair of works for prepared piano discussed in Chapter 2, and

27' 10.554" for a percussionist (1956). Cage's overall plan was to "compose many independent pieces for various media, each of which could be played as a self-contained work in its own right, or performed together with any number of the others" (Pritchett 1993, p. 96). The notation for these works is often complex, and points towards the virtuosity of the *Concert for Piano and Orchestra*.

But while "The Ten Thousand Things" are essentially traditional (albeit very demanding) concert works, the remaining series includes pieces that "do not describe events in either a determinate or indeterminate way, but which instead present a procedure by which to *create* any number of such descriptions or scores" (Pritchett 1993, p. 126); many are implicitly (if not explicitly) theatrical. Thus in *Variations I* (1958), the materials consist of several transparent squares notated with either points or lines, which are superimposed in order to produce "readings" of notational data. *Theatre Piece* (1960), meanwhile, requires that each of its performers make a collection of verbs and nouns, these serving as the raw data that are placed within individual time-bracketed scores. Given the potential dangers of up to eight individuals carrying out asynchronous actions within a confined space, Cage – ever the pragmatist – wisely instructs that "a rehearsal will have the purpose of removing physically dangerous obstacles [including, one might add from experience, other performers] that may arise due to the unpredictability involved."

Perhaps the most radical of these works – and the one that relates most closely to the idea of the cottage becoming a universe – is *Variations IV* (1963). The work is designated as being "for any number of players, any sounds or combinations of sounds produced by any means, with or without other activities" and can be performed anywhere – concert hall, theatre, apartment, open space, cave. Thus, where *4'33"* had in 1952 liberated ambient sound, and *0'00"* had a decade later achieved the same for everyday gesture, *Variations IV* goes the whole hog in liberating *everything*. The materials provided by Cage do not enable the performers to specify substance (i.e., sonic material), but rather the means by which the spatial sources of such substance may be determined. Thirty years previously, Charles Seeger (himself the teacher of Henry Cowell) had coined the term complete heterophony to describe "a polyphony in which there is no relation between the parts except mere proximity in time-space, beginning and ending, within hearing of each other, at more or less the same time," further noting that "Heterophony may be accidental, as, for instance, a radio-reception of Beethoven's 'Eroica' intruded upon by a phonograph record of a Javanese gamelan" (Seeger 1933, p. 111). In Cage's own recorded performance of the work's première – and it is important to acknowledge that Cage's performance practice is a vital element in helping us to understand

the intention in many of his pieces – there is extensive use not only of amplified ambient sounds (of street, audience, and radio), but also of discs of a
wide variety of extant musics. We never hear "Beethoven . . . intruded upon
by . . . Javanese gamelan" as such; but Schubert intruded upon by Japanese
shamisen music comes convincingly close.[7]

*

To a considerable degree, *Variations IV* is not just the "kitchen-sink sonata,
the everything piece, the minestrone masterpiece of modern music" jocu-
larly described by Eric Salzman (quoted in Kostelanetz 1971, p. 150). Rather,
it is in addition both a McLuhanesque example of what Salzman called
"instant communication with the entire experiential world, [in which] our
nervous systems are extended [and receive] messages from every corner of
the global village" (quoted in Kostelanetz 1971, p. 151) and – less optimisti-
cally – the end of conventional music history, in that it can both contain
everything that has existed previously, and predict everything that is yet to
come. In this context, it is therefore unsurprising that so much else of Cage's
music from the later 1960s (the remaining *Variations* pieces, *Musicircus*, and
HPSCHD) might seem like partial regurgitations of *Variations IV*; nor that
Cage himself, in the "Foreword" to *A Year from Monday*, confided that "I am
less and less interested in music" (Cage 1967, p. ix). At times, like Earle Brown
following the composition of *December 1952*, he must have wondered what
else, musically, there was that he could achieve. As Brown had put it, "The
extremely high degree of . . . freedom . . . seemed to be as far as I could go in
that direction" (Brown 1974). Indeed, as is discussed in Chapter 8, it was
only in 1969 that Cage found a new way of navigating through the infinite
space he had opened out six years earlier; and again, there is a direct parallel to Brown's experience, in that the breakthrough came through a kind
of compromise, for "the notational and performance process discoveries
were applied to [later] works in a far more normal compositional way . . . "
(Brown 1974). In both cases, though, the ability to move forward creatively
and with new vigor from an apparent impasse is major testament to the
composers' inventiveness and imagination.

7 Visual art

KATHAN BROWN

John Cage's visual art, done in the last section of his life, is a collection of forms whose purpose, he often said, is "to sober and quiet the mind." Cage developed his art with sustained attention, and it became original on its own terms. In a purely visual way it gives a sense of the direction and meaning of his mature thought.

Cage was sixty-five years old when, in 1977, I invited him to come to Oakland, California, to work with our printers at Crown Point Press to make etchings. In reply to my invitation, he told me that he had promised the composer Arnold Schoenberg (in 1934), as a condition of studying with him, to devote his life to music. And then he added another story. He had once received an invitation from a friend to walk with her in the Himalayas, and he had not accepted. "I have always regretted this," he added.

Because of that regret, he accepted my invitation, and beginning in January 1978, he worked with us for a week or two almost every year, fifteen times before his death fifteen years later. At Crown Point Press, which is now located in San Francisco, Cage produced twenty-seven groups of prints, mainly etchings, and these groups contain all together 667 individually composed works of art. Cage had begun his work as a visual artist in 1969 in New York with a print project, but it was nine years later, with his first Crown Point visit, that his sustained art activity began. After his introduction to etching on that first visit, he spent five years on four complex projects. Then, in 1983 he simplified his printmaking approach, and also began drawing. In the nine years after that until he died, he produced about 150 drawings at home in New York, in between regular work periods at Crown Point Press. In that period he also made 114 watercolors in two sessions at the Mountain Lake Workshop in Virginia. That is the bulk of Cage's visual art.

But there is more. He worked with others to produce several limited-edition books. He worked at the Rugg Road Mill in Boston to make three suites of handmade paper using edible materials. He designed complex room-sized works of installation art on several occasions, including an installation for the Carnegie International Art Exhibition in Pittsburgh (installed in 1991 and shown in early 1992). Finally, he created *Rolywholyover*, a traveling exhibition of his own art, along with works by other artists and a sampling of odd things from local museums. *Rolywholyover* was initiated by the Museum of Contemporary Art in Los Angeles and planned by Cage but realized after his death. In 1992, the last year of his life, Cage made a film, as well as completing his final etching project at Crown Point Press.

Cage worked with visual art in almost the same way he worked with music. His printers or assistants were something like musicians – he developed scores for them to execute. The printers were indispensable, but (cf. Chapter 9) this was not collaborative work – the vision was his; he was the artist. You could say, however, that the circumstances of accepting invitations to work were an integral part of Cage's art production: only his pencil drawings were made independently and they fit within a concept previously developed in his prints.

In a print studio, an artist can make art that would be impossible without techniques the printers have mastered. Many composers of music cannot play the violin but use violins in their work, and many artists who make prints cannot lay an aquatint. The composers know what a violin sounds like; the artists know what an aquatint looks like. In the course of his work, Cage grew to understand the print processes and he developed excellent skills in engraving, and in drawing with pencils and brushes. Because he worked with others, he was able to borrow some additional necessary skills.

There is one type of skill that he could not borrow or quickly learn, however, and that is skill in understanding the important issues of the art field. In this, Cage was not a novice when he began his visual work. In his youth, during the Depression years, he sold lectures on the history of music and art door to door, and studied those subjects to keep abreast of his students. Before his commitment to Schoenberg, he both painted and composed music. His friend David Sylvester has written that Cage recalled those early paintings as having been inspired by images reflected in curved surfaces; he quotes Cage as saying he used "not a brush, but steel wool, so that I was rubbing the paint onto the surface of the canvas" (Sylvester 1989, p. 50).

After Cage gave up painting, his contact with artists influenced his music. Although his approach to chance came from Asian philosophy, he was aware that Marcel Duchamp, whom he met in 1942 and greatly admired, used elements of chance in making sculpture. Duchamp's first use of chance was in 1912, the year Cage was born. Mark Tobey, whom Cage met in 1939, was a long-term influence. A favorite story of Cage's involved Tobey asking students to draw with their noses and toes pressed against a wall.

One of the reasons Cage adopted chance operations for his music in 1951 was his desire to step away from the philosophy of the Abstract Expressionist artists. He edited a one-issue art and literary magazine with Robert Motherwell in 1950, and was part of the Artists' Club where the Abstract Expressionists met. "I was with de Kooning once in a restaurant,"

Cage recalled in a 1978 interview. "He said, 'If I put a frame around these breadcrumbs, that isn't art.' And what I'm saying is that it is. He was saying that it wasn't, because he connects art with his activity – he connects with himself as an artist, whereas I would want art to slip out of us into the world in which we live" (White 1978, p. 15).

The idea that framing breadcrumbs might make them art was a sacrilege in the early to mid-1950s, but Cage had a conviction that art and life are close together. Merce Cunningham, Jasper Johns, and Robert Rauschenberg shared his conviction, and in that period, the four saw each other almost every day. "The four-way exchanges were quite marvelous," Cage remembered. "It was the *climate* of being together that would suggest work to be done for each of us" (Kotz 1990, p. 89).

In 1952 – with Rauschenberg, Cunningham, and others – Cage created the first happening (see Chapter 9). In 1958 the highly visual score for *Concert for Piano and Orchestra* was exhibited at the Stable Gallery in New York. David Sylvester, in a catalog for a 1989 exhibition that included the same score, points out the visual character of Cage's manuscripts in general, but adds that "however beautiful [a score] may be to look at, it was not made as something to be looked at" (Sylvester 1989, p. 47).

Cage's visual art, by contrast to his scores, has no purpose but the visual. In developing it, the new forms he discovered were not a product of his will – he didn't invent them. Instead, he discovered them by opening an area of inquiry, as a scientist might do, and pushing that inquiry dispassionately to an extreme. "I always go to extremes," he once said to me, laughing.

"If you work with chance operations," he explained to Joan Retallack, who interviewed him in the last months of his life, "you're basically shifting from the responsibility to choose to the responsibility to ask. People frequently ask me if I'm faithful to the answers, or if I change them because I want to. I don't change them because I want to. When I find myself in the position of someone who *would* change something – at that point I don't change it. I change myself. It's for that reason I have said that instead of self-expression, I'm involved in self-alteration" (Retallack 1996, p. 139).

I watched Cage at work many times over many years, and I can testify that he was telling Retallack the truth. I saw him occasionally modify an approach to make it more practical to a situation, and usually he would accept an honestly made mistake, but I never saw him reject a chance-derived outcome once he had settled on a sequence of chance operations and set it in motion. Good science, also, does not modify results because of the wishes of the scientist.

Cage worked with individual units that he formed into an expanding space not limited by the traditional picture plane, and recently I discovered an article in the science section of the *New York Times* that seems especially relevant to his approach. It explains that energy is "not smooth and continuous but comes in discrete packets, the quanta"; it goes on to report on the work of a young researcher, Dr. Fotini Kalamara, in London. Dr. Kalamara thinks that "if we could look really close, space and space-time would turn out to be not smooth and geometrical, as in Einstein's theory, but 'bumpy' and made up of building blocks" (Johnson 2000, p. D6). "Bumpy" is a word I will use from time to time as I describe the development of Cage's art.

I am going to use some other isolated descriptive words, too, as I continue. They are words that Cage himself put forward in *Composition in Retrospect*, which he wrote in 1981 (Cage 1982, pp. 39–57). He listed these ten words that he said characterized aspects of his work: *method, structure, intention, discipline, notation, indeterminacy, interpenetration, imitation, devotion,* and *circumstances.*

The Plexigrams, 1969

Cage's first visual art project, done in 1969, was called *Not Wanting to Say Anything About Marcel*: two lithographs and a group of eight objects he called "Plexigrams," silk screen printing on Plexiglas panels. Each object consists of eight panels, 36 × 51 cm (14 × 20″), in a wooden base. The panels can be reordered at will and are covered with words and dictionary-like pictures, mostly fragmented. Cage started his graphic work with *imitation*: the Plexigrams look a lot like a Rauschenberg edition called *Shades* (1964) and also relate to *Revolver*, a larger-scale mechanized work on plastic panels that Rauschenberg did in 1967. Cage's Plexigrams are different in concept, however, in that he used his rigorous chance operations to compose them.

Altogether there are sixty-four panels, the number of hexagrams in the *I Ching*. To compose the Plexigrams, Cage used chance operations to determine whether words found in the Random House dictionary should be fragmented before appearing in the art, and whether they should change into images. If images were asked for, Cage used the dictionary illustration if there was one. Otherwise, he selected the picture by using chance operations on images from the New York Public Library Picture Collection of the World.

Every operation in Cage's work process was discrete, with coin throwing for each tiny step. Carl Solway, who with Alice Weston published the Plexigrams, reports that among the receipts for bills paid is one to an assistant for throwing coins. Irwin Hollander at the Hollander Workshop in New York did the printing, and Calvin Sumsion, whom Cage invited to participate, did the paste-up of the images in preparation for photographically transferring them to silk screens. "I composed the graphic work and he executed it, just as I would write a piece for a pianist and she would play it, or he would play it," Cage explained. "In other words, in moving from music to graphic work, I took with me the social habits of musicians, hmm? The division of labor, so to speak" (Retallack 1996, p. 93).

We can see *intention* in the Plexigrams. Cage intended to make a work of visual art using procedures he had established for writing music. In fact, looking back on Cage's visual art as a whole, it seems to me that he always started projects with intention. For the details, he would put the "intention of the mind out of operation" (Retallack 1996, p. 127) by using *indeterminacy*, or chance operations.

From my point of view, the most important aspect of the Plexigrams is the method Cage devised for placing images on a page. He laid a grid over the page, then asked the *I Ching* for coordinates on it. After locating an image on the grid at those coordinates, he would turn it against a protractor to the number of degrees specified by chance operations. He used this method, with or without the protractor, for most of his graphic works and some of his music over the rest of his life.

The first Crown Point prints, January, 1978

When Cage first arrived at Crown Point Press he brought with him a score that, as he said "was the door that opened from music, for me, back into the field of graphic – paying attention to how things are to look at" (Retallack 1996, p. 92; cf. Chapter 8 of the present volume). He had written *Score (40 Drawings by Thoreau) and 23 Parts: 12 Haiku* almost four years earlier. In composing it, he overlaid lines that control duration for the performers with images sketched by Henry David Thoreau at Walden Pond. Each musician performing this work receives one of twenty-three parts into which the drawings are fragmented. Cage had brought us the conductor's score in which the images appear whole, the score without parts. From this he made the etching *Score Without Parts (40 Drawings by Thoreau): 12 Haiku*. The plate size is 33 × 47 cm (13 × 18″), and it is printed on a 56 × 76 cm (22 × 30″) sheet. In his subsequent works on paper, Cage used the entire sheet so traditional distinctions between plate and sheet sizes do not apply.

To make *Score Without Parts*, Cage traced some of Thoreau's drawings and copied some freehand onto the plates, using different chance-decided techniques. There are little pictures of a skunk, a squirrel, an eddy in a pond, and other natural things, and they were his introduction to our world: hard ground, soft ground, drypoint, and engraving.

"I had the sense that I was not an artist, that I couldn't draw, really, anything; but that I had done this [score] and it would make an etching, and did," Cage said fourteen years later. "From now," he added, "I would say not a very interesting one but, nevertheless, something. And then I made a rather interesting thing there, which was the *Seven Day Diary*... Since I couldn't draw, I decided to close my eyes and draw... and if I dropped my tool someone would put it back in my hand for me. I was surrounded by helpers" (Retallack 1996, p. 95).

As he did in most of his projects at Crown Point, Cage started *Seven Day Diary* with what he called "the first thing," the paper. He chose one he liked from the ones we had. Each day, he chose a plate size by chance operations and oriented it on the paper using the method he had developed for the Plexigrams. The sheet size is 30 × 43 cm (12 × 17″).

The first day he used the first two techniques that we would teach any student, drypoint and hard ground etching. (He did a test with just one and found it too skimpy.) He numbered the different tools and asked which to use, then how many marks to make with each tool. Next he asked how many marks should be long, how many medium, how many short. He had with him a sheaf of pages showing *I Ching*-derived numbers, computer-printed and ready to use to get answers without the need to throw coins.

Each day we added a new technique. In this project, however, he couldn't use engraving, a technique he had especially liked in *Score Without Parts*, because engraving requires full attention: you must push the tool through the copper rather than drawing in the normal way.

Cage began his work at Crown Point Press, as he had his work on the Plexigrams, with *intention*. This intention involved *notation*. *Score Without Parts* is his only graphic work that uses music notation. *Seven Day Diary*, which followed *Score Without Parts*, focused on *method*, and also on *interpenetration*: lines long, medium, and short piled up and mingled with one another.

Signals, Crown Point Press, 1978

During eleven days in September, 1978, we made thirty-five prints for a project Cage called *Signals*, and we pulled only one impression of each. The prints were dispersed along with their plates, maps, drawings, notes, etc. to individual purchasers.

Here is the structure: three elements – Thoreau drawings, circles, and straight lines on a 33 × 50 cm (13 × 20″) sheet. Although images can over-lap, each one is an individual. Many of the Thoreau drawings partly fall off the plates, which Cage thought of as nets that probably would catch images, but might not.

Two prints in the series did not catch images of any kind and are blank. Cage asked us to ink them anyway, and he was delighted with the film of ink – the hand tone – and the few faint scratches that printed. "I'm producing a situation like what happens in nature," he explained to us. "Certain things happen, and then because of the concatenation, sometimes nothing results." This remark is preserved on videotape that I shot in the studio in 1979. Another remark on that tape, even more revealing, concerns Cage's interest in learning the difficult technique of engraving. In the *Signals* project, Cage had allowed the possibility of many engraved lines, an ambitious set-up for a beginner. This type of line shows every tremor of the hand, every lapse of attention. "It seemed to me that to be able to engrave required a certain calmness," he says on the tape. "And it's that calmness that I've been, one way or another, approaching in my music and writing and so forth. And then, it became physical, you see, with the engraving tool." In 1978, the first year of Cage's work at Crown Point in visual art, I think he arrived at the most irrevocable aspect of his work: *devotion*.

The big sets of prints, Crown Point Press, 1979–1982

Devotion was required, both on Cage's part and that of his printers, for the *Changes and Disappearances* project that came next. Cage was writing the *Freeman Etudes* at the time. In this work, he said, "I wanted to make the music as difficult as possible so that a performance would show that the impossible is not impossible" (Kostelanetz 1993, p. 245). The *Changes and Disappearances* prints, he remarked in another context "were as complicated as things could be. As complicated as, say, the *Freeman Etudes*. It was difficult for the printers to realize the work. I like them very much. They're probably the most musical, the most detailed work with very subtle changes in the colors and shapes . . . Just as music is made with lots of little notes, so this is made with all those little pieces of color" (Retallack 1996, p. 96).

Changes and Disappearances is printed on rectangular sheets of pale gray-blue paper, 28 × 56 cm (11 × 22"). The prints have what look like translucent panes of glass drifting across them, the light catching on slender images imbedded in the panes. The images are on sixty-six small plates, each with a curvy side, the curves made by cutting with a jig saw over strings that Cage had dropped on the plate. (He mentioned that he was imitating Duchamp who had dropped strings to obtain curves in a work of sculpture, *Three Standard Stoppages*, in 1913.)

There are many curving lines, since Cage also dropped string to get marks over which he engraved, and many straight ones that he scratched into the plates. Cage added the engraving and drypoint lines one by one as he

Figure 7.1 John Cage, *Changes and Disappearances 31* (1979–82). One in a series of thirty-five engravings with drypoint and photoetching printed by Lilah Toland at Crown Point Press in two or three impressions each. 28 × 56 cm.

added new prints to the series. Sometimes after lines were drawn and colors specified, when the plates were set out on the press bed, a line would fall outside the paper borders. Cage called this a disappearance. Nevertheless, there were many more additional appearances, or changes, than there were disappearances as the series progressed.

The first *Changes and Disappearances* print has fifty-four colors. The last one, number 35, done four years later, has 298. We printed only two impressions of each of these prints (with a third in a few cases for artist's proofs). (See Fig. 7.1.)

By Cage's fifth work period on *Changes and Disappearances*, in September 1980, we had begun training two new printers, and Cage had an idea for a set of prints that he proposed could be done by them at the same time as the project in progress. He wanted to use the beautiful hand tone he had discovered in working on *Signals*, and he wanted to add the concept of a horizon line.

The *On the Surface* prints are 46 × 61 cm (18 × 24″). The small individual plates appear as shards floating, overlapping, nudging one another against an implied horizon line that lowers in each print in the series. At a glance the paper seems blank except for the shadows of the embossed edges of the plates, but pale colors soon come into focus, along with many fine dashes, peppered dots, and other lovely accidental marks.

Sixty-five plates taken from our scrap pile were individually shaped each with one curved side and located according to chance operations. As the series progressed, whenever a plate poked up over the horizon it was cut from a point on the horizon line to a chance-determined point below. There was an exception, however. If a plate settled into a position where the portion below the line was too small to cut cleanly, it remained uncut and was lightly balanced above the others. We began the *On the Surface* project in 1980 and finished in 1982, with two impressions printed of each image.

Déreau, the last of the big sets and to me in some ways the most satisfying, was entirely done in 1982, the year we also finished both *Changes and Disappearances* and *On the Surface*. As I think back on *Déreau*, it is as if it somehow just grew up naturally as work on the other two enormous projects was coming to a close.

Cage made up the word "Déreau" using the first syllable of "décor" and the second of "Thoreau." Fixed Thoreau drawings provide a décor, or stage-set for free-floating elements. The prints are on 36 × 46 cm (14 × 18″) off-white Japan paper. We see some animal and bird tracks, part of a flower, something that might be a water bug. There are bubbles near the top of the page, and a lovely swirl of waving lines in several colors at the bottom. A circle dances onto this stage, and some bars. There's a little flag-like shape, and a large pale rectangle. The most active figures are the intricate engravings; they are taut with energy. There is a horizon line, but it doesn't relate to the forms. It moves up and down in the different prints in the series, changing everything by implying the sea below, the sky above.

The colors in *Déreau* are from five distinct palettes: black, yellow, red, blue and earth. Cage once told me he wanted his colors "to look like they went to graduate school," and they were always complex mixtures in chance-determined proportions. This is the only series, however, that sets out several distinct palettes; there are subtle but unmistakable passages of color change. (See Fig. 7.2.)

Changes and Disappearances (thirty-five prints), *On the Surface* (thirty-six prints), and *Déreau* (thirty-eight prints), are major works of Cage's visual art. He saw these sets as large complex single works, the parts of which, to his great delight, could be dispersed independently without disturbing the whole. For each of these works, at his request, we printed a "posterity" set that is kept together, and also one or two individual prints of each image.

In Cage's list of aspects of his work, it is the word *discipline* that most applies to the 1979–82 period of his art making. On that list, he said that he had originally included "form" but it was absorbed into "discipline." "The form – in other words, what happens – comes about through chance, and is, so to speak, not connected as a concern" (Retallack 1996, p. 209). What happened in these large works, I believe, is a new form, not seen in art before. This form is something akin to birds flying or fish swimming. It is released

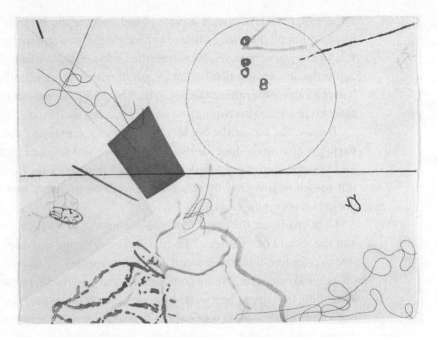

Figure 7.2 John Cage, *Déreau 19* (1982). One of thirty-eight engravings with drypoint, aquatint and photoetching printed by Lilah Toland at Crown Point Press in two impressions each. 36 × 46 cm.

from the picture plane, and doesn't pull people into it dramatically. When you first notice it, you wonder if it's really there.

After these works, Cage changed practically everything in his approach. He had learned to engrave with a skill few printmakers accomplish, but these are the last works in which he used engraving. They are also the last ones in which Thoreau drawings came into play. Finally, they are the last works he characterized as detailed in a way that he thought of as musical.

The first work with stones and fire, Crown Point Press, 1983–1987; and the *Ryoanji* drawings, New York City, 1983–1992

When Cage arrived at Crown Point Press on January 2, 1983, he brought with him a bag of stones, sixteen of them, each two to three inches across. He also brought an idea to buy some soft packing materials – cotton batting, jute pads, felt, and foam – and use those to make prints. This idea was realized as *HV*.

HV stands for Horizontal/Vertical, and these strange one-of-a-kind prints, in which irregular, unruly materials were asked to function geometrically, set the tone for all the work to come. Cage's intention in his January

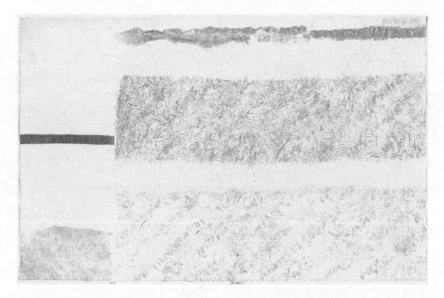

Figure 7.3 John Cage, *HV* (1983). Number 2 in a series of thirty-six monotype collagraphs, each one unique. Printed by Lilah Toland at Crown Point Press. 30 × 35 cm.

1983 work period at Crown Point, I believe, was to make something with a horizontal/vertical orientation that was also bumpy. (See Fig. 7.3.)

He used the stones he had brought with him to begin what turned out to be a large and absorbing body of work that he titled collectively *Ryoanji*. The *Ryoanji* prints are fairly small (23 × 59 cm, 9 × 23″) and have the proportions of the Ryoanji Garden in Kyoto, Japan. From his sixteen stones, Cage selected fifteen (the number in the famous garden; it is just rocks, moss, and raked sand). Then he located each stone individually on a test plate using his system of coordinates on a grid, but keeping a horizontal/vertical axis that did not require use of the protractor that had figured so prominently in the earlier work. He drew around the stones with a sharp drypoint tool. The first test failed. He wasn't satisfied with the way it looked, so he moved to more complex questions.

Later, I learned that Cage had made a *Ryoanji* drawing of fifteen stones on paper in 1982 as a cover design for one of a series of books called *Editions Ryoan-ji*. When he tried the same thing on metal, he wrote, "The mystery produced by pencils disappeared, reappearing only on copper when the number of stones was multiplied" (Kostelanetz 1993, p. 135). In the *Where R = Ryoanji* prints (and also the later drawings), R = 15 stones. In the first print, *2R + 13·14*, he drew around two stones fifteen times each, then drew around thirteen stones fourteen times each. He continued with three prints in which he squared the number of stone tracings, at first drawing lightly, then increasing the pressure. Since drypoint lines are simply scratched into

Figure 7.4 John Cage, *Where R = Ryoanji R8/15* (1992). Pencil on paper. 25.4 × 48.3 cm.

the copper plate, the tool throws up a burr that collects ink against it. As Cage's tool traveled around each rock, it threw up a thicker burr wherever he tipped it at an angle, so the lines are irregular and lively.

He was just getting started on R^3, which entailed 3,375 drawings around individually placed rocks, when it was time to leave. So he packed up his tool, the plate, and another plate and went back to New York.

Cage began drawing on paper after he finished work on the two plates he had with him in New York. Margarete Roeder, his friend and longtime art dealer, says that he used his drawing activity as a kind of meditation. He often spoke of writing music "instead of sitting cross-legged," and by the time he began drawing in 1983 some of the labor-intensive part of writing music had been taken over by the computer.

So far as the actual drawing activity was concerned, he must have been surprised at how easily his pencils moved around the rocks after having done so much scratching into copper with a sharp point. The ease shows. The drawings are not as bumpy as the prints. Cage drew them with pencils of varying hardness, from 6B to 9H, and the number of pencils used is shown as the last number in the title. *R8/15*, for example, means there are fifteen times eight stone tracings done with fifteen different pencils. He never used any other approach for his drawings – they are all *Ryoanji*. (See Fig. 7.4.)

There is *Ryoanji* music too; it provides flights of glissandi for the instruments involved. Probably the prints came first (they were begun in January 1983 and the music called *Ryoanji* is dated 1983–84), but in any case Cage points out to Retallack that the two are composed differently. "There [in the graphic work] I'm not dealing with time, so I can draw around the whole stone. Music is characterized by detail and by having to do things that work in time." He added that in drawing around the rocks for music he created curved lines that go "from left to right as music does. They don't go in a circle. Music doesn't go in a circle. The only way a circle could be expressed in music would be with two instruments, both of which went from left to right [one ascending, the other descending]" (Retallack 1996, p. 242).

Except for his drawing, music occupied Cage fully in 1984. In January 1985 he returned to Crown Point for a two-week period, bringing his stones. We used them for *Ryoku*, a set of thirteen lovely color drypoints that Cage associated with Haiku.

At the same time, he was looking for a direction that didn't include the stones. He thought it might be promising to try some experiments with earth, air, fire, and water. He cut up different papers and subjected them to the elements by burying them, burning them, soaking them in dirty water and tea, and driving over them with a car (he had done this long ago in helping Rauschenberg with a print of his). He also ran some through the press with damp teabags and branded some with heated iron teapots (he said he had brands all over the kitchen counter at home). We ended up with nine unique collages somewhat Rauschenbergian in feel, and two good ideas: using fire and using brands.

Right then, before he left, Cage made sixteen works called *Fire*, on narrow paper sheets approximately 50 × 30 cm (20 × 11″) that were subjected to fires we built on the bed of the press. The paper was damp, and running it through the press put out the fire and trapped the swirling smoke marks, to which Cage added branding. Chance operations dictated which teapots from a group we had assembled made the brand marks and how many to use in each print. Cage really loved the way these smoked paper surfaces looked, and he used fire as a medium for the next seven years until he died.

The following year, 1986, we spent the first day of Cage's work period in a junkyard pulling on massive pieces of twisted iron. Eventually we managed to separate one link from a chain that had been on a hoist, and that gave us a branding tool in the form of a large circle, an "en" in Japanese. "Enso" paintings, which Cage had in mind, are circles drawn by monks. "Ka" means "fire" in Japanese. The prints we did in 1986 are called *Eninka*.

At first, I wondered if we would get any prints. We made many tests, counting newspaper balls as instructed by chance operations and timing burns and brands, but despite the beautiful circle we couldn't seem to do anything that advanced the *Fire* prints from the previous year.

Cage thought we should try lots of different kinds of paper and even though it seemed impractical we tested a sheet of *gampi*, a skin-like Japanese paper so thin it can only be used for printing if it is mounted to something heavier. The big fire selected at first by chance demolished it, but Cage adjusted the parameters that controlled fire size and soon we were able to pull some large pieces out of the pile of ashes on the press. Cage was fascinated that the paper was so sensitive that it picked up occasional imprints from the newspapers used for the fire. Still, he was dejected. "It's just a mess," he said.

"Wait," said his printer. She tossed the crumpled and burned papers into a bath of water. Soon they straightened out, and after mounting ("It's what we would normally do with this paper," the printer explained) suddenly we had a map-like form, or a seaside landscape. Cage was suffused with joy. "Oh, it's beautiful! Don't you think it's beautiful? I can't believe it. I couldn't sleep all night. I thought my whole life had been a waste!" He was laughing, of course, but it made me think. Once he got started on a path, he might make adjustments but he wouldn't set out in a different direction until the path got somewhere. Each time something seemed to be a mess did he wonder, if only briefly, if his whole life had been a waste?

In this group of prints, Cage concentrated on *structure*. I think his underlying question was how soft or hard the structure needed to be. In the following year, 1987, when he did a series called *Déka*, it became clear that structure was somehow in his mind. As in *Déreau*, the first part of the title stands for "décor." The second part, "ka," is the Japanese word for "fire." Before and after 1987, Cage used fire simply by smoking the printing paper. Here, he etched into a plate the residue of soot and smoke from a fire. Then he combined that plate with another that contained a "stage," a chance-decided geometric shape running along the bottom of the sheet.

The watercolors, Mountain Lake Workshop, Virginia, 1988 and 1990

In 1983, the year Cage did the first prints and drawings in which he drew around stones, he was invited to Virginia to lecture at an exhibition of his etchings at the Virginia Polytechnic Institute and State University. At the last minute, Cage had asked that some of his new drawings be included. Ray Kass, an instructor at the Institute with a specialty in watercolor, was very taken with them, and invited Cage to do some similar work in watercolor.

During Cage's 1983 visit to Virginia, Kass did two things to lay the groundwork for the future watercolors. He took him to the nearby New River and showed him the large round rocks there, and he prepared what he called a "studio practice" with rocks, papers, brushes, and watercolors in place. He hoped Cage would locate the rocks using his chance operations and then draw around them using the watercolors, and also he "suggested [Cage] apply some surface washes in order to experience the transparency of the medium and its layering effect" (Kass 1988, p. 2). Cage did some tests. Five years later he did a full-fledged workshop. He spent eight days in 1988 working with Kass and a few students. He drew around the rocks, which were so beautifully round the marks can be seen as circles, and he added washes using large flat brushes, several of which Kass designed and had constructed especially for him. He made fifty-two works, and he collectively titled them the *New River Watercolors*.

In 1990, in his second (seven-day) workshop at Mountain Lake, Cage produced sixty-one works titled *River Rocks and Smoke*. He used smoke instead of washes to give tone to the watercolors. "This work has a great sense of quietness, and the stone tracings are especially energetic and free," commented Margarete Roeder, who placed many of the watercolors with clients of her gallery. Cage did some of the watercolors when he was seventy-six, some when he was seventy-eight. They range in size from 46 × 91 cm (18 × 36″) to almost two and a half meters (eight feet) tall and nine meters (thirty feet) long. I can almost hear him saying, "Isn't it amazing?"

Cage did have some doubts about the watercolors at first (Kass 1988, p. 9) but after the second workshop, he told Retallack he had no more reservations. "Now my experience has changed," he said, "so that I feel all right with watercolor and brushes. In fact, I wouldn't be averse to working with them again. The reason is that in the workshop it's quite impossible to see what you're doing. It's flat rather than vertical, and you're not far away enough to see if it's very big. But I was at an exhibition in Wisconsin where I was able to see that [large] watercolor from a distance. And I liked it, just as others did. I enjoyed it" (Retallack, 1996, p. 141).

Cage's final prints, Crown Point Press, San Francisco, 1989–1992

Because of his experience at Mountain Lake, in 1989 Cage used brushes at Crown Point for the first time. In his work with us that year, he made eight *Stones* prints, two of them quite large as etchings go (137 × 104 cm, 54 × 41″). Like the watercolors that immediately preceded and followed them, the *Stones* prints are concerned with *method*. Cage was learning about brushmarks, and working them into his ideas about *structure*. But these prints and watercolors were a prelude to work that leaves structure largely behind. (See Fig. 7.5.)

Smoke Weather Stone Weather, a group of thirty-seven prints made in 1991, is a turning point between the structured watercolors and *Stones*

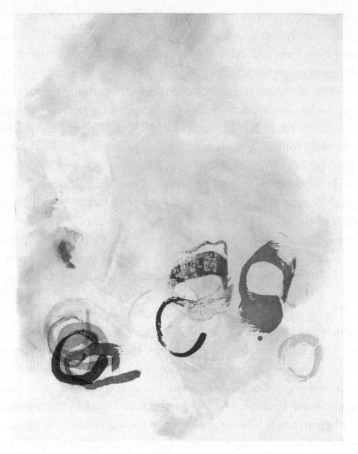

Figure 7.5 John Cage, *10 Stones 2* (1989). Aquatint printed on smoked paper by Pamela Paulson at Crown Point Press in an edition of twenty. 58 × 46 cm.

prints and the simple openness of Cage's last works. Like *Déreau, Smoke Weather Stone Weather* seemed just to happen, and anticipated a change. We used unusual handmade paper (38 × 63 cm, 15 × 25″) and the number of sheets available determined the number of prints; we made only one impression of each image.

Cage combined brush drawings with a line that emphasizes the irregular quality of the stones. Eleven to fifteen stone tracings occupy each print and the images, without fragmenting, move around the paper and up to the edges. The colors are fragile and the paper smoked, so the figures both submerge into and emerge from the whole.

Cage's title, *Smoke Weather Stone Weather*, shows his thinking at the time. The stone-drawings normally would provide structure, but here most of them slip away from structure and, like the smoke, become parts of the weather. Just one or two drift into prominence in any single print. As Cage said in 1992, "Weather remains the weather no matter what is going on . . . so that the structural elements that do appear don't change the way we *see* weather." He added that he was "having more and more the feeling of not being involved with structure" (Retallack 1996, p. 97).

After fifteen years of art-making, Cage's attitudes had shifted. Here, again, are the ten words he listed in *Composition in Retrospect*: *method, structure, intention, discipline, notation, indeterminacy, interpenetration, imitation, devotion,* and *circumstances*. Over time, his art had become simpler as *method, structure, intention, notation,* and *imitation* waned in influence. *Discipline* had become less labored, but not less present. *Interpenetration* had become stronger as images integrated with "weather." And *indeterminacy, circumstances,* and *devotion* had remained steady, always at the center of his work.

I read an interesting remark recently in a *New York Times* interview with a famous novelist. The novelist said, "If you're writing, you're not living, and if you're living, you're not writing" (Gussow 2000, p. E1). She neatly defined the way many artists make art. They retreat into a separate world of their own creation, and then – if they are good enough – entice us into that world through their work. Cage's approach was exactly the opposite. His work was part of living. It was more concentrated in its detail and more refined in its discipline than everyday life, but nonetheless it was integral to it, as the spirit is integral to the body.

Cage was not the only contemporary artist to integrate art and life – think of the artists who most influenced him, Marcel Duchamp and Mark Tobey. Following them are others, some of whom are influenced by Cage. Their work does not manipulate the viewer. Nothing tells you how you are expected to react. Seduction by this type of art is gradual, and is likely to occur only after a person has taken some time with a first encounter. If it does occur, it can change the way you look at other things besides art by adding a spiritual, or out-of-the-ordinary, dimension that gives pleasure and quiets the mind's chatter.

Cage often said that the music and art he most enjoyed encouraged paying attention as a way of being present in the world. He explained the idea to Joan Retallack like this: after leaving an exhibition of Mark Tobey's work, he "happened to look at the pavement, and – literally – the pavement was as beautiful as the Tobey, hmm? So the experience of looking at the Tobey was instructive about looking at the pavement . . . Art became *identical* with life" (Retallack 1996, p. 101).

In Cage's work period with us in January, 1992, he used his stones but (relaxing some structure) he did not use a grid to locate them. On the press bed, he centered each mark in the lower third of a defined space the size of the paper. Then, before printing, he moved the paper: up, down, left, or right (or a combination) according to chance operations. Instead of drawing around the stones, he drew along their edges. He made a series of fifty-seven prints 18 × 20 cm (7 × 8″) on handmade gray smoked paper printed with black and gray inks. The series is called *Without Horizon*. Each print has one, three, four, or five marks which move independently to create an enormous landscape-like form in a very small space.

Cage did another series that January, also. He worked with plates that had been marked accidentally and with them he made a set of prints called *HV2*. He returned to using plates from our scrap pile, as he had done for the large set called *On the Surface* ten years earlier. The two sets are very different. *HV2* does not have the "musical" intricacy and internal movement of *On the Surface. HV2* is, in fact, not intricate, and it is very still. Its movement is something like breathing and drifts out beyond the paper's boundaries, then pulls inward again. Of all Cage's prints, I think this series does the most perfect job of sobering and quieting the mind, placing it, as he said to me on my first meeting with him, "in accord with what happens."

Each 28 × 35 cm (11 × 14″) sheet is filled completely with horizontal and vertical rectangles of varying sizes in transparent colors, all the colors essentially the same density. The plates were left uncleaned prior to etching,

Figure 7.6 John Cage, *HV2, 14c* (1992). One of fifteen aquatints printed by Pamela Paulson at Crown Point Press in three impressions each. 30 × 35 cm.

and the accumulated oils from fingers and hands that touched them before and after they were taken from the scrap pile left permanent marks. The colors glow evenly except for these lighter smudges and fingermarks. Other marks, darker ones, are the nicks and scratches and occasional lines that Cage expected to come, as he said, "from existence."

Cage had asked us that year, 1992, to plan the work so everything could be completed in the two weeks he was with us. That is why *HV2* is a small set, only fifteen prints. In constructing an image, Cage first pulled plates from the scrap pile, working quickly and not studying them, but not using his *I Ching* materials. He laid the plates out horizontally and vertically on paper the size of the sheet we would use for printing. If he picked up a plate that was unwieldy or obviously already marked, he put it on the plate cutter, jumped on the treadle to lower the blade, and cut off the part he could not use.

He subjected each plate to chance operations to obtain its color mixture, and recorded the mixtures in a score the printers could follow. Then he drew a map showing the positions of the plates. After the plates had been etched and inked by the printers, he used the map as a guide for reassembling the image on the press bed. We made three prints of each of the fifteen images. One set, at Cage's request, has been kept together. (See Fig. 7.6.)

While work on *HV2* was going on, we were also working on *Without Horizon*, the small gray prints that resemble landscapes. We made as many of these as possible in the time we had, and printed only one of each. It turned out that these were the last etchings John Cage would do. He died later that year, on August 12, twenty-four days before his eightieth birthday.

8 Music II: from the late 1960s

WILLIAM BROOKS

Composition as process

John Cage is rightly celebrated for instructing us all in the pleasures of individuality, variety, and the unexpected. But it is also undeniable that certain consistencies underlie his work, from the earliest pieces to the last. Prime among these was his inclination to partition the act of composing into discrete processes or tasks, undertaken sometimes concurrently and sometimes in sequence. He sought above all to rationalize the creative impulse, to devise techniques and procedures which could be applied in an orderly fashion and which would allow the construction of engaging, useful works regardless of the composer's circumstances or state of mind. In this he differs importantly from other American experimentalists with whom his name is often linked: Cowell, whose theories were often applied intuitively and whose characteristic medium is the sketch; or Ives, a gifted improviser whose basic medium is collage.[1]

Cage's best-known and most enduring systematization of the creative process was his reduction of composition to asking and answering questions: "as a comPoser / i shouLd / gIve up / makiNg / choicEs / Devote myself / to askIng / queStions / Chance / determIned / answers'll oPen / my mind to worLd around / at the same tIme / chaNging my music" (Cage 1988a, p. 15). But this position was preceded in the 1940s by a formalization of almost equal importance, which divided composition into four conceptual domains: *materials, method, structure,* and *form.* The sources and implications of this aesthetic are discussed in detail elsewhere in this volume,[2] and its application in Cage's music until the early 1950s is easily traced. It is perhaps less obvious that it also illuminates many of Cage's later works, and that differing relationships between its four components helped shape compositional techniques from the 1960s onwards.

Cage's first full account of his four-fold aesthetic was presented in the lecture "Defense of Satie" (Cage 1948b). There he sets *structure* and *form* in dialectical opposition: *structure* defines a class of entities having common properties; *form* distinguishes each member of that class from all the others. "We all have in common the fact of our structure as human beings," he wrote, "but the way in which we live, that is, the form of our life, is individual" (Cage 1948b, p. 79). *Method,* a systematic way of generating continuity, and *materials,* the sounds and silences of a work, mediate between these opposites: each is capable of defining a class of works (twelve-tone pieces, music for prepared piano) but each can also be newly invented to make pieces individual without violating a class's structural consistency.

Almost immediately, however, Cage's application of *structure* and *form* became more narrowly circumscribed: both had to do with the organization of time. Thus the parts that "interact in such a way as to make a [structured] whole" were conceived to be lengths of time (not, for instance, the "parts" of an ensemble); and *form* was "the morphological line of the sound-continuity" (not, for instance, the distribution of overtones in a complex timbre) (Cage 1948b, p. 79).

Ten years later, in one of the Darmstadt lectures, Cage tracked the evolution of these notions through several works from the 1950s. He observed that he had generally applied chance in the domain of *method*; and he observed further that when he applied it to *structure* (as in the *Music of Changes*), "structure became indeterminate" and therefore "not necessary." Being unnecessary, he noted, "in *Music for Piano*, and subsequent pieces, indeed, structure is no longer a part of the composition means." *Materials*, however, remained chosen; the composer's mind was "the agent which established the boundaries" for the sounds of *Music for Piano*. For materials to become indeterminate "something more far-reaching" was necessary; and in the score of *Variations*, Cage explained, chance operations were used to define only properties of the sounds (frequency, duration, etc.), rather than the sounds themselves (Cage 1958a, pp. 20–22, 27).

In the works of the 1950s, then, *structure* was gradually subsumed into *method*; the *materials* remained largely determined either by Cage's choices or by circumstances. In the 1960s, materials too were subsumed, so that scores like *Variations* became simply descriptions of methods, with neither sounds (materials) nor durations (structure) specified. The place of *form* in these works is problematic. If form is an account of change over time (a "morphological line") then it too was dissolved into method; but if it is that collection of properties which distinguishes one composition from another (as "the form of [a] life is individual"), then it persisted. Indeed, in *Musicircus*, for which no score exists, it could be argued that even *method* has dissolved; there remains only *form*, in the latter sense, manifest in the act of naming.

The first *Musicircus* took place in 1967. As Cage approached the 1970s, then, he contemplated abandoning (or transcending) all the components of his original aesthetic. However, *form* in its essential sense would remain unless Cage refused even to circumscribe an event (or class of events) by naming it – that is, unless Cage renounced composition itself. This was a step he was unwilling to undertake. What followed instead entailed in part a reconsideration of the four components in his earlier aesthetic. His willingness to undertake this reconsideration was encouraged by three important experiences of the late 1960s.

First, in 1967 Cage was reintroduced to the writings of Henry David Thoreau.[3] Cage's social and philosophical thought had become increasingly fragmented in the early part of the decade, as he attempted to integrate – or at least to commingle – writers as diverse as Norman O. Brown, Buckminster Fuller, and Mao Tse-Tung. The fragmentation extended to Cage's own thinking; he began to distinguish between political and philosophical or aesthetic domains (as in the continuing "Diary: How to Improve the World (You Will Only Make Matters Worse)"), rather than integrating them (as in the "Lecture on Nothing"). And his writings themselves grew fragmentary: disconnected thoughts (the "Diaries"), lists of ideas ("Talk I"), and eventually dismantled syntax (the Mesostics) and words themselves ("Mureau").

Thoreau stood somewhat in opposition to this: a writer whose focus ranged freely between society, art, nature, and daily life, and who manifested (especially in the *Journals*) the integration of disciplined method, structural consistency, and openness towards material that Cage himself had espoused. Cage found in Thoreau not only an invitation to reintegrate his own thinking, but a demonstration that such a reintegration need not be reactionary. One of the most striking results was the performance-text "Empty Words" (1973–78), structured in four large parts, assembled with an intricate method for selecting materials from Thoreau's *Journal*, and shaped by an overall form that creates "a transition from language to music" (Cage 1980, p. 65).

The other two experiences of the late 1960s both occurred in conjunction with *HPSCHD* (begun in 1967). The first was the creation of a computer program which generated *I Ching* hexagrams as if by throwing coins (and, later, translated the chosen hexagram into a selection from a specified number of alternatives). Cage's life had become increasingly hectic; he toured with Cunningham, lectured on and off campuses, and was constantly asked to participate in interviews and performance events. He no longer had the time or energy necessary to apply the "coin oracle" thousands of times in a complex method such as that used to make the *Music of Changes*. Computer printouts containing strings of hexagrams, however, offered a striking gain in efficiency; methods that had grown impractical for Cage became useful again. *HPSCHD* thus marks the beginning of a process of automation which accelerated through the remainder of Cage's life; by the 1990s his work was facilitated by over twenty computer programs (generating outputs like mesostics and lighting charts as well as *I Ching* selections) and a collection of assistants and technicians to help convert outputs into scores.[4]

HPSCHD is also the first of Cage's works to incorporate specific excerpts from historical music. (In several earlier compositions he had used

recordings as sound materials, but the choice of music for a particular realization was largely arbitrary.) In *HPSCHD* the most prominent *material*
was the "Dice Game" attributed to Mozart, inflected with "substitutions"
from later composers and embellished with computer-generated microtonal tapes; it followed that the notation of the harpsichord parts was more
conventional than in any piece since the *Sixteen Dances* (1951). Moreover,
although the components of *HPSCHD* were distributed unpredictably
in performance, the *structure* (the time-lengths and proportions) of each,
and the relationships between them, were considered and precise. As a
whole, the work's *form* was not linear but concentric, with layers of
material distributing themselves outward from the pervasive, repetitive
"Dice Game."

In a variety of ways, then, *HPSCHD* marked the reintroduction of concepts and techniques that Cage had seemingly abandoned. It sounded fresh
rather than reactionary both because it was so unexpected and because the
sheer quantity of events mediated the character of each taken alone. But
Cage's next major work, *Cheap Imitation* (1969), embraced poverty, not
abundance: one melody on one piano, derived again from a pre-existing
work (Satie's *Socrate*) by simply transposing individual pitches or melodic
fragments. The rhythm, phrasing, and structure of the source were preserved; Cage even modified his method slightly so that exact repetitions of
phrases in the original would be preserved in the *Cheap Imitation*. Nothing mediates the retrospective quality; *Cheap Imitation* looks and sounds
far more like pieces from the early 1940s than like any of its immediate
predecessors.

In both *HPSCHD* and *Cheap Imitation*, then, Cage embraced the past, not
only by recalling and reusing historical artifacts but by accepting repetition
and resemblance as properties of the resulting music. The *Song Books*, which
followed in 1970, elevated recollection and repetition to a central position;
moreover, they took as their prime source material Cage's own corpus of
work. Cage reviewed his earlier music, made a list of procedures he had
used, and then asked (for each song) whether he should introduce, repeat,
or vary the composing technique. Some of the introduced techniques were
altogether new, but a substantial number were transparent reapplications
of methods that reached back as far as the early 1940s.[5]

The *Song Books* mark the true beginning of the final phase of Cage's
work. In effect, during the twenty years after 1950 Cage had worked through
in his own music the aesthetic transformations he had described in the
"Lecture on Nothing" and the "Lecture on Something": first the abne-
gation of taste, control, and even materials in favor of – quite literally –
nothing ("everybody has a song which is no song at all"); and then ("if one
maintains secure possession of nothing") the reacceptance of all that had
been discarded ("there is no end to the number of somethings and all of

them . . . are acceptable") (Cage *c.* 1949–50, p. 126; Cage *c.* 1951–52, p. 132). Having reached *nothing* in works like *0'00"* and *Musicircus*, Cage was able to find *something* acceptable in *HPSCHD* and *Cheap Imitation*; the *Song Books* affirmed that acceptance explicitly and joyously.

In the twenty years that followed, Cage returned to most of the some-things that had formerly been central to his composition. In a sense, the process used to make the *Song Books* was reused throughout the remainder of his career: each new piece either introduced, varied, or repeated an exist-ing compositional procedure. In 1980 Cage observed:

> I work in many ways in a given time period . . . Some ideas that I have
> I drop, and others I pick up from the past, and so on. So it's not a linear
> situation. It's more like overlapping layers.   (Kostelanetz 1988, p. 94)

To some extent the conceptual underpinnings – the four-fold aesthetic – also returned, although with a significant difference: in the works after 1970 Cage became steadily less preoccupied with distinctions between aes-thetic components and more concerned with their interrelatedness. It is almost as though Cage's entire career exemplified one of his favorite Zen stories: Before studying Zen [before 1950], men are men and mountains are mountains. While studying Zen, things become confused [1950–1970]. After studying Zen [after 1970], men are men and moun-tains are mountains – *but*, Suzuki said, *the feet are a little off the ground* (paraphrased from Cage 1961, p. 88; see also Kostelanetz 1993, p. 156).

Thoreau

The first major work after the *Song Books* was *Score (40 Drawings by Thoreau) and 23 Parts*, written in 1974. It is quite easily partitioned by means of the four-fold aesthetic: the *materials* are the Thoreau drawings, placed ran-domly into a *structure* consisting of twelve staff-systems each partitioned into seventeen (5:7:5) units, and shaped by a *form* in which the perfor-mance of each system is followed by a silence of approximately the same length, with the whole followed by "a recording of the dawn at Stony Point, New York, August 6, 1974" equal in length to all that has preceded it. Chance procedures (a *method*) were used to orchestrate the drawings (that is, to as-sign portions of each to the twenty-three parts) and to determine the number of attacks supplied by each player during each structural unit.

It is worth tracing the compositional antecedents of this complex mix of techniques. Cage had used drawings (sometimes his own) in a variety of previous scores (*Aria*, for instance), and in the *Variations* he had recon-ceived materials to be notational (rather than sonic) gestalts. However, the immediate predecessors for *Score* are solos 3 and 5 in the *Song Books*. In these, graphic materials related to Thoreau (a portrait, a map of Concord) are used to derive a melodic line; in each case, moreover, the performance of the melody is coupled with a tape recording of natural sounds. Structures that divide a total time-length into patterned sections and subsections are fundamental to virtually all the celebrated works from the 1940s; and in the 1950s Cage had decoupled tempo from the notational canvas, so that structured space (in the notation) need not be correlated with structured time (in performance). In the case of *Score,* the notation is structured by proportions derived from the syllabic structure of a Japanese poetic form, the *haiku,* which Cage had used similarly in the *Seven Haiku* of 1952. The form of *Music for Carillon No. 5* (1967) consisted of alternating sections of sound and silence (the same work derived pitches from the grain in a piece of plywood) (Kostelanetz 1988, p. 73). Two years before *Score,* Cage had orchestrated the monophonic *Cheap Imitation* by randomly assigning notes or phrases to the available instruments, producing a timbrally inflected unison. Melodic articulations had been regulated by counting attack-points as early as the 1940s, in works for percussion and prepared piano.

Score resembled most of Cage's early music in that the act of composition was partitioned into several distinct procedures; but it is different in that the procedures were drawn from sources that ranged widely both chronologically and stylistically. The *form* of *Score* – that which makes it what it is – has less to do with the morphology of its continuity than with the ways in which these separate procedures were combined. *Score* applies to the domain of technique the kind of recontextualization practiced on the materials of *HPSCHD,* accepting familiar *somethings* but allowing them to interact in ways that transform their meanings.

The compositional components of *Score* recur individually in dozens of subsequent works, but Cage never reused the exact combination that constitutes *Score* itself. In still more works certain components recur in variation, and sometimes a combination of variations produces a closer resemblance to *Score* than an exact reuse of a particular component. Moreover, variation techniques themselves recur both exactly and in variation; the notion of variation is itself variable. The result of all this is an extensive and complex network of works that are somehow related to *Score,* a network more like an ethnographer's kinship chart than a biographer's lifeline.

Score's haiku-based structure, for example, recurs exactly in the two sets of *Haikai* for flute and zoomoozophone (1984) and for gamelan (1986). However, in these works the structure (5 : 7 : 5) is manifested not in lengths of time but in numbers of events; that is, the structure is married to attack-points rather than lengths of time. (That Cage nonetheless considered the works structured is confirmed by the use of bar lines which,

according to a note in the first *Haikai*, "merely indicate the 5 : 7 : 5 structure.")
A closer kinship with *Score* is manifested by *Renga* (1976), in which reappear both Thoreau drawings and a durational structure, but the latter is now
based on a different poetic scheme, the *renga*, which contains thirty-six iterations of a 5:7:5:7:7 pattern. *Two*^{2} (1989) also uses the *renga* structure
but, like the *Haikai*, manifests it in attack-points rather than durations.
More distantly related to *Score* are *Etcetera 2/4 Orchestras* and the derived
Hymnkus (both 1986), in which each solo contains seventeen events but
the 5 : 7 : 5 pattern is not evident either distributively or durationally. On
the periphery, perhaps, is a work like *Child of Tree* (1975), in which a time
structure unrelated to either haiku or renga is derived by the performer
according to Cage's instructions; the structure in this case is made clearly
audible through required changes in instrumentation.

There are other works that could be linked with the family of pieces in
which structure plays a prominent role, but it may be more useful to explore
a second family, defined by a different attribute: the use of graphic materials.
Thoreau's drawings, from which the notation for both *Score* and *Renga* is
constituted, are used in a quite different way – as projected images – in *Empty
Words* (1973) and *Lecture on the Weather* (1975). But despite the connection,
neither of these works resembles *Score* substantially; it is a later set of pieces,
the various *Ryoanji* (begun 1983), in which the resemblance is evident. In
the *Ryoanji*, however, the graphic notation is derived from tracings made
around rocks, and the cultural antecedents are Japanese (Zen) rather than
American (Thoreau).

The use of ambient sounds creates yet another family of near and distant
relations. *Etcetera* (1973) and *Etcetera 2/4 Orchestras* (1985) closely resemble *Score* in that both call for recordings made in Cage's own composing
environments (Stony Point and his New York loft). The recording in *Inlets*
(1977), in contrast, is of "burning pine cones," not a specific location; but
formally it functions much like the recording in *Score*, in that it is preceded by a silence and heard in the second half of the piece. *Lecture on the
Weather* calls for recordings of wind, rain, and thunder, but the motivation in this case is neither contextual nor formal, but programmatic. An
altogether different collection of variations, more distantly related, consists
of pieces in which one or more listeners are asked to experience or record
the ambient sound at several linked locations: 147 addresses in New York
(in *49 Waltzes for the 5 Boroughs*, 1981) or 430 addresses in and around
Chicago (in *A Dip in the Lake*, 1978); or even the hundreds of ambient
recordings, gathered world wide, that make up one conceptual layer of
Roaratorio (1979).

As a final illustration of kinship networks one might consider the alternation of sound and silence that is fundamental to the form of *Score*. Exactly

this alternation, but with the durations of the silences determined by chance, characterizes the form of *Branches* (1976), which is thus a close relative in this domain (though in all others it differs greatly). In *Litany for the Whale* (1980), differing melodic phrases alternate with a melodic refrain which is set off by a short silence; in *ear for EAR* (1983), Cage writes "antiphonies" for "single voices, one visible, the other(s) not." In these works, then, alternation between sound and silence is gradually extended to include alternation between two categories of sound events. Again this leads to a different, more distantly related collection of variants, in which different types of music appear in irregular succession. In *Music for . . .* (1984) "each part is a sequence of 'pieces' and 'interludes'"; the "pieces" themselves contain two kinds of music, and one of these two kinds consists of a single held tone "preceded and followed by silence, repeated any number of times." Thus there is created a complex form comprised of pairs of alternatives nested in three levels. The *Thirty Pieces for String Quartet* (1983) contain no nested forms, but each part alternates irregularly among "three kinds of music . . . tonal, chromatic, and microtonal."

One could trace many more links, giving rise to further collections of related works, but for present purposes these examples must suffice. It is evident that, in effect, each of the works written after 1970 is defined by a unique assembly of characteristics – a kind of compositional DNA – within a community of related works. Just as that which makes a person an individual is in part a complex of traits linked to greater and lesser degrees with close and distant relatives (eyes like her mother, nose from her great-aunt, hair resembling a distant cousin), so the individuality of each composition (its *form*, in the broad sense) derives from characteristics and variants traceable in greater and lesser degrees to other compositions, near and distant.

If there must be a single progenitor for this entire community of compositions, let it be Thoreau. Certainly Thoreau's presence is felt in the extent to which nature is a source for many of the materials; and the art which Cage married to nature is direct and essential: structures derived from Japanese poetry, simple forms constructed from alternation and repetition. "I went to the woods because I wished to live deliberately," wrote Thoreau; and in many of these compositions Cage seems to be recapitulating Thoreau's journey (recorded above all in his journal) into the art of life by way of nature. In this sense a large body of Cage's compositions after 1970 are directly indebted to the first of the three important discoveries he had made in the late 1960s.

The second and third discoveries also each gave rise to a family, a community, of compositions. *HPSCHD*, it will be recalled, demonstrated for Cage that existing music could be incorporated into new works without invalidating the principles of non-intention on which Cage's aesthetic rested.

It also required the creation of computer programs that could apply *I Ching* decisions at speeds and in quantities that had become wholly impractical for Cage himself; it allowed Cage to automate important aspects of his compositional process. Each of these discoveries was extended, varied, and intermarried with others in the communities of compositions that Cage subsequently created.

History

For Cage, the use of pre-existing music entailed, as always, determining what questions to ask; and the questions, in turn, often depended upon reconceiving the nature of the received material. Thus, in *HPSCHD*, the Mozart "Dice Game" in effect creates not a composed continuity but a structure to be filled: twenty iterations of sixty-four (8 × 8) measures. The "Dice Game" fragments that initially fill these measures function as sonic background – a kind of silence, if you will – into which are placed materials drawn from other works by Mozart and others. The technique is one of substitution – the "Dice Game" is gradually replaced by other material – but the conception rests on redefining the "Dice Game" to be an empty structure.

Similarly, in constructing the first *Cheap Imitation* from Satie's *Socrate*, "seeiNg / It / as polyModal" (Cage 1988a, pp. 27–28) allowed Cage to overwrite the note-to-note continuity with one that was different but related. Working phrase-by-phrase, Cage used chance techniques to choose a mode (seven pitches) and a transposition; then he rewrote the pitch content to conform to the mode and transposition chosen. The result preserved the *structure* (phrases and proportions), *materials* (the twelve chromatic pitches), and *form* (rhythm and dynamics) of the original; but Cage reapplied what he took to be Satie's *method* in a way that generated a fresh but familiar outcome.

The first movement of *Cheap Imitation* is unique in that Cage chose each note within a phrase independently, so that in effect every pitch was a fresh start. In the two movements that follow (and, indeed, in all the succeeding "imitations"), the replacements were made in units no smaller than a half-measure, so that interval content and contour was preserved. The resemblance to the original is much greater, and it may be that Cage had found that choosing the pitches independently transformed the form of the original ("the morphological line") too greatly. It is certainly the case that in other "imitations" which followed (notably the "Queen of the Thunder" in the *Song Books*) the relationship between the transformation and the original is so close as to approach parody.

The *Song Books* contain several other "Cheap Imitations," including some which vary the method used to transform the original. Song 80, for example, presents the rhythms, phrases, and dynamics of a Satie song, thus preserving the same properties as in the first *Cheap Imitation*; but rather than applying modal transposition, phrase by phrase, Cage asks that the pitches be supplied by drawing the notes of the original one-by-one from a hat. In Song 85, the Satie *Chorals* are the basis for a "rubbing": a larger staff like that used in *Atlas Eclipticalis* is placed over the score and the note-heads inscribed on it. The effect is to preserve the contour of the original (although in a very restricted range) but to transform the rhythm, phrasing, and inflection. Though the song uses pre-existing material and is thus closely related to the *Cheap Imitations*, in Cage's scheme for the *Song Books* it is actually listed as a variant of star-chart pieces like *Solo for Voice I*.[6] It is thus also close kin to another community of pieces to be discussed shortly.

Both the original *Cheap Imitation* and the "rubbing" were later transcribed (arranged) for other forces. However, most later works that are based on earlier music use a different technique, one not present in the *Song Books*. Cage first applied this technique, which he called "subtraction," in *Apartment House 1776*, a commission to celebrate the American bicentennial. Using chance techniques he chose a collection of forty-four early American choral pieces; in each piece he selected certain pitches from each of the vocal lines and extended these through an arbitrary number of succeeding notes, with the sustained note replacing the original pitches. After each such sustained pitch there followed a silence which extended, similarly, through an arbitrary number of succeeding notes.

Cage arrived at this method after several false starts. His objective was clear from the start: "to do something with early American music that would let it keep its flavor at the same time that it would lose what was so obnoxious to me: its harmonic tonality." His first attempts failed because "the cadences remained recognizable"; in contrast, using the successful method, "the cadences and everything disappeared; but the flavor remained . . . you get the most marvelous overlappings" (Kostelanetz 1988, pp. 85–86). In effect, Cage's transformation preserved the *structure* (proportions), *materials* (pitch content), and even aspects of the *method* (the rhythmic placement of the retained pitches); but the *form* (the morphology of the continuity, grounded in this case on the predictive aspects of harmonic logic) was altered substantially.

Cage was sufficiently enamored of "subtraction" to apply it with only slight variations in several pieces that followed: *Some of "The Harmony of Maine"* (1978), *Hymns and Variations* (1979), and *Thirteen Harmonies* (1986). But it resonated in more subtle ways in other works. In *Dance/4 Orchestras* (1982) Cage worked with "conventional" materials distributed into short sections which are repeated an unspecified number of times (Kostelanetz 1988, p. 96). The music is metric and relatively simple, but Cage asks that each of the four conductors work "independently of the others, with respect particularly to his beginnings and his tempo" (Kostelanetz 1993, p. 134). Though nothing was "subtracted" from pre-existing works, the music has a familiar, derivative quality; but again *form* was reconceived to undermine the predictive implications of meter and repetition. In *Music for . . .* (1984) repetition and prediction are almost entirely decoupled, so that the forms (morphologies) associated with repetition appear only as a kind of ghost, suggested but not actualized in the musical continuity.

There is one further group of works that Cage derived from existing materials, in this case literary rather than musical. Again the *Song Books* mark a turning point: in several of the *Solos* texts were created by fragmenting passages from Thoreau or Satie. There followed larger text-pieces, such as "Mureau" (1970) and "Empty Words" (1973–78), intended for both publication and performance. At about the same time Cage reconceived the nature of his invented "mesostic," changing it from a structure around which a poem could be written to a method for "writing through" pre-existing texts (*Finnegans Wake, Howl*, the writings of Duchamp). These texts then became the basis for explicitly musical works, primarily the series whose titles all end in "kus" (by reference to hai*ku*). In certain of these (*Sonnekus²*, 1984; *Mirakus²*, 1985) there is an embedded musical quotation as well, which runs down the center of the musical fragments just as a word runs down the center of a mesostic.

With certain of these works we find ourselves back in the community of pieces associated with Thoreau and with nature. Thus the large community of pieces associated with pre-existing works not only arranges itself in a network of close and distant relations, but also intermingles on its periphery with the network encompassed by a different community. The distribution of pieces in the multi-dimensional field defined by Cage's various structures, methods, materials and forms is by no means uniform; the pieces "clump" into families with differing degrees of proximity. But no piece is a stranger; there are no anomalies, no works unrelated to all the others.

Automation

Much the same is true for the pieces most profoundly affected by the third of Cage's 1960s discoveries: the possibility that composition could be automated in varying degrees. The first of several *I Ching* programs was written by Ed Kobrin for use in composing *HPSCHD*, and thereafter Cage kept handy a stack of printouts, each page containing several dozen hexagrams.

To make a choice he referred to the next available hexagram, then crossed it out. As time passed this basic procedure was supplemented by tables which related hexagram numbers to the number of options available; and in the *Song Books* and many subsequent works Cage actually included a selection of these tables, to facilitate chance operations required of the performer. Thus, for instance, the instructions for *Child of Tree* (1975) read in part:

> Divide the eight minutes into parts by means of the coin oracle of the I Ching.
>
> | | |
> |---|---|
> | 1–16 = 1 | 33–48 = 3 |
> | 17–32 = 2 | 49–64 = 4 |
>
> ... Reserving the 10th instr[ument] for the last part, ascertain by means of the coin oracle of the I Ching how many and which of the remaining 9 instruments are used in the other part(s) ... obtain an I Ching number, and interpret it acc[ording] to the table for 8.
>
> | | |
> |---|---|
> | 1–8 = 1 | 33–40 = 5 |
> | 9–16 = 2 | 41–48 = 6 |
> | 17–24 = 3 | 49–56 = 7 |
> | 25–32 = 4 | 57–64 = 8 |

In works such as this the gain in efficiency is small, since only a few *I Ching* choices need be made; but other pieces required so many decisions that working through the alternatives manually would have been wholly impractical. For many such pieces Cage devised methods by which his copyists could generate scores from his own cryptic instructions, which essentially noted the *I Ching* choices and their implications.

In an important body of such pieces *I Ching* decisions were combined with tracings made from star charts. Again Cage was hearkening back to earlier methods; to determine the pitches of *Atlas Eclipticalis* (1961), he had inscribed staves on tracing paper that had been laid over pages of astronomical maps. He reapplied this technique, with several variations, in the *Song Books*; then, in 1974, he used it on a massive scale to create the dense and difficult *Etudes Australes*. The *Etudes* differ importantly from the earlier works, however, in the extent to which the tracings were transformed during the compositional process. In effect, Cage used the star charts only to generate a string of pitches that he then displaced and embellished according to decisions made using the computerized *I Ching*. Each pitch (each traced dot) was assigned to one of the available octaves; then it was decided whether the pitch was to be played alone or as part of an aggregate (a chord), and if the latter, how many notes it would contain; and finally the aggregate itself (if needed) was chosen from a list of all the physical possibilities (Kostelanetz 1993, p. 100). Though the details differ, this transformation of one continuity into another is not unlike the transformations that made the *Cheap Imitations*, with the borrowed melodies of the *Imitations* replaced in the *Etudes* with a kind of "cantus" derived from star charts.

The *structure* of the *Etudes Australes* is simple: four books, each containing eight etudes, with each etude occupying two facing pages. The structure is thus spatial, as in *Score* and many roughly contemporaneous works; but Cage asks that an effort be made to realize the proportions in time as well: "In a performance the correspondence between space and time should be such that the music 'sounds' as it 'looks.'" (Ever the realist, he adds, "However, as in traveling through space, circumstances sometimes arise when it is necessary to 'shift gears' and go, as the case may be, faster or slower.") The *materials* of the *Etudes* as a whole are the notes on the piano, played conventionally; but because of the two-stage compositional process, each individual *Etude* is also defined by a more limited set of materials (the star-chart "cantus"). In addition, as a set the *Etudes* have a distinct *form*: "the whole work . . . moved from an etude in which the likelihood . . . of arriving at aggregates was small . . . to the thirty-second etude, where the likelihood of there being aggregates was almost equal to there not being. So it went from simplicity to complexity" (Retallack 1996, p. 202).

The *Etudes Australes* occupied an extreme position at the time of their composition. They demanded greater virtuosity than anything Cage had written since the 1950s; their notation was relatively conventional; their composition required a method that included computers and copyists; and they manifested a clear reinstatement of the four-fold aesthetic, and particularly of *form*.

Two other sets of *Etudes* followed, the *Freeman Etudes* (1977–80) and the *Etudes Boreales* (1978), each notably different from the others. The *Freeman Etudes*, for violin, entailed note-by-note consultation with Paul Zukofsky to determine possible aggregates and conjunctions as needed; they were also fully notated with respect to timbre and dynamics as well as pitch and time. In the *Etudes Boreales* the cello part resembles the *Freeman Etudes* but the piano part, played with beaters on the frame and body of the instrument, specifies locations rather than pitches. Though each is individual, all three sets of *Etudes* together constitute a close-knit family characterized by the use of star charts, a complex, computer-assisted method, and attention to form. Collectively they are also linked with more distant families or communities: with *HPSCHD* and the *Song Books*, of course; with Thoreau by the derivation of notation from nature; with history in their acknowledgement of convention and virtuosity; and with borrowed material through the application of transformational processes to something akin to the Satie "rubbings."

Several works occupy a somewhat intermediate position between the *Etudes* and these distant relations. Two other important families of pieces derive pitch notation from templates or transparencies. The various *Ryoanji*, discussed earlier, contain pitch contours which were traced onto transparencies from templates made by drawing around rocks. In this case the notation contains curves, rather than dots; but more importantly, the *Ryoanji* differ from the *Etudes* in that the contours appear on the score exactly as traced: there is no second stage to the method. Somewhat more closely related is *Thirty Pieces for Five Orchestras* (1981), in which pitches are derived from holes punched in cardboard templates that were placed randomly on staff notation. *I Ching* techniques then transformed the pitches in two different ways: some were consolidated into chords and articulated in chance-determined rhythmic ostinati; others were elaborated monophonically with dynamics and other indications. In the closely related *Thirty Pieces for String Quartet* (1983) the second stage of composition produced *three* outcomes: ostinati, irregular melodies with a single dynamic, and virtuosic passages which (in Cage's own words) "resemble the *Freeman Etudes*."

The two sets of *Thirty Pieces* also exemplify early applications of what became called "time-bracket" structures. With time-brackets Cage returned to one of his most striking techniques of the 1940s: partitioning the performance length into structural units of time ("the division of a whole into parts") (Cage 1958a, p. 18). In the earlier pieces he had applied mathematical schemes (notably the "square-root" principle) to accomplish this; in time-bracket pieces chance determines the lengths of the structural units. Moreover, in most time-bracket pieces, the start and stop times for each unit are expressed in ranges (time-brackets), not specific values. Thus, for example, the first unit of the first violin part of *Thirty Pieces for String Quartet* is to begin at any time in the first forty-five seconds; it is to end any time between thirty seconds and one minute fifteen seconds into the piece. The second unit begins no earlier than the one-minute mark; if the material in the first unit ends at, say, forty-five seconds, there will be at least fifteen seconds of silence before the second unit starts.

In time-bracket structures, then, the whole is divided in an irrational fashion, using chance techniques; the *structure* is determined (at least in part) by the *method*. Moreover, in performance the structure can vary, so that the exact placement of sounds in time, and the small-scale order of events produced by many players together, is unpredictable. Cage had anticipated these kinds of structural freedom in works like *Child of Tree*, in which the total time-length is partitioned by the performer as part of preparing the score. He had also structured the notational *space* (in *Score*, for instance), leaving duration unspecified. Time-brackets reinstated time as a structural domain, and they allowed greater consistency in successive performances; though variable, the range of permissible outcomes is relatively small. Using time-brackets Cage was able to conceptualize composition much as he had in the 1940s: first the total time-length was *structured*, and then the structural units were filled with *materials* (which could of course include silence). The essential difference was that *method* (chance procedures) determined the details of the structure as well as the note-to-note continuity.

The newly rationalized compositional process was both facilitated and required by the computers Cage increasingly used. In 1988, while working on *Music for . . .* (one of the first time-bracket pieces), Cage imagined that he would continue to add parts to the work as needed, so that the possible instrumentation would grow over the years. To facilitate this Andrew Culver created a program that replicated Cage's method, generating "time brackets, pitches, dynamics, [and] specials for the . . . series" (Retallack 1996, p. 315). Cage continued to use this and other programs in subsequent years, so that his manuscripts began to merge with computer outputs:

> My notation for various reasons has become very, very sketchy. It's largely a result of making use of computer facilities . . . I use time brackets; and in the time brackets I place not notes, but letters . . . The pitch is given by its letter and is associated with a mark describing the octave . . . Fortunately the copyists have learned to read this kind of computer printout that I give them, which they then turn into something much more conventionally musical . . .
> (Retallack 1996, p. 177)

In his last few years Cage composed over three-dozen time-bracket pieces. In many ways these are very close kin (having in common, as they do, "the fact of [their] structure"); but the material that fills the structure ("the form of [each] life") is individual. Dynamics are generally soft, and in nearly half the pieces the brackets contain only single tones or short phrases. Parts written for percussion or unconventional instruments generally specify only a number (of sounds, of instruments) in each time-bracket. But even pieces that look very similar can sound quite different. Discussing this with Joan Retallack, Cage commented:

> I can now write long pieces quite quickly because of the "time brackets." The question arises, are they all going to sound the same, or are they going to be different? . . . in the spirit of speed, you see . . . it's very apt that they may all sound the same. And I don't want that to happen. It doesn't seem right.
> (Retallack 1996, p. 122)

Instrumentation changes, of course, but each piece is also characterized by differences in tessitura, timbre, and scalar content. Some pieces are microtonal; some are not. In some the time-brackets are coordinated and the materials conceived harmoniously; others present structural or sonorous conflicts between members or parts of the ensemble. Because time-brackets, like square-root proportions, can contain literally anything,

Cage could even recapitulate within these late works certain techniques from the previous decade. Thus, for instance, both *Four³* (1991) and *Two⁶* (1992) contain fragments from *Extended Lullaby*, essentially a "cheap imitation" of Satie's *Vexations. Two³* (1991) incorporates amplified conch shells, used exactly as in *Inlets*. A substantial subset of pieces uses microtones in ways not unlike the "rubbings" or the *Ryoanji*.

Cage also shaped the form (the morphology) of certain works (or at least allowed form to emerge during the composing process). Thus *Three* (1989) is a suite in which the first and final pieces Cage imagined to be respectively "a chorale" and "more lyrical." *Fourteen* (1990) places a bowed piano in the foreground by assigning silence to many time-brackets in the other parts; "let the bowed piano part be an unaccompanied solo, one which is heard in an anarchic society of sounds," Cage explains. The prefatory note to *101* includes a lengthy description of the piece's shape, which reads in part:

> [*101*] opens with a ragged burst of high, loud sound from the brass and all
> of the woodwinds except the flutes and clarinets . . . Towards the end, but
> not at the end, . . . the brass and all the woodwinds except the flutes and
> clarinets are heard *fortissimo* and in their highest range, a second and last
> time, falling apart, so to speak, rather than holding together as a group.
> (Kostelanetz 1993, p. 198)

In the time-bracket works, then, Cage both differentiated and integrated the four components of his early aesthetic. The differentiation is evident in both the compositional procedure (time-brackets : materials : morphology) and the extent to which each piece sounds truly individual. The integration arises because all components of the aesthetic are mediated by a single method – chance techniques – refined to a degree of precision sufficient to allow virtually the entire process to be described in a computer program. The time-bracket pieces form the largest single community of work in Cage's entire output, and in many ways they are the most distinct and tightly unified collection produced during his final quarter-century. As always, however, they are also linked with relations near and far in other communities; they stand *with* (not in contrast to) the community of pieces derived from pre-existing material and the collection of works grouped loosely under the influence of Thoreau.

Composition in retrospect

The works written since *Song Books*, then, are distributed throughout a field, a galaxy; and though certain groups, certain systems, can be distinguished, each influences and is influenced by all the others. Or: the works written since *Song Books* are shaped into families, communities, with each individual revealing a different combination of traits drawn from the collective history; but though some individuals are close kin and some are distant, there is none for which no link can be traced, no ancestor found. Or, again: each of the works written since *Song Books* is a node, a terminus, in a network of emerging and dissolving relationships; but though the paths that link them are newly determined with each encounter, nothing stands alone, nothing leads nowhere.

The metaphor may be natural, historical, or cybernetic, but it is in any case non-linear – which makes situating this body of work in a chronology particularly treacherous. Nevertheless, it does seem that the persistence of *method* throughout Cage's career offers at least one thread, one line by which all his music may be joined. And Cage approached method, fundamentally, as a reductionist: he brought discipline to the chaos of composing, creating categories of techniques, behaviors, and decisions, so that the entire process could be articulated as a series of discrete steps, parallel activities, answerable questions. In the 1940s this approach produced a quite rigorous four-fold aesthetic; after the 1960s, the interpenetration and mutual modulation of the four components led to multiple manifestations, compounds, and hybrids that both complicated and enriched the earlier scheme.

Cage attempted a summary of his aesthetic for a final time in *Composition in Retrospect* (and its companion piece, *I–VI*). Each of these texts is comprised of mesostics constructed upon fifteen words that encapsulate, Cage says, "aspects of my work in musical composition":[7] *method, structure, intention, discipline, notation, indeterminacy, interpenetration, imitation, devotion, circumstances, variable structure, nonunderstanding, contingency, inconsistency,* and *performance. Composition in Retrospect* glosses each word with Cage's own comments; in *I–VI* the mesostics are constructed of chance-derived fragments taken from a variety of sources.

"Method" and "structure," taken verbatim from the four-fold aesthetic, reappear as the first two words. But each has by now also given rise to related concepts. A mesostic on "method" provides a list of examples: "iMitations / invErsions / reTrograde forms / motives tHat are varied / Or / not varieD" (Cage 1988a, p. 6). Then, in the mesostics on "imitation" themselves, Cage makes the nature of that particular method clear: ask "what questIons / will Make the past / alIve / in anoTher / wAy." He continues with examples taken from the family of works described above: the *Cheap Imitations,* subtractions, and rubbings (Cage 1988a, pp. 27–28). "Imitation," then, is a descendant of *method,* an individual (or group of individuals) in a lineage *method* long before engendered.

"Variable structure," on the other hand, is presented as an alternative, not an example – a cousin, not an offspring. "Structure" Cage describes in the terms of the 1940s: "the diviSion of a whole / inTo / paRts / . . . / a Rhythmic / structurE / in which the Small / parTs / had the same pRoportion to each other / that the groUps of units the large parts had to the whole" (Cage 1988a, p. 7). "Variable structure" is associated specifically with time-brackets: "These time-brackets / are Used / in paRts / parts for which thEre is no score no fixed relationship / . . . / music the parts of which can moVe with respect to / eAch / otheR / It is not entirely / structurAl / But it is at the same time not / entireLy / frEe" (Cage 1988a, pp. 35–36).

Materials does not appear, as such, among Cage's fifteen "aspects"; instead it has been split into two components: "circumstances" and "notation." As before, Cage described the domain upon which a composer's method operates; but rather than containing sounds, this now contains visual objects, notations: "turNing the paper / intO / a space of Time / imperfections in the pAper upon which / The / musIc is written" (Cage 1988a, p. 18). "Circumstances" intermixes *materials* and *method* even further: "aCt / In / accoRd / with obstaCles / Using / theM / to find or define the proceSs / you're abouT to be involved in / the questions you'll Ask" (Cage 1988a, p. 31). *Materials* remains, then, but not as a separate concept; *materials* has been married, in effect, to *method*.

Form has been dispersed even more widely. Its earlier metaphoric description ("the way in which we live") is echoed provocatively in a mesostic on "intention": "doiNg / someThing / that diffErs / liviNg / in The same town / fInding life / by nOt / liviNg the same way" (Cage 1988a, p. 9). But in the same set Cage makes clear that in the late aesthetic form is not imposed, but emerges "to satIsfy / a particular Need / Though having no control / ovEr / what happeNs / accepTance / sometImes / written Out / determiNate / sometImes / just a suggestioN" (Cage 1988a, pp. 10–11).

Other sections of *Composition in Retrospect* create alloys from two or more of the original four components. Thus, for instance, "discipline" is linked to *method* ("Suzuki / the magiC square / and then chance operatIons") and to *structure* and *form* ("It / iS / Complete / goes full cIrcle the structure of the mind / Passes / from the absoLute / to the world of relatIvity") (Cage 1988a, p. 12). The mesostics on "contingency" include accounts of three pieces in which *materials, method*, and *form* are largely interdependent. "Indeterminacy," clearly an aspect of *method*, also confirms that *materials* are now notational (not sonic); describing the *Variations*, Cage offers a metaphor: "not to supplY / a partIcular photograph / but to thiNk / of materials that woulD / makE / iT / possiblE / foR / soMeone else / to make hIs / owN" (Cage 1988a, pp. 20–21). And "indeterminacy" is linked with *form*, especially as articulated by "discipline": "pay atteNtion / to Daily work or play / as bEing / noT / what wE think it is / but ouR goal" (Cage 1988a, p. 23).

Still other "aspects" of *Composition in Retrospect* reach out from the domain of art to society and politics: "interpenetration," "nonunderstanding," "inconsistency," "performance." Sprinkled through these (and the others) are references to thinkers who had been important to Cage: Suzuki, Joyce, Wittgenstein and, above all, Thoreau. Other passages incorporate references to some of Cage's favorite anecdotes, or to his earlier writings.

In effect, the construction of *Composition in Retrospect* parallels that of the entire body of work with which it is contemporaneous. Cage's aesthetic, like his compositional technique, came to include diverse families of related concepts. And like the compositions, these families both derived from and incorporated previous concepts and materials. The four-fold aesthetic became fifteen-fold; but the fifteen are all kin to the four that began, and to each other. The aesthetic describes itself: interpenetration, contingency, devotion, discipline. All that has been part of Cage's work remains present, distributed and reconfigured by accident and intent. *No difference,* says Suzuki, *but the feet are a little off the ground.*

When a composer dies, we lose the pleasure of surprise. Cage's extraordinary mind – part quicksilver, part abacus, part salmagundi – can no longer baffle our inclination to order his work, to classify inconsistencies, to account for the unexpected. In Cage's case, however, we are consoled by an evident multiplicity of applicable explanations. At the very least, it seems, we need three distinct models to account for the strategies Cage used to reconcile continuity with the unforeseen.

In the 1940s each new work built upon its predecessors; each piece represented an extension, a refinement, a clarification of the principles that underlay what came to be called the four-fold aesthetic. These works can be situated in a linear (though not strictly chronological) history; they can be associated with print (notation), with growth, with progress. In the 1950s and 1960s, new works stripped away the properties and frameworks of their predecessors; each piece contained less, in some sense, to make room for the unpredictable, erratic contributions of collaborators and circumstances. These works suggest an ecological history in which decay provides space and nourishment for new, unanticipated growth; they can be associated with media (electronics), with abundance, with anarchy. The works made after 1970 fill the space thus created with assemblages of ideas, fragments, artifacts, recollections; they allow all the previous work to be revisited, recontextualized. They invite a non-linear, relational history, in which the line between past and future is dissolved; they are associated with networks (information), with equilibrium, with acceptance.

Together these three approaches could constitute the tale of one man's life: an ordinary life, even a cliché, moving from growth through crisis to wisdom. They could also reprise the history of American culture in the middle and late twentieth century: Cage was nothing if not a student of his time. But for we who continue they are both an invitation and a challenge: do we recapitulate the same progression, following Vico through endlessly iterating cycles of history (Joyce)? Do we improve, grow, advance towards a world which *works*, designing new solutions to problems of distribution, access, equality (Fuller)? Or do we seek a transparency in which present histories mix and reconfigure themselves, so that we and our artifacts dissolve into a nature not of our making but informed by our presence (Thoreau)? And what is the relationship between these alternatives? Are they mutually exclusive, or are they mere aspects of an underlying singularity?

A composer's work is best gauged not by what it tells us but by what it does not. Cage repeatedly declared that his task, as a composer, was to determine the proper questions to ask. The work he has left us – notably but not exclusively in the final twenty years of his life – asks the same of us: find the right questions. We shall not lack for answers.

PART III

Interaction and influence

9 Cage's collaborations

LETA E. MILLER

"It is not really natural for artists to work together... There is only one certainty: before the collaboration is through, you will have revealed yourselves to each other; you will be absolutely exposed. A certain blind courage is necessary..." (Graham 1963, p. 4)

In the summer of 1952, a remarkable theatrical presentation took place in the dining hall of Black Mountain College in rural North Carolina. The audience – students and faculty at the school's summer session – were seated in a square broken by aisles into four triangles whose apexes merged toward the center.[1] On each chair sat an empty cup, purpose unspecified; many people used them as ashtrays. John Cage (according to his recollections a decade later) stood on a ladder at one edge of the square dressed in a black suit reading from his "Juilliard Lecture." Another ladder served as a podium for M. C. Richards and Charles Olson, who ascended it to read poetry. Suspended from the ceiling were four all-white paintings by Robert Rauschenberg, providing the backdrop for slides and a film by Nicholas Cernovitch. Rauschenberg stood below them operating an Edison horn record player, switching scratchy recordings on and off. Merce Cunningham danced down the aisles followed by a dog, and David Tudor played the piano. According to Cage, the performance lasted 45 minutes (the time it took to read his lecture), at the end of which the cups – even those used as ashtrays – were filled with coffee.[2]

In later years, Cage's 1952 *Black Mountain Piece* would assume epic proportions, touted as the first of many mixed-media, multi-disciplinary, anti-establishment "happenings." At the time, though, it seemed far less momentous. "I laughed a lot," recalls Lou Harrison. "There was so much going on and it seemed so absurd" (Harrison 1995).

Descriptions of this first happening – which vary widely in estimates of time, activities, seating, and nearly everything else – often suggest an impromptu event. But in fact, it was far from random. Though indeterminate in details, the production took place in the context of a predetermined time framework. Participants (except the dog) were assigned fixed slots: Cunningham recalls having two; M. C. Richards remembers one. The projectionist had three: 16′–23′, 24′ 30″–33′45″, and 38′20″–44′25″ (Fetterman 1996, p. 103). Performers could fill their "compartments" (Kirby 1995) with whatever materials they chose. The poetry Olson and Richards read, the records Rauschenberg played, the piano composition Tudor performed, or the (equally acceptable) possibility of filling one's time with silence, were decisions determined independently, without consultation. The interactive result – in a sense, the artistic *product* – was left to chance, while overall time-management was pre-planned: in Cage's terms, freedom within limitations (Kirby & Schechner 1995, p. 53).

The Black Mountain happening was in the broadest sense a collaborative artwork – Cage, Rauschenberg, Richards, Olson, Cunningham, Cernovitch, and Tudor contributing segments that were assembled linearly or simultaneously by prior plan. But instead of creating a fixed work, they collaborated in a *process*, governed by rule but free in its realization. This event has often been cited as a watershed in Cage's career, marking a change in his compositional procedures. But though it was a beginning, it was also a culmination: the logical extension of a history of interdisciplinary collaboration that had engaged his attention for years.

Recent articles on Cage's early West Coast years (Stevenson 1982; Hines 1994; Miller 2002) detail numerous collaborative activities, particularly with modern dancers. In Los Angeles (pre-1938), Cage noted wryly, dancers showed greater interest in his compositions than did musicians. He accompanied a concert dance group at U.C.L.A. under Martha Deane (Miller 2002) and wrote music for an aquatic ballet that led to his discovery of the "water gong" (lowering a gong into water produced an alluring sliding tone). His first full-time job – in Seattle beginning in 1938 – was as dance accompanist to Bonnie Bird at the Cornish School.

The most important of Cage's Seattle innovations arose directly from his collaborations with Bird. His first piece for prepared piano (*Bacchanale*, 1940) was composed for her student Syvilla Fort. In fact, Cage discovered the *concept* of the prepared piano during one of Bird's dance classes[3] and was able to apply it to a practical, logistical problem: the stage for Fort's recital at the Repertory Playhouse was too small for his percussion ensemble.

Similarly Cage's first electronic composition (*Imaginary Landscape No. 1*, 1939) was written for a Bonnie Bird choreography: a humorous piece highlighting detached arms, legs, and heads – an effect Bird created by hiding dancers' bodies behind rectangular or triangular shields (photographs in Miller 2002 and Vaughan 1997, p. 18). Cage used electronic sliding tones in this work, a result of his association with Bird's husband, Ralph Gundlach (Miller 2002). A psychology professor at the University of Washington, Gundlach had acquired single-frequency test-tone recordings for his research in musical perception. When their usefulness was past he gave them to Cage, who discovered sliding tones by changing the turntable speed while experimenting in the Cornish School's radio studio. It would prove to be but the first of many instances in which he applied emerging technological developments to imaginative aesthetic ends.

On the same recital with *Imaginary Landscape No. 1* (March 24/25, 1939), Bird presented a new version of Jean Cocteau's *Marriage at the Eiffel Tower*. Cage mimicked the collaborative compositional process of Les Six (though in this case with only Les Trois) by providing music by Henry Cowell, George McKay of the University of Washington, and himself. McKay composed the *General's Speech*, *Trouville Bathing Beauty*, and *Promenade and Ode to a Customer*. Cowell, who was at the time in San Quentin prison (Hicks 1991), sent a *Hilarious Curtain Opener* for piano, a *Train Finale* for six percussionists, and three keyboard *Ritournelles*. Bird used Cowell's opener and closer, but found the *Ritournelles* too metrically regular.[4] Cowell, upon hearing of the problem, replied with typical modesty, adding, "I had somehow gathered the idea that the music was meant to flow along regularly, while you did irregular things – a relationship which is sometimes very effective" (Cowell 1939) – an interesting harbinger to the separation of music and dance metrics that would later characterize Cage–Cunningham collaborations (though to a far greater degree than Cowell probably envisioned).

Cage's contributions to the work included wedding-march music (subtitled "Rubbish music"), a toccata "and subsequent mow-down,"[5] a "Quadrille that is a barn dance," "Sad music in the modern minor," and a series of toy orchestra interludes. Among the surviving score fragments is a "Massacre for piano 4 hands" (probably the "mow-down"), which is a nearly minimalist score based on a repeating two-note motive. The toccata features the same figuration. Cage's wedding march is a pastiche of quotes (discarded rubbish?) from the Mendelssohn and Wagner wedding marches (*Midsummer Night's Dream* and *Lohengrin*), Dvořák's *Humoresque*, the opening salvo of Rachmaninoff's c♯ minor prelude, and Massenet's *Aragonaise*. Similarly, the quadrille quotes the "Popeye" hornpipe, *Yankee Doodle*, and *Turkey in the Straw* played in octaves. Most interesting are the toy orchestra interludes, calling for fife, trombone, ratchet, harmonica, toy piano, tom-tom, snare drum, siren, and various whistles: a "yellow green whistle," a "flat whistle," a police whistle, and a slide whistle.

Marriage was a musical collaboration only in the loosest sense: as in the Parisian original, the composers merely divided the movements among them. But two years later Cage completed a true collaboration – a percussion quartet composed jointly with Lou Harrison. Cage had been composing percussion works for autonomous performance as well as dance accompaniment since 1935 in Los Angeles. Aside from the limitations of his unexceptional piano skills, he found the percussion medium attractive because of its communal (collaborative) nature: his amateur groups in Los Angeles and Seattle included both musical colleagues and non-musician friends.

Cage concluded that of the four basic musical elements – pitch, timbre, amplitude, and duration – the last was most basic, since only duration applies to both sound and silence.[6] In Seattle he began to use rhythm as the organizing principle in his percussion pieces, favoring micro-macrocosmic forms – structures in which the lengths of larger sections mirror those of their component parts. When Cage and Harrison began work on *Double Music* in 1941, Cage proposed the same type of structure.

The collaboration began by fixing compositional limitations. Cage wrote for players 1 and 3, Harrison for players 2 and 4. Together they developed a vocabulary of rhythmic cells that could be enchained in any manner, and agreed on an overall duration that translated into $200 \times {}^4_4$ measures. Each of them then divided the total length into equal parts as he saw fit. Harrison chose twenty-one units of nine-and-one-half measures. Cage chose fourteen units of fourteen measures (leaving a four-measure coda), and arranged each section into figuration patterns of 4–3–2–5 (See Example 9.1). At Harrison's request, instrumentation was all metal (in admiration of Cage's *First Construction (in Metal)* of 1939). They then went about the compositional process independently, and when finished, put the parts together without changing a note.

At social gatherings in New York in the mid-1940s, Harrison and Cage, along with Cowell and Virgil Thomson, explored a *linear* approach to collaborative composition. One composer would write a measure plus a note, fold the paper on the bar line, and pass it to his neighbor, who did likewise. Originally titled "Sonorous or Exquisite Corpses" in imitation of the surrealist word-game, twenty of these short pieces were later arranged for quintet by Harrison's student, Robert Hughes, and published under the title *Party Pieces.*[7]

In this same period Cage began to apply micro-macrocosmic principles to his increasingly frequent collaborations with Merce Cunningham. On their first shared program (April 5, 1944), they coordinated choreographic and musical frameworks for most of Cunningham's six solo dances (Cunningham 1982, pp. 107–108). Cage's music – for prepared piano – was built from various permutations of his rhythmic principles. *Spontaneous Earth*, one of the most straightforward, consists of nine sections of nine measures, most of which are subdivided as 3–2–2–2 (See Example 9.2). *Tossed as it is Untroubled* (seven sections of fourteen) and *The Unavailable Memory of* (built from patterns of eight) are more intricate:

Tossed as it is Untroubled
|| 14 || 14 || 14 || 14 || 14 ||:7 :||<u>7</u>||<u>7</u>||
                                       =14   =14

The Unavailable Memory of
||: 16 :|| 8 || 16 | 24 | 8 | 16 || 1 m. conclusion

Example 9.1 John Cage and Lou Harrison, *Double Music* (1941), measures 1–33

Example 9.2 John Cage, *Spontaneous Earth* (1944), measures 1–18

Root of an Unfocus, the most complex of the group, is a tripartite work with a different rhythmic organization in each section (see Example 9.3). The first part is 7 × 7; in the middle section, units of $^4_4$ are juxtaposed with $^3_4$ measures; and in the last, 100 half notes are divided into two units of twenty-three (repeated) with a final coda[8] (See Example 9.3). Cunningham, who was "still concerned with expression" at the time, describes the work's subject as fear: awareness of the unknown, struggle, and final defeat (Cunningham & Lesschaeve 1985, p. 79). Cage's music builds in rhythmic motion in the center, resolving into a pseudo-minimalist closing as Cunningham executed a series of falls and crawled offstage.[9]

Though collaborative in concept and overall form, the music and dance elements in these compositions coordinated only at structural guideposts. Within individual sections, Cage and Cunningham developed materials and metrics independently. This approach to music–dance collaboration offered a fresh answer to an old question: how to reconcile the potentially competing roles of the two arts.

For some years, modern dancers had been railing against "interpretive dance" – the process of fitting choreography to previously composed music. Some of them danced to silence. Others turned the compositional process on its head, developing independent choreographies to which composers would fit a score by noting the dancers' "counts." While satisfying to chore-ographers, this method merely reversed the problem. Nevertheless, many composers worked in this manner. Cage wrote *Bacchanale* this way, as well as several dances for Jean Erdman.[10]

Henry Cowell addressed the problem in a series of articles published in dance periodicals from 1934 to 1941, proposing (among other solutions) elastic musical structures with units that dancers could expand, contract, re-peat, omit, transpose, invert, or interchange in various ways (Cowell 1934, 1937, 1938, 1941a, 1941b; Miller 2002). His suggestion to Bird that the meter of music and dance need not match may well have sparked Cage's own experiments aimed at increasing their independence. Cage's confession

Example 9.3 John Cage, *Root of an Unfocus* (1944), structure diagram; measures 1–28

Section I: 7 sections of 7 bars

‖: 7 + 7 :‖ (= 4 sections of 7)

‖: 7 :‖ (= 2 sections of 7)

‖ 7 ‖ (= 1 section of 7)

Section II: Juxtaposition of 4/4 units with 3/4 bars

A:
4 + 4 bars │1 bar │2 + 2 + 2 + 2 bars │1 bar│
(4/4)   (3/4)   (4/4)   (3/4)

B:
4/4-3/4 — 4/4-3/4 — 4/4-3/4 — 4/4-3/4
(1 bar each)   (silent)

A (D.C.):
4 + 4 bars │1 bar │2 + 2 + 2 + 2 bars │1 bar │
(4/4)   (3/4)   (4/4)   (3/4)

Coda:
4 + 4 bars │1 bar │
(4/4)   (3/4)

Section III: 23♩ X 4 plus coda

‖: 6 bars (4/4) │1 bar (2/4) │5 bars (4/4) │6 bars (4/4) │1 bar (2/4) │5 bars (4/4) :‖ 4 bars (4/4)
    12♩   1♩   10♩   12♩   1♩   10♩   8♩
└————————— 23♩ —————————┘ └—————————23♩—————————┘ └_8♩_┘

Example 9.3 (*cont.*)

to Harrison that he hated dance accompaniment (Cage 1939) reflected in part his resistance to the role of composer as servant of the choreographer. By matching music and dance only at structural pillars, however, he and Cunningham could collaborate while retaining autonomy, creating, in essence, a cooperative interdependency (Cunningham 1952). Although the

Black Mountain event expanded this independence, its governing principle remained duration. Cage set up a temporal frame within which he permitted independent choice of materials. *Process* was predetermined; *product* admitted chance interaction. At the same time, the happening set the stage for a further (radical) extension of Cage's "time compartment" procedures. Cowell had advocated equality between music and dance. Cage and Cunningham ultimately achieved that goal by separating them entirely. In their later works, the two arts coexist in the same time period with no dependent relationships.

After 1950, Cage's work became increasingly collaborative. In fact, it would not be an exaggeration to say that the majority of his pieces after the Black Mountain period involved some type of compositional "working together" – with technicians, performers, or other composers. But though Cage deliberately ceded authorial control by welcoming such input (often from many collaborators at once), he usually established a framework within which they operated. In the words of composer Gordon Mumma, who collaborated with Cage on numerous projects between 1963 and the early 1990s:

> [Normally] Cage set up the architecture but then allowed the internal decor to be subject to chance operations – [that is, there were] defined structures that permitted internal maneuverability. Cage was incredibly disciplined. He planned what he was going to do – or what was going to *be* done – the results of which were often beyond predictability. He dealt with details almost as obsessively as Schoenberg did.
>
> His works were like a field with a fence, in which one could move as one wished. But there was a line: you couldn't just fool around. You had to do what he said you could do and not what he didn't say you could do.
>
> (Mumma 2000)

It would be impossible, in the limited context of this chapter, to discuss all of Cage's later collaborative projects; they are simply too numerous. His approach to collaboration, however, and reasons for his attraction to it become readily apparent through examination of a few selected compositions.

In many cases, Cage's collaborator was another composer, or, more likely, several others: he often invited those he admired to join him in the creative process. The degree of interaction varied widely, from loose associations in which each participant wrote part of the work (as in *Marriage at the Eiffel Tower*) to compositions with interactive parts on the model of *Double Music*. The choice often reflected practical, rather than artistic, concerns: specifically, the amount of time and resources available.

In other cases, the collaborator was an engineer. Admittedly, the line between "facilitator" and "collaborator" becomes less distinct here. Yet some of Cage's technical consultants exerted so much control over the artistic output that they functioned as co-composers. After 1960 Cage became increasingly fascinated by the possibilities of technical-musical collaboration which were manifest in a number of gargantuan undertakings described below.

Compositional collaboration with performers raises even thornier questions. In some sense all musical performance involves collaboration with the composer. But contrasting renditions of a traditional score – while varying in details of tempo, dynamics, balance, and other matters – nevertheless result in recognizable variants of the same music. Many of Cage's compositions, in contrast, give performers such broad latitude that each performance creates a unique work. Even so, performers are never licensed to "just fool around," in Mumma's words. Guidelines are defined at the outset. As Cage says: "Permission granted. But not to do whatever you want" (Cage 1967, p. 28).

These three modes of collaboration – with composers, with engineers, and with performers – were not always independent. *Variations V* (1965) makes use of all three, requiring intricate cooperation among dancers, composers, filmmakers, and engineers (see Miller 2001). The première of this work (July 23, 1965), part of a two-and-a-half week French-American Festival at Lincoln Center, was blessed with a huge budget. Under the artistic directorship of Lukas Foss, the festival aimed "to tempt prominent artists to do things they don't ordinarily do" (Foss 1965). Cunningham and Cage gladly obliged.

"I hope John will forgive me in heaven, or wherever he is," says Mumma, "when I say that *Variations V* was the first Wagnerian thing he did. It was the beginning of an enormous operation of interaction between creative artists and engineers" (Mumma 2000). During the performance, the sound environment was activated directly by the dancers via two systems of electronic sensors on the stage (Mumma 1967). Engineers at Bell Labs, working under the Swedish research scientist Wilhelm (Billy) Klüver, built a set of small focused photocells, the light reaching them periodically interrupted by the intervention of the dancers' bodies (Klüver 2000). Meanwhile Robert Moog (developer of the Moog synthesizer) designed and built a set of twelve five-foot-high antennas – capacitance devices that responded to the proximity of the dancers in a manner similar to a Theremin.[11] Changes in the capacitance responses of the antennas and the light intensity on the photocells activated switching circuitry within a fifty-input mixer that controlled six loudspeakers spread around the auditorium.

The sounds feeding the mixer came from a series of tape recorders and radios operated by three composers: Fredric Lieberman, Malcolm Goldstein, and James Tenney. Lieberman was in charge of twelve recorders and twelve radios. Cage provided him with reel-to-reel tapes containing pre-recorded sounds, which Lieberman played, then rewound and replayed. But for the radio input Lieberman became a co-composer by devising his own score governing frequency changes (Lieberman 2000). Goldstein and Tenney recall operating tape recorders only. Goldstein notes that he "worked by improvisation in a non-patterned way, turning things on and off" (Goldstein 2000).

Cage and David Tudor operated the mixer, which had been designed and built the previous year by Max Mathews at Bell Laboratories for the New York Philharmonic's infamous performance of *Atlas Eclipticalis* (Mathews 2000). Each composer took charge of twenty-five inputs. Additional sounds came from contact microphones in objects handled by the dancers: the leaves of a potted plant, for instance, and a towel that served as a headdress. Though Lieberman, Tenney, and Goldstein created the sounds, they had little influence over the aural environment in the hall. They did not affect volume (Cage and Tudor's job at the mixer); nor could they control the movements of the dancers in relation to the photocell and capacitance sensors. In short, they generated a stream of diverse sounds, most of which were never heard.

Electronic visual stimuli completed the production. Distorted television images by Nam June Paik and film collages by Stan VanDerBeek (including images of the dancers themselves shot during rehearsal) were projected on a huge screen at the back of the stage. One reviewer complained that the films were so large, so surprising, and so amusing that they distracted one's attention from the dancers (Terry 1965).

After Black Mountain, Cunningham had routinely developed choreographies without music, rehearsing his dancers in silence, timing them with a stopwatch, and often hearing the music only at the first performance. But in *Variations V* such separation was impossible. Since the engineers were cluttering the stage with towers, wires, and photocells, planning was essential. "Merce and John had to share things that they didn't normally share," says Mumma, who substituted for Lieberman, Tenney, and Goldstein in later performances:

> Cage's music was going to litter the stage . . . Merce adjusted his choreography to take into account the antennas, which could cut and draw blood if you hit them. We supplied the musical materials, but how these materials were articulated and when they were heard, and where they were heard, resulted from the movement of the dancers, which, by means of the antennas and photocells, articulated the electronics. What came out in the music was completely surprising to everybody. (Mumma 2000)

The result was a musical and visual tour-de-force with dancers threading their way through the equipment. Cunningham used the antennas creatively in his choreography. He and Barbara Lloyd performed a delightful pas-de-deux around one of them; the dancers stretched a cord around the group of them; and at the end, he rode a bicycle through the whole set-up.

Variations V was an unlikely touring work, but Cunningham archivist David Vaughan has documented sixteen additional U.S. and Canadian performances from coast to coast (Washington, Oregon, British Columbia, Illinois, New York, Connecticut, Kentucky). And when the Norddeutscher Rundfunk television section invited Cage and Cunningham to film the work in Hamburg in the summer of 1966, they took the whole production to Europe. Mumma went along as composer and electronics guru and continued to work with the Cunningham Dance Company for the next eight years. On two separate European trips, they presented Variations V in St. Paul de Vence, Paris, London, Stockholm, and Lisbon. Despite the logistical nightmare of hauling the equipment around Europe, the touring version was only slightly less elaborate than that at Lincoln Center.

In the years following, Cage expanded his composer–engineer collaborations. Variations VII (1966) – presented on one of "9 Evenings: Theatre and Engineering" sponsored by Klüver's Experiments in Art and Technology (E.A.T.) – featured live sounds of New York, which Cage brought into the performance space in the Armory by arranging for ten telephone hookups, and dialing the SPCA, the New York Times press room, Luchow's German restaurant, the 14th Street ConEd power station, Cunningham's studio, and other locations. Additional sound sources included appliances (fan, blender, et al.), body sounds (heart, stomach, clothes, etc.), radio and television bands, Geiger counters, oscillators, and pulse generators. The photocells developed for Variations V transmitted these sounds to loudspeakers activated by four performers who walked around the equipment platform operating various devices (Klüver undated).[12]

Inspired by E.A.T.'s activities, Estonian-Canadian composer Udo Kasemets arranged a similar festival, "Sightsoundsystems," in Toronto (Kasemets 2000). The opening presentation, at the Ryerson Polytechnical Institute on March 5, 1968, was Reunion, a collaborative work in which sound was activated (choreographically, in a sense) by movements of game pieces on a chess board. Cage, Marcel Duchamp, and Duchamp's wife Alexina (Teeny) Duchamp played chess on a board hooked up with sixty-four photoresistors – one per square (Cross 1999). Sonic input included independent, unrelated compositions by Mumma, Tudor, David Behrman, and Lowell Cross (who also designed the circuitry). Since Cage had been taking periodic chess lessons from Duchamp in New York, the stage evoked his living room. Cross provided wine (but only one bottle since he knew Duchamp would defeat Cage quickly), and Duchamp sat in an easy chair. Cage squared off against Marcel Duchamp, who defeated him in twenty-five minutes, and then against Teeny, with whom he was more evenly matched. The second game was adjourned unfinished at 1 a.m., to be completed a few days later in New York.

As in *Variations V*, the four composers provided independent sound inputs but had no control over what reached the loudspeakers. Nor could the chess players (though they activated the sounds) influence what was heard. Cross, on the other hand, exerted considerable control in the way he designed the electronics. The thirty-two squares covered with chess pieces at the beginning were 'off' (they did not transmit a signal to the speakers) when they were covered. The remaining thirty-two squares operated the opposite way: they were off when *not* covered. The work thus began in silence, notably increasing in intensity as outside squares were uncovered and internal ones covered. As chess pieces were removed from the board, sound density gradually decreased again, but not to silence since the original thirty-two squares were never entirely covered again. Cross implies that he designed the system with this aural structure in mind: "With sixteen inputs (allowing four signals each from the four collaborating composers) and eight outputs (each directed to a loudspeaker system), the complexity of the sound environment enveloping the audience increased as the early part of the game progressed; it then diminished as fewer and fewer pieces were left on the board" (Cross 1999, p. 38). *Reunion* was Marcel Duchamp's last public performance; he died seven months later. Cage, however, performed the work on two subsequent occasions, at the Electric Circus in New York against an editor from the *Saturday Evening Post*, and at Mills College against Lowell Cross.

Cage apparently took delight in the interdisciplinary extravagance of *Variations V*, for four years later in 1969, when he was resident at the Center for Advanced Studies at the University of Illinois, he and Lejaren Hiller created *HPSCHD* – an even more grandiose multi-media event held in the university's cavernous Assembly Hall, a sports arena that seated 17,000 people. The production on May 16, 1969 involved 7 harpsichordists, 208 tapes, 84 slide projectors, 52 tape recorders, 52 speakers, 12 movie projectors, a 340-foot circular plastic screen, as well as amplifiers, additional plastic screens, slides, films, posters, and other materials (Husarik 1983). Hiller had completed his Ph.D. in chemistry at Princeton in 1947 while studying composition with Roger Sessions and Milton Babbitt. As a member of the Illinois chemistry faculty, he and Leonard Isaacson developed the Illiac computer with which Hiller generated the *Illiac Suite* for string quartet (1956–57). In 1958 he transferred to the Music Department. As his collaboration with Cage began, Hiller generated so many ideas for *HPSCHD* that Cage invited him to act as co-composer (Hiller 1970). Two additional collaborators – Calvin Sumsion and Ron Nameth – later joined them, to select the event's visual components. Forty other contributors were listed on the program.

HPSCHD began as an exploration of microtonal divisions of the octave. "The octave . . . has no more reason being divided into 5, 6, 7, 8, or 9 equal intervals than it has to be divided into 34, 43, or 56 parts . . ." reflected Cage in 1980. "It's just a question of establishing limits" (Husarik 1983, p. 2). He and Hiller produced fifty-one twenty-minute tapes of harpsichord sounds using computer-generated scales that ranged from five to fifty-six equal-tempered divisions per octave. They also permitted limited sharping or flatting of each pitch, resulting in a potential for 885,000 pitches (Husarik 1983, p. 10). Pitch choices, inflections, and time values for the taped sounds were determined by *I Ching* predictions, which Hiller's computer generated in such profusion that Cage obtained source material for hundreds of not-yet-envisioned compositions. (Max Mathews had generated similar *I Ching* data for Cage at Bell Labs several years previously.)[13]

The seven harpsichordists performed compositions that Cage and Hiller derived from Mozart's *Musikalisches Würfelspiel*, a dice game enabling amateurs to compose minuets in binary form (||: A :||: B :||) using chance procedures. Mozart wrote 176 measures that can be assembled in various configurations. Players create a sixteen-measure dance (eight in section A, eight more in section B) by tossing dice and choosing the appropriate measure from an accompanying table. Using Mozart's game, Cage and Hiller produced a one-minute-long, sixty-four-measure piece, comprising eight sections of eight measures (AABBaabb), a form reminiscent of Cage's early micro-macro organization. The two composers then created nineteen other similar minuets to form a twenty-minute composition. This piece was played by harpsichord soloist II. Solo parts III and IV were generated by the same procedure, but measures from Mozart's piano sonatas were substituted for the dice-game measures. In solo III right- and left-hand materials were aligned as in the original works; in solo IV they were decoupled. Continuing their historical survey for soloists V and VI, Cage and Hiller substituted measures from later keyboard works: Beethoven's *Appassionata Sonata*, Chopin's Prelude in d minor, *Reconaissance* from Schumann's *Carnaval*, Gottschalk's *The Banjo*, Busoni's Sonatina No. 2, Cage's *Winter Music*, and Hiller's Fifth Sonata. Harpsichordist VII plays any Mozart composition or any work the other soloists are playing. Harpsichordist I plays one of the tape parts, transcribed for a twelve-note scale, the only octave division not represented by one of the tapes.[14]

Calvin Sumsion, a graduate student at the time, selected technographic photographs from encyclopedias using Hiller's *I Ching* data; these images were projected onto semi-transparent screens. He also gathered 6,800 astronomical slides from NASA, the Mount Wilson Observatory, and other sources. Cage and associates handpainted an additional 1,600, totaling 8,400. Meanwhile Nameth previewed 400 films, choosing a group of scientific reels. Audience members wandered through the huge space during the production, many lying on the floor to observe the visual display. Their random conversation became "an extension of the sound, the random nature of their movements . . . an extension of the visuals" (Husarik 1983, p. 18).

Sometimes, as in *HPSCHD*, Cage built an architecture from diverse pre-existing materials. At other times, the architecture came first, to be completed by indeterminately selected materials. *Assemblage* (1968) exemplifies the former process, *Landrover* (1972) the latter. Both works involved collaboration among Cage, Mumma, and Tudor. For *Assemblage* (a film made by the Cunningham Dance Company in San Francisco's Ghirardelli Square), ample time, financial support, and space made intensive collaboration viable. KQED television provided a spacious factory loft equipped with tape recorders, allowing the composers to interact in a tight collaboration during a three-week residency. (Cunningham, meanwhile, worked independently.) "We knew there would be about fifty-eight minutes," recalls Mumma, "and John asked, 'What would you be interested in doing?' I said, 'I'm thinking about recording the sounds of San Francisco" (Mumma 2000). Tudor decided to use insect sounds, amplified and modified. Cage (in a precursor to *Roaratorio*, 1983) collected sounds from around the world. "John would go off to the library to get sounds like thunderstorms from Brazil. I was out on the trolleys and ferry boats. We brought all this material together and listened to what the others were doing. Then we established and agreed on a structural architecture for a big collective work" (Mumma 2000).

Landrover was quite another story. A few days before the première, Cunningham asked Cage for music. In the style of *Marriage at the Eiffel Tower*, Cage suggested that the total time be divided in thirds (hence the title *52/3*), each composer taking responsibility for one module. The dance, in contrast, had four sections (Vaughan 1997, p. 182). For different performances, the composer-team shuffled the order of the modules. Mumma chose his material in relation to what preceded him. "If David was raising hell and blowing the roof off, I might do something very different. If he was very quiet, I might do something a little more busy" (Mumma 2000). Cage, on the other hand, did not vary his part. He sat at the piano playing fragments of pre-tonal keyboard music, isolated by silence. He chose these selections by disciplined chance procedures – sometimes before, sometimes during the performance.

Compositional collaborations with performers span a similar gamut. At times Cage provides materials, licensing performers to build their own architecture; at other times, he predetermines the time scheme, leaving sound components to the player's choice. In some works (such as those in

Example 9.4 John Cage, *Music for...* (1984), flute part, beginning

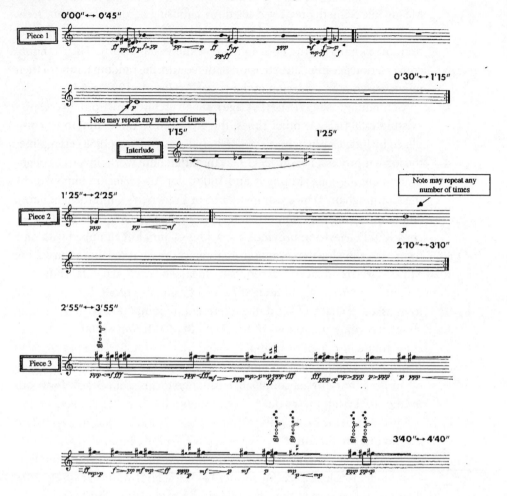

which a score is created by overlaying transparencies with lines, shapes, and dots), he predetermined only process. In all of these works, however, the governing factor is duration.

Cage never discarded his concept of time brackets, but in later years he used them in new ways. *Music for...* (1984), for instance, contains determinate sonic materials but performers are allowed considerable latitude regarding their temporal arrangement. Each part contains two types of sections (Example 9.4). "Pieces," two lines in length, are presented in proportional notation (space=time), or in single notes that may be repeated any number of times. Interludes contain noteheads without dynamics or durations. Time brackets specify compartments in which sound materials are executed, but performers may begin or end any time within them (see Example 9.4).

Performance parts are available for all orchestral instruments and voice, thus accommodating available resources – from solo to chamber orchestra. Players complete the work's title by supplying the number of performers (e.g., *Music for Four*). They also determine the composition's length. Although the entire work lasts thirty minutes, Cage invites players to create shorter versions. In such cases, participants may begin anywhere as long as they select an uninterrupted sequence of pieces and interludes. In a ten-minute version, for instance, the flutist might start with piece 3, whose first time bracket would become 0:00–1:00.

Performers operate as Cage and Harrison did in *Double Music*, preparing their parts without consultation. Thus each rendition of *Music for . . .* is unique, the players building a "product" from specified materials within Cage's temporal architecture. By allowing them to omit parts of the piece and determine instrumentation, length, and placement of materials, Cage removed his intentionality from the resulting composition. But by specifying that they construct their parts independently, he also removed theirs. The resulting work is a collaboration between Cage (who supplied materials and process) and the performers (who choose details of execution); but as in *Double Music*, the Black Mountain happening, *Variations V*, and *Reunion*, the intersection of these intentions is determined by factors out of the control of any individual contributor.

The social aspects of collaboration – manifest as early as the Los Angeles percussion works – pleased Cage. He quite deliberately dismantled barriers between professionals and amateurs, musicians and non-musicians. Doris Dennison, an instructor of eurythmics and member of Cage's Seattle percussion group, recalls him asking during one of their long, tiring rehearsals, "Do you delight in this?" (Dennison 1995).

But one of the main attractions of the collaborative process was the suppression of individual intentionality through the interaction of multiple egos. As early as 1948 Cage reflected on *Double Music*: "The peculiarities of a single personality disappear almost entirely and there comes into perception through the music a natural friendliness, which has the aspect of a festival" (Cage 1948a, p. 38). He so enjoyed this early experience that he anticipated writing a *Triple Music* with Harrison and Merton Brown, combining his "structural rhythm" with the dissonant contrapuntal style they were exploring in that period (Cage 1948a, p. 44).

Cage's model of un-connectedness – working together while severing linkages – ultimately allowed everything to be connected. He advocated "a flexible relationship . . . ; interpenetration . . . through non-obstruction . . ."; or, in more direct language, "a lot of people working together without getting in each other's way" (Cage 1981, pp. 52, 180). While he took delight in the free flow of ideas, and established guidelines within which the collaboration took place, the final work reflected the will of no single participant. "Buckminster Fuller ... describes the world to us as an ensemble of spheres between which there is a void, a necessary space. We have a tendency to forget that space. We leap across it to establish our relationships and connections," Cage reflected in 1976. "I think [that things] interpenetrate more richly and with more complexity when I myself do not establish any connection. That is when they meet and form the number one ... And since each one is itself, there is a plurality in the number one" (Cage 1981, pp. 93 and 78).

10 Cage and Tudor

JOHN HOLZAEPFEL

"The world is immense through him, has no limits, has only inviting horizons"
(Cage on Tudor, Quoted in Duckworth 1989, p. 27)

John Cage often noted that all of the music he composed between 1951 and the end of the 1960s was written with one person in mind, the pianist and composer David Tudor (1926–96). Unique among Cage's many collaborators, Tudor was a driving force, in ways both concrete and intangible, in the development of Cage's music during its most revolutionary phase, a phase that began soon after Tudor appeared at a pivotal moment in Cage's career.

Cage and Tudor first met at the end of 1949, when the composer was looking for a pianist to make a rehearsal recording for Merce Cunningham. As Cunningham's accompanist, Cage would normally have taken on this task himself. But the piano reduction of Ben Weber's *Ballet*, Op. 26, subtitled "The Pool of Darkness," lay beyond his abilities at the keyboard, so he looked for help. His search took him to the dance studio of his friend and colleague Jean Erdman, who introduced him to her accompanist, the twenty-four-year-old David Tudor. Cage had recently heard Tudor and Frances Magnes perform Stefan Wolpe's Sonata for Violin and Piano, and he knew that the pianist was capable of negotiating music far more difficult than Weber's *Ballet*. Subsequently, he appeared at the door of Tudor's apartment on the lower east side of Manhattan with his request. Tudor consented and, Cage later recalled, played the score with such beauty that Cage was surprised to learn that Tudor disliked it intensely. This brief episode, otherwise no more than a footnote, was the prologue to one of the most astonishing composer–performer relationships in the history of music.

More than eight months went by before Cage and Tudor had occasion to work together again. The circumstances were similar; Cage was again in need of a pianist to play a new work. This time, it was a work of a different magnitude altogether, the Second Piano Sonata of Pierre Boulez. Boulez had completed the sonata in 1948 and had played excerpts from it for Cage during the composer's visit to Paris in 1949, but the work had yet to be heard in public. Soon after his return to New York in the fall, Cage asked his friend William Masselos to give the première, and subsequently reported to Boulez, "William Masselos is going to play your sonata (2nd piano) but he has asked for a year to work on it. He is very busy" (Nattiez 1993, p. 48).

Cage went ahead with plans for the performance, scheduled for November 19 as part of the first of the League of Composers' three concerts devoted to "First Performances and Revivals." Sometime around the end of the summer, he went to Masselos for a progress report and learned that there had been no progress at all; Masselos had been taken ill, but he also confessed that he had been unable to make any headway into the sonata. When Cage told Morton Feldman of this development, the younger composer replied that the only pianist capable of performing Boulez's sonata was his friend David Tudor. Moreover, Feldman said, Tudor had borrowed his copy of the score in the spring and had been studying it on his own. This news must have come as a relief, no less to Masselos than to Cage, who quickly arranged an amicable exchange of responsibility for the performance. With three months remaining before the performance, now rescheduled for the second League of Composers concert, on December 17, Tudor set to work on the sonata in earnest.

But as the performance drew near, Tudor found himself in an alarming predicament. He could play everything in Boulez's sonata but the sonata itself: no matter where he began to play, within a few measures the music fell apart. For Tudor, this was an unprecedented dilemma:

> I'd always been well known for my ability to handle complex scores – it could be black as sin and I could still play it – but this time I found a sort of constant breakdown in the continuity . . . I became vitally concerned that it would be full of lapses and holes . . .   (Tudor 1972, p. 24)

As he looked for the cause of his difficulty, Tudor noticed something intriguing about the sonata:

> Boulez had written no counterpoints, no second voices, and you couldn't subordinate any voices at all, as there was nothing leading, nothing on which the music centered itself.   (Tudor 1972, p. 24)

Hoping to find help in Boulez's writings, Tudor made his way through two untranslated essays Cage had also brought back from Paris. To his dismay – the concert was now less than a month away – they were of no help at all, with a single exception. At the end of the 1948 "Proposal," an essay otherwise concerned with the need to establish a rhythmic basis for twelve-tone music, Boulez had made an oblique reference to the radical French dramaturge Antonin Artaud:

> I think that music should be collective hysteria and magic, violently modern – along the lines of Antonin Artaud and not in the sense of a simple ethnographic reconstruction in the image of civilizations more or less remote from us.   (Boulez 1948, p. 54)

Tudor quickly procured a copy of Artaud's best-known work, *Le théâtre et son double*. And in this collection of polemical essays, letters, and manifestos, Tudor found the key. "It has to do with violence," he observed many years later, "and it's quite different from Expressionism; it isn't that at all. It's aesthetic violence, and purposeful" (Tudor 1992).

> All of a sudden I saw that there was a different way of looking at musical continuity, having to do with what Artaud called the affective athleticism. It has to do with the disciplines that an actor goes through. It was a real breakthrough for me, because my musical consciousness in the meantime had changed completely . . . I had to put my mind in a state of non-continuity – not remembering – so that each moment is alive.
>
> (Tudor 1982)

Artaud had called for a new kind of theater requiring disciplined but un-reflective physical immediacy that would be grounded not in the author's script, in a text, but in the actor's body and the breath that supports it. True theater, Artaud believed with unflinching passion, lived not in the written word but in, and only in, its materialization in performance; the rest was just literature.

But immediacy was no longer possible when modern theater had lost the sense of "laughter's power of physical and anarchic dissociation," had "broken away from the spirit of profound anarchy which is at the root of all poetry." A renewal of theater demanded "true action, but without practical consequences" (Artaud 1958, pp. 42, 115).

"Anarchic dissociation" and "profound anarchy" were ideas that spoke directly to Cage when Tudor shared his discovery of Artaud during the frequent meetings between Cage, Tudor, and Feldman in the fall of 1950 and early 1951. And "true action, but without practical consequences" is what Cage would call purposeful purposelessness.[1] Even Artaud's concept of the spoken word and language found affinity with Cage's treatment of sound itself. Words for Artaud were no longer primarily symbols but objects; indeed, unique objects which "once spoken are dead and function only at the moment they are uttered" (Artaud 1958, p. 75).

Artaud claimed that theater was the only medium in which his revolution of aesthetics and performance could take place. But when David Tudor transformed his mind into "a state of non-continuity – not remembering," he became exactly the musical performer Cage was looking for – exactly the performer Cage needed, one can say, if the composer was to hear his new and radical ideas come to life. For by substituting "pianist" for "actor" and "musical performance" for "theater," we can grasp how Tudor applied his reading of Artaud to his performances of the music of the post-war avant-garde and to the music of John Cage in particular. The purpose of what Tudor called purposeful aesthetic violence was to disrupt traditional musical continuity – musical syntaxes, in other words – so that the life of the music is in each moment rather than in the connections between them. "I recall this as a definite breaking point," Tudor later said, "as the moment I became aware that another kind of musical continuity was possible, and from then on I began to see all other music in those terms" (Tudor 1982). The aftermath, Tudor noted, was "a change in the perception of music" (Harris 1987, p. 182) that took place in the years after 1950.

For Cage, this change began when he decided to compose music through the systematic use of chance operations. He first used chance techniques in late January 1951 to compose the third movement of the Concerto for Prepared Piano and Orchestra (see Chapter 11). After completing the concerto the following month, Cage turned to a project that would occupy him for the remainder of the year. It would be a full-length work in which he could apply chance techniques at every level of the compositional process. That it would be called *Music of Changes* was a tribute to the source of its compositional technique. That it would be for piano was a matter of necessity, if Cage wanted to hear it performed at all. That it would represent a quantum leap in the performance difficulties of Cage's music was because Cage was now composing for David Tudor.

Tudor's stupendous gifts as a pianist would have been a blessing to any composer of difficult new music. For Cage they were a godsend as he embarked on a journey of musical exploration that would for at least a decade place him beyond the pale even of his previous colleagues ("even that music estranges my former friends," he wrote to Tudor in the summer of 1951, after an informal performance of his delicate *Six Melodies for Violin and Keyboard* of 1950, "what will they feel next year?" [Cage 1951a]). By his own frequent admission, he could not have made the journey without David Tudor. "One assumed he could do everything," Cage later said of the pianist. "In fact, hearing him perform was proof" (Cage 1989a). On that assumption Cage proceeded to compose, over the course of the next two decades, a series of works whose continual experimentation increased in direct proportion to Tudor's involvement in them.

As he came to know the young pianist in the fall of 1950, Cage found, as he told Boulez in a letter written on the day after Tudor's performance of the Second Piano Sonata, "an extraordinary person" (Nattiez 1993, p. 77). Tudor's secretive, often mysterious personality and his taciturn demeanor stood in marked contrast to Cage's natural gregariousness. "He seemed to me to be a mystery," Cage later said, "to *wish* to be a mystery, which shouldn't be looked at" (Cage 1989a). But in the self-contained spiritual nature of Tudor's character – an aspect that struck everyone who knew him – the composer found an empathetic soul. Tudor shared, or quickly came to share, Cage's belief in the spiritual properties of sounds independent of any expressive character a composer might attempt to place upon them by fashioning musical relationships. This belief carried over into Tudor's profound sense of responsibility as a performer. He wrote to a friend:

> For me music exists as a spiritual reality which will continue to exist after every composer and every page of notes and dynamics are destroyed, and every performer must struggle to make the positive facts of this reality audible to a listener. Otherwise, what excuse has the poor pianist for existing? (Tudor undated)

At the same time, Tudor's firm faith in the sacred nature of music – "music must be a direct spiritual experience!!" he insisted (Tudor undated) – was grounded (in William Blake's arresting phrase) in a love for "the holiness of the minute particular." Upon anything that attracted his interest – music, cooking, the labyrinths of electronic circuitry, even window-shopping – Tudor bestowed an unhurried, sustained, and awesomely comprehensive attention. When Cage sent him a list of errata in the first part of *Music of Changes*, Tudor replied that he had already discovered them, then presented the composer with a long list of questions about additional ambiguities he had found in Cage's score. After responding to these queries, Cage confessed that the notation of *Music of Changes* "is inadequate since it does not refer to relations (but only seems to) . . . " (Cage 1951b). Both Cage and Tudor recognized that this was the result of using conventional notational signs within a new notational framework that equated space on the page with musical time. The composer's simple advice for surmounting the obstacles he had placed before the performer reflected his trust in Tudor's skill and imagination: "let it be lively," he told the pianist (Cage 1951b).

For his part, Tudor's preparation of *Music of Changes* led to more than eighty pages of charts, lists, computations, and timings. To solve the puzzling notational problems of Cage's score, he enlisted the aid of the mathematician Hans Rademacher, who devised two formulas for calculating the durations of each of the work's structural units, one formula for those units in which the tempo remains constant, another for those in which it is internally modified by an *accelerando* or *ritardando*. Tudor then copied the resultant timings into his copy of the score, and in performance read the notation proportionally by referring to a stopwatch placed on the music rack.

His performances of *Music of Changes* led Tudor to two decisive insights about musical time and space in the work. "I was in a different musical atmosphere," he would recall. "I was *watching* time rather than *experiencing* it. That difference is basic" (Tudor 1972, p. 24). And after performing the first part of the work on a recital that also included Boulez's Second Piano Sonata, he wrote Cage, "There is an important difference between it and Boulez: in Boulez the space seems to be in front of one, in one's line of aural vision, as it were; in your piece space is *around* one, that is, present in a new dimension" (Tudor 1951).

Completed on December 13, 1951, and performed by Tudor on the auspicious date of New Year's Day 1952, *Music of Changes* inaugurated what the artist and psychologist Irwin Kremen has called "a working partnership of exquisite accomplishment" (Kremen 2000). One such accomplishment has come to stand for Cage's entire aesthetic. In the latter part of August, Cage returned to New York from Black Mountain College, where he had viewed Robert Rauschenberg's series of all-white paintings. If it was the implications of Rauschenberg's radical act – that a canvas need include neither image nor even, as the abstract expressionists had hoped, gesture – that emboldened Cage to begin composing the piece, it was Tudor's interest in performing it that persuaded him to finish it. When the composer expressed doubts about presenting, as a serious work of music, a chance-generated sum of silences, the pianist replied that he hoped Cage would complete the composition in time for a recital he was planning to give in Woodstock, NY, at the end of the month.

When he received the score of *4′33″* a few days later, Tudor gave careful consideration to its place in the program, experimenting with the program order several times before placing the new work (the only première on the program) in the penultimate position. To delineate the three movements of the work, either Cage or Tudor (accounts, including the latter's own, vary on this point) thought of raising and lowering the keyboard lid to signal the three time-lengths of 30″, 2′23″, and 1′40″. Whether this gesture clarified the structure of *4′33″* to the audience who heard its first performance is doubtful. The printed program for the recital at Maverick Concert Hall on August 29, 1952, shows *4′33″* consisting of "Four Pieces." Whether this was simply a printer's error (this is not as obvious as some commentators have assumed), it was an additional source of confusion for listeners already baffled by the music itself.

Tudor always insisted that Cage composed *4′33″* on staff paper in a score now lost. He said that the composer laid out the three movements in proportional notation on empty staves whose silence Tudor read by a stopwatch, just as he had read the sounds (and silences) of *Music of Changes*, the parent work of *4′33″*. For performances he gave of the work many years later, Tudor made two reconstructions of Cage's score that support his claim; moreover, they differ not only from the published editions of *4′33″* but from each other as well. In the first reconstruction, he equated one-half inch to M.M. = 60, or one second, and partitioned the single continuous staff running through the three movements into measures of seven and one-half inches long; one measure equals fifteen seconds, and proportionally shorter measures represent the leftover time-space in the second and third movements. In the second reconstruction, Tudor used a grand staff, complete with treble and bass clefs and a time signature of $^4_4$. And tellingly, each measure is now ten centimeters long, and the tempo marking shows that a quarter note equals both two and one-half centimeters and M.M. = 60. Since this is the same system of measurement Cage used in notating *Music of Changes*, it seems that if Tudor's recollection of an earlier version of *4′33″* was correct, the later reconstruction accurately reproduces Cage's lost score. The question is not only important to establishing the genesis of Cage's most challenging artistic statement. It also points to the question of notation as Cage used it in the 1950s and early 1960s – the period of his greatest dependence on the participation of David Tudor.

In notating his early chance music, Cage employed two basic techniques. The earliest was the space-time method used in *Music of Changes*, *4′33″*, and the "time-length" pieces such as *34′46.776″ for a Pianist* of 1954. In the summer of 1952, Cage devised a quicker means of generating a chance composition by placing the notes on the page either with random templates, as in the *Music for Carillon No. 1*, or where he found tiny pocks and bumps in the paper he used to write the work, as in the *Music for Piano* series of 1952–56.

Yet both methods resulted in scores that are no less (and no more) fixed in their notation than are Cage's pre-1951 works. With a few variations, the composer continued to use the two techniques through the spring of 1956, when he composed the last of the *Music for Piano* pieces. Then, Cage's productivity suddenly dropped off. His works list for the remainder of that year is empty.

"His interest in puzzles invited the whole thing of indeterminacy. And so what you had to do was to make a situation that would interest *him*. That was the role he played."

(Cage 1989A)

Cage dated the score of his next composition "January 1957," but since he and Tudor gave the first performance of *Winter Music* on January 12, he probably began working on this large and ambitious work before the beginning of the year. Whatever the date of its genesis, *Winter Music* both looks back to the compositional and notational techniques Cage had developed in the early 1950s and marks the path he would explore for the next decade or more: it is the first work in which he extended indeterminacy from the composition of his music to its performance. Consequently, it also marks a new phase in David Tudor's approach to preparing his performances of Cage's scores.

In the early 1950s, Tudor had no reservations about playing Cage's music from the composer's idiosyncratic but functional notation. This was no more than a reflection of Tudor's general philosophy of performance. Not only did he wish to read all music from its composer's notation, he also wanted his scores to be, as he put it, "clean as a whistle" (Tudor 1992). Indeed, one finds in his library of music, both old and new, remarkably few annotations, usually nothing more than a few timings (especially for dance pieces); fingerings are next to non-existent. He needed, he said, unobstructed access to the printed page; anything other than what the composer had placed there was a distraction. As a pianist, Tudor read music as if its life depended on it, as if the art of performance was in reviving what notation held in temporary suspension.

But as other composers joined Cage in giving increasing freedom to performers of their music, Tudor found himself faced at times with an overabundance of choice to make in the reality that is musical performance. No friend to improvisation, he undertook instead a series of rigorous preparatory steps, including measurements, computations, conversion tables – whatever he found useful to the task – whose results he translated into a more or less conventional notation for his own use in performance. He began writing these realizations in 1954 for his performances of Morton Feldman's *Intersection 3* and Earle Brown's *Four Systems*. Three years later, he applied the practice again.

Winter Music is a set of twenty pages of notations based on the same method Cage had used to write the *Music for Piano* series: wherever he found an imperfection in the paper, he placed a solid note head, then overlaid the results with a staff that turned the note heads into notes. So far, this was nothing new. But in *Music for Piano* he had fixed the notes with clefs on two staves; now Cage used chance to "float" the clef signs in front of a single staff, thereby rendering the pitch content of *Winter Music* indeterminate. To aid the performer in deciding which notes to assign to which clef, he provided a pair of chance-determined numbers. The first number applies to the higher of the two clef signs, the second to the lower. For example, the first page of *Winter Music* includes a ten-note chord or "aggregate," to use Cage's term, preceded by a bass clef above a treble clef and the numbers 1 and 9 instructing the pianist to read one note in the bass clef and the remaining nine notes in the treble.

Reading from Cage's notation can make for rough going in performance (see Example 10.1). Nor are the composer's performance instructions entirely helpful:

Example 10.1 John Cage, *Winter Music* (1957), page 4

The 20 pages may be used in whole or part by a pianist or shared by 2 to
20 to provide a program of an agreed upon length. The notation, in space,
5 systems left to right on the page, may be freely interpreted as to time. An
aggregate must be played as a single ictus. Where this is impossible, the
unplayable notes shall be taken as harmonics prepared in advance.
Harmonics may also be produced where they are not so required.
Resonances, both of aggregates and individual notes of them, may be free
in length. Overlappings, interpenetrations, are also free. The single staff is
provided with two clef signs. Where these differ, ambiguity obtains in the
proportion indicated by the 2 numbers notated above the aggregate, the
first of these applying to the clef above the staff. Dynamics are free. An
inked-in rectangle above a pair of notes indicates a chromatic tone-cluster.
The fragmentation of staves arose simply from an absence of events.

For their duo performances of *Winter Music,* Cage himself entered readings of his own notations (readings based, of course, on his performance
instructions) alongside them in his copy of the score. Tudor, on the other
hand, took more elaborate measures.

Working from a pre-publication copy in which Cage had not yet numbered the twenty pages of the score, he assigned the pages letters from A
through T. Because these letters do not always correspond to Cage's later

pagination of the score, I will refer to a given page both by Tudor's letter-name and its number in the published edition (Peters Edition 6705 [1961]). Page A (3), for example, means Tudor's A/Peters page 3; B (4) refers to Tudor's page B/Peters page 4, and so on.

Tudor then sorted out a pitch content for his realization by compiling an index of his readings of all of Cage's notations. If a notation was sufficiently straightforward, he simply transcribed it, at times clarifying it enharmonically and frequently dispensing with Cage's numerous ledger lines. These lines show the correspondence between the notations and the paper imperfections, which are their source, but in performance they are an obstruction to reading. Tudor replaced the lines with *8va* signs and two modified clefs, a treble clef with an arrow pointing up to show *8va sopra*, and a bass clef with a downward arrow for *8va bassa* (see Example 10.2). The index identifies each group of readings by the page and system in which the notations appear. Individual note heads represent single notes and aggregates; two note heads connected by a stem signify a chromatic key-cluster. In the first entry for page A (3), the circle number 1 refers to the first system on that page of Cage's score, the ten-note aggregate to which I have referred above. In all this, Tudor was proceeding according to Cage's performance instructions. But his pitch index also shows that rather than simply reading one note in one clef and then assigning the remaining nine notes to the other clef by default, Tudor wrote out complete readings in both clefs, then added the appropriate numeral to go with each. This extra step allowed him to consider the pitch content of both readings before selecting those ingredients, so to speak, which would go into his realization.

Next, Tudor needed to determine the timing, or attack point, of each notation in *Winter Music*. Observing that all of Cage's notations fall within a horizontal span of sixteen inches, he used a scale of inches in tenths to measure the distance of each note head or aggregate from the beginning of the page in a module of sixteen, or mod. 16. The first aggregate on page A (3), for example, appears in system two and is 1.05 inches from the beginning of mod. 16. The second aggregate appears in system four at 13.6 inches. Tudor began entering the measurements in his pitch index but stopped after the first system of page B (4) and instead drew up a list of complete measurements for all twenty pages of Cage's score. As in his pitch index, he arranged the measurements by page, system, and order of occurrence (see Example 10.3).

Tudor was now ready to write out his realization. If a page of *Winter Music* contained numerous notations, he transcribed his readings to gatherings of staff paper cut and folded into small bifolios. Each gathering consists of five bifolios, one for each system on a page of Cage's score. On each half of a bifolio, Tudor marked a horizontal span of eight inches, so that a complete

Example 10.2 David Tudor, realization of *Winter Music*: first page of pitch index

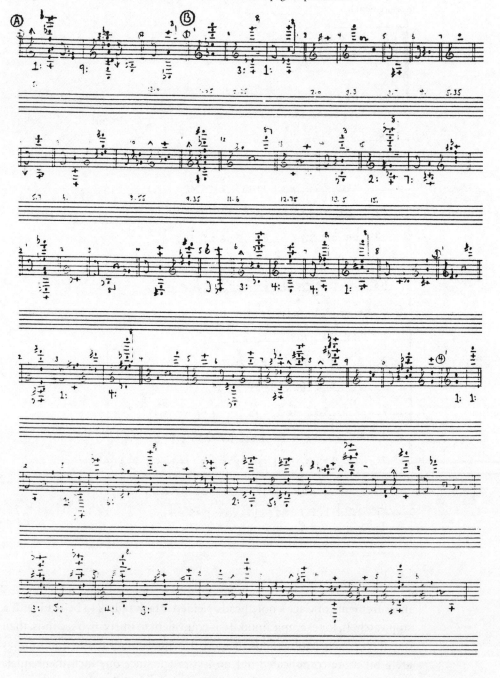

bifolio is equivalent to sixteen inches, corresponding to the mod. 16 of his measurements. Then he entered the readings from his pitch index, adding short strokes at the top of the page to ensure each reading's proper position in his score. In this way, the module of 16 inches became a time line, and the

Example 10.3 David Tudor, realization of *Winter Music*: first page of measurement list

measurements of Cage's note heads yielded attack points to be read with a stopwatch. If, for example, mod. 16 is equivalent to thirty-two seconds, then one inch equals two seconds. If mod. 16 equals one minute, the timings are a bit more complicated but no less exact, since one inch then equals one-sixteenth of sixty seconds, or 3.75 seconds[2] (see Example 10.4).

In those cases where Tudor combined elements of two readings of a single notation, we can identify their sources by referring to Tudor's pitch index. Cage's second notation in system one of page B (4), for example, consists of four note heads, a treble and a bass clef, and the numbers 3 and 1; i.e., the performer is to read three notes in the treble clef and one in the

Example 10.4 David Tudor, realization of *Winter Music*, page B(4), first bifolio

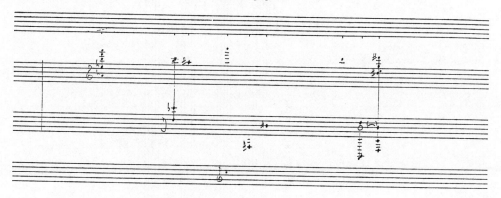

Example 10.5 David Tudor, realization of *Winter Music*, page B(4): reading of system 1, notation 2 in pitch index (1) and realization in performance score (2)

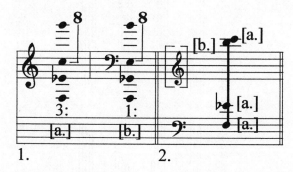

bass. In his pitch index, Tudor wrote this aggregate in both clefs, renotating them for ease of reading, then entered the appropriate numbers below each. The realization shows that he selected the notes f, eb′, and c‴ from his treble-clef reading and the remaining note, b″, from his reading in the bass clef (see Example 10.5).

This step reflects Tudor's understanding of Cage's stipulation that "[o]verlappings, interpenetrations, are . . . free", by which the composer probably meant that sustained sonorities may mingle with new ones, since he also wrote, "[r]esonances . . . may be free in length." But Tudor also extended the meaning of "interpenetration" by combin2ing several readings of two or more pages of Cage's score into composite realizations. Probably because they contain comparatively few notations, he combined the five pages A (3), L (13), O (1), R (19), and T (18) in this way. The first bifolio of the gathering marked "ALORT" contains Tudor's readings of the first systems in which notations appear on each of these pages. Combined readings of the second systems are combined in bifolio 2, of the third systems in bifolio 3, and so on (see Example 10.6).

Example 10.6 David Tudor, realization of *Winter Music*: composite realization of systems 2, pages A (3), L (13), O (1), R (19), and T (18), first bifolio

In two of his composite realizations, those of pages J (11) and Q (16) and of pages E (7), F (6), and I (9), Tudor used a somewhat different notation, replacing his homemade bifolios with small music manuscript books whose pages are overlaid with coordinate graph squares, or *Hilfslinien*, as the German manufacturer called them. Each square is roughly one-half centimeter long, and there are thirty-four squares on a page. On each page, Tudor bracketed thirty-two of these squares, leaving one square empty at either end of the resulting frame. This gave him thirty squares in which to place his notations. To make a time frame corresponding to his measurements of Cage's score, he grouped the squares in units of five, with sixteen units representing one of Cage's systems in mod. 16.

The new format offered several advantages. The larger-sized paper contained six staves instead of two, and Tudor used four of these to correspond to his four clef signs. (He did not enter these clefs in his composite realizations, but they are easily inferable from his pitch index.) Bound notebooks meant that he could write out a realization of all five systems continuously rather than in individual bifolios. No longer needing small strokes to mark attack points, he divided the graph squares into four parts and entered his readings at their proper positions within the squares. It is possible that Tudor equated a graph square with a unit of time, perhaps one second, in which case he could read the four-part division of the squares even without relying on proportional notation, since a quarter of a second is equivalent to a conventional sixteenth note at the tempo M.M. = 60. This is admittedly speculation, but the procedure would be consistent with Tudor's methods in other realizations. What is certain is that he was less interested in the space measured by the slightly irregular graph squares, or even in any temporal-spatial relationship they might suggest visually, than in the alignment provided by their coordinates.

In Example 10.7, from Tudor's composite realization of pages J (11) and Q (13), I have identified the source of each reading and added the appropriate clef signs from Tudor's pitch index.

*

"David Tudor's qualities inspired many composers," Cage once wrote, "to introduce freedoms for the performer into their compositional means – indeterminate music which removes the conventional difference between composer and performer" (Cage undated). Yet during his years as a pianist, Tudor never considered himself a composer, or even a co-composer, of the music he played. And his realizations of even the most abstruse notations – the puzzles of which Cage spoke and which Tudor relished – are not compositions in themselves. In fact, they are not very different, in one

Example 10.7 David Tudor, realization of *Winter Music*: beginning of composite realization of pages J (11) and Q (13), first systems

»Sūnova« „Ideal" mit Hilfslinien - 6 zeilig, quer

sense at least, from written realizations of figured bass or of the diminutions of Baroque preludes; that is, they are practical solutions in the root sense, written with the aim of making a composer's notation practicable in performance.

They are also grounded in a concept of the relation of notation to performance that stems from the aesthetics of Ferruccio Busoni, whose example as a pianist and as an artist Tudor took as a model during his formative years. "There is a passage in Busoni," he told an interviewer in 1972, "which speaks of notation as an evil separating musicians from music, and I feel everyone should know this is true" (Tudor 1972, p. 24). Tudor shared Busoni's skepticism about the capacity of notation to convey what the earlier pianist had called, in the title of his most famous essay, the essence of music. And he despised the kind of literalism that came to dominate music-making, especially in the United States, after the Second World War, expressing on one occasion his "hatred of those academics whose music consists of accurately played notes, phrases, dynamics, etc., 'the logical relations between every note' – that kind of player" (Tudor undated).

Tudor's realizations are nothing if not accurate – as well as systematic, methodical, and meticulous, terms eloquent of Tudor himself. And they are more than a source of solutions to Cage's sometimes perplexing notations and his often unclear instructions for reading them. They are models, to borrow a phrase from George Steiner, "of nuance and scruple." They show, in example after example, how Tudor found in indeterminate music a means by which he could expand his own "sound imagination" by creating an equilibrium between responsibility and freedom, between the exigencies his close readings produced from a composer's text and the possibilities open to a virtuoso performer who could exercise a virtuoso imagination.

11 Cage and high modernism

DAVID W. BERNSTEIN

During a lively correspondence with John Cage that took place around 1950, Pierre Boulez recognized parallels between his own development of integral serialism and the systematic procedures Cage used in the *Music of Changes* (1951). Boulez noted that Cage "has been working on setting up structural relations between different components of sound, and for this he uses tables which organize each component into parallel but autonomous distributions. The tendency of these experiments by John Cage is too close to my own for me to fail to mention them" (Boulez 1952a, p. 135). At that time, with the composition of *Livre pour quatuor* (1949), *Polyphonie X* for eighteen instruments (1951), and *Structures* for two pianos (1951–52), Boulez was intensely pushing the limits of the serial system. He saw similarities between the development of total serialism and Cage's focus on the "individuality of sound," particularly because the latter took into account all the attributes of sound: pitch, amplitude, timbre, and duration. Cage had reached a crucial point in the evolution of his musical style and aesthetics, the beginning of a life-long preoccupation with chance and indeterminacy. Yet, despite the fact that, on the surface, the determinism of total serialism seems diametrically opposed to Cage's aesthetic agenda, Boulez and Cage had much in common. The relationship among the two composers is symptomatic of a larger historical issue, namely, Cage's place within the development of musical modernism after the Second World War. We shall return to this broader context after examining the evolution of Cage's musical style during the late 1940s and 1950s.

Static harmony in *The Seasons* (1947) and the *String Quartet in Four Parts* (1949–50)

Cage's studies of mysticism and Asian philosophy in the 1940s (see Chapter 3) inspired a transitional period that culminated with crucial changes in his musical style. He began to conceptualize the elements of his compositional processes in terms of four categories: structure, material, method, and form (Cage 1948b and 1949). Organized according to rhythmic proportions and the tenets of his "square-root" system, structure results from precompositionally determined temporal divisions. Cage defined form as the "morphological line in the sound continuum." Illustrating differences between structure and form, he explained that although poets may employ the same structure in constructing a sonnet, each realization has its own unique "word continuities." Similarly, in music, while structure may remain constant, form, or the musical content, must vary from work to work (Cage 1948b, p. 79). The method of composition is the means of controlling the note-to-note continuity. The composer's materials consist of both sounds and silences.

In "Defense of Satie" Cage noted a new contemporary awareness of form which he described as "static, rather than progressive in character." He attributed the beginnings of this new approach to the music of Anton von Webern and Erik Satie, composers who, according to Cage, sought to define musical structure in terms of time lengths rather than harmony (Cage 1948b, p. 81). He saw harmony as a means by which parts of a composition could be related to each other, a procedure "concerned with the point-to-point progress of a piece" rather than the relationships between the whole and its parts (Cage 1948a, p. 34). Cage later described harmony as a "forced abstract vertical relation which blots out the spontaneous nature of the sounds forced into it" (Cage 1954, p. 152). He also considered the possibility that harmony, freed from its structural responsibility, might also become a formal element, i.e., a component of a musical continuity, just as any other sound or silence (Cage 1949, p. 62). This reinterpretation of harmony opened up new possibilities for changes in his musical style. It focussed upon the individuality of each harmony, rather than on harmonic progression. The resultant static harmony lacked the strong linear continuity that Cage had found objectionable in music since Beethoven. It also fostered a more restrained, understated musical style that resonated with Cage's evolving aesthetics.

Earlier, Cage had recognized that a composer working with the "total field of sound" might begin with a "sound row" – a precompositional collection of sound elements (Cage 1942, p. 66). In writing percussion music, this might consist of an array of percussion sounds and, as was the case with his *First Construction (in Metal)*, a series of rhythmic motives. Cage employed a similar approach in his music for prepared piano; each work drew from a fixed collection of preparations or "gamut." Depressing a key produces an element of this collection, which might consist of a single frequency, an interval, or a more complex aggregate of frequencies and timbres (Cage 1958a, p. 25).

Beginning in 1946, Cage extended this idea to compositions with conventional sounds. *The Seasons* (1947), an orchestral work commissioned for a ballet choreographed by Merce Cunningham, was the first major work to apply this technique. *The Seasons* attempts to portray the Hindu conception

of the seasons as a cyclical progression from quiescence (winter), to creation (spring), preservation (summer), and destruction (fall). Each of the
four seasons is set as an individual movement, preceded by a prelude.
The final movement, "Fall" is followed by a return to the opening prelude. The work's nine movements deploy a rhythmic structure based upon
19 × 19-measure units organized according to a rhythmic proportion of
2:2:1:3:2:4:1:3:1 (although as was the case in Cage's *Three Dances*
(1945), the number of measures in each movement changes when there is
a change in the tempo).

Apparently Cage had help from others (including Lou Harrison and
Virgil Thomson) orchestrating *The Seasons* (Vaughan 1997, p. 40). This does
not, however, detract from the originality of the score.[1] Cage recognized
the possibility of creating unique timbral combinations with traditional
orchestral instruments and was keenly interested in writing for orchestra
(Cage 1948a, p. 44). The gamut for *The Seasons* includes single pitches,
intervals, and more complex chordal configurations or "aggregates." He
deployed these sounds quite freely; their orchestration varies and they often
appear with new elements not contained in the gamut. Example 11.1, from
"Prelude III" illustrates Cage's technique. The alternating trichords in the
left and right hands are components of six-note sonorities which appear,
for example, at rehearsal number 13 in "Winter." Similarly, the bass notes
in measures 11 and 13 stem from the first sonority in Example 11.1. Cage
was willing to segment the elements of his gamut. He also allowed for
changes in register. The trichord in measure 2 appears in a higher register
in measures 11 and 12. In addition, one of its notes changes from D to E.
A flexible approach to the gamut also allowed Cage to create melodies,
as in "Prelude IV," consisting of sustained notes from a given aggregate
which remain after the others drop out (see also Pritchett 1993, p. 44). This

Example 11.1 John Cage, *The Seasons* (1947), Prelude III, measures 1–13

technique is particularly pervasive in "Fall," where individual extended notes combine to form triadic arpeggios and melodic fragments.

In *The Seasons*, Cage began to approach his ideal of static harmony and fragmented form in movements such as the work's first and third preludes. Other movements are more traditional. For example, "Fall" builds to a climactic crescendo culminating at rehearsal number 122, gradually diminishing thereafter, thus completing a prototypical "Romantic" arch form. *The Seasons* is clearly a programmatic work matching its subject matter from the "quiescent" to the "destructive." These extremes are expressed in part through exploiting contrasting diatonic and chromatic elements in Cage's gamut. Note, for example, how the b minor chord begins to slowly emerge seven measures after rehearsal number 123 as the tumult of "Fall" dissipates, paving the way for a return to the restraint of "Prelude I" and a renewal of the seasonal cycle. In general, the work's curious, yet original and effective, juxtaposition of "Webernesque" pointillism and diatonic passages reminiscent of Satie shows the influence of two composers whom Cage would acknowledge as important models for his work during this period.

The *String Quartet in Four Parts* (1949–50) and, to a lesser extent, the *Six Melodies for Violin and Piano* (1950),[2] represent the next stage in the development of Cage's gamut technique. As in *The Seasons*, the gamut for the String Quartet consists of single sounds, intervals, and aggregates. However, in this later work Cage decided to render these elements "immobile" by maintaining their register, manner of production (bowing, harmonics, etc.), string, and instrument. The gamut (see Example 11.2) for the String Quartet consists of a variety of string timbres (including several notes produced by the cello on its D and G strings tuned a half-step lower).[3] It contains diatonic as well as chromatic aggregates. The reader may refer to the score and Example 11.2 to observe how Cage deployed these sonorities. For example, the first movement begins with a succession consisting of sonorities 21, 18, 13, 16, 27, 42, 43, 42, and 32. Although in a few instances Cage chose to build new sonorities with elements from his collection, he largely avoided the superimposition of gamut elements in the String Quartet. In fact, he described the String Quartet in terms of a "single melodic line without accompaniment" (Cage 1962, p. 51), a "single line in rhythmic space" (Nattiez 1993, p. 55). While the fourth movement and, to a lesser extent, the first movement contain "melodies" made up of the highest voice in Cage's sonorities, the inner movements more fully realize Cage's idea of a "harmony" dependent upon the distinct characteristics of each sound (whether single tones or more complex timbral aggregates).

Like *The Seasons*, the four movements of the String Quartet depict a seasonal progression, this time beginning with summer. The work as a whole consists of 22 × 22 measures arranged according to a rhythmic structure of

Example 11.2 John Cage, *String Quartet in Four Parts* (1949–50), "gamut"

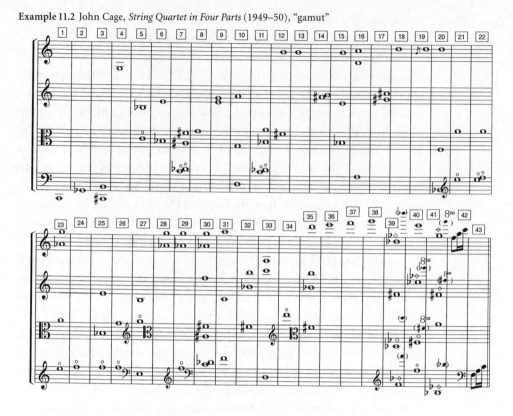

2½ : 1½ : 2 : 3 : 6 : 5 : ½ : 1½ with two components of the proportion assigned to each movement on the macro-level. The rhythmic structure is often articulated through dramatic changes in timbre (such as the beginning of the first of the group of three twenty-two-measure units in the second movement [m. 133]). Particularly striking is Cage's use of changes in harmonic rhythm to articulate his rhythmic structure. For example, the alternation of two members of the gamut (nos. 7 and 27 in Example 11.2) has an almost "cadential" effect bringing the initial twenty-two-measure unit in the first movement to a close. Similarly, the gradual liquidation of the repeated D–B (nos. 18 and 13) accompanied (a rare instance of superimposition in this work) by a changing background of sustained aggregates articulates the conclusion of the final twenty-two-measure unit of the same movement.

There is a gradual slowing down of harmonic rhythm across the first three movements of the String Quartet, culminating with the near stasis of the third movement. Cage's instructions in the score for each of the first three movements range from "Quietly Flowing Along" for the first movement, to "Slowly Rocking" for the second, to "Nearly Stationary" for the third. The third movement consists of the two largest components of Cage's

Table 11.1 John Cage, *String Quartet in Four Parts* (1949–50), iii, gamut "series"

22-bar Units	Gamut "Series" in the String Quartet in Four Parts, Third Movement
1: mm 199- 220	21, 28, 32, 28, 21, 28, 32, 28, 21, 28, 32, 28, (21), **7, 16, 7, 21, 7, 16, 7, 21, 7, 16, 7, 21** *m. 210* "retrograde inversion"
2: mm 221- 242	21, 29, 41, 29, 21, 19, 21, 29, 41, 32, 19, 32, 41, 32, (19), **32, 41, 32, 19, 32, 41, 29, 21, 19, 21, 29, 41, 29, 21** *m.230* retrograde (rhythm and pitch)
3: mm 243- 264	30, 2, 30, 21, 14, 21, 30, 2, 16, 14, 16, 2, 16, (14), **16, 2, 16, 14, 16, 2, 30, 21, 14, 21, 30, 2, 30** *m. 253* retrograde (rhythm and pitch) also "inversionally" related with section 2 (above)
6	4: mm 265- 286	23, 29, 31, 28, 4, 21, 25, 21, 9, 17, 11, 4, 33, (1), 33, 4, 11, 17, 9, 21, 25, 21, 31, 25, 31, 32, 27, 21, 13 *m. 275*
	5: mm 287- 308	13, 21, 27, 32, 31, 25, 31, 21, 25, 21, 9, 17, 11, 4, 33, (1), 33, 4, 11, 17, 9, 21, 25, 21, 4, 28, 31, 29, 23 *m. 297* retrograde (rhythm and pitch) of section 4 (above)
	6: mm 309- 330	**14, 21, 28, 21, 14,** 19, 21, 7, 21, 19, 21, 7, 21, 19, **19, 21, 7, 21, 19, 21, 7, 21, 19,** 14, 21, 28, 21, 14, 21, 28, 21, 14 "retrograde inversion" *m. 320* "retrograde inversion" "inversion" (and retrograde)
	7: mm 331- 352	23, 29, 31, 29, 9, 21, 12, 11, 17, 9, 12, 11, 17, 9, 35, 15, 19, 27, 35, 15, 21, 21, 35, 15, 19, 27, 35, 21, 21
	8: mm, 353- 374	21, 21, 35, 27, 19, 15, 35, 21, 21, 15, 35, 27, 19, 15, 35, 9, 17, 11, 12, 9, 17, 11, 12, 21, 9, 29, 31, 29, 23 retrograde (rhythm and pitch) of section 7 (above)
5	9: mm 375- 396-	30, 2, 30, 21, 14, 21, 30, 2, 16, 14, 16, 2, 16, (14), **16, 2, 16, 14, 16, 2, 30, 21, 14, 21, 30, 2, 30** *m. 384* retrograde (rhythm and pitch)
	10: mm 397- 418	29, 41, 29, 21, 19, 21, 29, 41, 32, 19, 32, 41, 32, (19), **32, 41, 32, 19, 32, 41, 29, 21, 19, 21, 29, 41, 29** *m. 407* retrograde (rhythm and pitch) also "inversionally" related with section 9 (above)
	11: mm. 419- 440	21, 7, 16, 7, 21, 7, 16, 7, 21, 7, 16, 7, (21), **28, 32, 28, 21, 28, 32, 28, 21, 28, 32, 28, 21** *m. 430* "retrograde inversion"

rhythmic structure: a section of six twenty-two-measure units followed by a section of five twenty-two-measure units. The continuities in the movement result from a method of deploying gamut elements that Cage referred to as "canons in retrograde and inversion" (Nattiez 1993, p. 92). Table 11.1 lists the successions of gamut elements in each of the twenty-two-measure units in the third movement and illustrates Cage's technique.[4] For example, in the opening six-unit section of the macrostructure, the second twenty-two-measure unit (mm. 221–242) contains a series of gamut sonorities which appears in retrograde (as indicated in bold type in Table 11.1) in both pitch and rhythm beginning in measure 230. A similar organization occurs in section 3 (mm. 243–64). Section 5 (mm. 287–308) is a retrograde (pitch and rhythm) of section 4 (mm. 265–86).

As Pritchett (1993, p. 50) points out, Cage's use of "inversion" in the third movement of the String Quartet did not entirely conform to the traditional definition of the term. In post-tonal theory, inversion entails an equidistant disposition of pitches above and below an axis. Cage chose such an axis for the third movement of his String Quartet: sonority number 21

(Example 11.2), approximately at the mid-point of his gamut. However, his gamut is asymmetrical. Moreover, his selection of "inversionally" related pairs of gamut sonorities was arbitrary, and not according to their distance around the axis of inversion. The result was a scale (Pritchett 1993, p. 53) yielding the following "inversionally" related pairs of gamut sonorities: (2, 41); (7, 28); (14, 19); (16, 32); (21, 21); (29, 30). Considered in this way, the first and second halves (in bold) of the initial twenty-two-measure unit are "retrograde inversions." The second and third units are "inversions," except for the first and last sonorities in the second unit. The sixth twenty-two-measure unit (mm. 309–330) has an interesting layout: its first and second halves are divided into two segments (as indicated in bold) that are "retrograde inversions." Moreover, the first half is an inversion of the second half; the two halves are also retrogrades. Section 6, flanked on both sides by five twenty-two-measure units, constitutes the mid-point of the movement, serving as an axis for its large-scale structure. Accordingly, the rhythmic and pitch retrogrades in sections 4 and 5 correspond to those between sections 7 and 8. Sections 3 and 9 are equivalent. Except for its first and last sonorities, section 2 uses the same gamut sonorities as section 10. Finally, in terms of successions of gamut sonorities, the first half of section 1 appears as the second half of section 11; the second half of section 1 appears as the first half of section 11. These systematic procedures not only allowed Cage to come close to his goal of a static, non-functional harmony; they also, as we shall see below, foreshadowed future developments in his compositional style. Cage did not realize the implications of the third movement in the final movement of his String Quartet. The work concludes with music in his "melodic" style, largely made up of diatonic sonorities from the gamut.

In the essay "Forerunners of Modern Music" (1949), Cage considered the elements of his compositional processes, explaining which of these elements could be consciously controlled and which were "unconsciously allowed to be." Structure is invariably controlled by the composer's intellect; it results from an objective decision to divide a composition into precompositionally determined units of time. "Form wants only freedom to be. It belongs to the heart; and the law it observes, if indeed it submits to any, has never been, and will never be written." Both the method of composition and the composer's materials may either be controlled through rational decision or result spontaneously from improvisation and inspiration (Cage 1949, p. 62; see also Nattiez 1993, pp. 38–39). For example, the quasi-serial manipulations in the third movement of the String Quartet provided Cage with a systematic, rational basis for determining the successions of gamut sonorities. In contrast, the deployment of gamut sonorities in the first, second, and fourth movements of the same work resulted from Cage's musical tastes, and in a certain sense, were arbitrarily chosen in the same manner that the composer selected his piano preparations: "as one chooses shells while walking along a beach" (Cage 1958a, p. 19).

"Freedom and control" in the Concerto for Prepared Piano and Chamber Orchestra (1950–51) and *Sixteen Dances* (1951)

Cage viewed composition as an activity integrating opposites: the rational and the irrational. He juxtaposed the composer's ideas of order on the one hand, his or her spontaneous actions and inspiration on the other. Cage thematicized this dialectic between freedom and control in his next major work, the Concerto for Prepared Piano and Chamber Orchestra (1950–51). He described the first movement in dualistic terms: a drama based upon the opposition of the prepared piano and the orchestra. The prepared piano part was freely composed much in the same manner as Cage's earlier works for the same instrument. The orchestra part resulted from systematic procedures. As in his earlier gamut compositions, Cage composed a collection of single sounds, intervals, and aggregates. However, rather than laying out the sonorities in his gamut linearly, he arranged them into a chart with fourteen columns and sixteen rows. Each row favors a particular instrument. Example 11.3 is a graphic representation of the entire chart.[5] Example 11.4 includes a portion of Cage's actual chart. The chart contains a

Example 11.3 John Cage, Concerto for Prepared Piano and Chamber Orchestra (1950–51), i, graphic representation of the orchestra chart

Fl.	A1	A2	A3	A4	A5	A6	A7	A8	A9	A10	A11	A12	A13	A14
Ob.	B1	B2	B3	B4	B5	B6	B7	B8	B9	B10	B11	B12	B13	B14
Cl.	C1	C2	C3	C4	C5	C6	C7	C8	C9	C10	C11	C12	C13	C14
Bn.	D1	D2	D3	D4	D5	D6	D7	D8	D9	D10	D11	D12	D13	D14
Tp.	E1	E2	E3	E4	E5	E6	E7	E8	E9	E10	E11	E12	E13	E14
Hn.	F1	F2	F3	F4	F5	F6	F7	F8	F9	F10	F11	F12	F13	F14
Tb.	G1	G2	G3	G4	G5	G6	G7	G8	G9	G10	G11	G12	G13	G14
Tu.	H1	H2	H3	H4	H5	H6	H7	H8	H9	H10	H11	H12	H13	H14
Perc.	I1	I2	I3	I4	I5	I6	I7	I8	I9	I10	I11	I12	I13	I14
Perc	J1	J2	J3	J4	J5	J6	J7	J8	J9	J10	J11	J12	J13	J14
Perc	K1	K2	K3	K4	K5	K6	K7	K8	K9	K10	K11	K12	K13	K14
Perc	L1	L2	L3	L4	L5	L6	L7	L8	L9	L10	L11	L12	L13	L14
Vn.	M1	M2	M3	M4	M5	M6	M7	M8	M9	M10	M11	M12	M13	M14
Va.	N1	N2	N3	N4	N5	N6	N7	N8	N9	N10	N11	N12	N13	N14
Vc.	O1	O2	O3	O4	O5	O6	O7	O8	O9	O10	O11	O12	O13	O14
Db.	Q1	Q2	Q3	Q4	Q5	Q6	Q7	Q8	Q9	Q10	Q11	Q12	Q13	Q14

Example 11.4 John Cage, Concerto for Prepared Piano and Chamber Orchestra (1950–51), i, segment of the original orchestra chart variety of timbral combinations using both conventional instruments and percussion. It also calls for a selection of electronic sounds, including a buzzer, a recording of a generator, an amplified coil of wire, and a radio, some of which appear in Cage's earlier works.

The rhythmic structure of the Concerto consists of 23×23 measures arranged according to the proportion $3:2:4:4:2:3:5$. The first movement takes up nine twenty-three-measure sections, the first three units of the proportion $(3:2:4)$. In composing the orchestral part for the first movement, Cage used his chart as if it were a "checker board" on which he made moves of a "thematic" nature (Nattiez 1993, pp. 78, 93). For example, the movement opens with the following succession of "cells" from the chart: F1, C8, G12, E5, E6. Each progression from cell to cell incorporates two moves: one along the vertical axis and one along the horizontal axis. Referring again to Example 11.3, we may represent the initial progression in terms of a series of ordered pairs in which the initial number stands for a move up or down and the following number a move to the left or the right: (3,7) (4,4) (2,7) (0,1). Cage observed that each series of moves may be followed by either corresponding or non-corresponding moves on his chart. The former is mostly the case in the first movement; when the moves do not exactly correspond, the sounds are still selected from the same columns. Table 11.2 lays out the progressions for the entire movement. The first unit of the macrostructure repeats the progression, starting from a new cell each time. The second unit of the macrostructure (rehearsal numbers 7–13) also uses the progression, except for the last five-measure phrase, which contains a new progression: A1 A2 A7 A12 A13 A14 D2 D9. The first movement largely consists of "transpositions" of the two progressions.

Cage recognized that the compositional method used in creating the orchestral part for the first movement of his Concerto involved what he described as an "unaesthetic choice"; the music for orchestra was less the result of his own decisions than it was the byproduct of systematic procedures (Nattiez 1993, p. 78). However, it is important to point out that Cage did not entirely relinquish his compositional control. In setting each progression according to the phrases of the microstructure, the duration of each cell results from compositional choice, constrained only by the requirement that each progression fits into a single phrase. In the first twenty-three-measure unit, for example, the first progression lasts three measures, the second two measures, and the third four measures. The fourth phrase consists of four free-composed measures for the prepared piano, followed by progressions in the orchestra of two, three, and five measures.

Cage avoided the superimposition of cells, in order to draw attention to their unique timbral characteristics. On several occasions, however, he did choose to superimpose and overlap cells to create interesting effects, such

Table 11.2 John Cage, Concerto for Prepared Piano and Chamber Orchestra (1950–51), i, cell progressions

	rn	Macrostructure 3	rn	Macrostructure 2	rn	Macrostructure 4
3		F1 C8 G12 E5 E6	21	Piano Solo	35	C1 C2 C7 C12 C13 C14 F2 F9
2	1	C1 F8 D12 B5 B6	22	Piano Solo	36	M1 M2 M7 M12 M13 M14
4	2	G1 D8 H12 F5 F6	23	Q1 M8 A12 O5 O6	37	Q2 Q9 G1
4	3	Piano Solo	24	N1 L8 O12 M5 M6	38	G2 G7 G12 G13 G14
2	4	E1 B8 F12 D5 D6	25	I1 F8 J12 H5 H6	39	K2 K9
3	5	D1 A8 E12 C5 C6	26	F1 I8 G12 E5 E6	40	E1 E2 E7 E12 E13 E14
5	6	B1 O8 C12 A5 A6	27	I1 F8 D12 B5 B6	41	H2 H9 C8 O1
3	7	G1 J8 H12 F5 F6	28	L1 L2 L7 L12 L13 L14 O2 O9	42	Piano Solo
2	8	J1 G8 K12 I5 I6	29	A8 N1	43	Piano Solo
4	9	H1 K8 I12 G5 G6	30	Piano Solo	44	O1 L8 Q12 B5 B6
4	10	K1 H8 L12 J5 J6	31	N1 A8 E12 C5 C6	45	Piano Solo
2	11	Piano Solo	32	B1 D8 Q12 C5 C6	46	B1 E8 I12 K5 K6
3	12	Piano Solo	33	B1 B2 B7 B12 B13 B14	47	I1 L8 H12 F5 F6
5	13	A1 A2 A7 A12 A13 A14 D2 D9	34	E2 E9	48	D1 A8 O12 A5 A6
3	14	A1 N8 B12 Q5 Q6			49	A1 N8 Q12 B5 B6
2	15	O1 L8 Q12 N5 N6			50	B1 E8 I12 K5 K6
4	16	L1 O8 C12 A5 A6			51	Piano Solo
4	17	Piano Solo			52	D1 A8 O12 A5 A6
2	18	Piano Solo			53	Piano Solo
3	19	Piano Solo			54	Piano Solo
5	20	L8 I1			55	O1 L8 N12 Q5 Q6
					56	Piano Solo
					57	Piano Solo
					58	Piano Solo
					59	Piano Solo
					60	Piano Solo
					61	Piano Solo
					62	O1 L8 N12 Q5 Q6

rn = rehearsal number

as the trombone glissandi (from cells G1 and D8) in measures 6–7 and the downward trombone slide accompanied by a rising water gong glissando (from cells Q9 and G1) one measure before rehearsal number 38 (Pritchett 1988b, pp. 62–64). Cage also manipulated the "harmonic rhythm" to underscore points of arrival in the rhythmic structure. For example, the final five-measure phrase (rehearsal number 20) at the end of the first section (three twenty-three-measure units) of the macrostructure contains only two cells (L8 and I1), extended in long rhythmic values (see Example 11.5). A similar slowing down of the harmonic rhythm occurs at rehearsal number 34, the five-measure phrase preceding the next division in the macrostructure. In the opening of the movement, Cage seems to have navigated from the top to the bottom of his chart while choosing "transpositions" of the opening progression. The first twenty-three-measure unit primarily uses cells from the top seven rows of his chart; the bottom of the chart is reached by rehearsal number 23. The last two twenty-three-measure units close with

Example 11.5 John Cage, Concerto for Prepared Piano and Chamber Orchestra (1950–51), i, final five-measure phrase

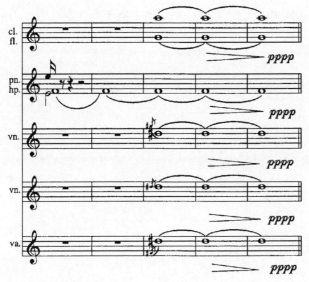

the same progression: O1, L8, N12, Q5, Q6. This, along with the extended piano solo in the final unit (rehearsal numbers 56–62), brings the movement to an effective close.

The piano preparation for the Concerto, among Cage's most elaborate, calls for a moveable plastic bridge that produces some startling micro-tonal pitch combinations. This added innovation notwithstanding, the music for prepared piano in the first movement contains passages, such as the ostinato two measures before rehearsal number 11, that sound very much like Cage's prepared piano works from the 1940s. At times, however, the prepared piano plays passages (such as those beginning at rehearsal number 12 or three measures before rehearsal number 42) made up of isolated gestures rather than continuous phrases and, as a result, sounds more like the orchestra part. The stylistic dissimilarity between the two parts continues to disappear in the second movement, where Cage decided to use charts for both the piano and the orchestra. He also added a new method: rather than making moves on his charts he employed a series of concentric circles and squares for selecting the gamut sonorities. Example 11.6 includes a sketch (Example 11.6a) that accompanied Cage's working materials for the second movement and a partial transcription (Example 11.6b). Beginning with the smallest square and a circle contained within it (Example 11.6b), the points of intersection yield cells C9, D10, E9, and D8. The circle then expands, circumscribing the square at the

Example 11.6 John Cage, Concerto for Prepared Piano and Chamber Orchestra (1950–51), ii; sketch (Ex. 11.6a) and partial transcription (Ex. 11.6b) of a page from the working materials

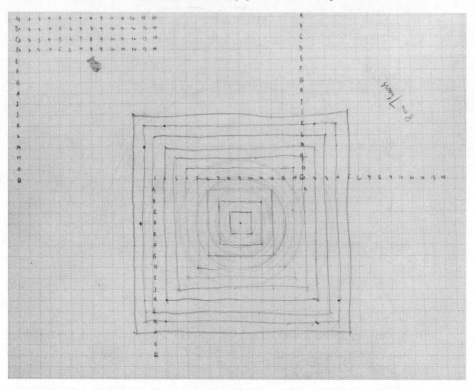

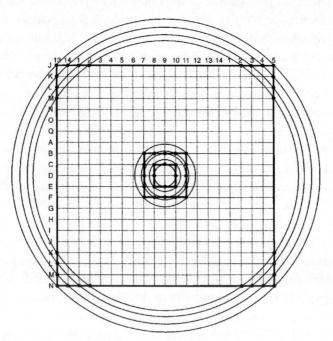

points corresponding to cells C10, E10, E8, and C8. Cage then proceeded to the next square and circle. As the circle expands, the following sequences result:

B9, D11, F9, D7
B10, C11, E11, F10, F8, E7, C7, B8
B11, F11, F7, B7

Example 11.6b also illustrates the final steps of the procedure, which continued until a circle circumscribed the largest square (yielding cells J5, N5, N13, and J13). Cage used a single progression of either four or eight cells for each phrase in the microstructure. Although it was not necessary to use the cells produced via the final two circles in Example 11.6b, he extended the vertical and horizontal axes of the chart in order to generate enough cell sequences for the entire movement. As Pritchett points out, in generating his list of cell sequences Cage proceeded from the smallest set of circles and squares and moved outward. However, in setting the sequences in the actual score, he reversed this process and deployed the cells in reverse order. The movement closes with D8, E9, D10, and C9 – the smallest circle and square at the center of the chart. This amounts to a technical representation of the "gradual coming together of the piano and the orchestra," which the composer himself acknowledged (Pritchett 1988b, p. 67).

Cage began another project after completing the second movement of his Concerto, a chamber work for flute, trumpet, violin, cello, piano, and percussion written for a dance by Merce Cunningham and entitled *Sixteen Dances* (1951). As he did in the *Sonatas and Interludes,* Cage attempted to portray the permanent emotions or *rasas* of East Indian aesthetics in his *Sixteen Dances.* Each odd-numbered movement represents a specific emotion and is followed by an interlude. The final movement depicts "tranquility." The work uses Cage's chart system with the added innovation of what he called chart "metamorphosis" (thus, as shown below, anticipating the approach applied in the Concerto's final movement). Composing from a chart consisting of eight columns and eight rows, he replaced eight sounds in his chart after finishing each pair of dances. As a result, all the sounds in the original chart were replaced by the time he began the last set. The extant sketches for *Sixteen Dances* include two charts, one marked "Original," the other "Metamorphosis."[6] The charts contain the same sorts of materials found in the charts for the Concerto. In describing the compositional technique used in composing his *Sixteen Dances,* Cage mentioned making moves on a "magic square" as he did in the first movement of the Concerto (Nattiez 1993, p. 94). Comparison of the score and the first chart, given in Example 11.7, shows that this is in fact the case. In addition, the manuscript for the score contains several pages with lists of cell progressions used in the

Example 11.7 John Cage, *Sixteen Dances* (1951), chart marked "original"

first movement. These show that the movement was composed according to a series of progressions involving two, three, and six cells (as indicated by underlines below). The rhythmic structure of the movement consists of 7 × seven-measure units. The progressions used in each of the units are as follows:[7]

$$\underline{I^1, VI^7, V^6} \quad \underline{II^4, VI^5} \quad \underline{VI^1, II^4, II^5, I^5, VI^3, VI^4} \quad \underline{VII^8, III^1}$$
$$\underline{V^6, II^4, I^3}$$
$$\underline{VI^8, III^6, II^5} \quad \underline{VII^3, III^4} \quad \underline{III^8, VII^3[VII^4, VI^4]^* \ III^2, III^3}$$
$$\underline{IV^7, VIII^8} \quad \underline{II^5, VII^3, VI^2}$$
$$\underline{VI^2, III^8, II^7} \quad \underline{VII^5, III^6} \quad \underline{III^2, VII^5, VII^6, VI^6, III^4, III^5}$$
$$\underline{IV^1, VIII^2} \quad \underline{II^7, VII^5, VI^4}$$
$$\underline{VIII^2, V^8, IV^7} \quad \underline{I^5, V} \quad \underline{V^2, I^5} \text{ (continued into next section)}$$
$$\underline{I^6, VIII^6, V^4, V^5} \quad \underline{VI^1, II^2}$$
$$\underline{IV^7, I^5, VIII^4}$$

Several authors have noted, without having an opportunity to refer to Cage's sound charts, that not every movement in *Sixteen Dances* follows the sort of systematic procedures in the first movement of Cage's Concerto (Pritchett 1988a, pp. 94–97). Examination of the charts and the manuscript provides additional evidence that this is the case. Comparison of the second movement with the chart in Example 11.7 shows that, while Cage drew from the sounds in his chart, he apparently did not proceed in a systematic manner. Since Cage decided to renew eight cells after every two movements, the extant charts apply only to the first and last pairs. It is thus not possible to ascertain definitively whether the remaining movements were composed systematically or not. A noteworthy exception is the fifth movement, which in the manuscript contains positive and negative numbers above each system suggesting that the sounds were selected by single moves along the vertical and horizontal axes of the chart. Several movements appear to have been written in Cage's "free" style; others do not. The "melodic" writing in movement 12 clearly looks back to the style of the last movement of the String Quartet: the sounds were obviously selected by Cage according to his own musical tastes. The repetitions in movements 4, 8, and 9 suggest a "free" approach to selecting cells from the chart. The latter movement is also noteworthy for its silences, some as long as eleven measures. Similar empty measures appear elsewhere in *Sixteen Dances*; all look forward to the third movement of the Concerto.

Cage returned to composing the third movement of his Concerto after completing the *Sixteen Dances* (Nattiez 1993, p. 94). The final reconciliation of the piano and orchestra took place in this movement by combining the two charts used in the previous movement into a single chart. This was accomplished by consulting the *I Ching*, the ancient Chinese oracular "Book of Changes."[8] The notion that the universe is organized according to two basic qualities – *yin* and *yang* – constitutes the philosophical foundation for the *I Ching*. *Yin*, represented by a broken line, is "female," passive and nurturing; *yang*, represented by a solid line, is "male," active, and dominant. The *I Ching* is organized according to sixty-four hexagrams, each consisting of six lines. The oracle is consulted by tossing three coins (or yarrow stalks). Two heads and a tail is a solid line; two tails and a head is a broken line. Three tails is a solid line moving to a broken line; three heads is a broken line moving to a solid line. Six tosses generate a hexagram; if any of the lines is "moving," then a second hexagram results with the appropriate changes.[9]

Cage was undoubtedly attracted to the juxtaposition and interrelationships between opposites underlying the *I Ching*, since this was analogous to similar oppositions at the core of his aesthetic philosophy (see, for example, the earlier discussions of "freedom" and "law," the "rational" and the "irrational"). In the case of his Concerto, the opposition between *yin* and *yang* was an apt metaphor for the dramatic interplay between the prepared piano and the orchestra.

In the third movement, Cage adapted the *I Ching* to merge the two charts used in the second movement into a single chart. Proceeding cell by cell, he selected a sound from the orchestra chart for a solid line, a cell from the prepared piano chart for a broken line.[10] For "moving" lines Cage composed new sounds for the piano and orchestra. A solid line changing into a broken line resulted in a sound for the orchestra followed by a sound for the piano; a broken line changing into a solid line yielded a sound for the piano followed by a sound for the orchestra.

This procedure resulted in a new chart with the same 14 × 16 format as those used for the first two movements. Cage also used the *I Ching* to select sounds from the new chart. According to Pritchett, he constructed two additional charts for this purpose, each containing eight rows and columns of cells corresponding to the sixty-four hexagrams in the *I Ching* (Pritchett 1988b, p. 70). The charts consisted of empty cells and cells containing a simple two-part move, a move down followed by a move to the right. The number of cells traversed by each move ranged from zero to seven. Both charts contained moves in only thirty-two cells; one chart had moves for only odd-numbered cells, the other for only even-numbered cells. Referring to the *I Ching*, Cage generated a hexagram for each measure. If the corresponding cell on his chart contained a move, he then chose the sound from the appropriate cell in his sound chart; if the cell corresponding to the hexagram was empty, he added a silence to the score.

Cage followed the rhythmic proportion for his Concerto in deploying the sounds for the third movement. Aside from the final number, this proportion is symmetrical: 3 : 2 : 4 : 4 : 2 : 3 : [5]. He used the same chance-generated hexagrams for the corresponding units of the proportion; each "3" used the same hexagrams as did each "2" and "4" respectively. However, in referring to his two charts of "moves," he changed from one chart to the other for each of the corresponding phrases. Since one chart contains empty cells in odd columns, the other in even columns, where one of the symmetrically related phrases contains a sound, the other contains a silence. Example 11.8 illustrates the results of Cage's procedure in the opening eighteen measures,

Example 11.8 John Cage, Concerto for Prepared Piano and Chamber Orchestra (1950–51), iii, measures 1–18, cell durations

showing only the duration of each cell. In each corresponding phrase a silence replaces a sound and vice versa.

The final five-measure phrase at the end of every twenty-three-measure unit in the third movement contains only silence. Through the use of chance operations and the proliferation of silence in the third movement of the Concerto, Cage took a step beyond static harmony to a revolutionary redefinition of musical form. From this point on, he remained committed to the use of chance, thus letting "sounds be themselves." Musical continuity, for Cage, now avoided relationships between sounds other than their mutual coexistence in musical space and time. The resultant "no-continuity," as he put it, "simply means accepting that particular continuity that happens" (Cage *c.* 1951–52, p. 132). Perhaps the most insightful description of this radically new form of musical continuity appeared in a contemporary assessment of Cage's music in the early 1950s by none other than his former teacher Henry Cowell:

> To John Cage, a brief series of sounds, or even single combination of them, has come to seem complete in itself, and to constitute an audible "event." But he does not use the conventional organization of music, in which such events are related through planned rhythmic, melodic, and harmonic succession to produce what we are accustomed to consider an organic musical development. Instead, since Cage conceives each musical "event" to be an entity in itself that does not require completion, he simply places them one after another and sees them as being related through their co-existence in space, where they are set in a planned order of time.
> (Cowell 1952, p. 124)

Chance operations: the *Music of Changes* (1951) and *Williams Mix* (1952)

The *Music of Changes* (1951) was Cage's first work composed entirely with chance operations. It employs the most elaborate system of precompositional charts used thus far: eight charts containing sounds and silences, eight charts with durations, eight charts with amplitudes (dynamics) and single charts for determining tempi and the number of contrapuntal layers. Sound chart 8, duration chart 6, and amplitude charts 5 and 6 appear here in Examples 11.9a–c.[11] The format of the charts corresponds to the sixty-four hexagrams in the *I Ching*; each chart has, in principle, eight rows and eight columns of cells. However, since the sound charts have both thirty-two sounds and thirty-two silences, only the odd-numbered cells, those containing the sounds, appear in each chart. The tempo chart has sixty-four cells, but contains tempi in only thirty-two; a blank cell indicates that

Example 11.9 John Cage, *Music of Changes* (1951), sound chart 8 (Ex. 11.9a), duration chart 6 (Ex. 11.9b), and amplitude charts 5 and 6 (Ex. 11.9c)

the tempo remains constant. The amplitude charts have only sixteen cells; a change in amplitude thus occurs in every fourth cell.

The sound charts for the *Music of Changes* consist of single pitches, intervals, aggregates, and constellations (more complex rhythmic combinations). The more traditional "pitched" aggregates and constellations are largely dissonant combinations, which give the work a distinctive chromatic sound. The high degree of chromaticism in *Music of Changes* was guaranteed by Cage's precompositional decision that the vertical and horizontal

Example 11.9 (*cont.*)

axes of his sound charts must include all twelve tones of the chromatic scale
(Cage 1952b, p. 58). He considered the sound charts in terms of two squares
with four columns and four rows. Each axis must contain all twelve tones
(repeated pitches were allowed). Note, for instance, in sound chart 8
(Example 11.9a) that row 3 contains all twelve tones plus two repetitions
(A and D); likewise row 4 contains all twelve tones plus two repeated pitches
(A♯ and D♯). The first four cells in column 1 include the entire chromatic
scale, plus five repetitions (C, F, G♯, B♭, and B).

Example 11.9 (*cont.*)

The sound charts for *Music of Changes* have a wide variety of innovative piano sounds such as clusters, harmonics, and "string-piano" techniques used by Cage and Henry Cowell. See, for example, the "arm clusters" in cell 5, and the instruction in cell 29 for the performer to run his or her fingernails lengthwise along the strings (a practice recalling Cowell's *Banshee*) in sound chart 8 (Example 11.9a). (Note that the numbering takes into account that the chart contains only odd-numbered cells.) In *Music of Changes* there are also more "unconventional" sounds produced by slamming the keyboard lid closed, striking various parts of the piano with a wood stick, and dropping a cymbal beater vertically into the piano so that it hits the sound board.

Cage observed a lack of rhythmic differentiation in his Concerto for Prepared Piano and Chamber Orchestra (Nattiez 1993, p. 95); the durations in the third movement, for example, consist largely of half and whole notes. For *Music of Changes*, he composed charts with varied durations generated by the addition of rhythmic values (which included sixteenths, eighths, quarters, halves, and wholes, as well as units based on thirds, fifths, and sevenths) from as small as a thirty-second of a beat to a whole note. As can be seen by referring to the slurs in duration chart 6 (Example 11.9b), each unit is segmented into what Cage termed "nodes" (Cage 1952b, p. 59). The durations in the actual score are notated spatially, a quarter note equaling 2.5 centimeters; there are four quarters in each measure.[12] Fractions in the score indicate a part of a quarter note or, in spatial terms, a portion of 2.5 cm. The placement of each note in space, indicated by its stem (for whole notes, to the left of the note head), corresponds to its location in time. Thus, a sound 5 cm to the right of a measure's beginning occurs after two quarters; a sound at .625 cm after a sixteenth.

The *Music of Changes* consists of $29\,^5/_8 \times 29\,^5/_8$ measures divided into phrases and sections according to the proportion $3;\ 5:6\,^3/_4;\ 6^3/_4;\ 5:3^1/_8$.[13] As indicated by the semicolons in the proportion, the work is divided into four parts, each comprising either one or two units of the macrostructure. For example, the first part consists of three $29\,^5/_8$-measure units. The fourth part comprises five $29\,^5/_8$-measure units followed by three-and-an-eighth $29\,^5/_8$-measure units.[14]

His earlier experiments with the "metamorphosis" of one chart into another notwithstanding, Cage was disturbed by the "static" situation inherent in the precompositional charts used prior to *Music of Changes*. In the Concerto, for example, he observed that "although movement is suggested in the metamorphosis-idea underlying it, each part is like a still picture, rather than a movie" (Nattiez 1993, p. 94). This seemed to contradict the very dynamic nature of life and the fact that the *I Ching* oracle often calls for one hexagram to change into another (Nattiez 1993, p. 94). In *Music of Changes*, Cage sought a kind of perpetual variation resulting from the continued renewal of his material through what he termed chart "mobility." During the compositional process certain elements in Cage's charts were designated as either "mobile" or "immobile"; "immobile" elements remained in the charts to be used once again; "mobile" elements passed "into history" and were replaced (Cage 1952b, p. 58). This procedure guaranteed a high degree of entropy; the relative absence of repetition in the *Music of Changes* contrasts with his earlier chart compositions.

As James Pritchett's path-breaking research demonstrates, the realization of the score for *Music of Changes* was a complex and meticulous process (Pritchett 1988, pp. 107–156). Cage composed the piece according to the phrase and section lengths of its rhythmic structure. At the outset, a single hexagram determined the number of contrapuntal layers (from one to eight) and the tempo for the initial phrase. (Cage noted that introducing the possibility of tempo changes in *Music of Changes* lessened the importance of its temporal structure, since the actual phrase lengths changed [Cage 1958a, p. 20].) After determining the tempo and the number of layers, he composed a layer at a time, tossing the coins, referring to the *I Ching*, and selecting the appropriate elements from his sound, duration, and amplitude charts. This was by no means an entirely mechanical process. For example, when the same pitch occurred simultaneously in two different layers, a situation which Cage called "interference," he left out one of the pitches (Cage 1952b, p. 58). He also shortened, lengthened, and segmented the duration of the sounds, manipulated the dynamics, and used pedaling to alter the results of his chance operations in order to yield more musical results (Pritchett 1988a, pp. 132–152). Odd-numbered sound and duration charts and even-numbered amplitude charts were mobile for the initial $29\,^5/_8$-measure unit. Whether the hexagram selected for the tempo and number of layers at the beginning of each subsequent unit was odd or even determined if this situation would remain the same or be reversed.

During 1951 and 1952 Cage composed several works with methods and working materials similar to those employed in the *Music of Changes*. His *Seven Haiku* (1951–52) for piano utilizes the same sound charts and most likely the same layer, duration, and amplitude charts as the earlier work (Pritchett 1988a, p. 173). *Two Pastorales* (1951–52) for prepared piano, was realized with charts for layers, sounds, durations, tempi, and amplitudes; it is reasonable to conclude that charts were also used for composing *Waiting* (1952), a piece for piano with or without preparations (Pritchett 1988a, pp. 192–193). Cage added a variety of dramatic actions to his sound charts for *Water Music* (1952), a composition scored for pianist also performing with a radio, whistles, water containers, and a deck of cards. The theatrical component of this work looks forward to Cage's *Black Mountain Piece* (1952), the famous "proto-happening" performed at Black Mountain College the following summer. (For score, see page 104.)

Cage's *Imaginary Landscape No. 5* (1952) is a score consisting of instructions for making a recording of eight layers of sounds taken from forty-two records on magnetic tape. Cage viewed this as an "inconsequential work"

(Nattiez 1993, p. 130); it is more importantly a precursor for *Williams Mix* (1952). Of the pieces composed during this period *Williams Mix* (1952) has a complexity rivaling the *Music of Changes*. A tape piece scored for eight mono tape recorders, it was part of the "Project for Music for Magnetic Tape" initiated by Cage and David Tudor and supported financially by the architect Paul Williams. In collecting the materials for his sound charts, Cage enlisted the help of sound engineers/composers Bebe and Louis Barron. He organized the sounds according to six categories: city sounds (A), country sounds (B), electronic sounds (C), "music" and especially manually produced sounds (D), wind-produced sounds and vocal music (E), and "small" sounds requiring amplification (F). These sounds were further classified according to whether three of their characteristics – frequency, timbre (overtone structure), and amplitude – were "controlled" (c) or "variable" (v). Thus, as Cage explained, "Dvvv" could be jazz or Beethoven with variable frequency, timbre, and amplitude (Nattiez 1993, p. 131). Controls could be imposed upon any of these characteristics through filters or reverberation. Such decisions, in addition to the selection of the sounds themselves, were entirely left up to Cage's sound engineers. After collecting the sounds in the form of segments of tape – some arranged into tape "loops" (as indicated by an underline, such as <u>Fvvv</u>), others mixed with another sound, a so-called "double source" (such as BvcvCvv) – Cage incorporated them into sixteen sound charts.[15]

As in the *Music of Changes*, coin tosses determined the number of layers (from 1 to 16) in *Williams Mix*. When there were greater than eight layers, two sounds were mixed for one or more of the eight tape recorders. In such cases, "interference" was eliminated by adjusting one sound so that it accommodated the other on a single track. Charts for attack and decay contained indications as to how to cut the ends of the tape segments including single and double cuts to or from a specific point on the tape as well as curves freely made at the moment of cutting (Nattiez 1993, p. 131). The rhythmic structure based upon inches of tape (at a speed of fifteen inches per second), rather than measures, is 46×46 arranged according to a proportion of $5:6:16:3:11:5$. The tempo charts called for distinct values for multiplying the phrase lengths by a factor "n," which distorted the rhythmic structure (Pritchett 1988a, p. 200). Cage realized only eleven of the forty-six sections of *Williams Mix*, completing only the first two sections of his macrostructure (5 and 6) (Pritchett 1988a, pp. 200–202). *Williams Mix* amounted to a little more than four minutes of what could have been a much longer work. Even so, its composition was an extremely time-consuming and laborious process in which many of Cage's colleagues and friends participated.

Cage, Boulez and the aesthetics of high modernism

Cage's encounters with Pierre Boulez were not based upon an "aesthetic mis-understanding," as one scholar has maintained (Nattiez 1993, p. 15). Rather, they were the result of two young composers working along similar lines, inspired, in part, by the same intellectual and cultural changes after World War II. The post-war period saw the emergence of a new, "radicalized" or "high" modernism in the arts. This occurred during a period of eco-nomic, moral, political, and social upheaval, the conclusion of a devastating modern "Thirty Years War." Europe had little time to recover from the catas-trophic events associated with World War I before hostilities were renewed with exponentially more destruction and butchery. The modernism of the previous half-century had lost its credibility as a revolutionary movement. It was replaced by a technocratic, positivistic, and rationalistic high mod-ernism, which was, above all, de-politicized. High modernist art was au-tonomous, formalist and anti-representational, as exemplified by the purist high-modernist architecture of Le Corbusier.

Cage and Boulez clearly fit into this historical context. Both composers, for example, in search of an autonomous anti-representational art, endorsed the objectification of sound. Boulez praised Cage for "conceiving rhythmic structure as dependent on real time, expressed through numerical relation-ships in which the personal element plays no part" (Boulez 1952a, p. 135). Cage rejected the notion that music is a means by which a composer ex-presses his or her emotions. In 1952 he stated:

> The most that can be accomplished by the musical ex-pression of feeling is to show how e-motional the composer was who had it. If anyone wants to get a feeling of how emotional a composer proved himself to be, he has to confuse himself to the same extent that the composer did and imagine that sounds are not sounds at all but are Beethoven and that men are not men but are sounds. Any child will tell us that this simply is not the case. A man is a man and a sound is a sound.   (Cage 1952a, p. 97)

Cage sought to withdraw his own subjectivity from the creative process through the use of chance and indeterminacy. The result was a seemingly depersonalized musical style, emphasizing the objectification of musical sound.

Similarly, in his *Structures* for two pianos (1951–52), Boulez was inves-tigating the limits of integral serialism "to see how far one could pursue the automaticism of musical relationships without allowing individual choice to intervene other than on really basic levels of organization" (Jameaux 1991, p. 58). He was experimenting with an "expressive nadir," a pure and objective musical style devoid of the composer's personality and intent.

Cage and Boulez focussed their investigations on all of the physical aspects of musical sound. In 1949, Boulez had praised Cage's *Sonatas and Interludes* (1946–48) for its exploration of complex frequency patterns, which "proved the possibility of creating non-tempered sound spaces, even with existing instruments." He even went so far as to declare that Cage's work called "into question the whole notion of acoustics as it has gradually stabilized in the evolution of western music" (Nattiez 1993, p. 134). Boulez had been working along similar lines, exploring quarter-tone tuning in *Le visage nuptial* (1946–47), an interest he would later pursue in his *Polyphonie X* (1951).

Both composers sought to control all the parameters of musical sound: Cage applied chance operations to elaborate systems of charts for each aspect of sound; Boulez developed similar materials in expanding the application of the twelve-tone system to intensity, attack, duration, and pitch. Boulez completed the first of his *Structures* (*Ia*) in 1951, the same year in which Cage finished his *Music of Changes*. In fact, the correspondence between the two composers during this period includes an interesting exchange concerning the compositional methods employed in the two works. Boulez's letter to Cage dated August 1951 contains some of the working materials used for *Structures* (Nattiez 1993, pp. 98–103). His charts are strikingly similar to Cage's.

Ironically, although the ironclad determinism of total serialism seems diametrically opposed to music based on chance, the mechanical "automaticism" of the former procedure appeared to all but eliminate the composer's role, just as did the latter. Despite this seemingly paradoxical congruence, Boulez had reservations concerning Cage's use of chance operations,[16] which culminated in 1957 with his well-known article entitled "Alea" in which he denounced the overuse of chance in composition (Boulez 1957). He attributed the overuse of chance to a weakness in compositional technique, claiming that a composer working with chance:

> feels no responsibility for his work, but out of unconfessed weakness and confusion and the desire for temporary relief, simply throws himself into puerile mumbo-jumbo. In other words, everything just happens as it will, without control (an intentional but not meritorious omission, since there is no alternative), BUT within a fixed network of probabilities, since even chance must have some sort of outcome.   (Boulez 1957, p. 26)

Boulez was unwilling to allow for what he referred to as "accidental chance." He believed that the wholesale adoption of such methods amounted to an abandonment of the creative process.

This characterization, however, does not apply to Cage's music. Indeed, it is a common misunderstanding that Cage's use of chance operations entails a lack of compositional control. Certainly, Cage's introduction of chance into the compositional process amounts to a revolutionary development. Nevertheless, aspects of Cage's approach to composition before he began using the *I Ching* remained the same. Whether composed using chance operations or not, each of the works examined here utilizes an elaborate precompositional plan realized through mechanistic procedures. Cage exercised control in carefully designing these strategies. A significant portion of the actual composing took place before he turned to the final score. From early in his career, Cage's emphasis upon the initial stages of the creative process helped him cultivate an acute sense of the potential of his methods and musical materials.[17] This remained a fundamental aspect of his compositional technique. These observations point to the importance of analyzing Cage's precompositional sketches – an issue raised elsewhere by several scholars (Pritchett 1988a; Van Emmerik 2001) – that informed the analytical investigations presented here.

Cage's commitment to letting "sounds be themselves" resulted in a radically new form of musical continuity devoid of intentional relationships between sounds:

> It is thus possible to make a musical composition the continuity of which is free of individual taste and memory (psychology) and also of the literature and "traditions" of art. The sounds enter the time-space centered within themselves, unimpeded by service to any abstraction, their 360 degrees of circumference free for an infinite play of interpenetration.
>
> (Cage 1952b, p. 59)

His redefinition of form entailed a rejection of an organicist assumption that a musical work should be a unified whole. This aesthetic criterion was as relevant for the high modernist composers exploring the limits of integral serialism during the 1950s as it was for composers during the nineteenth century. Cage rejected the "totalizing" organicism underlying high modernist art, demonstrated as a case in point by his critique of the modular architectural designs and theories of Le Corbusier (Joseph 1997). Cage's concept of musical form was revolutionary. To be sure, this development amounted to a break with certain modernist modes of thought. In fact, recent scholarship in literary criticism, cultural studies, and musicology has emphasized the vital role that Cage played in the development of musical "postmodernism" (see Chapter 13).[18] But, as we have seen, the radical results of his compositional processes were achieved through more conventional means, namely, through modernist precision with its systematic attention to detail and control of the materials used in composition. Finally, we should also consider these issues with respect to Cage's evolving political and social philosophy. Cage viewed the "no-continuity" of his compositions from the early 1950s as an early, purely musical formulation of his political beliefs. By "letting sounds be themselves," he had created musical works that offered models for alternative forms of social and political organization. The de-politicized high modernism of the 1950s was in a sense replaced by an older "heroic" modernism more prevalent in the earlier part of the twentieth century.

12 Music and society

WILLIAM BROOKS

John Cage's first substantive essay was written in 1928 and delivered in Los Angeles as a prize-winning speech at the Southern California Oratorical Contest. Entitled "Other People Think," it addressed "American Intervention in Latin America" – in particular, the control of Bolivia's finances by a cartel of American bankers and the Marine Corps' military intervention in Nicaragua. It was hortative and predictive: "We must learn that the day is coming when no one will need our aid . . . our posterity must not be slandered as the devotee of a Golden God" (Kostelanetz 1971, pp. 48–49). Cage liked it.[1]

Cage was revising his final essay, "Overpopulation and Art," at the time of his death, having delivered it at Stanford in January 1992. It too is hortative; indeed, it is remarkably directive in its admonitions: "**first** the wOrld's prime / Vital / problEm is how / to multiply by thRee . . . / . . . / . . . the overall / Performance realizations of the world's / comprehensive resoUrces . . . / . . . / **next** instead Of ownership / indiVidual / 24 hour usE of facilities / . . . / **and then** stOpping / the remoVal / of fossil fuEls / fRom the earth / . . . / **third** alOng with / the remoVal / of nations thE / Removal of schools . . . " (Perloff & Junkerman 1994, pp. 28–30).

Slightly over midway between these two essays Cage began the series of texts (also delivered as lectures) which he titled "Diary: How to Improve the World (You Will Only Make Matters Worse)." Fragmentary and disordered, these range from oblique remarks ("Without intending to, I'm going from lake to lake") to sober imperatives ("We had the chance to do it individually. Now we must do it together: globally"). But a social subtext constantly surfaces: "Art's obscured the difference between art and life. Now let life obscure the difference between life and art" (Cage 1965a, pp. 6, 9, 19).

At no time, it would seem, was Cage unconcerned about society and politics and about the relation of these to art. Yet Cage was rarely a "political" artist in the usual sense; he resolutely avoided affiliations and causes, and he created music in support of social endeavors primarily as gestures of friendship, not endorsements. His was a music not of solutions but of questions, and his hope was that the right question at the right time would precipitate a change of mind that would have social as well as artistic reverberations.

[214]

There were, however, pieces with unmistakable political messages. Two works can be taken as paradigms: *Credo in Us* (1942) and *Lecture on the Weather* (1975). Though separated by over thirty years, both these pieces are pointed critiques of American society. Both include texts; both use ancillary media; both are theatrical. Cage later described *Credo in Us* as "a suite of satirical character," written for a dance choreographed jointly by Jean Erdman and Merce Cunningham (Dunn 1962, p. 35). "Us," he explained to Charles Amirkhanian in 1983, stood for the U.S. as well as for "you and me" (Kostelanetz 1988, p. 62). The music's structure was determined by the dance, as was Cage's practice at the time: four "facades" separated by three "progressions." "There are many holes in the music," Cage explained much later, "and in the holes there were words of a text that Merce Cunningham had written" (Kostelanetz 1988, p. 62). An early program provides more details and also gives some sense of the kinds of texts involved:

A dramatic playlet for two characters:
   Husband – Shadow
   Wife – Ghoul's Rage
Place: Westward Ho!
Time: Three Generations

They are happied husband and wifed. They have harmonious postures. They facade their frappant ways across a sacred spot.

Ah, but what! This breakage of pattern. And he on-and-ons – is he only machine? – with her unreality. But soon breakage too.

So he searched for the Glory that was Greeley's, and she wandered after. It killed time.

Ghoulish, however, digging back, this thing in her broke through to ancestral gold; and he was stampeded after. But that was no elixir.

Boiling both and retching, now finally with fruitful efforts; a caraway! "Ah, such eyes."

But still a zombie.[2]

Credo in Us was scored for four performers: the first and second play tin cans, gongs, a tom tom, and an electric buzzer; the third plays piano, wood (with hands), and a tom tom; and the fourth plays a "radio or phonograph." For the latter, Cage advises in the score, "use some classic: e.g. Dvořák, Beethoven, Sibelius, or Shostakovich." Cage had used phonographs before, notably in the *Imaginary Landscape No. 1* (1939), but in this case he is interested not in sound *per se*, but in parody. The placement and amplitude of the phonograph events (at the very beginning, for example, alone and *fortissimo*) establish them clearly as symbols of bombastic self-importance and ambition. The buzzer and tin cans, similarly, serve not as simple percussion instruments (as they do in the *Constructions*, for instance), but as intrusive, noisy irrelevancies. And the piano (unprepared but sometimes muted) offers a "cowboy solo" (in the first progression) and a "jazz solo" (in the third) (Kostelanetz 1988, p. 62).

Everything in *Credo for Us*, then, *means* something; everything is to be heard as *other* than pure sound or pure structure. In its invocation of judgment, taste, and memory to undercut cultural assumptions, *Credo in Us* seems far removed from the works and aesthetic positions most commonly associated with Cage.

However, it is paralleled somewhat by *Lecture on the Weather*. Here too things *mean* other than they *are*: fragments of line drawings extracted from Thoreau's *Journals*, reversed to become white images on a black background, become flashes of lightning. These are conjoined with recordings of breeze, rain, and thunder to convey the effect of a gathering storm; but again, these recordings are not simply sounds but harbingers of change, signals of danger and opportunity. Concurrently twelve speakers declaim excerpts from Thoreau's writings at times determined by chance operations; and once again, the result is not only not discernibly Thoreau, it is not even a sonic collage: it suggests mutterings of discontent, a groundswell of protest.

The whole is preceded by a detailed written preface, to be read aloud, which is unambiguously critical of government as practiced in the United States:

> what is called balance between the branches of our government is not balance at all: all the branches of our government are occupied by lawyers...
>
> ...the law...is concerned with precedent, not with discovery...When the law is corrupt, it is corrupt because it concentrates its energy on protecting the rich from the poor...That is why not only aspiration but intelligence...and conscience...are missing in our leadership.
>
> Our leaders are concerned with the energy crisis. They assure us they will find new sources of oil. Not only will Earth's reservoir of fossil fuels soon be exhausted: their continued use continues the ruin of the environment. Our leaders promise they will solve the unemployment problem: they will give everyone a job. It would be more in the spirit of Yankee ingenuity, more American, to find a way to get all the work done that needs to be done without anyone's lifting a finger. Our leaders are concerned with inflation and insufficient cash. Money, however, is credit, and credit is confidence. We have lost confidence in one another. We could regain it tomorrow by simply changing our minds.   (Cage 1975, p. 4)

In the course of the "Preface" Cage recalls his prize-winning speech from four decades before: "*Other People Think*...proposed silence on the part of the U.S.A. as preliminary to the solution of its Latin American problems.

Even then our industrialists thought of themselves as the owners of the world, all of it, not just the part between Mexico and Canada. Now our government thinks of us also as the policemen of the world, no longer rich policemen, just poor ones, but nonetheless on the side of the Good and acting as though possessed of the Power" (Cage 1975, p. 5).

So there *is* an "agit-prop" Cage, an impassioned critic of the *status quo*, a trenchant satirist and polemicist. What can this Cage have to do with the open Cage, the joyous observer of all around him, defender of the unexpected?

It is worth noting that there are several other works, roughly contemporaneous with either *Credo in Us* or *Lecture on the Weather*, that have important political components. From the earlier period, there is *In the Name of the Holocaust* (1942), for prepared piano, written for a dance by Merce Cunningham; the title is a clear indictment of both government-sponsored genocide and institutional religion, and the piece moves from quiet plucked sounds through more dramatic sections exploring more abrasive preparations to a raging *fortissimo* conclusion built primarily of massive forearm clusters. Another score was written for Pearl Primus's dance *Our Spring Will Come* (1945); one's perception of the rather gentle prepared piano music is transformed when one learns that over it was to be declaimed a Langston Hughes poem addressing the condition of Black people in America.[3]

Lecture on the Weather was preceded by *Les Chants de Maldoror Pulverisés par l'Assistance Même* (1971), a wickedly satirical mis-application of democracy. Excerpts from Lautréamont's novel *Les Chants de Maldoror* are distributed among the audience, which then must vote to decide questions such as whether to read in a high or low voice. In some cases the minority rules; in all cases Cage's instructions specify an approved method for those who wish to rebel: "rebellion can take the form of song or plainchant . . . "; "rebellion can take the form of repeatedly calling out the name of the author (Lautréamont) . . . "; "rebellion can take any form whatever . . . " This in turn had been preceded by the seminal *Song Books* (1970), a collection of nearly ninety "solos," one of which (Solo 35) had been singled out by Cage for multiple renderings during any single performance. Solo 35 is a collection of melodies setting a text by Thoreau: "The best form of government is no government at all, and that is what men will have when they are ready for it." Cage asks that the flag of the whole earth, or the black flag of anarchy, be raised before each rendering, so that at the end of a fairly long performance the stage will be virtually littered with flags.

These two periods (the early 1940s and the early 1970s) have in common American engagement in major wars (World War II and Vietnam). The second was also a time of radical social protest, in part against the war but also against politics as usual; surely *Les Chanson de Maldoror Pulverisés par l'Assistance Même* in part comments on the notorious 1968 Democratic convention in Chicago and the ensuing legal spectacle, the trial of the Chicago Seven. *Lecture on the Weather* is preferably performed "by American men who had become Canadian citizens" (Cage 1980, p. 3); in 1975 that meant draft evaders. As late as 1979 Cage was still reacting to the preceding decade: "I am an optimist. That is my raison d'être. But by the news each day I've been in a sense made dumb. In 1973 I began another installment of my *Diary: How to Improve the World (You Will Only Make Matters Worse)*: it remains unfinished" (Cage 1980, p. ix). And the earlier war touched even Cage's more abstract pieces:

> Being involved in the complexities of a nation at war and a city in business-as-usual led me to know that there is a difference between large things and small things . . . Two of my compositions . . . suggest this difference. One of them, the *Third Imaginary Landscape*, used complex rhythmic oppositions played on harsh sounding instruments combined with recordings of generator noises, sliding electrical sounds, insistent buzzers, thunderous crashes and roars, and a rhythmic structure whose numerical relationships suggested disintegration. The other, four pieces called *Amores*, was very quiet . . . My feeling was that beauty yet remains in intimate situations; that it is quite hopeless to think and act impressively in public terms.   (Cage 1948a, pp. 39–40)

Cage's overtly political pieces, then, appear to be something of an aberration, a "public" effort undertaken only when situations are wholly intolerable. His more usual practice was indirect: the creation of a music which would open people's minds to other possibilities, social as well as musical. He sought to bring about what he often described as "anarchy": not mindlessness or riotous self-indulgence but "non-obstruction," applied in art to prevent taste and judgment from obscuring "the very life we're living," and applied in daily life as a self-discipline by which one's desires are prevented from impeding another's actions (Cage 1957, p. 12). The complement to "non-obstruction" is "interpenetration," and Cage constantly links the two terms: "Living for a thing is to be at the center. That entails interpenetration and non-obstruction" (Cage 1981, p. 91). "All of / creatioN / enDless / interpentetrAtion / togetheR / wiTh / nOnobstruction . . ." (Perloff & Junkerman 1994, p. 16). It was in his study of Zen that Cage first encountered this duality, but he later explored it in Buckminster Fuller's concept of design, Thoreau's writings about nature, and Marshall McLuhan's interpretations of technology. In all cases what he proposes is to position the self consciously in the *nothing* between separation and continuity: "Buckminster Fuller . . . describes the world to us as an ensemble of spheres between which there is a void, a necessary space. We have a tendency to forget that space. We leap across it to establish our relationships and connections . . . In reality, we fall down and we don't even realize it!" (Cage 1981, p. 93).

Analogously, the leap to relationships in society – manifested above all in the imposition of law by governments – forgets the *necessary* space between individuals. Cage rails constantly against the imposition of uniformity, the assertion implicit in the very word "politic" that change comes about only through the concerted efforts of groups of individuals. But willful autonomy is equally pernicious; to blindly indulge one's own desires is to create an even more sweeping distinction, between oneself and all others. Anarchy requires that every individual remain poised between autonomy and connectedness, refusing obstruction of self or others but not refusing interpenetration. The anarchic citizen strives to be "as careful as possible not to form any ideas about what each person should or should not do," but at the same time "to appreciate, as much as possible, everything [each person] does do – even down to [the] slightest actions" (Cage 1981, pp. 99–100). "Anarchy," Cage writes, "really does have The future / people are talkIng abOut / it is creative coNduct / As opposed to / subordiNate / conDuct it is positive / individuAlism to follow a way of thinking / that pRoposes you can assume / for your own acTs / respOnsibility / Visibly / rEsponsible / fiRst to yourself and then to society . . . " (Perloff & Junkerman 1994, p. 37).

Anarchy is made practical, Cage asserts, by the organization of daily life: provide for basic needs, eliminate useless work, distribute resources sensibly and ecologically. These are the tasks which "utilities" should undertake; one of Cage's favorite metaphors is the telephone, which allowed social interaction to take place without physically carrying messages from one place to another. "Don't change Man (Fuller): change his environment. Humanities? Save them for your spare time. Concentrate on the Utilities" (Cage 1969, p. 83). An anarchy that is motivated by conflict only perpetuates the impossibility of change: "An *impracticable* anarchy is one which provokes the intervention of the police . . . If the object is to reach a society where you can do anything at all, the role of organization must be concentrated on the utilities" (Cage 1981, p. 53). To bring about the "revolution", it is *usefulness*, not ideology, that serves to test ideas and actions: "I'm not interested in objecting to things that are wrong. I'm interested in doing something that seems to be useful to do" (Kostelanetz 1988, p. 274).

Cage was a composer, and if he was to do something *useful*, he could do it (at least) in the realm of music. In this sense virtually every piece he made after 1950 was intended to further, one way or another, changes of mind and in society. The range of strategies is astonishing; with each new notation, with each novel technique, could be associated a parallel social intervention. Each work, like each individual, is rightly situated in the *nothing* between relatedness and autonomy; and the experience of the work – always in and of the present – invites contemplation of that nothingness. However, viewing the works as historical artifacts (not as momentary art), it is possible to generalize, to group, to relate; and in retrospect it seems that Cage's strategies fall into three large categories.

In a substantial number of works spanning almost his entire career, Cage attempted to present a model of or analogue to one or more aspects of utopian society. Arguably such pieces reach back at least as far as *Double Music* (1940), which Cage wrote with Lou Harrison, each independently of the other but in conformance with an agreed-upon structure. The results are two musics which are both autonomous and interpenetrating; as Cage explained in 1948, before his anarchic ideals were fully formed: "there is a deeply rewarding world of musical experience to be found in this way. The peculiarities of a single personality disappear almost entirely and there comes into perception through the music a natural friendliness, which has the aspect of a festival. I hereby suggest this method of composition as the solution of Russia's current musical problems. What could better describe a democratic view of life?" (Cage 1948a, p. 38).

A more generally recognized landmark is the Concerto for Prepared Piano and Orchestra (1951–52). In conversation, Daniel Charles asked Cage how he moved from the expressive aesthetic of the *Sonatas and Interludes* "to *non-obstruction* and *interpenetration*, in Suzuki's sense"; Cage replied by citing the Concerto, which was "a drama between the piano, which remains romantic, expressive, and the orchestra, which itself follows the principles of oriental philosophy. And the third movement signifies the coming together of things which were opposed to one another in the first movement" (Cage 1981, p. 41). Later, Cage made the utopian implications more explicit: "The pianist, who, in the second movement, followed the orchestra as a disciple follows his master, in a sort of antiphony, then comes to join the latter in his impersonality. At the same time I grant more and more space to silences. Which may signify that I ceased being a composer. The silences speak for me, they demonstrate quite well that *I* am no longer there . . . They say nothing. Or, if you prefer, they are beginning to speak *Nothingness!*" (Cage 1981, p. 104). The Concerto, then, models a process by which the soloist (an individual) learns to transcend *ego*, to enter into the ensemble (an anarchic community); in the utopia of the third movement sounds (individual actions) are positioned in silence (nothingness), which allows them to be both non-obstructing and interpenetrating.

The relationship between individual and ensemble is especially problematic for Cage, and he went to considerable lengths to avoid vesting authority in either conductors or soloists. The *Concert for Piano and Orchestra* (1957–58) contains both soloist and conductor; the position of the former is undercut both by Cage's refusal of the word "concerto" and by the essentially irrelevant character of the soloist's music. The conductor (Merce Cunningham, in the first performance) serves simply as a clock, with no interpretive or directive power whatsoever; in effect, the conductor is transformed from government official to utility technician. In several later works, notably *Etcetera* (1973) and *Etcetera 2/4 Orchestras* (1985), conductors, soloists and ensemble are interdependent: a conductible ensemble is created only when a subset of individuals (acting in effect as soloists) chooses to bring it into being (Pritchett 1993, p. 193). In all these and many other works, the interplay of individual initiative and collective responsibility is meant in part to represent the workings of a more ideal society.

Probably the most striking model of anarchy is offered by *Musicircus*, a work so anti-authoritarian that Cage never even wrote a score for it. Since no performing forces are specified, no time lengths, no coordination, no director, *Musicircus* is an invitation rather than a directive: musicians of whatever persuasion are invited to occupy a certain space (or spaces) for a certain time. This brings about neither ensemble nor counterpoint, but rather simple coexistence. Sounds are both discrete and interconnected; both musicians and spectators have the opportunity to situate their understanding at any point on the spectrum between individuation and aggregation. Charles Junkerman has written a probing account of a 1992 *Musicircus* in which he notes that four principles seemed to govern the event: a non-hierarchical distribution of sounds and performers; a non-commercial basis for participation; an absence of distinctions or categories; and a deliberate lack of focus. All these are necessary corollaries of anarchy as Cage conceives it; *Musicircus* becomes, in fact, not so much a *model* of anarchy as an *example* of it (Perloff & Junkerman 1994, pp. 44–48).

The performers in a *Musicircus* confront, among other problems, the absence of authority: no one will tell them they are too loud or soft, too responsive or inflexible. They are entirely on their own, without guidance or regulation, and they must confront the necessity of determining rules for governing their own behaviors. In this sense *Musicircus* also belongs to a second large category of compositions: those which seek to produce change by asking (never requiring) performers to confront the absence or breakdown of conventional ways of working. Very broadly speaking, the confrontations occur in three types of situation.

The first is created by the sheer virtuosity required by many of Cage's scores. In some of the earlier works, like the *Concert*, the demands are deceptive; the novelty and richness of the notation conceal the formidable effort required to prepare and execute a satisfactory performance. But in several later pieces – especially the series of *Etudes* – the notation is relatively conventional and the near-impossibility of a correct performance is immediately evident. Cage's motivation for making such extraordinary demands was explicitly social:

> I had become interested in writing difficult music, etudes, because of the world situation which often seems to many of us hopeless. I thought that were a musician to give the example in public of doing the impossible that it would inspire someone who was struck by that performance to change the world, to improve it, following, for example, the clearly outlined projects of Buckminster Fuller. That has not happened but I remain optimistic and continue to write music, which is, after all, a social art – it is not finished even when other people play it; it requires listeners too, and among them even sometimes the composer. Thus pieces of music can be taken as models for human behavior, not only proving the possibility of doing the impossible, but showing too, in a work performed by more than one person, the practicality of anarchy. (Kostelanetz 1993, p. 106)

A performer undertaking such a work, then, is asked to exemplify a commitment not to beauty or understanding or technique but to sheer tenacity. In its very intractability the music is meant to build the skills needed to transform the impossibilities of our social situation: persistence, resourcefulness, discipline.

A different kind of impossibility arises in other works, in which performers confront situations which are literally uncontrollable. In pieces such as *Inlets* (1977) and *Child of Tree* (1975), it is the instruments themselves which control events, so that a player's efforts to produce desired effects are almost certainly frustrated: "In the case of the plant materials [in *Child of Tree*] . . . the instrument is unfamiliar. If you become very familiar with a piece of cactus, it very shortly disintegrates, and you have to replace it with another one that you don't know. So the whole thing remains fascinating, and free of your memory as a matter of course. In the case of *Inlets*, you have no control whatsoever over the conch shell when it's filled with water . . . So the rhythm belongs to the instruments, and not to you" (Kostelanetz 1988, p. 91).

In other circumstances, players work independently of each other and often at cross-purposes; one performer may control the amplitude of the sounds created by another, for instance, so that a sound intended to be very soft is actually quite loud. Even when no direct interaction takes place, the overall effect of activities undertaken by several individuals simultaneously is not predictable by any one person alone. Again performers confront the breakdown of conventional, musicianly behavior, in that their responsibility is to themselves and their own actions, not to an imagined totality; and again, the implications are social and anarchical, as Cage made clear in conversation with Nikša Gligo: "[My performance with Tudor] is a very simple example of anarchy because two of us were working together, but independently.

I was not telling David Tudor what to do, nor was he telling me what to do, and anything that either of us did worked with everything the other did ... When we have the facility to do and to work without constraint, or when we have the things that we need to use, I think we have all that we need. We do not need to have the laws that tell us not to do this but to do something else" (Kostelanetz 1988, p. 266).

A third sort of confrontation occurs when the requirements of Cage's music are simply incompatible with the conventional circumstances of a musician's situation. Throughout Cage's career he produced work which simply could not be performed by professional ensembles without a substantial change of mind. "Have you heard that Town Hall recording of my *Concert for Piano and Orchestra?*" Cage asked Geneviere Marcus in 1970. "At one point, one of the woodwind instruments quotes from Stravinsky ... He was just going wild – not playing what was in front of him, but rather whatever came into his head. I have tried in my work to free myself from my own head. I would hope that people would take that opportunity to do likewise." Marcus then commented, "Yes, but it's like society. You want to give people freedom, to have an anarchic situation, and now you're saying that they do tend to misuse it sometimes, and this is what people are afraid for society too, that they will misuse freedom in an anarchic situation." To which Cage responded, "Well, the reason we're afraid is because we have this overlap situation of the Old dying and the New coming into being. When the New coming into being is used by someone who is in the Old point of view and dying, then that's when that foolishness occurs" (Kostelanetz 1988, pp. 68–69). Only two years later Cage observed yet another confrontation, which he again framed in societal terms:

When I arrived ... I discovered that not only was the orchestra's final rehearsal [for *Cheap Imitation*] their first but that many of the musicians had not bothered to look at the music ... After hearing a few miserable attempts to play the first phrases, I spoke to the musicians about the deplorable state of society (not only of musical society), and I withdrew the piece from the evening's program. By having written *Cheap Imitation*, I've provided, I think, a means for opening the ears of orchestral musicians and enabling them to make music instead of, as now, only money to pay their bills. I am convinced that they play other music just as badly as they play mine. However, in the case of *Cheap Imitation*, there are no climaxes, no harmonies, no counterpoints in which to hide one's lack of devotion. This lack of devotion is not to be blamed on particular individuals ...; it is to be blamed on the present organization of society; it is the raison d'être for revolution.   (Cage 1972, pp. [xii]–[xiii])

All three of these situations – impossible virtuosity, uncontrollable circumstances, intransigent professionalism – invite performers to enter into new relationships with each other and with the sounds they make. For listeners the music may or may not model new social relations; but its social implications are equally profound. For if the tasks of the performers are reconceived, if a workable anarchy can come to inform their music-making, and if the music they make can enter into daily life, then surely the transformation of daily life itself is at least conceivable.

A third and final category of compositions which address social change could plausibly be said to encompass all the works written using chance techniques – that is, essentially everything Cage wrote after 1950. Chance techniques shift the focus of composition from result to process, from intention to acceptance. They select one alternative from a field of possibilities, but with no presumption that that alternative is in any way preferable. "Chance operations are not mysterious sources of 'the right answers,'" Cage wrote. "They are a means of locating a single one among a multiplicity of answers, and, at the same time, of freeing the ego from its taste and memory, its concern for profit and power, of silencing the ego so that the rest of the world has a chance to enter into the ego's own experience whether that be outside or inside." And, he added: "The desire for the best and most effective in connection with the highest profits and the greatest power led to the fall of nations before us: Rome, Britain, Hitler's Germany. Those were not chance operations" (Cage 1975, p. 5).

For a performer, however, chance operations create an interpretive dilemma, most evident in the works having relatively conventional notation, such as the series of *Music for Piano* from the 1950s. The third note of *Music for Piano 4* is A♭; but why play that note? It was, after all, selected randomly from the eighty-eight possibilities the keyboard offers. Any other note could just as well have been chosen. Were this a Mozart minuet, one would presume that a different note would be *wrong*, would detract from the beauty of the work, would violate the composer's intention and hinder a listener's opportunity to discern that intention. But this is not Mozart, and there is no intention. Why play A♭?

No satisfactory answer exists in the domain of aesthetics; judgment, taste, interpretive insight are all irrelevant to *Music for Piano 4*. The use of chance operations shifts performance too, willy-nilly, from product to process, from object to action. If a response is to be found, it will be situated in the domain of *ethics* (the rightness of actions) rather than *aesthetics* (the rightness of objects). A performer's work is thus relocated in life itself, and especially in the life of a society: determine the right thing to *do*; act so as to further the general good. Music interpenetrates with life.

Cage's answer with respect to recomposition is clear: any alterations – even ones intended as improvements – are manifestations of *ego*, and therefore to be avoided. Ego is inherently conservative, inherently limited, and to impose a judgment shrinks the realm of the possible, obstructs the possibility of change. "The *I Ching* promises a completely sad lot to anyone who insists on getting a good answer. If I am unhappy after a chance operation, if the result does not satisfy me, by accepting it I at least have the chance to modify myself, to change myself. But if I insist on changing the *I Ching*, then it changes rather than I, and I have gained nothing, accomplished nothing!" (Cage 1981, pp. 94–95).

But what of accident? Cage embraced the unexpected, accepted the incongruous: "Value judgments are not in the nature of this work as regards either composition, performance, or listening... A 'mistake' is beside the point, for once anything happens it authentically is" (Cage 1952b, p. 59). Is a performer, then, to be similarly open? Need a performer practice? Is it *wrong* (ethically, of course, not aesthetically) to play (in error) something not written?

Cage provided a partial answer: "Minimum ethic: do what you said you'd do" (Cage 1965a, p. 4). To undertake a performance is to declare, in effect, that one will perform what is written. The *ethical* position (again, aesthetics are irrelevant) is to do all that one can to bring that about; a mistake *is* a mistake, even if it is also beside the point. But this still begs the question, at least in part: in performance does one approach the immediate future (the next musical event) with the same attitude, the same anxieties, that would be brought to the next event in a fully *intended* composition? Or is a certain insouciance about the outcome acceptable, if not inevitable? If all is acceptable, why attempt to shape the future at all?

Such questions have exact parallels in Cage's views about society and change. On the one hand he offered a seemingly endless stream of proposals for the future, means by which change – of a very specific sort – could come about. On the other hand he insisted on accepting the present *as it is*, without judgment or regret – most famously, perhaps, in a story that still retains some of its power to shock:

> I went to a concert upstairs in Town Hall. The composer whose works were being performed had provided program notes. One of these notes was to the effect that there is too much pain in the world. After the concert I was walking along with the composer and he was telling me how the performances had not been quite up to snuff. So I said, "Well, I enjoyed the music, but I didn't agree with that program note about there being too much pain in the world." He said, "What? Don't you think there's enough?" I said, "I think there's just the right amount." (Cage 1961, p. 93)

This anecdote, seemingly about pain and the world, actually focuses on the word *is*: Cage says nothing about the amount of pain tomorrow, nor does he preclude efforts to reduce pain in the short or long term; he simply asserts that *at this moment*, this very *now* instant, the world *is* as it should be – not because it conforms to a judgment made yesterday about today, but because any effort to affect its condition tomorrow is futile unless its *present* state is accepted, in full and without qualification. Again and again, in his writing and his thought, Cage distinguishes the present from the future, acceptance from action, arguing *against* contradiction: "Between your availability to experience whatever happens (what I called aesthetic openness . . .) and the desire to change the world (an active responsibility for the littlest things) there is no break or reversal" (Cage 1981, p. 97). "I can work in the society as it intolerably structured is, and I can also work in it as hopefully unstructured it will be in the future" (Cage 1972, p. xiii). Or, most compactly: "World's O.K. as is: work to make the world O.K." (Cage 1966, p. 57).

At the heart of Cage's social thought, then, is a reconception of *time*: not a continuum, in which past flows into future through the present, but three distinct conditions: past / present / future. The self is poised in the nothingness between these, so that they interpenetrate without obstruction; in a condition of constant readiness, the self both accepts and imagines (and so also for Cage's music)

All of

creatioN

enDless

interpenetrAtion

togetheR

wiTh

nOnobstruction. . .

. . .

from failUre

to faiLure

right up to the finAl

vicTory

. . .

aNarchy   it promises nothing

minD

up to the finAl

victoRy

creaTive mind

(Perloff & Junkerman 1994, pp. 16, 37, 38)

13 Cage and postmodernism

ALASTAIR WILLIAMS

Postmodernism is best understood as an ensemble of discourses that is not only internally diverse but also contradictory in its relationship to modernism. For postmodernism is both a rejection of modernism, because it jettisons the modernist fascination with system and form, and a transformation, in the sense that it reveals aspects of modernism that were previously undervalued. Given that the range of influences which contributed to the career of John Cage is as tangled as the diverse currents that feed postmodernism, it is not difficult to find parallels between Cage's aesthetics and the postmodernist ethos.[1] Add to this Cage's apparent appetite for unresolved paradoxes, and it is tempting to argue that this is the sense in which Cage is most consistently postmodernist. However, not all Cage's contradictions are postmodernist contradictions. Indeed the difficulties presented by trying to decide whether Cage is modernist or postmodernist, demonstrate just how hard it is to draw a rigid line between the two mindsets.[2]

Before considering further the affinities between Cage and postmodernism, it is necessary to map some of the salient features of postmodernism, while noting that Cage's activities are not only described by this category but also contribute to its formation. The postmodern response to the rationalizing processes of modernity falls into two main strands. One offers an intensification of modernity, drawing on the energy of post-industrial new technologies and comfortably inhabiting the increasingly manufactured worlds we have created. The other strand counters the incursions of technocratic systems on nature and communities and is characterized by, for example, the ecology movement and new-age beliefs. Of course, there are many shades and variations of opinion between these hyper-modern and anti-modern extremes.

Both aspects can be found in Cage. The first in his commitment to the new, in his ability to escape the restraints of the past, in his willingness to generate new compositional systems, and in his capacity to use procedures in a detached way. The second in his challenges to systematic control, in his political and cultural anarchy, and in his sensitivity to the particular. The cultural politics of postmodernism in its second mode also pay much attention to the particular, typically by examining issues of gender, ethnicity and sexuality that are usually ignored by the grand historical narratives of modernity. In this respect Cage's postmodernism is idiosyncratic since, while these themes are by no means absent, attention to the particular for him is expressed in the more abstract sense of releasing sounds from governing concepts. *4'33"* (1952), which simply invites audiences to listen to the sounds around them, offers perhaps the most extreme example of this tendency. It does, however, contain a nascent environmentalism, in which Cage anticipates one of the most pressing concerns of the late twentieth and early twenty-first centuries. We encounter in his output, therefore, both the excitement of the new and a sense of resistance to social mechanization.

Within a narrower cultural domain, modernism and postmodernism are typically held apart by distinctions between closed, structured works and open, indeterminate texts. The former, the argument goes, value structure but refuse to see themselves as embedded in cultural values; the latter, meanwhile, will probably reflect on their own strategies and encourage the listener to do likewise. When rigidly adhered to, such dualities run into problems for two reasons: first, because postmodernism is as much an interpretive ethos as a way of creating art/music, it follows that apparently opaque modernist scores can be read in a postmodernist frame; second, because most artifacts display mixed characteristics, rigid distinctions between modernism and postmodernism are difficult to maintain. This overlapping is particularly intense in the case of Cage's output, where there is a rub (some would say a tension) between detached procedure and the specific moment.

From his earliest days (those of, for instance, the *Sonatas and Interludes* for prepared piano of 1946–48), Cage exhibited traits that would now be described as postmodernist. One such feature was a willingness to detach notation from the sounds that resulted, something Cage increasingly learned to accept because working with the prepared piano gradually taught him not to expect identical outcomes from different pianos.[3] This openness came about because, as a pupil of Henry Cowell, he was situated in an American experimental tradition that enjoyed some independence from the constraints of the western canon, despite his lessons with Arnold Schoenberg. This American way of thinking imbued him with a willingness to start from basic principles, without requiring a precedent, and enabled him to react to his surroundings in a direct way. This said, however, his earliest music shows a recognizably modernist fascination with system and process, and even though he parted from its initial manifestations, this interest remained active throughout his life. It is tempting to attribute this characteristic to the influence of Schoenberg and of Europe in general, but it is also characteristic, in an idiosyncratic way, of the American tradition. These influences, together with his aspects of his own personality, enabled Cage to organize material in a rigorous way without being constrained by established practice.

Construction and contingency

The constructionist trait apparent throughout Cage's career is especially marked in those scores using the "square-root form" that he employed from 1939 to 1956. The *First Construction (in Metal)* (1939) is the first of a group of scores to use a proportional number scheme in which the large-scale and small-scale number schemes mirror each other, in this case by using sixteen units of sixteen bars (though the mechanism is not exactly applied). Furthermore, each unit of sixteen bars is subdivided into small groups, in the sequence 4, 3, 2, 3, 4, which as a ratio is also used at the macro level to organize sixteen-bar units.[4] Despite the rigorous organization of instrumentation in this score, however, several of the instruments, including the gongs, brake drums and thundersheet, use unspecified pitches, and by doing so occupy a dimension beyond the reach of system-based composition. There is, then, what might be called an unrationalized dimension to the music in a juxtaposition of the system and the contingent that was to become perhaps the most defining feature of Cage's creative output.

This interplay took a decisive turn in the early 1950s when Cage started making choices by using chance techniques. Specifically, he used the *I Ching*, or Chinese *Book of Changes*, to make decisions about how to fill spaces in the chart for the third movement of the Concerto for Prepared Piano (1951). A tool for making chance-based decisions, the *I Ching* produces very precise instructions without closing the gap between structure and sound already noted in earlier scores. The combination of detailed instructions with unspecified content becomes extreme in the case of *Imaginary Landscape No. 4* (1951) for twelve radio receivers. Using an elaborate chart technique, Cage was here able to construct a score that specified tunings and volume settings. However, these precise instructions led to unpredictable results since the tunings would produce different outputs at different times of day and in various places. In some ways this score is thoroughly postmodernist since it produces sounds in space without providing a schema by which to understand them;[5] in other ways, at least as conceived by Cage, it is distinctly modernist. By broadening the discussion to include the *Music of Changes* (1951), which employs the same chart techniques as used in *Imaginary Landscape No. 4*, this paradox can be explored more extensively.

Like earlier scores, this four-volume set for piano uses a proportional number scheme to determine both the number of units and the bars within them, while employing the sixty-four hexagrams of the *I Ching* to construct charts for sound objects, durations, dynamics, tempi, and density of superimposed events. In this regard, the approach to composition is not unlike that of serial composition – and we know from their correspondence that Cage shared many concerns with Pierre Boulez in the late 1940s and early 1950s.[6] Significantly, this agreed preference rubs against the aesthetics of the bourgeois music tradition, since it indicates that a modernizing rationality can penetrate the sanctified realm of art – it suggests, that is to say, that art, too, can be exposed to the type of anonymous steering mechanisms that control industrialized societies. This sort of detachment has, of course, been bitterly criticized by advocates of postmodernism for its negation of subjectivity. At the same time, however, it heralds the frustration with humanist values that is so characteristic of the postmodernist ethos.

Cage made one of his most uncompromising statements in this regard when writing of the chart technique deployed for *Music of Changes* and *Imaginary Landscape No. 4*. He commented: "It is thus possible to make a musical composition the continuity of which is free of individual taste and memory (psychology) and also of the literature and "traditions" of the art. The sounds enter the time-space," he continues, "centered within themselves, unimpeded by service to abstraction" (Cage 1961, p. 59). This assertion, we can now see, hinges on a tension between modernism and postmodernism. For while the idea of sound unimpeded by abstraction fits well with the notion of a postmodernist decentered text, the attempt to unleash art from taste and memory is thoroughly incompatible with an ethos that seeks to understand art as embedded in a range of discourses. The first part of Cage's statement, therefore, falls into the modernist trap of seeking an aesthetic experience that resides in pristine procedures, free of personal traits. The second part of his proclamation, in which Cage claims to have turned to the sounds themselves, is also somewhat misleading, especially when considered in relation to *Imaginary Landscape No. 4*. For while this piece may indeed turn sounds away from established semantic frameworks and towards new configurations, listeners may equally well simply follow the conventions of whatever can be extracted from the mix of radio transmissions. Overall – despite relinquishing the control of sounds – by denying that sounds are socially embedded, Cage finds himself at odds with the tenor of much postmodernist aesthetics which searches for human agency in music.

Yet our experiences of these pieces need not be governed by Cage's sentiments, especially since a form of human agency does emerge in this music. What distinguishes Cage's aesthetics from high modernist aesthetics in general is its acceptance of the contingency of structure – its willingness to place controlled systems and unpredictable processes side by side. (And his interest in anarchy would suggest that he also applied this view to systems of social organization.) We have seen this intersection of control and chance at work in *Music of Changes*, which might be described as a determinate score produced by indeterminate means because the result is precise even though chance was used to make decisions. At the same time, however, the compositional procedures produce notational configurations that are sometimes unplayable and which frequently require much interpretation. Consequently, a pianist performing *Music of Changes* may well intervene, contra Cage, in a manner that is richly informed by memory and taste. In this respect, Cage's much later *Freeman Etudes* for solo violin echo the strictures of *Music of Changes*. Composed in two groups (1977–80/1989–90), these thirty-two studies used star charts to determine pitches and rhythms thereby producing music so difficult that the violinist is forced to make decisions in order to render the music playable. In both cases the performer assumes at once some authorial responsibility and intervenes as an active human agent. In both cases the interplay of the system and the contingent produces unexpected results when Cage's sentiments of the 1950s are confronted with the actuality of performance.

Discourses

Issues such as authorial control and the role of the reader (and performer, in the case of music) occupy central positions in modernist and postmodernist debates. That they should emerge so clearly in Cage's scores of the 1950s is a mark of his (not always intentional) ability to tackle prescient themes. In the range of debates about textuality there is a certain overlap between the modernist doctrine of structure – of something automated and remote from humanist values – and the postmodernist notion of text as something built on contingency, even as it espouses human agency. From the postmodernist side, much of the contingency stems from the fact that different listeners bring different values to bear on music.

Cage is situated somewhere between these positions. For him, automated procedures dissolve authorial intention and encultured meaning, thereby releasing sounds from the grip of authority. By taking a performer to be a kind of reader, if not deliberately, there is a sense in which Cage does indeed facilitate the kind of active reader envisaged by postmodernist theory. He certainly blurs the distinction between composer and performers in a multi-media piece such as *Variations IV* (1963), in which the performers create their own score by using instructions provided by Cage. Furthermore, he facilitates (though he does not actively envisage) the kind of listener who listens from a particular subject position. As we shall see, this dimension is especially notable in those scores that organize objects, especially other musics, with built-in associations. This is because, by using automated procedures to separate his own sensibility from his compositions, Cage (perhaps unwittingly) creates a space for active listening. In doing so, he paved the way for later figures such as Pauline Oliveros (*b.* 1932) to create a type of performance art that actively engages situated subjectivities. For all his idiosyncrasies, Cage, like much postmodernist criticism, shows that aesthetic meanings are negotiable and far from immutable.

This said, Cage clearly expected his instructions to be obeyed, since they were intended to exert on others the same distancing effect that he imposed on himself. He expressed disappointment with the commercial recording of *Variations IV* precisely because, by taking liberties with his instructions, it not only obscured the sense of distance and space that the directions were designed to create but also negated the tranquility and silences characteristic of more faithful performances (Cage 1981, p. 133). He also made clear his frustration with the orchestral musicians in a performance of *Europeras 1 & 2* for performing medleys of operatic tunes instead of playing the parts assigned to them.[7] Cage therefore remained an intentional composer to the extent that he expected the underlying idea of a work to be respected.

Another guiding theme that informs many of Cage's procedures was the goal of music becoming the everyday, or put the other way, of the everyday becoming music. The underlying affinity with postmodernism here is a shared willingness to dissolve an aesthetic sphere into the world it claims to transcend. Cage tells us we do not need to look for art, for it is all around us: we only need to throw off a (European) aesthetic mantle, open our ears, and we will hear music. It is, however, necessary to balance this position by pointing out that when we heed this summons our perception of the everyday is altered precisely because Cage encourages us to experience it aesthetically. Furthermore, it bears repeating that when we encounter the everyday, we encounter mediated sounds – sounds that are already socially encoded. By attuning us to our sonic environments, however, Cage enables us to appreciate the ways in which various sounds encode different spaces – a tendency that has become even more pronounced in recent times, with a lifestyles industry tying particular sounds to particular furnishings and decor.

Cage's most famous score, *4'33"*, is about silence, about finding that silence is not silent, and about learning that the sounds in which we are immersed can be perceived as art, while *0'00"* (1962), which Cage dubbed *4'33" No. 2*, more actively turns the everyday into an aesthetic experience. The score, to which Cage subsequently added further instructions, reads: "In a situation provided with maximum amplification (no feedback), perform a disciplined action." In a 1965 performance of this score, the audience heard sounds generated by Cage sitting on a squeaky chair, typing letters, and occasionally taking a sip of water. Even when described as performance art, such events continue to perplex and will often be dismissed on the basis that they are not music. Such a rejection can, however, be countered because what matters in this case is that an everyday occurrence is experienced aesthetically. As Cage himself put it: "I am speaking of nothing special, just an open ear and an open mind and the enjoyment of daily noises" (quoted in Pritchett 1993, p. 145).

Does Cage's preoccupation with the everyday presume that we can have some direct encounter with sound that aesthetic tradition has connived to eradicate? Practices designed to allow the sounds to speak for themselves would indeed seem to be predicated on the notion that sounds can be experienced in a more fundamental sense than we are accustomed to believe. The result of such an assumption is that the authenticity of the sounds becomes substituted for the revered authenticity of the composer's intention. And, like many of Cage's stances, we find that this outlook is more compatible with some facets of postmodernism than others. This is because in one sense this perspective stands in stark contrast to the value that postmodernist musicology attributes to the ways in which music is culturally situated. Yet in another sense we have seen that there is a nascent environmentalism and politics of the particular in the way that pieces such as *4'33"* and *0'00"* challenge us to open our ears. Indeed, nature imagery comes to the fore in *Inlets* (1977), which includes the sounds of water gurgling in conch shells, of a burning pinecone, and of a blown conch shell trumpet.

In the everyday one encounters popular culture in a variety of guises, yet Cage made no particular commitment to popular culture and played only an indirect part in the events that since the 1970s have combined to make the boundaries between popular and high culture more fluid. Like Andy Warhol, he challenged the limits of what institutions deem to be art, but, unlike this artist, he did not do so primarily through the media of consumer culture. Even though Cage's attempts to collapse the institutions of art into everyday experience inevitably allow for the possibility of popular music to be heard, such music is regarded with as much neutrality as any other. Because neutrality is distrustful of the mechanisms by which music becomes an active shaping force in the subjectivity of any community, no genre is treated preferentially.

Like popular culture, Cage only indirectly made space for non-western culture, which likewise was most likely to be heard as a result of remote procedures; unlike popular culture, however, non-western cultures exerted an influence on Cage at a procedural level. Again, his activity in this area was more characteristic of some aspects of postmodernism than of others, since by looking east he moved outside the normative sphere of western art but did so mainly on his own terms. Rather than becoming immersed in, for instance, Indian culture, he took principles from it and applied them to his own avant-gardist tendencies. As documented in Chapter 3 of the present volume, Cage was influenced variously by the ancient philosophies of India, China, and Japan. An early influence was Ananda Coomaraswamy, a scholar and advocate of Indian culture, who not only argued against the values of originality and self-expression that had prevailed in western art, particularly since the nineteenth century, but also distrusted the fetish of autonomy that separated art from life.[8] At first glance, Cage's high modernist procedures derive from the values that Coomaraswamy sought to reject, yet at some level Cage found congruence between a critique of originality and the internal contradictions of system-based composition. Used in tandem with these detached principles, the influence of Zen Buddhism also allowed Cage to move outside the expressive domain of bourgeois art, even if this detachment has more obvious affinities with an American experimental tradition than with the traditions of Buddhist music. Even *Ryoanji* (1983–85), which takes its name from a stone garden attached to a Zen temple in Kyoto, Japan, re-creates the eponymous garden in a different medium rather than evoking it musically. The garden itself comprises fifteen stones set in raked sand, thereby creating an emptiness that aids contemplation, and it is this emptiness that Cage seeks to emulate.

By re-creating an aesthetic experience in another medium, Cage demonstrated the extent to which his sensibility was attuned to the idea of art as experience; and this affinity resonates with an anthropologically influenced strand of musicology's desire to overcome what is seen as a modernist preoccupation with music as an object. The complaint from which this perspective arises is that positivist musicology looks at music as a thing to be catalogued, edited and historically placed, while formalist analysis concerns itself with organic coherence. Both tendencies, it is argued, reduce human artifacts to the status of objects, and this leveling is thought to be particularly inappropriate when it involves subjecting non-western culture to western procedures. Cage was certainly aware of how music atrophies; indeed, James Pritchett observes that a "distinction between objects and processes is at the heart of the change in Cage's music from the 1950s to the 1960s" (Pritchett 1993, p. 146). To which, one can add, much of Cage's music from the 1960s hinges on an overlap between processes and the human agencies they encounter. Arguably, all scores are instructions for doing something but when, in the 1960s, Cage's priorities moved from organizing material to establishing processes, he made this property explicit. *Variations IV*, for example, asks performers to map their performance space, to drop plastic transparencies on this map, and to use the sounds that occur along the resulting trajectories; thereby setting in motion processes with unknown outcomes. In this particular case, the method helps to make the building in which a performance takes place become an active agent in the array of sounds, rather than remaining as a static spatial entity.

Part of the reason music can seem object-like is that it can become frozen into its notation by musicological searches for the manuscript (*Urtext*) that most closely indicates the composer's original intention. Such endeavors can, however, only achieve accuracy in one dimension because notation itself is rooted in performance traditions that are handed down in less specific ways. Given the importance attributed to notation, it is not therefore surprising that it was a central preoccupation for someone as iconoclastic as Cage. We have already seen that the score of *Music of Changes* mirrors modernist preoccupations in its desire to include an enormous amount of information; we have also seen that there is a certain amount of contingency in how this manuscript is interpreted because the performer has to make decisions. Notation was at the heart of Cage's concerns because he constantly faced the challenges of translating ideas into charts and of translating charts into something that could be used by performers. This attention to the medium produced sometimes spectacular results, as seen in the *Concert for Piano and Orchestra* (1957–58), celebrated for its array of notations, which reflects on the notational system rather than treating it as a given. Using the terminology of semiotics, one might say that when scores start to be appreciated as visual artifacts, then signifiers start to achieve a life of their own detached from their normal signifying function: this is to say, they are appreciated for what they look like rather than standing for something else. And when these scores receive attention, beyond their function as visual artifacts, as instructions for performance, they require active interpretation, thereby drawing performers into the creative process. This process contrasts with some of the fixed views that have accrued to western ideas of notation, but Cage confronts the dominant codes of the European tradition more directly in his *Europeras*, to which I now turn.

Multi-media

After the system building of the 1950s many composers sought broader conceptions of semantics and identity in music; and this process can be detected in some of Cage's work, despite his willingness to subject the richest resources to distancing chance procedures. Generalizing, there are two main strands in Cage's output from the late 1970s (the time at which postmodernism became a mainstream ethos) to his death in 1992. One strand offers a series of instrumental compositions such as the *Freeman Etudes* and the "number pieces"; the other constitutes major multi-media works such as *Roaratorio* and the five *Europeras*, which draw on existing materials that contribute significantly to the meaning of the music. Each strand can be related to earlier periods in Cage's creative life, with *Roaratorio* and the *Europeras* re-exploring a dimension that developed from the happenings. The difference is that in the last twenty years of his life Cage seemed to have felt the pull of postmodernism towards meaning and identity. Even though the continued use of chance procedures somewhat obscures this shift, the multi-media scores dating from this time strip procedure from established meaning, thereby creating the potential for new meanings to arise.

The five *Europeras* constitute Cage's major multi-media offerings of the 1980s. A Joyce-like compound, *Europera* combines the words "Europe" and "opera" and sounds like "your opera" when spoken. *Europeras 1 & 2* (1987) were Cage's response to a commission from the Frankfurt opera, while *Europeras 3 & 4* (1990) and *Europera 5* (1991) were written on a less grand scale, with piano accompaniment making them suitable for performances outside the opera house. Cage found the materials for *Europeras 1 & 2* by plundering the New York Metropolitan Opera's archives for repertoire operas that were out of copyright. These excursions provided sections from instrumental scores that could be combined, using chance procedures, with the result that much of the instrumental writing is taken from accompanying patterns that are familiar only in a general sense (though there are some recognizable snippets). Similar procedures also yielded arias to be sung in no particular order by the cast of nineteen singers. Sets and costumes were likewise extracted from archives and distributed randomly, while lighting was organized by chance operations that made any highlighting of a character accidental. Because the quantity of chance decisions that fed into these procedures was huge, a more technological solution than Cage's tried and tested coin-tossing procedures was required. In the event, a computer program was designed to simulate the chance procedures of the *I Ching* on a large scale, generating a typically Cagean paradox: a very precise set of instructions generated by a sophisticated, random methodology.

Cage's work with existing materials, like some contemporary conceptual art, is shocking because it employs organizational methods that are alien to the internal configurations of the existing object. It touches on the Lacanian schizophrenic subject, as described by Fredric Jameson, for whom the world is made up of disconnected, fragmented codes (Jameson 1991, pp. 26–28). Applied to opera, chance procedures block and defamiliarize many learned responses to the genre, and in doing so may either cause offense or offer release from the dead weight of tradition. At the same time the *Europeras* are dependent on the genre of grand opera, almost in the way a parasite is dependent on the host it simultaneously depletes.[9] There is, therefore, a tension between a genre associated with intense expression and the automated procedures Cage applies, which were forged from a desire to negate exactly that legacy. Indeed there is plenty of irony in a figure who rejected the pomp of the European tradition working in its most extravagant genre: even as we see and hear cherished practices fall apart, we are left with the knowledge that only a figure with the international reputation of Cage, and with his professional ability to pursue a task to its logical outcome, could have ever staged such an event.

The conventions used in opera have received much attention recently from research focused on constructions of gender and ethnicity, with a view to understanding better the cultural work done in opera and perceiving it in ways that are not exclusively dominated by established traditions. Clearly, the *Europeras* lack the focus of such critical reception; yet by disturbing expectations, they demonstrate the contingency of the regime that governs stereotypical plots and encourage us to reflect on familiar assumptions. Put another way, they throw in the air precisely the semiotic conventions that cultural theorists are now so busily trying to understand. Because the *Europeras* are caught in a semantic tension between established associations and the new configurations produced by chance procedures, they raise all sorts of questions about the western canon, even though they utilize only one of its genres.

Cage once said he preferred to hear all Beethoven's symphonies simultaneously, though he apparently overcame his hostility to this composer later in life. This antipathy stems from Beethoven's central position in the culture of the masterpiece that served to provide models for what music should be, offering a model of structural closure and heroic struggle inimical to Cage's sensibility. In the first half of Cage's career, his attitude to the canon would have been unusual for a professional composer. In later years, however, as the canon lost its institutional grip, his sense of its dwindling cultural authority would have been more widely shared. Consequently, if we return our focus to grand opera, the *Europeras* are less shocking in these post-canonic times, when the operatic repertoire cannot take for granted the prestige it used to enjoy, than they would have been had Cage composed them in the 1940s. Moreover, Cage's habit of reorganizing classical music in ways alien to its own tradition shares some features with the ways in which classical music is now being increasingly marketed by unfamiliar mechanisms derived from the pop industry. In this respect, the snippets and collisions of the *Europeras* share features of contemporary multi-media advertising and display qualities of the diverse situations in which we encounter music in everyday life. Both Cage and the turn-of-the-century music industry seek to reconfigure musical identities, yet do so with the crucial difference that Cage leaves these subjectivities in a state of flux, whereas marketing pursues the opposite course in trying to nail them to specific categories.

If issues of identity are unavoidable in the *Europeras*, the same is equally true of *Roaratorio* (1979), with its dominant Irish theme. During the 1970s Cage wrote a series of mesostic poems: poems, that is, with a keyword in capital letters running through the middle of the typescript. Not only did Cage create poems using this technique, he also employed it as a method of rewriting existing texts.[10] The results include a series of readings of James Joyce's *Finnegans Wake*, with the words "JAMES JOYCE" running through the center. "Writing for the Second Time through Finnegans Wake" forms the basis of *Roaratorio*, which was commissioned as a radio play by West German Radio. Here is a randomly selected extract; the numbers refer to lines in *Finnegans Wake*.

> 169   Jem is
>   jAcob
>   he was of respectable steMming
>   an outlEx
>   between the lineS of
> 170   Juicejelly legs
>   mOlten mutton
>   greekenhearted Yude
> 171   attouCh
>   what happEns when
>   (Cage 1982, p. 44)

Cage responded to the commission by re-creating Joyce's text in a different medium. To do this he made recordings of sounds referred to in the novel and also recorded at places mentioned in Ireland. These sounds, along with recordings of Irish traditional musicians and Cage's reading of his mesostic text, were then mixed down to a stereo tape for radio broadcast (in concert performance the text can be read and the traditional music played live). The result on the CD recording, which used sixty-two-track tape, is a jumble of sounds of varying density fading in and out, with Cage's expressionless reading taking place in the sometimes inaudible background (Cage 1992).

The full title, *Roaratorio. An Irish Circus on "Finnegans Wake"*, provides a clue as to what Cage had in mind. For him, the word "circus" conveys simultaneously existing events, while "roaratorio" is one of Joyce's invented words, combining the words "roar" and "oratorio." Envisaged like this, the piece is neither about Joyce nor an interpretation of him but, rather, a presentation of him.[11] On the semantic plane, the result draws on a specifically

Irish-American identity – even though Cage's procedures work against concrete modes of interpretation – that emphasizes predominantly rural sounds
and traditional music. We may conclude, then, that whatever the novelty
of Cage's re-creation of Joyce, *Roaratorio* draws sustenance from romantic
perceptions of Ireland and pulls us into a politics of identity. Indeed its
success depends on the ways in which these themes emerge in unexpected
ways, playing on subjectivity in a manner unimagined by Cage's aesthetics
of the 1950s.[12]

Institutions

As I suggested at the beginning of this chapter, Cage is perhaps nowhere
more in tune with postmodernist thinking than in a pluralism that allows
multiple events to stand alongside each other within the same space. Instead of espousing a dominant culture, he welcomed multiple perspectives
and was content to let events coexist, seeking neither a prevalent voice nor
an overall synthesis. In this respect, he anticipated the idea of a museum
without walls, in which cultures from diverse times and places are all available in the historical present. He was, however, less attuned than are some
millennial artists to how the multiple, contested perspectives characteristic
of late twentieth-century societies impact on actual lives, pulling people in
diverse directions simultaneously. Cage's neutrality in the face of diverse,
sometimes incommensurate, worldviews offers few resources for inhabiting
such an environment.

We have seen that postmodernist musicology is preoccupied with
demonstrating how so many aspects of music that are taken as "natural" are
in fact constructed in ways that represent particular establishment interests.
In a more general sense, it seeks to show that because musical meaning is
propelled by these discourses it cannot simply reside in the music itself.
When viewed from this perspective, Cage's 1950s preoccupation with creating music free of all external associations, I have argued, is dismissive of
these ways in which music is encoded. Yet, this outlook represents an extreme stance in his career; and perhaps more importantly, from an early
stage, Cage seems to have had an intuitive sense of how to work with these
discourses at, one might say, an institutional level. In this respect, he has
much in common with, and possibly inspired, contemporary artists, such
as Cindy Sherman, who work with codes rather than with traditional materials. And it is certainly true that Cage has always been more widely accepted
by visual artists than by musicians. At an institutional level, cultural practice
becomes reflexive because instead of operating within boundaries, it queries
whatever defines these borders and limitations. Like many contemporary

practitioners and theorists, Cage also had an acute sense that his activities were performative: that by doing certain things they redefined musical discourses.

Cage lived through the peak of mass industrial production and it is arguable that his automated procedures in the 1950s to some extent mirror the detachment of mass manufacturing processes from individual experience. He also lived through the subsequent shift to supply side production, which uses flexible process to respond rapidly to demand from particular markets. Unlike economic history, Cage managed to practice both types of "manufacture" simultaneously, and his skills at adapting to demand were always considerable. In the final years of his life, for example, he wrote a series of so called "number pieces," scores that hark back to the sparse, isolated sounds that characterize his compositions in the 1950s. Using a widely adaptable time-bracket method of composition, these pieces were made up of fragments for which duration ranges were given, along with time ranges that determine when passages should occur in the piece. One of these, *Four* (1989), was composed for the Arditti Quartet. The players are instructed to distribute the parts amongst themselves in any way and then to redistribute them, with the result that the same material is played twice (see Pritchett 1992, p. 4). The resulting music is still, with gaps and single notes fading in and out, sometimes forming chords, sometimes occupying lonely space. Clearly this was a technique that allowed Cage to respond rapidly to commissions of a wide variety, adapting a single technique to a range of circumstances – a condition to which the knowledge economy still aspires.

And if Cage's artistic activity was at once pragmatic and performative, so was his life. Cage, to a considerable extent, invented himself and his own reception history by being acutely aware of the ways in which these profiles are assembled. His autobiographical remarks certainly emphasize those aspects of his life that fit with the way he chose to be perceived. The frequency with which we hear the comment, attributed to Schoenberg, that he was not a composer but an inventor of genius shows just how successful he was in this regard. Since there is no record of Schoenberg saying this – other than Cage's own – we have to consider Cage himself to be an active agent in making this comment stick. (For further details, see Hicks 1990.) This is not to suggest that Cage was dishonest; it is only to indicate that in providing his own reception history, as it were, he displayed a shrewd understanding of how such narratives affect interpretation.

If Cage's development had coincided with the axis of modernism and postmodernism, as it is often plotted, then it would have taken a postmodernist turn in the 1970s. As I have suggested, this chronological scheme does indeed have some relevance for the multi-media works that cast more concrete identities. Nevertheless, it remains the case that characteristics which would usually be attributed to postmodernism are to be found in his music of the 1930s, and qualities that would normally be attributed to modernism are to be located in his music from the 1990s. This is so because neither the extended creative life of Cage nor the complex intersections between modernism and postmodernism partake of simple schemata. If we understand postmodernism to be a dialogue with modernism that brings out some features that were once suppressed, as well as pushing beyond its limitations, then it is a dialogue in which Cage was a very active participant.

14 No escape from heaven: John Cage as father figure

KYLE GANN

In June 1975, John Cage was a guest composer at Morton Feldman's first "June in Buffalo" seminar. At regular meetings during the week he had the attending young composers talk about and play their music, and he would comment. Since there were too many composers for the allotted time, Cage assigned everyone a number and used the *I Ching* to choose which composers should speak. One young woman was incensed by the arbitrariness of this method, and every day became more vocal opposing it. The other young composers, myself included (for I was there), regarded Cage's slightest whim as divine mandate and considered the young woman a pain in the neck. Opinions that she should shut up abounded between sessions. Finally, at one of the sessions Cage entered and began by saying, "I've been thinking it over, and I've decided that Mary's right. We'll drop the chance operations, and whoever wants may talk about their work."

Of all the lessons I learned from Cage, that was the biggest, the most startling, and the most profound: the Confucian principle that ideas exist for the sake of people, not the other way around. Mary probably *was* right, but our unquestioned assumption of Cage's greatness threw any disagreement from so obscure a source into relief as a falsehood not worthy of examination. Cage was more open-minded than any of us. Nor was the lesson primarily, or at least exclusively, an ethical one. If chance procedures could be thrown aside when they interfered with a social situation, shouldn't they – or any other musical device or principle – all the more easily be thrown aside when they interfered within a musical situation? With the kind of aesthetic/ethical unity Cage so loved drawing attention to, the event was a composition lesson and a life lesson at the same time. To this day not a week goes by in which the imprint of that lesson fails to influence my composing and dealings with people.

I begin with autobiography not because I had any special relationship with Cage, but for the opposite reason: because, as a young composer, my relationship with him seemed typical, echoed by hundreds, perhaps thousands of others. Also because when discussing the special case Cage always is, it is necessary to start by breaking down some of the usual modes of discussing influence. The common wisdom is that he is one of the most influential composers of the twentieth century. And yet, looking through music of composers born after 1940, it is rarely easy to say wherein that influence consists. Cage's influence is everywhere and nowhere: so pervasive that it can seem trivial to call attention to, and so non-existent that it can sometimes be impossible to find an idea or device borrowed from Cage in the scores of even young composers devoted to him.

Those young composers, at least composers young relative to Cage, will be the subject of this chapter. The composers contemporaneous with Cage knew him as a provocateur, someone whose unconventionality grabbed attention in *Life* magazine, but whose music seemed irrelevant to the mainstream; and subsequently as someone who achieved a resentable celebrity after the publication of *Silence* in 1961. Composers born after 1940, however, experienced no such split. As they came of age artistically, they encountered Cage as full-blown celebrity, as humorist, as philosopher-saint, as composer of mind-blowing chance and indeterminate scores, as spokesperson for egolessness in a decade (the 1960s) that made egolessness seem a charming possibility.

And yet where will one look for egolessness among those young composers today? How many of them relinquish control over their own music in the way Cage did, bypass their own taste as he did? The official establishment statement on Cage, intended to circumscribe his importance while grudging him his undeniable due, is that he was important as a philosopher, not as a composer. But which young composers still subscribe to Cage's philosophy? Cage was part of a generation – one could mention Milton Babbitt and Conlon Nancarrow, close contemporaries of Cage, as others – for whom music was simply a pattern of sounds, incapable of expressing or eliciting emotion except by some willing self-delusion on the part of the listener. As a philosophy of music, this one seems short-lived and relatively insignificant.

Yet how to explain the fact that, for hundreds of composers, Cage remains one of the central musical figures of the mid-twentieth century, if not *the* central one? The question already creates a distinction between types of younger composer. For thousands trained in America's conservatories, Cage is merely an historical irritant, a charlatan against whom their teachers warned them. For another type, Cage is a model, a basic paradigm for a composer's life. In America, this is probably the most reliable distinction between what is called the Uptown composer (Uptown as in Manhattan) and the Downtown composer. Uptown composers mention Cage with anger or contempt or condescension; Downtown composers talk of him with reverence, respect, and seriousness. Perhaps no other composer in history elicits such extremes of approval and disapproval.

What we will find is that Cage's influence is not what we typically think of as influence: as in, say, those influenced by Nancarrow will use different tempos at the same time, or those influenced by Copland adopt a rhythmically lively pandiatonicism in their music. Cage-influenced composers diffract out along a rainbow of types: those who are influenced by specific Cage works, those influenced by specific techniques, those influenced by the general sound of his music, those to whom he transmitted influences picked up from earlier composers such as Cowell, those influenced by what Cage said and wrote, those influenced by his attitudes, those influenced by the example of his life, and those who simply found knowing him a life-changingly powerful experience. Because of the immense diffusion of Cage's impact, it may be most interesting to discuss at length the composers who were conventionally influenced by him, who actually began with Cage's composing style and developed it into their own individual manner. But, starting from the specific and moving to the general, we will try to give the flavor of every mode in which this remarkable man's musical, ethical, and personal example had a positive impact on composers of the late twentieth and early twenty-first centuries.

Since so little is written on the music of composers born after 1940 – a regrettable deficiency for which publishing companies have much to answer – the primary basis of this chapter is personal interviews and statements elicited from several dozen composers whose music has been conspicuous for its relation to what is generally understood as the post-Cage avant-garde.

Influence of the early works

There is an interesting distinction among Cage-influenced composers between those who cite his early, pre-*4′33″* works as influential, and those who are impressed instead by the late, chance- and indeterminacy-oriented works. Many composers claim to prefer the early works and not care for the later ones; hardly anyone will say the opposite. Champions of the early works remark most of all on Cage's use of rhythmic structure as the basis for music – especially as opposed to European music's emphasis on harmony – and also on his ability to create a kind of stable tonality through a fixed pitch gamut rather than through functional chords or voice-leading. Curiously, composers who cite the early works usually name specific pieces, while the champions of Cage's late music mention techniques or materials without reference to specific works.

For instance, many composers, including David Garland, Larry Polansky, John Luther Adams, and myself, consider Cage's *String Quartet in Four Parts* of 1950 a seminal work. The fact that Cage worked with a finite gamut of harmonies or sound complexes rather than with individual notes, both in the Quartet and in the earlier prepared piano works, pointed the way to a more holistic approach to composing with complex sounds rather than the atomistic way of dealing with individual notes, and even individual parameters of notes, heavily favored by serialism. One could say that this holistic approach appeared synchronously with the development of magnetic recording tape, and that the use of whole recorded sound complexes by the *musique-concrète* composers could have led, and did lead, to the same results.

The development of the sampler in the 1980s, however, has brought the Cagean aspect of holistic sound complex composing into a new light. The capacity of the keyboard sampler for summoning a different timbre with each key – prominent in the keyboard works of Linda Fisher, Henry Gwiazda, and Annie Gosfield, for example – makes the instrument a close analog of Cage's prepared piano. With the recent widespread appearance of prepared piano samples in music for samplers, pioneered by Mikel Rouse and others, the debt to Cage seems explicitly acknowledged. It can be argued that the invention of the sampler itself would have brought about a more holistic approach to sound composition; appearing against the background of a cultural memory of Cage's works of the 1940s, however, the use of sampling seems conditioned by the magnetism of *Sonatas and Interludes* and the *String Quartet in Four Parts*.

Of course, the prepared piano was itself Cage's own invention, and has passed into conventional musical use: perhaps the most mainstream example by a well-established composer is the use of (prerecorded) prepared piano with string quartet in *John's Book of Alleged Dances* by John Adams. The example of using everyday objects to alter the sound of an instrument has spread to other instruments, most significantly the guitar: James Emery, Jeffrey Schanzer, Nick Didkovsky, and Roger Kleier are only a few of the guitarists who have applied paper clips, pencils, and other objects to guitar strings to alter the sounds, most of these with the prepared piano as the seminal impetus.

Cage's use of limited pitch gamuts in the early works to create a quasi-tonality, evident not only in the works already named but in the *Nocturne* (1947), *Dream* (1948), *In a Landscape* (1948), the *Sixteen Dances* (1950–51), and other early period works, has had a pervasive influence, yet one not easy to trace. One can clearly see that by the mid-1980s, the limiting of a gamut of harmonies was standard procedure in works of postminimalist and totalist composers. One could cite Michael Gordon's *Thou Shalt/Thou Shalt Not* (1983), Julia Wolfe's *Windows of Vulnerability* (1991), certain scenes in Mikel Rouse's opera *Dennis Cleveland* (1996), and much of William Duckworth's music as examples of this technique. In all of these examples, a semblance of tonality, or at least harmonic stability, is created by the recurrence of sonorities coming back again and again, sometimes in alternation or even dissonant conflict with other recurring sonorities.

However, it would be saying too much to claim that this tendency comes directly from Cage, or even that he originated it. The use of limited and recurring sonorities to create harmonic stability became common in the Stravinsky-influenced American works of the 1930s, particularly those of Aaron Copland (*Appalachian Spring, Billy the Kid* and many others), William Schuman, even Roger Sessions. In fact, while the practice may have originated in the moment form of Stravinsky's early ballets, this harmonic technique has been a basic factor of certain strains of American music ever since, held dear not only by Cage followers but also by composers of the most conservative stripe. The most one can say is that for some young composers, the idea was transmitted through Cage's works of the 1940s; Larry Polansky, for example, claims to have picked it up from the *String Quartet in Four Parts, Sixteen Dances*, and the *Nocturne*.

A more superficial but more easily pinpointed result of Cage's 1940s music was the acceptance into new music of the toy piano. Its use by David Garland (in "My Pony's Falling" and other songs) and Bernadette Speach (in *Chosen Voices*) is attributed by the composers directly to having heard Cage's *Suite for Toy Piano* of 1948. Many other composers, including Jerome Kitzke (*The Animist Child*), Wendy Mae Chambers, Jed Distler, and myself (*Paris Intermezzo, So Many Little Dyings*) have used the toy piano with at least knowledge of Cage's prior use. Again, the toy piano seems destined to have found serious use within contemporary music with Cage or without, but he seems undeniably to have accelerated its acceptance.

The most widely cited effect of Cage's works of the 1930s and 1940s, however, is his use of rhythmic structure rather than pitch as the underlying basis of music. It would be difficult to determine whether this influence stemmed more from the works Cage wrote in predetermined rhythmic structures, such as the *String Quartet in Four Parts* and the *First Construction (in Metal)* for percussion, or from his statements in *Silence* such as the following:

> Sound has four characteristics: pitch, timbre, loudness, and duration. The opposite and necessary coexistent of sound is silence. Of the four characteristics of sound, only duration involves both sound and silence. Therefore, a structure based on durations (rhythmic: phrase, time lengths) is correct (corresponds with the nature of the material), whereas harmonic structure is incorrect (derived from pitch, which has no being in silence).
>
> (Cage 1961, p. 63, n. 2)

I know of no works written by other composers using what James Pritchett has called Cage's "macro-microcosmic" rhythmic structure, by which each part of a composition is divided into the same proportions as the piece is as a whole. Such works undoubtedly exist. More pervasive, however, is a general tendency to begin composing by setting up a rhythmic structure and then filling each section with sounds.

John Luther Adams admits to close study of Cage's numeric rhythmic-structuring methods, and has used similar ones in his works for percussion such as *Strange and Sacred Noise* and the "Three Drum Quartets" from *Earth and the Great Weather* (1993). More common in Adams's music, in works such as *Dream In White on White* (1992), *In the White Silence* (1998), and *Clouds of Forgetting, Clouds of Unknowing* (1990–95), is the use of overlapping rhythmic structures, by which, say, a string quartet changes chords every eight beats, a string orchestra every $10\,{}^2/_3$ beats, and the harp starts a new phrase every $6\,{}^2/_5$ beats. However, this overlapping of structures relates less directly to Cage than to the "Rhythm" section of Henry Cowell's *New Musical Resources* (1930) a book that had its own impact on Cage's thinking. To an extent Cage was the conduit through which Cowell's rhythmic tradition passed, and the rhythmic influences of Cowell and Cage are not always separable.

William Duckworth has also evolved a style of composition in which time structures are precomposed and then filled in. In his middle-period works, the rhythmic structures are often determined by the Fibonacci series, the series in which any two numbers of the series are added together to obtain the next number (0, 1, 1, 2, 3, 5, 8, 13, 21, 34, 55, 89...). Example 14.1 shows the use of predetermined rhythmic structure to determine phrase length in a passage from Duckworth's *Time Curve Preludes*. More will be said of Cage's influence on Duckworth below.

Example 14.1 William Duckworth, *Time Curve Preludes*, No. 8, measures 1–13

Since predetermined rhythmic structure can rarely be picked out by listening or even analysis, it seems safe to assume that many more pieces bear the imprint of this kind of structuring than is known. In one respect, however, composers born in the 1950s have veered away from Cagean usage. In the quotation above and throughout *Silence*, Cage defines the rhythmic aspect of sound as duration. Composers who grew up surrounded by rock music have tended to define the rhythmic aspect of sound in relation to a beat, not in terms of a sound's mere length, but rather of the relationship of attack points, often with respect to the grid of a steady tempo. The insistence on duration as the time aspect ties Cage to the thinking of the mid-century serialists, and limits his relevance to new music of the 1980s and 1990s.

Influence of the post-*4′33″* music

When considering the influence of Cage's late music, we turn to ideas and techniques rather than specific works. A few specific late Cage works have identifiable lines of descent. His use of radios in *Imaginary Landscape No. 4* (1951), *Water Music* (1952), and *Variations IV* (1963, presaged by his use of phonograph recordings in *Credo in Us* and *Imaginary Landscape No. 2* of 1942) sparked an interest in using commercial recordings as recontextualized musical materials. Some of the influence of these works undoubtedly detoured through Europe, as the use of radios and recordings was popularized by Karlheinz Stockhausen in his *Kurzwellen* (1968), *Opus 1970* (1970), and other works.

To the Cage fan, it would be gratifying to claim that the explosion of so-called postmodern music in the 1980s and 1990s based, via samplers and DJ performances, on recordings was the direct result of Cage's early experiments. Doubtless few in the DJ-as-artist field would ascribe the entire phenomenon to him, though many would certainly credit him as a precursor. The ubiquitous recording, as broadcast by radio or played on turntable or hot-wired CD player, was fated to become widely used in the late twentieth century as a musical instrument in its own right, the original music being thus bracketed as though in quotation marks. Cage may have been the first to sense this potential, and he certainly led many other university-trained young "serious" composers to the same thought. Many young urban pop musicians, however, had probably never heard the name John Cage until long after they had begun spinning records on turntables by hand.

It is documentable that some young composers inherited an interest in recordings as a direct result of Cage. Chief among these may have been Nicolas Collins. Collins's *Devil's Music* (1985), an early landmark in his output, is a collage of fragments of radio broadcasts that are digitally sampled, looped, and sometimes reversed or retuned. His ingenious theater piece *It Was a Dark and Stormy Night* (1990) has most of its music drawn from a recording of a Peruvian folk tune which is gradually revealed in its entirety at the end. Most reminiscent of *Credo in Us* is Collins's *Broken Light* (1991), scored for CD player and string quartet. The CD soloist subverts the recordings by looping them and jumping around within the disc on a hot-wired CD player, and the movements are named by the Baroque composers whose music is thus violated: Corelli, Locatelli, and Torelli.

Likewise, Joshua Fried has used radios and recordings in a live performance idiom. In his early days of performing in New York's East Village, he would run several radios or prerecorded tracks simultaneously, and trigger sounds from them by hitting piezo-electric discs with drumsticks; the faster he would drum, the more continuously the sound would emerge. Carl Stone has also made a career from manipulating recordings. His *Shing Kee* puts a recording by Japanese pop star Akiko Yano through a minimalist additive process; in an amazing demonstration of gradual recognition, her breathy tones over consonant piano chords are gradually revealed to be a Schubert lied. His *Hop Ken* rearranges samples of a recording of Mussorgsky's *Pictures at an Exhibition* and his *Mom's* (all of Stone's pieces are named after restaurants) realigns digital shards of Asian music into rock rhythms.

Examples are easily multiplied. Most famously, Christian Marclay's on-stage creation of record collages from his tremendous vinyl record collection can be traced back to Cage through several channels. Related to Marclay's is the work of Canadian composer John Oswald, whose infamous CD *Plunderphonics* was forced out of business by a court order on dubious charges that it violated copyright laws (dubious, because Oswald had never allowed the disc to be sold, only given away). Oswald had whimsically rearranged bits of Stravinsky's *Rite of Spring* and Beethoven's Seventh Symphony, digitally lowered Dolly Parton's voice to sound male, and made a digitized parody of Michael Jackson's hit *Bad*, called *Dab*. Neil Rolnick's *Sanctus* (1990) effectively layers and juxtaposes recordings over various classical mass movements. The keyboard sampling artist Annie Gosfield credits her early interest in performing with prerecorded sound to Cage's example.

Imaginary Landscape No. 4 had a more abstract influence on non-electronic composers as well. Beth Anderson credits it with giving her the idea for her series of *Swales* which are composed collages for acoustic instruments. Collage as an acoustic form flourished in the 1960s and 1970s with works like Luciano Berio's *Sinfonia* (1968), the "Concord" String Quartets (1972–79) of George Rochberg, and the polystylistic orchestral works of William Bolcom. Some of these composers would have avowed little or no interest in the kind of experimentalism that Cage's followers represented, and one can only speculate whether *Imaginary Landscape No. 4* or *Credo in Us* had any conscious, unconscious, or grudging impact on their tendency toward collage.

It is when we turn to the subject of chance processes, however, that we come to the central question of Cage's influence. The rhythmic, harmonic, and formal aspects of Cage's music he shared with other composers, who in ambiguous cases might be credited with equal influence. But chance composition is the concept most closely identified with Cage, and not so identified with any other composer (with the single exception of Iannis Xenakis's stochastic processes, the lesser influence of which might be seen as running closely parallel to Cage's). If Cage was as influential a composer as he is credited with being, we should expect to find that chance processes have entered the musical vocabulary in a widespread and pinpointable way. Certainly chance was Cage's most controversial innovation, one widely disparaged by composers with no sympathy for the Cagean avant-garde, and even one rejected by many younger composers who otherwise considered Cage a hero.

There are, however, many composers for whom chance processes have become a viable compositional technique – less so in the acoustic world than in the electronic, where chance is indeed a pervasive principle. Beginning in the 1970s it became common to set up synthesizers to run from random voltage control circuits, and the practice continues among thousands of electronic music students who use random algorithms in Max and other software. For the electronic composer more interested in testing the limits of his or her software than in creating a lucid result for the listener, chance processes are an everyday fact of life.

More important, if we are looking for true influence and not mere convenience or imitation, is that several composers have developed their own deliberate approach to chance composition, with results that sound not at all like Cage's own music. For instance, William Duckworth, as mentioned before, is one of the leading inheritors of Cage's aesthetic, having been influenced by both Cage's early rhythmic structures and his late chance procedures. Nevertheless, Duckworth's own music – postminimalist in style with simple melodies, jazzy rhythms, and clearly outlined forms – could hardly sound less Cagean. Especially in his recent works collected as part of the mammoth work *Cathedral,* Duckworth has used chance as a large formal determinant, and also to determine detailed elements within each section of a work.

One of Duckworth's most notable works in this respect is *Mysterious Numbers,* an orchestral work also available in a chamber version. The piece is in three jaunty, dancelike movements, with melodies that flirt with the

Example 14.2 William Duckworth, *Mysterious Numbers*, i, measures 236–242

octotonic scale. Yet Duckworth used chance procedures to determine: (1) the length of each section; (2) the scale on which each section would be based; (3) the tonic within that scale; and (4) which rhythmic figures, out of a repertoire of pop-music-based rhythms, would be used in each section. Example 14.2 shows a juncture in the first movement at which the tonality, scale, and rhythmic figures change.

Duckworth has used similar chance-determined changes of key and rhythmic texture in his pieces for piano(s) and percussion ensemble, *Gathering Together* and *Revolution*. Also, in a vocal work titled *Their Song* he subjected texts by F. Scott Fitzgerald, Henry Miller, Gertrude Stein, and Thomas McGrath to chance operations, choosing passages from one to sixty-four words in length, and fashioning the resulting passages into the text of the song. In applying chance procedures to large structural divisions, rather than note-by-note as Cage usually did, Duckworth has expanded the scale on which chance operates. The transformation is something like what Stockhausen did to serialism in such works as *Gruppen*, *Hymnen*, and *Telemusik*, applying the row concept to sectional divisions rather than (or in addition to) the textural and melodic details. The effect is to use chance not as a texture-creating device, but almost as a philosophical tool for deciding the direction of a piece, perhaps more in keeping with the original divinatory intention of the *I Ching*.

Richard Kostelanetz has written of "non-hierarchical form" as being the primary legacy of Cage's chance procedures, though he notes that few composers have adopted it (personal correspondence to the author, c. 1988). Perhaps the composer most closely associated with this idea is Petr Kotik, who was born in Prague, came under Cage's spell early, and has lived in America since 1969. Kotik used chance processes from early in his career, though at first without Cagean rigor. Then in 1971, he rescued a box of graphs that a science professor friend was about to throw away, graphs that charted the results of experiments measuring rats' reaction times to the ingestion of alcohol. Liking the undulating shapes, Kotik used these graphs to determine melodic contours in all of his major works from 1971 to 1982, including *There Is Singularly Nothing* (1971/73), *John Mary* (1973–74), and the several-hour vocal work *Many Many Women* (1975–78), all with texts by Gertrude Stein. The lines in the last-named work, in particular, interweave in random counterpoint. Kotik also fell into the distinctive habit of doubling his melodic lines in parallel fifths or fourths, almost like medieval organum.

In the 1980s Kotik began to abandon the rat charts as unnecessary, having internalized the kind of shapes they suggested. Nevertheless, his more recent music is still characterized by a sense of non-hierarchical form, as melodies in parallel fifths overlap in fluid textures and non-cumulative, non-directional forms. Example 14.3 shows a page from Kotik's *Quiescent Form* of 1995, freely written, but with lines overlapping in apparent randomness, the feel of the entire work still marked by a Cagean lack of focal points and an acceptance of silence.

The Cagean aspects of Neely Bruce's music usually have to do with collage features not determinately synchronized in performance, such as in *Short Sentences* (1999), a set of three, simultaneously performed operas. Several Bruce works use playing cards or dice to determine the order of notes or sections, and his *Furniture Music in the Form of Fifty Rag Licks* (1980) is put together from shuffled ragtime phrases selected in order by an audience member. As Bruce points out, the collage features of his larger works such as *CONVERGENCE* for multiple bands, multiple choruses, two orchestras, jazz ensemble, and so on, come as much from the example of Henry Brant as from Cage. However, Bruce wrote his *Trio for Bands* (1995) explicitly to illustrate Cage's conviction that two or three rock bands playing at the same time would be more interesting than one.

One of the younger New York composers most concerned with chance processes is Nick Didkovsky, whose ensemble Doctor Nerve plays weirdly angular computer-composed music in a high-energy, rock/jazz instrumentation and style. Didkovsky generates music for the band through software

Example 14.3 Peter Kotik, *Quiescent Form*, measures 372–385

that uses chance operations, though conditioned by mathematical algo-rithms that direct the results into certain probabilities according to Myhill distributions, Markoff chains, and recursive systems. Didkovsky then shapes the results according to his own taste, deleting notes and adding repeat signs so that odd note assemblages will become more familiar through repetition. The chance-determined musical data with which Didkovsky begins are free of his own taste and prejudices, but he uses his own judgment to alter them for ensemble playability. In this way Didkovsky software-generated works such as *Nerveware No. 1, 2, 3* and *8* for Doctor Nerve, *Take Your Ears As the Bones Of Their Queen*, *Ironwood* for drum solo, *She Look He Spit*, *Flesh Comes Out* for string quartet, *Far Away Scares Him*, *Arnalia's Secret*, and *Caught By The Sky With Wire*. Example 14.4 shows a typical page of *Take Your Ears As the Bones Of Their Queen* (Didkovsky's titles are sometimes

Example 14.4 Nick Dikovsky, *Take Your Ears as the Bones of their Queen*, measures 6–8

arrived at by subjecting texts to the same randomizing algorithms he uses for notes). Didkovsky's Doctor Nerve CD *Beta 14 ok* is also designed to be played in shuffle (random-access) mode.

Before going into her "swale" period, Beth Anderson relied much on chance techniques. In her oratorio *Joan* (1974), based on transcripts of the

Example 14.5 Beth Anderson, *Joan*, phrase transformation

```
They will catch her if they can by her own words.
faed bbee cafca aed bf faed cag bd aed abg badde

They will catch her if they can by her own words.
bbea ecff cabcb bef cf bbea cab ba bef ceb ecfda

They will catch her if they can by her own words.
ecee cdbb caecc cec da ecee cad be cec ecd cecdd

They will catch her if they can by her own words.
ddaa cadd cadcd dab ab ddaa cab ba dab ccb ccbdc

They will catch her if they can by her own words.
bbba bccc cabcb bbc cc bbba cab ba bbc cbb bccaa

They will catch her if they can by her own words.
bbaa aabb aabab bab ab bbaa aab ba bab aab aabba
```

trial of Joan of Arc, she derived melodies for the instrumentalists by assigning letters of the words in the text to the seven natural notes of the scale: a being assigned to a, b to b, and so on, then h to a again, i to b, on a rotating basis. As the piece progresses, notes are dropped from the scale, so that the alphabet is mapped onto only six pitches, then five, four, three, and two, for an increasingly minimalist texture of melodies derived by the chance contours of the text. Example 14.5 shows the progressive transformation of one phrase as it runs through the work.

What all of these composers have in common is that they started out using chance processes with a Cagean aim: to bypass their own subjective responses and arrive at musical results they might never have come up with out of their imagination. Each of them, however, has gradually abandoned chance to steer the musical results toward their own creative taste, though with a nugget of chance at the center, like the grain of sand around which the oyster shapes a pearl. Kotik and Anderson used chance early in their careers and left it behind; Duckworth and Didkovsky renew the process with each piece, starting with chance processes, but going on to make music very recognizably in their own respective styles. And the diversity of styles among these composers is enough to show how versatile a technique chance processes can be.

The number of composers whose works exhibit this kind of direct Cage influence is relatively small. Vastly larger is the group that have inherited general attitudes from Cage, and his most widespread influence of all was probably his insistence that any sound could be music. One of

his most famous texts was "The Future of Music: Credo" which opens
Silence:

> I BELIEVE THAT THE USE OF NOISE TO MAKE MUSIC WILL
> CONTINUE AND INCREASE UNTIL WE REACH A MUSIC
> PRODUCED THROUGH THE AID OF ELECTRICAL INSTRUMENTS
> WHICH WILL MAKE AVAILABLE FOR MUSICAL PURPOSES ANY
> AND ALL SOUNDS THAT CAN BE HEARD.   (Cage 1961, pp. 3–4)

Many composers list this idea first above all others, and its spread is too vast
to be estimated or traced. This may have been a shocking (though not entirely
unprecedented) opinion *c*. 1940, but, in the worlds of experimental and
popular musics alike, it has turned out to be the truest prediction Cage ever
made.

Extramusical aspects of influence

It is instructive to note what aspects of Cage's work have not had an impact
on younger composers. His desire to escape from intentionality has not
found much resonance; many young composers single this out as an aspect
of Cage they can't identify with, and few point to it as a positive feature. The
use of chance processes to generate notes has been taken over as a textural
device, but rarely with a Cagean disregard for the results. As Joshua Fried
puts it in a typical statement:

> Chance operations can help make a work sound "better" . . . if the context
> and the chance operation is sensitively and intelligently controlled . . .
> When the situation is such that a Set of chance operations yields the best
> results, those results are likely to be especially beautiful, because nature
> works that way.   (e-mail to the author, July 13, 2000)

To think in terms of better and worse, however, Fried adds, "makes me,
arguably, anti-Cage, conservative . . . "

Then again, for other composers Cage's gravitational force was so immense that they had to consciously flee from his influence. Collins writes,

> In a sense, Cage ruined my life. By the end of the term [first semester at
> Wesleyan] I had come so fully under the spell of the credo that "any sound
> can be a musical sound" that I found it quite impossible to choose one
> over another.   (e-mail to the author, July 14, 2000)

I can echo this sentiment; for two years in college I had to temporarily put
Cage's writings and music out of my mind and pretend I hated them, so
that I could nurture a personal sense of my music.

Elodie Lauten, who has worked closely with the *I Ching* throughout her career, disagrees with Cage's use of it as a random number generator.

> The most important aspect of the *I Ching* in my view is its hierarchical aspect; in other words it is a cosmological mirror. There is nothing really left to chance. The chance aspect is an illusion . . . The *I Ching* actually works with a nearly scientific precision.
>
> > (e-mail to the author, July 15, 2000)

The fact that Cage used only the numbers of the *I Ching* in his music while ignoring the complexly nested meanings of the hexagrams is a problem for some devotees of eastern thought. The fact is, in his modernist, often abstract, generally non-emotive approach to music, as in his sunny personality, Cage was not a mystic. He seemed to dabble in occult and eastern philosophies for the numbers and concepts he could cadge from them for his music and writings. Nevertheless, for many artists of my generation his writings were the first signal that there was something interesting to be found in Zen, Chinese philosophy, Christian mysticism (Meister Eckhardt), Jungian psychology, astrology (though he didn't mention it often, Cage was a client of the astrologer Julie Winter), and other phenomena exotic to traditional western spirituality. He made these disciplines sound approachable and intellectually fascinating, and thousands of young artists checked them out for themselves. Of course, many others can take credit for the interest in occultism in the 1960s, but for musicians, stereotypically isolated in their practice rooms, Cage was a crucial source.

Many young composers who admired Cage claimed not to have been musically influenced by him. "I'm sorry to say that Cage didn't directly influence any of my work," says Mary Jane Leach; "I like as few pieces of his as of some of my least favorite composers," adds Janice Giteck. "I've always presumed all sound as music," claims Henry Gwiazda; "I don't think this came from Cage." For many of these people, Cage's importance was as a personal example. Leach drew inspiration not from imitating Cage but in following a parallel path: "The lesson I drew," she says, "was not to copy him, but to find . . . a way that worked for me and be comfortable with that and not worry how it would be regarded." Gwiazda speaks for many when he says, "I've greatly admired Cage's artistic courage . . . To be able to remain steadfast in the face of almost universal condemnation takes a degree of fortitude that I aspire to. I think about that from time to time, and it has had a most positive influence on my thinking" (e-mail to the author, August 10, 2000).

William Duckworth writes:

> At first, I thought Cage had given me the permission to do anything I wanted to – a benign anything goes. But lately, I've been feeling that Cage's

real influence was the instilling of an understanding that dedication, and the committing of time to what you believe in, is of the utmost importance, and creates a very different kind of composer than one focused on fame or fortune. Music was important to John in a spiritual way; it transcended the politics of the moment. That feeling, more than any other, is with me every day. So his major influence on me has been philosophical; the shaping of my basic artistic attitudes at a fundamental level.

(e-mail to the author, July 21, 2000)

And John Luther Adams: "Cage's gentle humor and generosity of spirit was a vivid model of how to live as an artist, with honesty, dignity, and grace."

This might be Cage's most important legacy of all: he provided an alternative paradigm for young composers to imitate in their attitude toward the life of the artist. From the 1960s on, the dominant personality paradigm in university music departments was that of Arnold Schoenberg, who equated popularity in music with stupidity and shallowness, who wrote, "if it is art, it is not for all, and if it is for all, it is not art" (Schoenberg 1975, p. 124) and further,

as soon as the war was over, there came another wave which procured for me a popularity unsurpassed since. My works were played everywhere and acclaimed in such a manner that I started to doubt the value of my music . . . Either the music or the audience was worthless.

(Schoenberg 1975, p. 51)

Schoenberg's example gave composers permission to indulge in the headiest *contemptus mundi*, to shut themselves up in music departments and vent their scorn at the ignorant public, to console themselves for their lack of performances with the posthumous adoration they would undoubtedly receive. To this neurotic "misunderstood genius" mindset, Cage – Schoenberg student though he was – provided a healthy, optimistic alternative.

A negative example that Cage mentioned in print and conversation was the composer Adolph Weiss, with whom Cage studied in preparation for going to Schoenberg. Weiss, Cage recounted to Jeff Goldberg, had a large stack of scores on his piano of works that had never been performed:

He was somewhat embittered because of this, and I determined then and there that if I did get to the point of writing music I would consider my responsibility only half-finished if I didn't get it performed. I don't think of music as finished when it's simply written down.

(quoted in Kostelanetz 1988, p. 101)

This was a tremendously important example, and thousands of younger composers have saved themselves from bitterness by following it. The Cagean attitude has led to the emergence of so-called "Downtown scenes" in many major American cities, milieux in which composers perform their own works, form their own ensembles, and in general take complete responsibility for getting their music to the public.

The anti-self-pitying attitude expressed here extends to every aspect of Cage's work. He detested radios, so he wrote *Imaginary Landscapes No. 4* for radios in order to overcome his dislike. He was irritated by minimalist music, so he wrote *Hymnkus* – a repetitive work using only two octaves' worth of pitches – to seek a minimalism he could be comfortable with. He considered television boring, so he incorporated it into *Europera 5* in an attempt to find what interest it had. Whatever his personality may have been like before his celebrity of the 1960s, we younger composers never saw him reject anything, and it made a vivid impression on us. We knew that if he didn't like something we did, his worst reaction would be to take it and make something more interesting out of it. We had no escape from his omnivorous tolerance.

A frequent Cage story concerns high compliments paid to young composers who were afraid that Cage wouldn't like their music. "One day in the mid-1980s," writes Janice Giteck, "I played a tape of my piece *Callin' Home Coyote* for Cage. He said, 'This music is so beautiful it makes me cry'; he had tears in his eyes. This was amazing for me to experience because I thought my music to be about as different as anything could be from Cage's. But he was so present and available, it was a terrific lesson in and of itself" (e-mail to the author, July 17, 2000).

Perhaps one would have had to attend music school in the 1960s or 1970s to realize how sharply this attitude contrasted with what one experienced from most well-known composers. The generation that had come to prominence in those years was dominated by composers – especially those in the grip of serialism – who wanted their style of music perpetuated by their students. Many of those composers withheld encouragement from young composers whose music represented a different aesthetic.

Not so Cage. No other composer over fifty was seen at so many New York concerts, and he was quick to run up to younger composers and tell them how much he had enjoyed their music. Today, it is considered a mark of pride among many university music professors to accept whatever style their students feel moved to write in, but the attitude was not common before 1985, and Cage was ahead of his time. No wonder thousands of young composers gravitated toward him. What raised him above other composers was not that we were interested in his ideas, but that he was interested in ours.

Cage's most potent influence was a direct transmission of behavior patterns, like children imitating Daddy. Thanks to his example, Cage-influenced composers do not write music for posterity, but for their immediate environment. They do not hold out for ideal performance conditions, but work with whatever is at hand, as Cage did when he invented the prepared piano. Cage-influenced composers do not base their career expectations on mythical accounts of honors that the European masters allegedly received during their lifetimes. They do not believe that great music can come only from the European tradition. They do not choose between Schoenberg and Stravinsky, nor do they necessarily choose Cage. Musically, they are Protestants. Each has a direct relationship to his or her own creativity that does not have to be mediated through a priesthood. Cage-influenced composers make no dogmatic statements about what a piece of music must or must not achieve or include. They do not despise audiences for not recognizing them. They are not threatened by what younger composers are doing. They do not wait to be discovered, but take responsibility for the performance and dissemination of their music. They do not passively wait for compositional systems or arts organizations to bail them out.

Cage was a walking, one-man healthy climate for new music. He was a handbook on how to be a non-bitter composer in a democracy. He was the only powerful, usable, contented father figure we had. And when we departed from his model and went off on our own paths, he didn't disown us or damn us or dissuade us – he gave us his blessing. Ultimately, his impact came not from the music he wrote or what he said, but from the person he had visibly become. That's why his presence sustained new music long after his techniques had ceased to occupy it. He made the world seem safe for creativity.

Endnotes

1 Cage and America

1 "Percussion Concert," in *Life*, 14 / 11 (March 15, 1943); reproduced in Kostelanetz 1971, illustrations 7–16. The programme for the concert appears as illustration 6.

2 For a contrasting view of Cage through 1938, see Hines 1994.

3 Paraphrased from Peyser 1976, p. 55.

4 For further details of Cage's ancestry, see Revill 1992, pp. 17–19, and for his early years, pp. 20–34.

5 The recording was presumably that of *Indeterminacy*, issued on Smithsonian-Folkways (40804/5).

6 The principal exception to this observation relates to Cage's high school years: see Hines 1994, p. 78.

7 Precise details are difficult to determine. Cage was certainly in Carmel, California, on April 5, 1934 (score of *Solo with Obbligato Accompaniment of Two Voices in Canon, and Six Short Inventions on the Subjects of the Solo*), and drove back to California in (late?) December with Cowell (Hicks 1990, p. 127). See also Chapter 2.

8 The only figures omitted here from Cage's list are Lou Harrison and Alan Hovhaness. The former met Cage, at Cowell's instigation, in 1938, while the work of the latter was only discovered by Cage (and Harrison) in 1945: see Miller & Lieberman 1998, pp. 17, 27.

9 For a fascinating discussion of the true origins of this remark, see Hicks 1990.

2 Cage and Europe

1 Rob Haskins located several such compilations including *Piano Pieces the Whole World Plays* (ed. Albert E. Wier), D. Appleton and Co., New York, 1915, 1918; *59 Piano Solos – You Like to Play*, G. Schirmer, Inc., New York, 1936; and *Robbins MAMMOTH Collection of Famous Piano Music* (ed. Hugo Frey, Series No. 1), Robbins Music Corp., 1936. These latter two postdate Cage's studies but also include the same kinds of pieces he describes. Moszkowski, for example, is represented in all three collections by his *Serenata*, and Grieg by *Anitra's Dance*. In addition the second collection has three other works by Grieg (*Album Leaf, To Spring, March of the Dwarfs*) and the third collection has one more, *The Butterfly*.

2 This would have been, in all likelihood, his first introduction to Satie, a composer whose work became enormously important to Cage in the 1940s. This later interest was, in turn, probably the result of Cage's interactions with Virgil Thomson, to be discussed below. There is no evidence to indicate that Cage took special liking to Satie before then. In fact, an article Cage wrote for *Dune Forum* titled "Counterpoint" suggests the opposite: "Satie, we're not so sure about. There has been a great effort to endow his Cold Pieces, his Reverie on the Infancy of Pantagruel, etc., with 'profondeur' " (Cage 1934, p. 44). One of his famous "housewife lectures" did concern three members of Les Six, a group of French composers connected to Erik Satie. The Friday, March 24, 1933 issue of the *Santa Monica Evening Outlook* (part of the "Of Interest to Women" section, page 12) contains the following: "Evelyn Paddock Smith, pianist, and Cornelia Maule, dancer, will perform tonight at the third of a series of lectures to be given by John Cage, composer pianist, on modern music in his studio, 211 Alta Avenue. His subject tonight will be 'Three Peaks of the Advanced Parisian School.' Arthur Honneger, Darius Milhaud, and Francis Poulenc are the composers about whom he will speak." If Cage did include Satie in the lecture, it is clear, at least from the advanced publicity, that he would not have been featured to any particular degree. My thanks to Catherine Parsons Smith for drawing this newspaper article to my attention.

3 I would like to thank Frans van Rossum, who read this chapter in its entirety, spent hours going over it with me on the telephone, and made numerous suggestions towards its improvement. Van Rossum thinks that the 1930s were "the most formative years of Cage's life." He also said that Cage told him the Bauhaus was an important influence. Van Rossum showed Cage the "Counterpoint" article (see n. 2) that includes, in part, the following, "I think of Music not as self-expression, but as Expression." The article ends with "I sincerely express the hope that all this conglomeration of individuals, names merely for most of us, will disappear; and that a period will approach by way of common belief, selflessness, and technical

mastery that will be a period of Music and not of Musicians, just as during the four centuries of Gothic, there was Architecture and not Architects" (Cage 1934, pp. 43, 44). Cage's response to the article: "it seems I've only had one idea in my life."

4 Van Rossum interviewed Harry Hay at his home, April 26, 1989. These songs were probably those mentioned by Cage in an interview with William Duckworth: "when I got to California, I began an entirely different way of composing, which was through improvisation, and improvisation in relation to texts: Greek, experimental from *transition* magazine, Gertrude Stein, and Aeschylus" (Duckworth 1989, p. 16). Three Songs (1933), which uses texts by Gertrude Stein, is from this period: see Chapter 4.

5 Adolph Weiss writes that Cage "came to New York with his friend, an artist" (George 1971, p. 46). On April 12, 1988, Harry Hay wrote about Cage and Sample's relationship and included the following: "John and Don – exhilarated with their stay at Carmel with Flora Weston and her entourage, with poetry readings at Robinson Jeffers' when Lincoln Steffens was a guest for the evening – eagerly set off in mid-April of 1934 for new adventures in New York" (Hay 1996, p. 322). Cage's return with Cowell is something Cage himself must have included in his conversations with Calvin Tomkins since it appears (although listed as fall rather than December, and for a year and a half rather than the several months Cage actually spent there) in Tomkins' account (Tomkins 1976, p. 84).

6 Conflicting dates in this case favor Michael Hicks' report which is used here (Hicks 1990, pp. 126–127). Thomas Hines writes that Cage left for New York in spring 1933 and returned in the fall of 1934 (Hines 1994, pp. 91–92). This corresponds to the account Calvin Tomkins gives (Tomkins 1976, p. 84) and to the dates found in George's dissertation on Weiss. Hicks' sources are likely more reliable in this case. As previously mentioned (see note 5) Harry Hay, who was close to both Cage and Sample prior to their trip to New York, corroborates their departure as being in "mid-April 1934" (Hay 1996, p. 322).

7 In his mesostic text "Themes and Variations" (1979–80), Cage lists fifteen men who he claimed "have been important to me in my life and work" (Cage 1980, p. 55). Only three of them were composers. One, David Tudor, was an American pianist and later a composer with whom Cage became acquainted after moving to New York in the

mid-1940s. Another was the French composer Erik Satie, whom Cage never met and whose music Cage became devoted to from the mid-1940s. The third was Arnold Schoenberg. For a look at how Schoenberg directly influenced Cage's compositions, see David Bernstein's "John Cage, Schoenberg, and the Musical Idea" (Bernstein 2002)

8 Cage, in conversation with Paul Cummings (1974) "that's where [Mills College] I met Moholy-Nagy and all those people from the School of Design in Chicago, and was invited to go to Chicago and join the faculty there" (Kostelanetz 1988, p. 9). The dates are given in an appendix, titled "John Cage, 1938–1954: A Preliminary Chronology," to Patterson 1996 (pp. 261, 264).

9 According to Kirstein, "I met Merce in 1938 in Seattle at the Cornish School and knew him when he was first working with Martha Graham. I admired him as a dancer, and I met and liked John Cage" (Klosty 1986, p. 89). He was also friends with Virgil Thomson who would, in all likelihood, have given Cage's work a strong recommendation prior to Kirstein's offering them the commission.

10 Schoenberg had himself applied for a Guggenheim in 1945, in order to complete his oratorio *Die Jakobsleiter* and opera *Moses und Aron*, two of the most important religious works of the twentieth century. His application was denied and the works remained unfinished at his death (Schoenberg 1964, p. 229).

11 As mentioned, Cage had already seen Duchamp's work in Los Angeles in the early 1930s through the acquaintance of Walter Arensberg, a friend of Duchamp and a collector of his work (Retallack 1996, p. 88). According to Cage, he first met Duchamp at the home of Peggy Guggenheim and Max Ernst (Tomkins 1976, p. 94). Duchamp is also one of the "fifteen men important to me in my life and work" used to form the mesostic strings of "Themes and Variations" (Cage 1980a, p. 55). In fact, besides Duchamp and Schoenberg, the only other European included on Cage's list is James Joyce.

12 Cage's work with James Joyce goes one step further. Joyce's writings become material that Cage used to create his own.

13 The work is in reality two pieces played together: 34' 46.776" itself, and 31' 57.9864". Both are for prepared piano.

14 This letter is located at the Internationales Musikinstitut Darmstadt. My thanks to the librarian at IMD, Wilhelm Schlüter, whose assistance was invaluable during my several visits to the library in Darmstadt. Materials

cited from the archive will be noted as "IMD" followed by the date.

15 Stockhausen had written Steinecke about Cage in March: "Please give him a course! He is worth ten Kreneks!" ("Geben Sie ihm bitte einen Kurs! Der wiegt 10 Kreneks auf!) Stockhausen 2001, p. 196.

16 According to Hans G. Helms, "Heinz-Klaus Metzger, Wolf Rosenberg and myself translated John's 1958 Darmstadt lectures during the nights preceding their performances . . . Although each of the three of us worked primarily on one of the three lectures, we continually discussed John's wording and their optimal German renditions in each of the lectures as we slowly progressed. Who actually did which lecture as the lead translator neither Metzger nor I remember with any certainty, and Wolf Rosenberg is dead. Because of the collective character of the translation process I am doubtful that a stylistic analysis would clarify who did what. While Metzger, Rosenberg and I were working on the translations (and all three of us had been asked by Wolfgang Steinecke to do this work), John was present to answer any questions we might have, now and then falling asleep in Khris's, my wife's, lap who also kept us awake both by asking critical questions regarding the finished pages and by providing us with coffee whenever the need for such a stimulant arose" (Helms 2001).

17 Helms confirms Metzger's opinion as follows: "Since the knowledge of English was not nearly as widespread in Germany and Latin countries as it is today, I am pretty sure that the translations were necessary to fully understand John's ideas and his way of thinking. Most Europeans attending the Darmstadt Summer Courses had a certain knowledge of the German language at that time because the centers for avant-garde music were Cologne, Darmstadt and Donaueschingen" (Helms 2001). English translations of German, unless otherwise noted, are my own.

18 The original typescript made for the lecture uses "ihnen" correctly for English third-person "they." In the recently reprinted lecture it is changed to "Ihnen" (formal "you") which will become problematic in the typescript later. There are other changes made as well, making it even more noticeable that the mistranslation to be discussed was not corrected (Cage 1958d, p. 168). The typescript is cited here because it is what the audience would have read in 1958.

19 Helms sent me this letter after reading the manuscript of this chapter in its entirety. His final words on the subject were as follows: "John thought – as did we – that at this point in time – to use your words – 'a direct personal attack' was necessary to wake up the sleeping minds." I am very grateful to Dr. Helms for the information he provided about the translations made of Cage's Darmstadt lectures, as well as other important facts that have been incorporated elsewhere in this chapter.

3 Cage and Asia: history and sources

1 This statement makes several appearances in Cage's prose, and may be found in Cage 1961, p. 100.

2 Cage 1948, p. 41. See also Cage 1954, p. 158, and Cage 1966a, p. 76.

3 Cage 1961b, pp. 138–139. See also Cage 1961, p. 127.

4 Additional citations from Sri Ramakrishna may be found in Cage 1949, p. 63; Cage 1958a, p. 45; Cage 1959, pp. 67–68; Cage 1958–59a, p. 272; Cage 1961a, pp. 117–118; Cage 1965b, p. 136.

5 This theme is reemphasized in another passage of the essay which Cage entitled "Refrain": "Activity involving in a single process the many, turning them, even though some seem to be opposites, towards oneness, contributes to good way of life."

6 This story is also one of several independent anecdotes found in Cage 1961, p. 88.

7 Other such references include those in Cage 1961, pp. 85, 93, and 273; and Cage 1967, p. 135.

8 See, for example, Cage c. 1951–52, p. 143.

9 "Suzuki's works on Zen Buddhism are about to be published." Letter from John Cage to Pierre Boulez, January 17, 1950. See Nattiez 1993, p. 50.

10 Ruth Fuller Sasaki, quoted in Fields 1992, p. 205. Sasaki was the wife of Zen teacher Sokeian Sasaki, who founded the First Zen Institute in New York City. She herself oversaw the translation of several Zen texts and was the first foreigner to be ordained a Zen priest in Japan.

11 See, for example, Kostelanetz 1971, p. 23.

12 See, for example, "Biographical Chronology," in Gena, Brent, & Gillespie 1982, p. 186.

13 Verification in the latter semester comes from Earle Brown, who recounts how he and Cage quit early each Friday afternoon while working on the arduous cut-and-splice assemblage of *Williams Mix* to attend Suzuki's lectures (Brown 1992).

14 For other anecdotal references to Suzuki, see for instance Cage 1961, pp. 32, 40, 67, 193, 262 and 266; and Cage 1967, pp. 67–68.

15 The internal quotation derives from Simone Weil, *La Personne et le Sacré* (Gallimard, 1957), as excerpted in Rees 1958, p. 45.

16 This manifesto reappears in edited form as part of the text for "Experimental Music: Doctrine" (Cage 1955), p. 17; "Why don't you realize as I do that nothing is accomplished by writing, playing, or listening to music?"

17 See, for example, "Kwang-tse points out that a beautiful woman . . . " in Cage 1967, p. 136; and on the succeeding page, "A Chinaman (Kwang-tse tells) went to sleep . . . "

18 This story also appears in the 1959 recording of *Indeterminacy: New Aspects of Musical Form*.

19 It is noteworthy that "The Ten Thousand Things" was Cage's private name for the series of pieces with unwieldy durational titles, including *26' 1.1499" for a string player* (1953) and *34' 46.776" for a pianist* (1954). See Pritchett 1993, pp. 95–104, and elsewhere in the present volume, for further discussion.

4 Music I: to the late 1940s

1 For an analysis of this movement and other early works by Cage, see Nicholls 1990, pp. 175–217.

2 The last two notes of the inversion should be reversed. Cage maintains this mistake throughout the movement.

3 Here and elsewhere, following Cage's practice, accidentals apply only to the notes they immediately precede.

4 See Bernstein, 2002 for a detailed discussion of Cage's studies with Schoenberg.

5 Cage was also familiar with Italian Futurism, particularly Luigi Russolo's manifesto *The Art of Noise* (1913), and also knew a more recent treatise on new sounds by the Mexican composer Carlos Chavez entitled *Toward a New Music* (1937). See Nicholls 1990, pp. 190–191.

6 Note that this is one of the proportions included in the above discussion of Seeger's "verse form."

7 See Bernstein 2001, pp. 22–29. The numbering and order of the motives correspond to the sketch for this work located in the New York Public Library John Cage Manuscript Collection (JPB 95–24, folder 37).

8 Cage later described this procedure in a letter to Pierre Boulez dated January 17, 1950. See Nattiez 1993, p. 49.

9 Cage's specifications indicate "phonograph or radio," but the actual score has passages for both.

10 See Miller 2002 for a detailed account of Cage's activities in Seattle.

11 For an analysis of *Bacchanale*, see Nicholls 1990, pp. 211–213.

12 The arithmetic here is simple. A metronome marking of 114 is 1.3 times faster 88; thirty-nine measures is 1.3 times longer than thirty measures. After determining the correct number of measures, Cage adjusted the rhythmic structure. This is only an approximation; a precise alteration would yield a more complex proportion with fractions. (Cage used complex proportions in his later works, as is discussed in Chapter 11.)

13 Cage stated that the cadences in *Sonatas and Interludes* would work if the piano were prepared correctly. See, for example, Cage's letter to Gregory Clough, dated January 18, 1968, John Cage Archive, Northwestern University Music Library, Evanston, Illinois cited by Deborah Campana in "As Time Passes," in Bernstein & Hatch 2001, p. 124.

14 Many of the movements in *Sonatas and Interludes* were arranged in such a way that, as Cage explained, "progress from the end of a section to its beginning would seem inevitable" (Cage 1958a, p. 19).

6 Towards infinity: Cage in the 1950s and 1960s

1 See, for instance, Chapters 2, 5, 7, 9, 10, and 11.

2 For a detailed discussion of the relationship between Cage and the other members of the "New York School" of composers, as well as their interaction with both the "New York School" of painters and a variety of other visual artists, see Nicholls 2001.

3 See also Dufallo 1989, pp. 107–109.

4 Given Cage's reactions to his new surroundings, the whole of Lu Yun's poem is worth quoting:

> The Valley Wind
> Living in retirement beyond the World,
> Silently enjoying isolation,
> I pull the rope of my door tighter
> And stuff my window with roots and
>   ferns.
> My spirit is tuned to the Spring-season:
> At the fall of the year
> There is autumn in my heart.
> Thus imitating cosmic changes.
> My cottage becomes a Universe.

5 Taken from "Music Lovers' Field Companion" (1954), in Cage 1961, pp. 274–276. It is odd, though, that Cage

refers to *4'33"* having been published, as this did not occur until the 1960s.

6 See also Chapter 14.

7 For further discussion of *Variations IV* and its implications, see Nicholls 1998, pp. 531–532.

8 Music II: from the late 1960s

1 I would like to thank Joan Dauber, my research assistant, for the invaluable help she provided in assembling materials for this chapter. Her persistence and formidable powers of organization are enhanced by the insights she brings as an intelligent and responsible performer of Cage's music.

2 See also Pritchett 1993, chapter 2.

3 See Revill 1992, p. 220.

4 A list of the computer programs used by Cage appears in Retallack 1996, p. 315.

5 See William Brooks, "Choice and Change in Cage's Recent Music," in Gena, Brent, and Gillespie 1982, pp. 82–100.

6 In Cage 1988a, p. 29, however, Cage directly links the "rubbings" with other methods of "imitation" (rather than with star charts).

7 Cage 1990, p. 2. *Composition in Retrospect* (Cage 1988a) first contained ten such words (1981); the other five were added when the text was expanded in 1988.

9 Cage's collaborations

1 For a diagram of the floor plan see Kirby & Schechner 1995, p. 53, and Fetterman 1996, p. 99.

2 This description relies most heavily on accounts by Cage and Cunningham, including Kirby & Schechner 1995; Cage 1961, p. x; Cage 1981, pp. 52, 166; Cunningham 1982, pp. 110–111. See also Harris 1987, pp. 226–228; Duberman 1993, pp. 370–379; and Kotz 1990, p. 76.

3 Cage claims to have discovered the prepared piano while placing various objects in his instrument at home, but Bird's recollection of a brass rod falling into the piano during class does not necessarily contradict his account. The accident in class likely led to the household experiments. See Fetterman 1996, p. 8, and Montague 1985, pp. 209–210.

4 The *Hilarious Curtain Opener* and one of the ritournelles were published in *New Music Quarterly* in October 1945.

5 The program lists toccata and fuge (*sic*).

6 Many variants of this concept appear in Cage's writings. See, for example, Cage 1961, p. 63 (n. 2).

7 Arrangement, 1963; published by C. F. Peters.

8 Cunningham's description of the form as 8×8, 10×10, 6×6 (Cunningham 1982,

p. 107), is not borne out by the musical score. Since he emphasizes that the music and dance coincided at structural points within a macro-microcosmic structure, it is likely that the discrepancy resulted from faulty memory.

9 During Cage's first visit to Black Mountain College in 1948, he worked with Louise Lippold (a Cunningham student and wife of sculptor Richard Lippold) the same way. *In a Landscape* is 15×15 with subsections of 5–7–3.

10 Cage met Erdman and her husband (author Joseph Campbell) through his wife Xenia shortly after arriving in New York in 1942. He composed several works for her, including *Forever and Sunsmell* (1942), *Daughters of the Lonesome Isle* (1945), *Ophelia* (1946), and *Imaginary Landscape No. 5* (1952).

11 Malcolm Goldstein and dancer Carolyn Brown recall problems with the functioning of the antennas. Moog (Moog 2000) notes that hundreds of small clips used to attach components to the antennas had a defective plating and the solder didn't take, requiring the disassembling and reassembling of every connection. He recalls fixing the problem by the time of the performance.

12 Performers were Cage, Tudor, David Behrman, Anthony Gnazzo, and Lowell Cross.

13 Cage says that Harrison introduced him to the *I Ching* in San Francisco during the 1930s (Kostelanetz 1993, p. 177), but Harrison himself only learned about it in Los Angeles in 1942–43 (Miller & Lieberman 1998, pp. 49–50). Although Harrison told Cage about the *I Ching* when he moved to New York in 1943, Cage did not use it until the early 1950s after Christian Wolff gave him a copy of the first English translation, published by Wolff's father.

14 The seven harpsichordists were David Tudor, Antoinette Vischer, William Brooks, Ronald Peters, Yuji Takahashi, Neely Bruce, and Philip Corner.

10 Cage and Tudor

1 Cage read *Le théâtre et son double* as a result of Tudor's engagement with the book. Artaud's ideas were a frequent topic of conversation in the Cage circle in the 1950s, and very much in the air at Black Mountain College when Cage and Tudor were in residence there during the summer of 1952. At their suggestion, Tudor's companion Mary Caroline ("M. C.") Richards prepared the first English translation of Artaud's book.

2 The durations of the three performances of *Winter Music* by Cage and Tudor for which I have found timings were four minutes, ten

minutes, and twenty minutes. Each of these durations lends itself easily to the method of timing I have described above, as does a two-hour version of *Winter Music* Tudor played, with a simultaneous performance of Cage's *Atlas Eclipticalis* by the Orchestra of the S. E. M. Ensemble, in New York in 1992.

11 Cage and high modernism

1 Harrison, in a conversation with the author in March 2001, explained that, although he suggested that Cage use the pentatonic scale in the "Spring" movement, he did not provide Cage with a great deal of help with the orchestration of *The Seasons*. He also mentioned the fact that Cage had a fine ear for instrumental combinations.

2 For the most part, both works use elements of the same gamut.

3 A slightly less extensive version of this gamut appears in Pritchett 1993, p. 49, which also includes an informative discussion of the String Quartet (pp. 47–55).

4 Campana 1993 also discusses the palindromic structure of the movement. She does not, however, refer to its "inversional" relationships.

5 Cage's charts for the orchestral part for the first and second movements and the charts for both the prepared piano and orchestra for the third movement are presently located in the John Cage Manuscript Collection, New York Public Library (JPB 94–24, folder 945). The following discussion of the Concerto was informed by Pritchett's extensive research on this important work (1988a, pp. 34–87; 1988b). Pritchett did not have access to the charts, but was nevertheless able to re-create them by referring to sketches and sound lists located in the David Tudor Papers at The Getty Research Institute in Los Angeles.

6 A manuscript score and the charts are housed in the John Cage Manuscript Collection at the New York Public Library, JPB 94–24, folder 167, and JPB 94–24, folder 949.

7 The bracketed cells, marked by an asterisk, were omitted in the score.

8 The history of Cage's first introduction to the *I Ching* is ambiguous. Cage stated that Christian Wolff gave him a copy of the book around the same time he was working on the Concerto (Cage 1981, p. 43), but he also acknowledged that Lou Harrison showed him the *I Ching* in the 1930s (Cage 1986, p. 177). Harrison remembers showing Cage the book in the late 1940s (Miller & Lieberman 1998, pp. 49–50).

9 Given that there are sixty-four hexagrams and any hexagram can change into any other, there exist 4,096 possible combinations (64 × 64).

10 Cage described this procedure in a letter to Boulez dated May 22, 1951 (Nattiez 1993, p. 88). Pritchett notes that Cage incorrectly assigned the piano part to a solid line and the orchestra part to a broken line in this letter (Pritchett 1988a, p. 74).

11 The charts and working materials for the *Music of Changes* are located in The David Tudor Papers now housed at The Getty Research Institute.

12 As John Holzaepfel observes in his liner notes to Joseph Kubera's recording of the *Music of Changes* (Lovely Music, LCD 2053), each measure should be 10 cm in length (4 × 2.5 cm). The published score is smaller than the autograph.

13 In the autograph of the score, the $^5/_8$ measure concluding each unit of the microstructure is 1.40625 cm long ($^5/_8$ × 2.5 cm).

14 As in the *Sonatas and Interludes* (see Chapter 4), fractions of each $29\,^5/_8$-measure unit are expressed as proportionally reduced phrases. The $^1/_8$ in the $3^1/_8$-measure unit, for example, appears as $^1/_8(3{:}5{:}6\,^3/_4{:}6\,^3/_4{:}5{:}3\,^1/_8)$ or $^3/_8{:}^5/_8{:}^{27}/_{32}{:}^{27}/_{32}{:}^5/_8{:}^{25}/_{64}$ (Pritchett 1988a, pp. 109–111).

15 Pritchett surmises, after examining the working materials and sketches for *Williams Mix*, that Cage used only 222 unique sounds (Pritchett 1988a, p. 209). Many of the sounds were used more than once, so as to arrive at the 512 (32 × 16) sounds initially required for Cage's sixteen charts. To allow for chart mobility, he arranged the sounds into a deck of 1,024 cards (Pritchett 1988a, pp. 205–209).

16 See, for example, his letter to Cage dated December 1951 (Nattiez 1993, pp. 112–113).

17 See, for example, the discussion of Cage's early instrumental music in Chapter 4.

18 See, for example, Ulmer 1985, pp. 101–107; Jameson 1991, p. 1; and Marjorie Perloff, *The Poetics of Indeterminacy* (Chicago: Chicago University Press, 1981). Perloff places Cage within a postmodernist literary tradition, which included Rimbaud, Stein, Williams, Pound, Beckett, Ashbery, and Antin. Musicologist Charles Hamm maintains that Cage's work from the early 1950s onwards was "postmodern" (Hamm 1997). In Bernstein 2001a, I discuss the relevance of both modernist and postmodernist aesthetics to Cage's music and thought.

12 Music and society

1 Cage read "Other People Think" again as part of a seventy-fifth birthday celebration in Los Angeles (September 9, 1987), and the title and other references are dotted through his writings.

2 Undated program, Bennington College Summer Session, in Wesleyan University archives. The resemblance of this synopsis to those Cage constructed for the *Europeras* many years later is uncanny, but surely coincidental.

3 David Patterson, "Modern Music/Modern Dance: Cage *without* Cunningham, 1940–1954," paper given at the Second Biennial International Conference on Twentieth-Century Music, Goldsmiths College, London, June 30, 2001. Cage revisited the politics of Primus's dance in 1971: "of course Spring will come. But before it does no amount of good weather keeps us from thinking we're in for a few more storms" (Cage 1970–71, pp. 114–115).

13 Cage and postmodernism

1 For further discussion of the postmodernist ethos, and of how it affects musicology, see Williams 2001, pp. 115–140, and Kramer 1995, pp. 1–32.

2 In this context, see also the concluding pages of Chapter 11.

3 A similar point is made by Hamm 1997, p. 280.

4 For more detailed discussion of the *First Construction*, see Pritchett 1993, pp. 6–19, and Nicholls 1990, pp. 206–208.

5 Hamm 1997 argues that *Imaginary Landscape No. 4* "leaves modernist modes of thought behind," p. 289.

6 See Nattiez 1993.

7 Cage's letter to the orchestra is reproduced in Swed 1994, p. 129.

8 For more on the influence of Coomaraswamy, see Hamm 1997, p. 287.

9 Cage's interest in mushrooms leads Ulmer to discuss the symbiotic relationship between host and fungus as a model for what he calls "post-criticism," Ulmer 1985, pp. 101–107.

10 For a discussion of the blurring between text and commentary, with particular regard to *Roaratorio*, see Danuser 1993, pp. 150–154.

11 For further discussion of this distinction, see Pritchett 1993, pp. 190–191.

12 For more detailed discussion of *Roaratorio*, see Williams 1997, pp. 95–103.

Bibliography

Anon. 1946, "Nuts and Bolts Make Music for John Cage" *PM's Sunday Picture News* [New York], March 24, 1946, pp. 1, 4

Artaud, Antonin 1958, *The Theatre and its Double* [*Le théâtre et son double*], trans. Mary Caroline Richards, New York

Bernstein, David W. 2001, "In Order to Thicken the Plot: Toward a Critical Reception of the Music of John Cage" in Bernstein and Hatch 2001, pp. 7–40

2002, "John Cage, Arnold Schoenberg, and the Musical Idea" in Patterson 2002, pp. 15–45

Bernstein, David W. and Hatch, Christopher (eds.) 2001, *Writings through John Cage's Music, Poetry, and Art*, Chicago

Blyth, Reginald Horace 1942, *Zen in English Literature and Oriental Classics*, Tokyo 1950–52, *Haiku* (4 vols.), Tokyo

Boulez, Pierre 1948, "Propositions" ["Proposals"] in Boulez 1991, pp. 47–54

1952a, "Eventuellement . . . " ["Possibly . . . "] in Boulez 1991, pp. 111–140

1952b, "Schoenberg est mort" ["Schoenberg is Dead"] in Boulez 1991, pp. 209–214

1957, "Alea" in Boulez 1991, pp. 26–38

1958, "Debussy" in Boulez 1991, pp. 259–277

1991, *Stocktakings from an Apprenticeship*, ed. Paule Thévenin, trans. Stephen Walsh, Oxford

Brand, Juliane, Hailey, Christopher, and Harris, Donald (eds.) 1987, *The Berg–Schoenberg Correspondence: Selected Letters*, New York

Brown, Earle 1974, "December 1952" in *Music by Earle Brown*, sleeve note accompanying vinyl disc, Composers Recordings, Inc. CRI SD 330

1992, interview with David Patterson, November 13

Brown, Kathan 2000, *John Cage Visual Art: To Sober and Quiet the Mind*, San Francisco

Cage, John 1934, "Counterpoint" *Dune Forum*, 1, pp. 42–44

c. 1938–40. "The Future of Music: Credo" in Cage 1961, pp. 3–6

1939, letter to Lou Harrison postmarked April 20, University of California, Santa Cruz, Library, Special Collections

1939a, "Goal: New Music, New Dance" in Cage 1961, pp. 87–88

1942, "For More New Sounds" in Kostelanetz 1971, pp. 64–66

1944, "Grace and Clarity" in Cage 1961, pp. 89–93

1946, "The East in the West" in Kostelanetz 1993, pp. 21–25

1948a, "A Composer's Confessions" in Kostelanetz 1993, pp. 27–44

1948b, "Defense of Satie" in Kostelanetz 1971, pp. 77–84

1949, "Forerunners of Modern Music" in Cage 1961, pp. 62–66

c. 1949–50, "Lecture on Nothing" in Cage 1961, pp. 109–126

1950a, "More Satie" in Kostelanetz 1971, pp. 92–94

1950b, "Satie Controversy" in Kostelanetz 1971, pp. 89–92

1951, "A Few Ideas About Music and Film" in Kostelanetz 1993, pp. 63–65

1951a, Letter to David Tudor, summer 1951 (unpubl. MS, The David Tudor Papers, The Getty Research Institute, Accession No. 980039)

1951b, Letter to David Tudor, August 5, 1951 (unpubl. MS, The David Tudor Papers, The Getty Research Institute, Accession No. 980039)

c. 1951–52, "Lecture on Something" in Cage 1961, pp. 128–145

1952a, "Juilliard Lecture" in Cage 1967, pp. 95–111

1952b, "Composition: To Describe the Process of Composition Used in *Music of Changes* and *Imaginary Landscape No. 4*" in Cage 1961, pp. 57–59

1952c, ["Manifesto"] in Cage 1961, p. xii

1953, ["Robert Rauschenberg"] in Kostelanetz 1971, pp. 111–112

1954, "45′ for a Speaker" in Cage 1961, pp. 146–192

1955, "Experimental Music: Doctrine" in Cage 1961, pp. 13–17

1957, "Experimental Music" in Cage 1961, pp. 7–12

1958a, "Composition as Process" in Cage 1961, pp. 18–56

1958b, ["On Earlier Pieces"] in Kostelanetz 1971, pp. 127–131

1958c, "Williams Mix" in Kostelanetz 1971, pp. 109–111

1958d, "Komposition als Prozeß: III. Kommunikation" trans. Hans G. Helms, Heinz-Klaus Metzger, and Wolf Rosenberg, in *Musik-Konzepte Sonderband: Darmstadt Dokumente I*, Munich, pp. 161–174

1958e, "Erik Satie" in Cage 1961, pp. 76–82

1958f, "Edgard Varèse" in Cage 1961, pp. 83–85

1958–59a, "Indeterminacy" in Cage 1961, pp. 260–273

1958–59b, "Preface to 'Indeterminacy'" in Kostelanetz 1993, pp. 75–79

1959, "History of Experimental Music in the United States" in Cage 1961, pp. 67–75

1960, "Form is a Language" in Kostelanetz 1971, p. 135

1961, *Silence*, Middletown, CT

1961a, "Lecture on Commitment" in Cage 1967, pp. 112–119

1961b, "List no. 2" in Kostelanetz 1971, pp. 138–139

1961c, "Rhythm Etc." in Cage 1967, pp. 120–132

1962, "Notes on Compositions" in Kostelanetz 1993, pp. 5–13, 51–62, 93–108, 133–142, 195–205

1962a, "Interview with Roger Reynolds" in Dunn 1962, pp. 45–52

c. 1962–66, "26 Statements Re Duchamp" in Cage 1967, pp. 70–72

1964, "Two Statements on Ives" in Cage 1967, pp. 36–42

1965a, "Diary: How to Improve the World (You Will Only Make Matters Worse) 1965" in Cage 1967, pp. 3–20

1965b, "How to Pass, Kick, Fall, and Run" in Cage 1967, pp. 133–140

1966, "Diary: How to Improve the World (You Will Only Make Matters Worse) Continued 1966" in Cage 1967, pp. 52–69

1966a, ["Memoir"] in Kostelanetz 1971, pp. 76–77

1966b, ["Letter to the Editor of the Village Voice"] in Kostelanetz 1991, p. 167

1967, *A Year from Monday*, Middletown, CT

1967a, "McLuhan's Influence" in Kostelanetz 1971, pp. 170–171

1968, "These Days" in Kostelanetz 1971, pp. 177–180

1969, "Diary: How to Improve the World (You Will Only Make Matters Worse) Continued 1969 (Part V)" in Cage 1972, pp. 57–84

1970–71, "Diary: How to Improve the World (You Will Only Make Matters Worse) Continued 1970–71" in Cage 1972, pp. 96–116

1972, *M: Writings '67–'72*, London

1973, "Foreword to *The Well-Prepared Piano*" in Kostelanetz 1993, pp. 117–119

1974, "The Future of Music" in Cage 1980, pp. 177–187

1975, "Preface to 'Lecture on the Weather'" in Cage 1980, pp. 3–5

1977, "Sixty-One Mesostics Re and Not Re Norman O. Brown" in Cage 1980, pp. 123–132

1979, "James Joyce, Marcel Duchamp, Erik Satie: An Alphabet" in Cage 1983, pp. 53–101

1980, *Empty Words: Writings '73–'78*, London

1980a, "Themes and Variations" in Cage 1993, pp. 53–171

1981, *For the Birds: In Conversation with Daniel Charles*, London

1981a, unpublished letter to David Nicholls, September 27

1982, *Roaratorio: An Irish Circus on "Finnegans Wake"*, ed. Klaus Schöning, Königstein

1982a, "Composition in Retrospect" [original version] in *John Cage Etchings 1978–1982*, San Francisco, pp. 39–57

1983, *X: Writings '79–'82*, Middletown, CT

1986, "Tokyo Lecture and Three Mesostics" in Kostelanetz 1993, pp. 177–194

1988, "interview with Miguel Frasconi" *Balungan* 3/2 (Oct. 1988), pp. 19–23

1988a, "Composition in Retrospect" in Cage 1993, pp. 3–51

1989, "An Autobiographical Statement" in Kostelanetz 1993, pp. 237–247

1989a, interview with John Holzaepfel, July 31

1990, *Method Structure Intention Discipline Notation Indeterminacy Interpenetration Imitation Devotion Circumstances Variable Structure Nonunderstanding Contingency Inconsistency Performance [I–VI]*, Cambridge, MA

1990a, "Mesostics" in *Äesthetik und Komposition*, ed. Gianmario Borio and Ulrich Mosch, Mainz, 1994, pp. 7–13

1991, interview with John Holzaepfel, August 26

1992, *Roaratorio: An Irish Circus on "Finnegans Wake"* [CD recording] mode 28/9

1993, *Composition in Retrospect*, Cambridge, MA

undated, draft of note or letter (of recommendation?) concerning David Tudor (unpubl. MS, The David Tudor Papers, The Getty Research Institute, Accession No. 980039)

Cage, John & Anderson, Laurie 1992, "Taking Chances: John Cage and Laurie Anderson" [a transcribed interview] *Tricycle: The Buddhist Review*, pp. 52–59

Cage, John & Kostelanetz, Richard 1987, "His Own Music: Ur-Conversation with John Cage" *Perspectives of New Music* 25, pp. 88–106

Campana, Deborah 1989, "A Chance Encounter: The Correspondence between John Cage and Pierre Boulez, 1949–1954" in Fleming and Duckworth 1989, pp. 209–248

1993, "On John Cage's *String Quartet in Four Parts*" in *Writings about John Cage*, ed. Richard Kostelanetz, Ann Arbor, MI, pp. 77–84

Conze, Edward (trans.) 1958, "The Heart Sutra" in *Buddhist Wisdom Books*, London, pp. 75–107

Coomaraswamy, Ananda 1934, *The Transformation of Nature in Art*, Cambridge
  1971, "Why Exhibit Works of Art?" *Studies in Comparative Literature* 5/3, pp. 173–183

Cowell, Henry 1930, *New Musical Resources*, New York
  1934, "How Relate Music and Dance?" *Dance Observer* 1/5, pp. 52–53
  1937, "Relating Music and Concert Dance" *Dance Observer* 4/1, pp. 1, 7–9
  1938, "A Discussion of Percussion" *Dance Herald* 1/4, p. 4
  1939, letter to Bonnie Bird, April 2 (private collection)
  1941a, "Creating a Dance: Form and Composition" *Educational Dance*, pp. 2–3
  1941b, "New Sounds for the Dance" *Dance Observer* 8/5, pp. 64, 70
  1952, "Current Chronicle" *Musical Quarterly* 38, pp. 123–136

Cowell, Henry and Cowell, Sidney 1983 [1955], *Charles Ives and His Music*, New York

Cross, Lowell 1999, "*Reunion*: John Cage, Marcel Duchamp, Electronic Music and Chess" *Leonardo Music Journal* 9, pp. 35–42

Cunningham, Merce 1952, "Space, Time and Dance" *Transformation: Arts, Communication, Environment* 1/3 pp. 150–151
  1982, "A Collaborative Process Between Music and Dance" in Gena, Brent, and Gillespie 1982, pp. 107–120

Cunningham, Merce & Lesschaeve, Jacqueline 1985, *The Dancer and the Dance*, New York and London

Danuser, Hermann 1993, "Die Postmodernität des John Cage. Der experimentelle Künstler in der Sicht Jean-François Lyotards" in *Wiederaneignung und Neubestimmung: Der Fall "Postmodern" in der Musik*, ed. Otto Kolleritsch, Vienna, pp. 142–159

Dennison, Doris 1995, interview with Leta Miller, December 5

Duberman, Martin, 1993 [1972], *Black Mountain: An Exploration in Community*, New York

Duckworth, William 1989, "Anything I Say Will Be Misunderstood: An Interview with John Cage" in Fleming and Duckworth 1989, pp. 15–33
  1995, *Talking Music: Conversations with John Cage, Philip Glass, Laurie Anderson, and Five Generations of American Experimental Composers*, New York

Dufallo, Richard 1989, *Trackings*, New York

Dunn, Robert (ed.) 1962, *John Cage*, New York

Emerson, Ralph Waldo 1982, "Self Reliance" in *Selected Essays*, ed. Larzer Ziff, New York, pp. 175–203

Ewen, David 1983, *American Composers: A Biographical Dictionary*, London

Fetterman, William 1996, *John Cage's Theatre Pieces: Notations and Performances*, Amsterdam

Fields, Rick 1992, *How the Swans Came to the Lake: A Narrative History of Buddhism in America*, Boston

Fleming, Richard and Duckworth, William (eds.) 1989, *John Cage at Seventy-Five*, Lewisburg & London

Foss, Lukas 1965, "Profile of a Festival," program booklet for concert of July 23, p. 7

Gardner, Howard 1993, *Creating Minds*, New York

Gena, Peter, Brent, Jonathan, and Gillespie, Don (eds.) 1982, *A John Cage Reader*, New York

George, William Bernard 1971, "Adolph Weiss," Ph.D. diss, University of Iowa

Giersch, Ulrich 1999, "Bauhaus Chronology" in *Bauhaus*, ed. Jeannine Fiedler and Peter Feierabend, Cologne, pp. 602–607

Goldstein, Malcolm 2000, interview with Leta Miller, July 31

Gowers, Patrick 1986, "Erik Satie" in *The New Grove: Twentieth-Century French Masters*, New York, pp. 127–148

Graham, Martha 1963, "Introduction" *Dance Perspectives* 16, pp. 4–5

Griffiths, Paul 1978, *Modern Music: A Concise History from Debussy to Boulez*, London
    1981, *Cage*, London

Gupta, Mahendranath 1942, *The Gospel of Sri Ramakrishna*, trans. and with an introduction by Swami Nikhilananda, New York

Gussow, Mel 2000, "Margaret Atwood on Vision, Sacrifice and Lyrical Complecities" *The New York Times* October 10, p. E1

Hamm, Charles 1995, "Epilogue: John Cage Revisited" in *Putting Popular Music in its Place*, Cambridge, pp. 381–385
    1997, "Privileging the Moment: Cage, Jung, Synchronicity, Postmodernism" *The Journal of Musicology* 15/2, pp. 278–289

Harris, Mary Emma 1987, *The Arts at Black Mountain College*, Cambridge, MA

Harrison, Lou 1993, interview with David Patterson, September 29
    1995, interview with Leta Miller, April 3

Häusler, Josef 1996, liner notes to *75 Jahre Donaueschinger Musiktage, 1921–1996*, trans. Diana Loos, Munich

Hay, Harry 1996, *Radically Gay: Gay Liberation in the Words of Its Founder*, ed. Will Roscoe, Boston

Helms, Hans G. 2001, private correspondence with Christopher Shultis, August 15

Hicks, Michael 1990, "John Cage's Studies with Schoenberg" *American Music* 8/2, pp. 125–140
    1991, "The Imprisonment of Henry Cowell" *Journal of the American Musicological Society* 44/1, pp. 92–119

Hiller, Lejaren 1970, "Music Composed with Computers – A Historical Survey" in *The Computer and Music*, ed. Harry B. Lincoln, Ithaca and London

Hindle, Brooke 1981, "The Machine in the New Nation" in *Emulation and Invention*, New York, pp. 1–23

Hines, Thomas S. 1994, "Then not yet 'Cage': The Los Angeles Years, 1912–1938" in Perloff and Junkerman 1994, pp. 65–99

Holzaepfel, John 1994, "David Tudor and the Performance of American Experimental Music, 1950–1959," Ph.D. diss., City University of New York

Huang Po 1947, *Doctrine of Universal Mind*, trans. Chu Ch'an (= John Blofeld), London

Husarik, Stephen 1983, "John Cage and Lejaren Hiller: HPSCHD, 1969" *American Music* 1/2, pp. 1–21

Jameaux, Dominique 1991, *Pierre Boulez*, trans. Susan Bradshaw, Cambridge MA

Jameson, Fredric 1991, *Postmodernism, or, the Cultural Logic of Late Capitalism*, London and Durham, NC

Johnson, George 2000, "Hardly Dead, Physics Lives Out a Permanent Solution" *The New York Times* June 20, p. D6

Jones, Caroline A. 1993, "Finishing School: John Cage and the Abstract Expressionist Ego" *Critical Enquiry* 19/4, pp. 628–665

Joseph, Branden W. 1997, "John Cage and the Architecture of Silence" *October* 81, pp. 81–104

Kasemets, Udo 2000, email letter to Leta Miller, July 31

Kass, Ray 1988, "The Mountain Lake Workshop" in *John Cage / The New River Watercolors*, Richmond VA, pp. 1–15 [originally published in *Drawing* 10/3]

Kentgens-Craig, Margret 1999, *Bauhaus and America: First Contacts 1919–1936*, Cambridge, MA

Kirby, Michael 1995, "Happenings: An Introduction" in Sandford 1995, pp. 1–28

Kirby, Michael, & Schechner, Richard 1995, "An Interview with John Cage" in Sandford 1995, pp. 51–71

Klosty, James (ed.) 1986, *Merce Cunningham*, New York

Klüver, Wilhelm undated, unpublished notes on performance of *Variations VII* (October 15/16, 1966) assembled by Klüver

    2000, interview with Leta Miller, July 28

Kostelanetz, Richard 1989, *On Innovative Music(ian)s*, New York

Kostelanetz, Richard (ed.) 1971, *John Cage*, London; revised and expanded as Kostelanetz 1991

    1988, *Conversing with Cage*, New York

    1991, *John Cage, An Anthology*, New York

    1993, *John Cage: Writer*, New York

Kostelanetz, Richard and Cage, John 1989, "A Conversation about Radio in Twelve Parts" in Fleming and Duckworth 1989, pp. 270–302

Kotz, Mary Lynn 1990, *Rauschenberg: Art and Life*, New York

Kramer, Lawrence 1995, *Classical Music and Postmodern Knowledge*, Berkeley and Los Angeles

Kremen, Irwin 2000, interview with John Holzaepfel, July 10

Lao-Tse, 1972 *Tao Te Ching*, trans. Gia-Fu Feng and Jane English, New York

Lieberman, Fredric 2000, interview with Leta Miller, July 12

Lippold, Richard 1993, interview with David Patterson, December 8

Mathews, Max 2000, interview with Leta Miller, July 24

Mead, Rita H. 1981, *Henry Cowell's New Music, 1925–1936*, Ann Arbor

Metzger, Heinz-Klaus 1996, "Fragment zum Thema 'Komet'" in *Von Kranichstein zur Gegenwart: 50 Jahre Darmstädter Ferienkurse*, ed. Rudolf Stephan, Lothar Knessl, Otto Tomek, Klaus Trapp, Christopher Fox, Stuttgart, pp. 250–251

Metzger, Heinz-Klaus and Riehn, Rainer (eds.) 1999, *Musik-Konzepte Sonderband: Darmstadt Dokumente I*, Munich

Miller, Leta E. 2000, "The Art of Noise: John Cage, Lou Harrison, and the West Coast Percussion Ensemble" in *Perspectives on American Music, 1900–1950*, ed. Michael Saffle, New York, pp. 215–263

2001 "Cage, Cunningham, and Collaborators: The Odyssey of *Variations V*" *Musical Quarterly* 85/3 (forthcoming)

2002, "Cultural Intersections: John Cage in Seattle (1938–40)" in Patterson 2002, pp. 47–82

2002a "Henry Cowell and Modern Dance: The Genesis of Elastic Form" *American Music* 20/1, pp. 1–24

Miller, Leta E. (ed.) 1998, *Lou Harrison: Selected Keyboard and Chamber Music, 1937–1994* (Music in the United States of America 8), Madison, WI

Miller, Leta E. & Lieberman, Fredric 1998, *Lou Harrison: Composing a World*, New York

Montague, Stephen 1985, "John Cage at Seventy: An Interview" *American Music* 3/2, pp. 205–216

Moog, Robert 2000, interview with Leta Miller, August 8

Morison, Samuel Eliot, Commager, Henry Steele, & Leuchtenburg, William E. 1977, *A Concise History of the American Republic*, New York

Mumma, Gordon 1967, "Four Sound Environments for Modern Dance" *Impulse*, pp. 12–15

2000, interview with Leta Miller, July 6

Naifeh, Steven and Smith, Gregory White 1989, *Jackson Pollock: An American Saga*, New York

Nattiez, Jean-Jacques (ed.) 1993, *The Boulez–Cage Correspondence*, trans. Robert Samuels, Cambridge

Nicholls, David 1990, *American Experimental Music, 1890–1940*, Cambridge

1998, "Avant-garde and Experimental Music" in *The Cambridge History of American Music*, ed. David Nicholls, Cambridge, pp. 517–534

2001, "Getting Rid of the Glue – the Music of the New York School" in *The New York Schools of Music and the Visual Arts*, ed. Steven Johnson, New York, pp. 17–56

Nyman, Michael 1999, *Experimental Music: Cage and Beyond* (2nd edition), Cambridge

Oja, Carol J. 2000, *Making Music Modern: New York in the 1920s*, New York

Patterson, David W. 1994, "Cage and Beyond: An Annotated Interview with Christian Wolff" *Perspectives of New Music* 32/2, pp. 54–87

1996, "Appraising the Catchwords, c. 1942–1959: John Cage's Asian Derived Rhetoric and the Historical Reference of Black Mountain College," Ph.D. diss, Columbia University

Patterson, David W. (ed.) 2002, *John Cage: Music, Philosophy, and Intention, 1933–1950*, New York

Perloff, Marjorie 1994, " 'A Duchamp unto my self': 'Writing through' Marcel" in Perloff and Junkerman 1994, pp. 100–124

Perloff, Marjorie & Junkerman, Charles (eds.) 1994, *John Cage: Composed in America*, Chicago

Peyser, Joan 1976, *Boulez: Composer, Conductor, Enigma*, London

Pritchett, James 1988a, "The Development of Chance Techniques in the Music of John Cage," Ph.D. diss, New York University

1988b, "From Choice to Chance: John Cage's Concerto for Prepared Piano" *Perspectives of New Music* 26/1, pp. 50–81

1992, liner notes to John Cage, *Four* on *The Complete String Quartets Vol. 2*, The Arditti Quartet, mode 27

1993, *The Music of John Cage*, Cambridge

Rees, Richard 1958, *Brave Men: A Study of D. H. Lawrence and Simone Weil*, London

Retallack, Joan (ed.) 1996, *Musicage: Cage Muses on Words, Art, Music*, Hanover, NH

Revill, David 1992, *The Roaring Silence: John Cage, A Life*, London

Sandford, Mariellen R. (ed.) 1995, *Happenings and Other Acts*, London and New York

Sarabhai Mayor, Geeta 1993, unpublished letter to David Patterson, July 4

Schoenberg, Arnold 1964, *Letters*, ed. Erwin Stein, trans. Eithne Wilkins and Ernst Kaiser, London

1975, *Style and Idea: Selected Writings of Arnold Schoenberg*, ed. Leonard Stein, trans. Leo Black, London

Seeger, Charles 1930, "On Dissonant Counterpoint" *Modern Music* 7, pp. 25–31

1933, "Ruth Crawford" in *American Composers on American Music: A Symposium*, ed. Henry Cowell, Stanford, pp. 110–118

1994, "Tradition and Experiment in (the New) Music" in *Studies in Musicology II, 1929–1979*, ed. Ann M. Pescatello, Berkeley, pp. 17–273

Shimomura, Torataro 1986, "D. T. Suzuki's Place in the History of Human Thought" in *A Zen Life: D. T. Suzuki Remembered*, ed. Masao Abe, New York, pp. 65–80

Stevenson, Robert 1982, "John Cage on his 70th Birthday: West Coast Background" *Inter-American Music Review* 5/1, pp. 3–17

Stockhausen, Karlheinz 2001, *Karlheinz Stockhausen bei den Internationalen Ferienkursen für Neue Musik in Darmstadt 1951–1996: Dokumente und Briefe*, collected and with commentary by Imke Misch and Markus Bandur, Kürten

Suzuki, Daisetz Teitaro 1958, "Zen in the Modern World" *Japan Quarterly* 5/4, pp. 452–461

Swed, Mark 1994, "Editor's Introduction to 'Synergetic Dynamics in John Cage's *Europeras 1 & 2*'" *Musical Quarterly* 78/1, pp. 127–130

Sylvester, David 1989, "Points in Space: John Cage" in *Dancers on a Plane*, London, pp. 47–52

Terry, Walter 1965, "Parting Shot Applause" *New York Herald Tribune* July 24, p. 4

Thomson, Virgil 1945, "Expressive Percussion" in Kostelanetz 1971, pp. 71–73

Timmons, Stuart 1990, *The Trouble with Harry Hay: Founder of the Modern Gay Movement*, Boston

Tomkins, Calvin 1976 [1965], *The Bride and the Bachelors*, London

Tommasini, Anthony 1997, *Virgil Thomson: Composer on the Aisle*, New York

Tudor, David 1951, draft of letter to John Cage, late July 1951 (unpubl. MS, The David Tudor Papers, The Getty Research Institute, Accession No. 980039)

1972, "From Piano to Electronics" *Music and Musicians* 20, pp. 24–26

1982, interview with Austin Clarkson, October 4

1992, interview with John Holzaepfel, January 17

undated, letter to unidentified correspondent (unpubl. MS, The David Tudor Papers, The Getty Research Institute, Accession No. 980039)

Ulmer, Gregory L. 1985, "The Object of Post-Criticism" in *Postmodern Culture*, ed. Hal Foster (first published as *The Anti-Aesthetic*, Port Townsend, WA, 1983), London, pp. 83–110

Van Emmerik, Paul 1996, "Thema's en Variaties: Systematische Tendensen in de Compositietechnieken van John Cage," Ph.D. diss., University of Amsterdam

2001, "Here Comes Everything" in Bernstein and Hatch 2001, pp. 157–166

Vaughan, David 1997, *Merce Cunningham: Fifty Years*, New York

White, Robin 1978, "An Interview with John Cage at Crown Point Press" *View*

Williams, Alastair 1997, *New Music and the Claims of Modernity*, Aldershot

2001, *Constructing Musicology*, Aldershot

Zimmermann, Walter (ed.) 1985, *Morton Feldman Essays*, Kerpen

Index